The State of the Nations 2001

The Second Year of Devolution in the United Kingdom

Edited by
Alan Trench

SCHOOL *of* PUBLIC POLICY

The Constitution Unit

IMPRINT ACADEMIC

Published in the UK by Imprint Academic
PO Box 1, Thorverton EX5 5YX, UK

Published in the USA by Imprint Academic
Philosophy Documentation Center
PO Box 7147, Charlottesville, VA 22906-7147, USA

ISBN 0 907845 19 3

British Library Cataloguing in Publication Data
A catalogue record for this book is available from the
British Library

Library of Congress Control Number: 2001096766

The State of the Nations 2001

ALSO OF INTEREST FROM IMPRINT ACADEMIC

Robert Hazell (ed.), *The State and The Nations:*
The First Year of Devolution in the United Kingdom
ISBN 0907845800

Keith Sutherland (ed.), *The Rape of the Constitution?*
ISBN 0907845703

TOCs, reviews and sample chapters:
www.imprint-academic.com/books

Contents

Contributors x

Figures xii

Abbreviations xiv

Foreword xvi

1   Introduction: Devolution's Second Year.
    But Mountains Left to Climb? 1
    Alan Trench

    Devolution and the General Election 2
    Devolution's Successes 4
    Devolution's Failures And The Unanswered Questions 6
    Bibliography 10

                    PART I: THE NATIONS

2   In Search Of Stability. Coalition Politics in the Second Year
    of the National Assembly for Wales 13
    John Osmond

    Legitimacy Without Power 13
    The Administration 16
        The Coalition 16
        The Economy 20
        A New Structure for the Welsh Health Service 21
        The Farming Crisis 22
        Education 23
        The Administration's Legislative Programme 2001-2 . . . 24
    The Assembly 26
        Office of the Presiding Officer 26
        The Assembly's Operational Review 27
    The Civil Service 29
    The Welsh Language Intervenes 31
        John Elfed Jones 32
        Dafydd Glyn Jones 33
    The Political Parties and the General Election 36
        The Political Parties 36
        The 2001 General Election 38
    The Future of Welsh Coalition Politics 41

Bibliography 43

3   Scotland: Maturing Devolution 45
    James Mitchell and the Scottish Monitoring Team

    Introduction. 45
    The Executive 51
        The Labour Leadership: Mcleish's Succession. 51
        'Team Mcleish' 53
        Institutional Innovation. 54
        All Change at Dover House 56
    The Scottish Parliament And The Parties. 57
        Executive–Parliament Relations. 57
        The Work of the Parliament's Committees 58
        The SNP and its New Leadership 60
        The Parliament as a New Model of Assembly 61
    Policy Development and Divergence. 63
        Legislation. 63
        Care for the Elderly 63
        Finance 65
            Barnett and the UK General Election. 66
            Local Government Finance and the CoSLA Crisis . . 67
            Tuition Fees, Care for Elderly and NHS Salaries . . . 67
        Symbolic Politics. 68
            Scotland Abroad: Europe and the Wider World . . . 69
        Normalisation 70
            Foot-And-Mouth Disease 71
            The Scottish Qualifications Agency Fiasco
                and Aftermath 71
            VisitScotland 72
            The Electronics Industry 72
    The UK General Election in Scotland 72
    Conclusion 73
    Bibliography 74

4   Northern Ireland: Endgame 77
    Robin Wilson and Rick Wilford

    Overview. 77
    The 'Peace Process'. 78
    The Executive 84
        The Absence of Trust. 84
        Rubbing Along. 86
    The Assembly 89
    Policy-Making and Legislation 96

Public Opinion. 100
The Media. 102
The Elections 103
Conclusion 104
Bibliography. 105

5   Reshaping the English Regions. 107
    John Tomaney

    Introduction 107
    The Regional Debate. 108
    Institutions of Regional Governance 111
        Regional Development Agencies. 112
        Regional Chambers and Assemblies 115
        Government Offices. 119
        Regionalisation 121
    Civil Regionalism 122
    Public Attitudes 122
    Parliament. 124
    Whitehall 126
    London 127
    Outlook 130
    Bibliography. 132

PART II: THE STATE

6   Finance — The Barnett Formula: Nobody's Child? 135
    David Bell and Alex Christie

    Introduction 135
    The Barnett Formula. 136
    Levels of Funding 139
    Changes in Funding 143
    The Barnett Formula and Other Funding Mechanisms. 147
    Conclusion 150
    Bibliography. 151

7   Intergovernmental Relations a Year On
    Whitehall still Rules UK? 153
    Alan Trench

    The Formal Apparatus for Intergovernmental Relations 154
        The Joint Ministerial Committee. 154
        The British–Irish Council and the North–South
        Ministerial Council 156

Concordats 157
The System at Work 158
    Ministers 158
    Officials 160
    The Territorial Offices 162
Legislation at Westminster 163
Finance 166
EU and International Matters 168
IGR In Crisis: Foot-and-Mouth Disease 170
Conclusions 172
Bibliography 173

8   Devolution and the Centre 175
    Roger Masterman and James Mitchell

    Introduction 175
    Devolution and the Courts 178
    The Impact of Devolution on Whitehall 180
    The Work of the Territorial Offices 181
        The Scotland Office 182
        The Wales Office 184
        The Northern Ireland Office 185
        The Continuing Roles of the Territorial Secretaries
            of State 186
    Government at the Centre 189
        HM Treasury 189
        Cabinet Office: The Constitution Secretariat . . 189
        The Mechanics of Devolution:
            Devolution Guidance Notes 191
        Remodelling the Centre 193
    Conclusion 195
    Bibliography 196

9   Devolution and Westminster 197
    Roger Masterman and Robert Hazell

    Introduction 197
    The House of Commons 199
        The State of the Parties, July 2001 199
        The End of Dual Mandates 200
        Nationalist Parties Form Joint Party Group . . . 202
    Westminster Legislation 203
        Legislating for Scotland 203
        Legislating for Wales 205
        Legislating for Northern Ireland 206

The Work of the Territorial Committees 207
    The Territorial Select Committees 207
    The Work of the Grand Committees 211
Changes in Procedure 213
The Role of Members of Parliament 214
The English Question 215
    English Votes on English Laws 216
    The Government's Position on the English Question . . . 217
    New English Structures at Westminster 218
The House of Lords 220
    The House of Lords Select Committee on the
    Constitution 221
Conclusion 223
Bibliography. 223

10 Hopes Dashed And Fears Assuaged?
    What the Public Makes of it So Far 225
    John Curtice

    Introduction 225
    Constitutional Arrangements 227
    Identity 236
    Devolution In Practice 240
    The 2001 General Election 248
    Conclusion 253
    Bibliography. 253

11 Conclusion
    The State of the Nations after Two Years of Devolution 255
    Robert Hazell

    The Beginnings of Policy Differentiation 255
    The Barnett Formula Comes Under Question 259
    Devolution is Here to Stay 262
    . . . and it is Reshaping the Party System 263
    The Devolution Dynamic Continues to Unfold 264
        The Welsh Start to Review the Settlement 264
        The English Regions Remain in Waiting 266
        Scotland's Policies Threaten the Budget 268
        Northern Ireland Falters then Falls: What Next? 269
    Whitehall and Westminster Carry on Much as Before 269
    Conclusion 271
    Bibliography. 272

Index 273

List of Contributors

David Bell is Professor of Economics, University of Stirling and co-director of the Scottish Economic Policy Network. He has carried out research as part of the Leverhulme Trust's programme on 'Nations and Regions: the dynamics of devolution, on the Barnett Formula, and was recently a member of the Care Development Group which looked into Long-Term Care of the Elderly in Scotland.

Alex Christie is a research fellow with the Scottish Economic Policy Network and previously worked on Leverhulme Trust-funded research into the Barnett formula and territorial public finance. His research interests lie in the field of public finance and he has provided information for the Scottish Parliament on EU funding and the Scottish Budget.

John Curtice is Professor of Politics and Director of the Social Statistics Laboratory at Strathclyde University. He is also Deputy Director of the ESRC Centre for Research into Elections and Social Trends and Head of Research, National Centre for Social Research Scotland. A frequent commentator on both British and Scottish politics in the media, he is co-author of L. Paterson et al, *New Scotland, New Politics?* (Polygon) and co-editor of J. Curtice et al, *New Scotland, New Society* (Polygon) and A. Park et al, *British Social Attitudes: the 18th report* (Sage).

Robert Hazell is the Director of the Constitution Unit and Professor of Government and the Constitution in the School of Public Policy, University College London. Originally a barrister, he spent most of his working life at the Home Office. He left Whitehall to become director of the Nuffield Foundation and founded the Constitution Unit in 1995.

Roger Masterman is a Research Assistant at the Constitution Unit, working on the Leverhulme Trust-funded project on 'Devolution and Westminster' and the ESRC-funded project on 'Devolution and Whitehall'.

James Mitchell is Professor of Politics and Head of the Department of Government, University of Strathclyde, and author of numerous books and articles on Scottish and UK politics and devolution.

John Osmond is Director of the Institute of Welsh Affairs, a policy think tank based in Cardiff. He is a former political journalist and television producer and has written widely on Welsh politics and devolution. His most recent books are *Welsh Europeans* (Serena, 1997); *The National Assembly Agenda* (Editor, 1998) and *Inclusive Government and Party Management:*

The National Assembly for Wales and the Work of its Committees (co-editor with J. Barry Jones, 2001) both published by the Institute.

John Tomaney works in the Centre for Urban and Regional Development Studies at Newcastle University. His research interests include the political economy of regional development and the politics of devolution in England. Among his recent publications is *A Region in Transition: North East England at the Millennium* (Aldershot, Ashgate), edited with Neil Ward.

Alan Trench has been a Senior Research Fellow at the Constitution Unit since February 2001. A solicitor by profession, he has also worked in local government and in private legal practice.

Rick Wilford is Reader in Politics, Queen's University Belfast. He has written extensively on both devolution and politics in Northern Ireland. His most recent works include the co-edited 'Politics in Northern Ireland' (Westview Press, 1999) and 'Designing the Northern Ireland Assembly', in *Parliamentary Affairs*, July 2000. He is currently researching devolution and health in Northern Ireland as part of the Constitution Unit's wider research programme in this area.

Robin Wilson is director of the Belfast-based think-tank Democratic Dialogue, which he founded in 1995. He has been intimately involved for many years in the debates around UK devolution, as well as the specific issues attaching to the Northern Ireland conflict, on which he has written numerous journal articles and book chapters. He was formerly editor of the current-affairs magazine *Fortnight*. He is a member of the Northern Ireland Community Relations Council.

List of Figures

WALES: IN SEARCH OF STABILITY

2.1 Key events in the National Assembly's second year 14
2.2 The coalition cabinet, October 2000 17
2.3 The Administration's four priorities for Welsh legislation in the 2001-02
Westminster parliamentary session 25
2.4 Independence for the office of the Presiding Officer 27
2.5 Cross-party consensus in the Operational Review 28
2.6 All-Wales election results for 2001, 1999 and 1997 39
2.7 NOP poll for BBC Wales June 2001 42

SCOTLAND: MATURING DEVOLUTION

3.1 Key events in the second year of the Scottish Parliament 46
3.2 Expectations of the Scottish Parliament 49
3.3 Team McLeish: the Scottish Cabinet, March 2001 54
3.4 The Scottish Parliament & public opinion 61
3.5 Bills passed in Scottish Parliament, December 2000-August 2001 63
3.6 Votes and seats in Scotland in the 2001 (1997) general elections 73

NOTHERN IRELAND: ENDGAME

4.1 Key events in Northern Ireland 79
4.2 Northern Ireland Executive Committee at 31 July 2001 89
4.3 Primary bills enacted in the 2000-01 session 98
4.4 Religion and the referendum vote 101
4.5 2001 UK general election results 103
4.6 2001 Northern Ireland local election results 103

RESHAPING THE ENGLISH REGIONS

5.1 Key events relating to the English regions 112
5.2 Spending allocations for RDAs in 2000 spending review 113
5.3 Regional chambers in England: basic data 117
5.4 Civic regionalism 2001 123
5.5 Attitudes to regional government in Sedgefield 125

FINANCE — THE BARNETT FORMULA: NOBODY'S CHILD?

6.1 Barnett-determined increases in assigned budgets resulting from £100 million
increase in funding to HEFCE 137
6.2 Per capita identifiable total managed expenditure by country and function
1999-2000 140
6.3 Per capita identifiable total managed expenditure by region and function
1999-2000 141
6.4 Identifiable public expenditure relative to "need" 1999-2000 142
6.5 The Barnett squeeze under planned departmental expenditure limits 145

INTERGOVERNMENTAL RELATIONS A YEAR ON

7.1 Key events in intergovernmental relations, 2000-01 154
7.2 Terms of reference of the Joint Ministerial Committee 155
7.3 Concordats concluded between July 2000 and July 2001 157

DEVOLUTION AND THE CENTRE

8.1 Key events in Whitehall: 2000-1 177
8.2 Ministers in the Scotland Office, at July 2001. 183
8.3 Ministers in the Wales Office, at July 2001 185
8.4 Ministers in the Northern Ireland Office, at July 2001. 185
8.5 Staff of the territorial offices 188
8.6 Devolution Guidance Notes published at August 2001 192

DEVOLUTION AND WESTMINSTER

9.1 Key events at Westminster, July 2000–July 2001 199
9.2 Territorial and party strength in the new House of Commons, July 2001 . . . 200
9.3 Westminster MPs with experience of the devolved institutions. 200
9.4 Dual-Mandate MPs in the 1997-2001 Parliament who did not contest
    their seats in 2001 201
9.5 MPs holding seats in the Northern Ireland Assembly, July 2001 202
9.6 Territorial extent of legislation passed during 1999-2000 session 203
9.7 Territorial extent of legislation passed during 2000-2001 session 203
9.8 Acts passed for which Sewel resolutions made by the Scottish Parliament . . 204
9.9 Welsh Affairs Committee reports published, 2000-1. 208
9.10 Northern Ireland Affairs Committee reports published, 2000-1 209
9.11 Scottish Affairs Committee reports published, 2000-1 209
9.12 Meetings of the Welsh Grand Committee, 2000-1 212
9.13 Meetings of the Northern Irish Grand Committee, 2000-1. 212
9.14 Meetings of the Scottish Grand Committee, 2000-1. 212
9.15 Parliamentary questions to the Welsh Office and Wales Office, 1997-2001 . 214
9.16 Parliamentary questions to the Scottish Office and Scotland Office
     1997-2001. 214
9.17 Parliamentary questions to the Northern Ireland Office, 1997-2001 215
9.18 Membership of the Standing Committee on Regional Affairs,
     announced 13 March 2001 219
9.19 The members of the Constitution Committee at July 2001 221

HOPES DASHED AND FEARS ASSUAGED?

10.1 Constitutional preferences in the devolved territories 228
10.2 What England thinks about Scotland and Wales 231
10.3 Two perspectives on English devolution 233
10.4 The West Lothian Question 234
10.5 National identity in England and Scotland 238
10.6 National identity in Northern Ireland. 239
10.7 Constitutional preference by national identity in England and Scotland . . . 240
10.8 Perceptions of the impact of devolution 241
10.9 Expectations of devolution 242
10.10 Perceptions of Power: Where do people think power lies? 244
10.11 Has devolution improved government? 245
10.12 Attitudes towards the Belfast Agreement 246
10.13 The 2001 general election result in Great Britain 248
10.14 The 2001 general election result in Northern Ireland 251

CONCLUSION

11.1 Policy divergence in health 256

Abbreviations

ABI	Area Based Initiative
ACE	Arts Council of England
BIC	British-Irish Council
CNA	Campaign for a North East Assembly
CFER	Campaign for the English Regions
CoSLA	Convention of Scottish Local Authorities
CSG	Consultative Steering Group
CSR	Comprehensive Spending Review
DCMS	Department of Culture. Media and Sport
DEFRA	Department for the Environment, Food and Rural Affairs
DEL	Departmental Expenditure Limit
DETR	Department for Environment, Transport and the Regions
DfEE	Department for Education and Employment
DGN	Devolution Guidance Note
DTLR	Department for Transport, Local Government and the Regions
DPM	Deputy Prime Minister
DTI	Department of Trade and Industry
DUP	Democratic Unionist Party
DWP	Department of Work and Pensions
EEDA	East of England Development Agency
EERA	East of England Regional Assembly
EPFs	Executive Programme Funds
ERMA	East Midlands Regional Assembly
EU	European Union
FCO	Foreign and Commonwealth Office
GLA	Greater London Authority
GO	Government Office
HEFCE	Higher Education Funding Council for England
IWA	Institute of Welsh Affairs
IGC	Intergovernmental Conference
IGR	Intergovernmental Relations
IICD	Independent International Commission on Decommissioning
IRS	Integrated Regional Strategy
JMC	Joint Ministerial Committee
MAFF	Ministry of Agriculture, Fisheries and Food
MoU	Memorandum of Understanding

NECC	North East Constitutional Convention
NAW	National Assembly for Wales
NHS	National Health Service
NILTS	Northern Ireland Life and Times Survey
NIO	Northern Ireland Office
NIUP	Northern Ireland Unionist Party
OFMDFM	Office of the First Minister and the Deputy First Minister
PC	Plaid Cymru – The Party of Wales
PPP	Public Private Partnership
PSA	Public Service Agreement
RABs	Regional Arts Boards
RCU	Regional Coordination Unit
RDA	Regional Development Agency
RES	Regional Economic Strategy
RUC	Royal Ulster Constabulary
SDLP	Social Democratic and Labour Party
SEEDA	South East England Development Agency
SERA	South East Regional Assembly
SF	Sinn Féin
SNP	Scottish National Party
SO	Scotland Office
SQA	Scottish Qualifications Agency
TfL	Transport for London
UDA	Ulster Defence Association
UKIP	United Kingdom Independence Party
UUP	Ulster Unionist Party
WJEC	Welsh Joint Educational Council
WO	Wales Office

Foreword

This is the second in the Constitution Unit's series of yearbooks on devolution. Like last year's volume, *The State and the Nations: The First Year of Devolution in the United Kingdom*, it draws on the work of the Constitution Unit and a network of research partners from across the UK who are collaborating with the Unit on a variety of research projects. The backbone of the work is provided by research projects linked to our five-year research programme on 'Nations and Regions: the Dynamics of Devolution', which is funded by the Leverhulme Trust. My thanks, and those of all my colleagues, go to them for their support.

This yearbook does two things that no other publication on devolution does. First, *The State of the Nations 2001* tries to provide a full account of what has happened over the last year (or more accurately, the year from July 2000 to July 2001), a period chosen to coincide with the sessions of the devolved assemblies and legislatures. Our aim is that this should be the first source of reference for those wanting to know about devolution during that period. Second, it seeks to look at devolution not just as it affects the areas affected by devolution (or, in the case of the English regions, which may be affected by it); it also looks at devolution as it affects the UK as a whole and particularly the central institutions of the state.

To produce the book so quickly, while the material it contains is still current, is necessarily a collaborative effort. It draws on the knowledge of a wide range of specialists, from all parts of the United Kingdom and across several academic disciplines. The book has been edited in an attempt to produce a coherent whole, rather than simply a collection of essays.

The book is divided into two parts. The first part, subtitled 'The Nations' looks at the progress of devolution in the various territories of the UK over the last year. It draws heavily on the work of the monitoring teams funded by the Leverhulme Trust and the ESRC who, every quarter, produce detailed monitoring reports on developments in Scotland, Wales, Northern Ireland and the English Regions — and indeed each chapter was written or edited by the leaders of those teams. Our profound thanks for all their hard work over the course of the year go to all the members of those teams – in Scotland, Professor James Mitchell, Barry Winetrobe, Dr Mark Shephard, Professor Philip Schlesinger, Professor John Curtice, Dr Alex Wright, Neil McGarvey and Professor David Bell; in Wales, John Osmond, Denis Balsom, Nigel Blewitt, Jane Jones, Adrian Kay, Professor Martin Laffin, Mark Lang, Nia Richardson, Gerald Taylor and Alys Thomas; in Northern Ireland, Robin Wilson, Rick Wilford, Michael Brennan, John Coakley, Lizanne Dowds, Liz Fawcett, Greg McLaughlin, Professor Elizabeth Meehan, Duncan Morrow and Graham Walker; and for the English regions, John Tomaney, Peter Hetherington and Lynne Humphrey. The monitoring reports are a great resource and are available on the Unit's website, at:

www.ucl.ac.uk/constitution-unit/leverh/index.htm

They appear every February, May, August and November.

The second part is subtitled 'The State' and deals with how the UK as a whole has been affected by, and how the centre has responded to, devolution. Several of the chapters are concerned with institutional issues; hence we have chapters by David Bell and Alex Christie on finance, Roger Masterman and James Mitchell on the centre, drawing on their ESRC-funded project on 'Devolution and Whitehall', Roger Masterman (again) and Robert Hazell on Westminster, and myself on intergovernmental relations. The latter three have drawn on our fifth series of quarterly monitoring reports, on devolution and the centre, which are written by Roger Masterman. This part concludes with a review by John Curtice of how public opinion toward the UK and the devolved institutions has developed over the year.

Production of this book has been a team effort, and the team involved goes far beyond the contributors and members of the monitoring teams. At the Constitution Unit, I am indebted to Professor Robert Hazell, Director of the Unit, for his guidance, support, and trust in asking me to take on this project; to our invaluable administrators, Rebecca Blackwell and Gareth Lewes, who make the machinery work in a wholly admirable manner; and to all my other colleagues, including Meg Russell, Ben Seyd, Roger Masterman, Jo Murkens, Scott Greer and Mark Sandford, who have read chapters or dug up facts at the drop of a hat. For production of the book I am particularly grateful to Lucinda Maer, who has copy-edited the manuscript with a speed and efficiency that has been quite astonishing, and Keith Sutherland and his colleagues at Imprint Academic for producing the book at a speed exceeding even that of last year's volume, and with great good humour.

I would repeat Robert Hazell's plea in his foreword last year: please tell us what you think is valuable about the book, and what you think could be improved. Is there information you think we should have included, but have not? Are there any subjects we should have covered but have not? My e-mail address is a.trench@ucl.ac.uk, and I would be glad to hear from you about what you think of the book and how we might improve it for next year.

Alan Trench
October 2001

School of Public Policy
University College London

1

Introduction: Devolution's Second Year

But Mountains Left to Climb?

Alan Trench

"Labour says that devolution would promote the Union and give the Scots and Welsh more say over their own affairs. Whether it truly believes this I cannot say. I do know that devolution is more likely to break up the Union than promote it and that, in so far as it may offer the Scots and Welsh marginally more say over their own affairs in a few areas, this advantage is swamped by the disadvantages the advocates of devolution seek to hide..."

"Devolution would also have a devastating effect on business . . . The extra tier of government would delay decisions and burden firms — it would create uncertainty and hence cut investment and cost jobs. As Scotland and Wales became uncompetitive, they would become once again the unemployment blackspots that Conservative Governments removed over the past 18 years. So devolution would hurt business. It would hurt people. It would take power away from individuals and mean higher taxes for Scots. It would eventually lead to the break-up of the United Kingdom."[1]

Only the most hard-bitten aficionado could claim that devolution's second year has been exciting. While it has been a year full of incident, it is hard to find a clear and distinct theme to what has happened in devolution (or indeed elsewhere in public affairs) during the past twelve months. This is partly because the year has been overshadowed by other domestic events – most notably the UK general election in June 2001, but also the Foot-and-Mouth crisis during the late winter and spring, the ongoing travails of the Northern Ireland peace process, and reform of the EU treaties and UK membership of the Single Currency. That is to say nothing of matters in the wider world. It is also because devolution has, with the best will in the world, become rather boring. In many respects it is a very different year to 1999-2000.

There may have been few big devolution stories over the last year, but many detailed changes and events have occurred. The sheer quantity of what can seem like unconnected details can often hide the patterns of what is happening underneath. What has happened in Scotland, Wales or the English regions is often little known about outside those areas, and one aim of this

[1] From John Major, 'Say no to this doomed enterprise', *The Times* 30 August 1997.

book is to bring these events to a wider audience and to put them into a broader context. While what happens in Northern Ireland is much more news-worthy in the conventional sense, here too much of what is of interest is not well known. The big issues of devolution are in fact there, and things have been happening concerning them. Regardless of whether they become front-page news in the next year, the next decade or never, what has happened in the past year will shape the course of devolution in the UK for a long time to come.

Even if one accepts that devolution has become boring, that is in fact a considerable achievement. John Major's warning quoted above was only one of many predictions that devolution was a catastrophe waiting to happen. The major accomplishment for devolution's first year was that devolution happened, and happened smoothly. It went (to crib from Ron Davies) from being a process, to being an event that had happened, to being just normal. If the euphoria surrounding it has since evaporated and devolution has become a rather unremarkable part of the landscape of British public life, that is an even greater indication of how devolution has succeeded. It is no mean achievement, and one can easily forget both how extensive and how quick the change has been.

While the landscape of the British state changed in 1999, we still lack a reliable topography of that new landscape, and the official maps are not always accurate. The other task of this volume is to explore what that landscape looks like now we have had at least a little time to get used to it.

DEVOLUTION AND THE GENERAL ELECTION

The year was to a large degree overshadowed by the UK general election, the first since devolution. The ramifications of the general election are a recurrent theme throughout this book, discussed in all the 'Nations' chapters in Part I as well as several chapters in Part II, particularly those on Westminster and public opinion and attitudes. It still merits discussion here. Devolution itself was not much of an election issue; all the major British parties declared their commitment to it, now that it had happened, and all responded to it by issuing separate manifestos for Scotland and Wales as well as the UK as a whole.[2] The Liberal Democrats and Conservatives did have some ideas about developments in the framework of devolution, particularly in their Scottish and Welsh manifestos, and the nationalist parties in Wales and Scotland wanted to see dramatic increases in the autonomy of the devolved institutions in those nations (although the SNP was unclear about whether independence was an immediate objective or one to be achieved after a

---

[2] For a detailed analysis of the manifesto commitments of the Labour, Liberal Democrat and Conservative parties, the SNP and Plaid Cymru on devolution matters, see Trench 2001a.

transitional period). The outcome of the election was in little real doubt, however, which made Labour's manifestos the real focus of attention. Each of these included an identical section on devolution noting the achievement of implementing devolution and indicating that nothing would change except in the case of the English regions. Here Labour repeated the promise of elected regional assemblies for regions where there was support for them in a referendum, which was first made in 1997.[3] For Labour, then, devolution was largely finished, a box ticked on Tony Blair's list of commitments. Would that it were so simple.

There were differences in the election campaigns in England and in Scotland and Wales.[4] Aspects of devolution were themselves issues, for one thing, and the existence of coalition governments also affected campaigning. Both the Scottish Executive and National Assembly Cabinet had to establish principles to enable ordinary government activity and inter-party co-operation to continue.[5] Despite this, what was most striking about the UK general election was probably how little it had changed from those conducted before devolution. For one thing, having devolved institutions does not appear to have significantly affected turn-out in Scotland or Wales (or Northern Ireland, for that matter); while turn-out across the UK was lower than ever before, the reductions in Scotland, Wales and Northern Ireland were in line with those in England. It appears that the electorate across the whole of the UK continued to regard Westminster as being as important as it always had been.[6]

If devolution affected the issues that were at stake in the UK general election, however, it did so in a curious way. The logic of devolution implies that devolved matters should not be treated as election issues in a UK election — they are issues in the elections for the devolved assemblies and legislatures, but not for Westminster. However, in Scotland and Wales as much as England, health, education, and crime were prominent election issues even though these were devolved matters.[7] While all the political parties were offenders in this, the worst were the Conservatives (across the whole of the UK) and in some ways the SNP. Only the Liberal Democrats distinguished between what was a UK matter and what was for the devolved institutions — although they did that by an all-purpose disclaimer in the British manifesto.[8]

[3] The three manifestos were entitled *Ambitions for Britain*, *Ambitions for Scotland* and *Ambitions for Wales*. Labour also published a manifesto for the English regions, *Ambitions for the English Regions*, and at least one English regional manifesto, *Ambitions for the North East*, as well. The pledge regarding regional government is on pp. 34-5 of *Ambitions for Britain*. For the 1997 pledge, see *New Labour: because Britain deserves better* (Labour's 1997 manifesto), pp. 34-35.

[4] See Electoral Commission 2001, especially pp. 68-72.

[5] See McGarvey 2001, sections 1.1-1.3, for what this involved in Scotland.

[6] See Electoral Commission 2001, pp. 69-70, and chap. 10 .

[7] For a detailed assessment of 'devolution literacy' as demonstrated in the election manifestos, see Trench 2001*b*.

[8] *For a Liberal And Democratic Britain: Freedom Justice Honesty.* The party's Welsh manifesto, *A real chance for real change: Freedom Justice Honesty: the Liberal Democrat programme for Wales*

One could interpret this as showing that when it came to translating devolution from a 'policy' into the constitutional framework within which policy had to operate, the parties simply did not understand it. That view has a good deal to commend it; politicians would scarcely be alone in not understanding how devolution works let alone what it means. Perhaps a more sympathetic approach would be to say that the parties are aware of the restrictions devolution means for action by the UK Government. They are not disregarding those restrictions, but they are also conscious that they have to fight elections for the Scottish Parliament and National Assembly for Wales in 2003, and want to ensure consistency between their programmes now and their programmes then. They are also aware that these are the issues that concern the electorate. Even in Scotland and Wales, health and education are high on the list of voters' concerns, and a party which did not reflect that would be running a grave electoral risk. This view is supported by the fact that Labour's Scottish and Welsh manifestos set out distinctive positions from that in the UK manifesto on such key devolved issues as health and education – for example, neither embraced the private finance initiative with the enthusiasm of the British party.

The problem is that while this may reflect political reality, it also means that the parties collectively missed an opportunity to explain what devolution means to the public at large. The understanding of devolution is limited already, particularly outside the areas directly affected.[9] A clear explanation of what the UK Government could, and could not, do after devolution would have done much to explain the nature of the changes to the general public particularly in England. That opportunity was missed, and with it a chance both to improve understanding of devolution and to parade Labour's achievement in delivering it.

The outcome of the UK general election means that what little doubt there was about the durability of devolution has gone. If we accept the judgement that so far devolution is a success, that raises the question, though, of the nature of this success. In 2000-2001 what have been the areas where devolution has succeeded?

DEVOLUTION'S SUCCESSES

Scotland and Wales are the clearest areas of devolution's success. In both countries new devolved institutions are established and are now up and running. Both have coalition governments, a first for modern Britain in peacetime, and in both the coalitions appear to work well. In the short time

---

and the UK deserves credit for carefully distinguishing which level of government would do what, including (in the case of the UK Government) making funds available or altering the powers of the National Assembly.

[9] See Chapter 10 below, and also Curtice 2000 and Curtice and Seyd 2001.

since devolution took effect both have also coped with a change of First Minister, probably rather sooner than anyone expected in 1999 (and in Scotland's case in very sad circumstances). Both are now making their own distinctive policies in the areas devolved to them. All this is devolution working as it was expected to.

Both nations are starting to constitute themselves as distinct polities. This is much more obvious in Scotland than in Wales, as Scotland had retained or developed so many institutions that were separate from those south of the border. As a consequence Scotland has its national mass media, which have long kept an eye on national institutions such as education and the law. The extensive areas of policy devolved to Scotland have meant this has started to happen to a greater extent. Wales, of course, starts from a much lower base than Scotland, with fewer Welsh newspapers and magazines and less Welsh broadcasting. Yet it too has started the slow process of developing a distinctive Welsh approach to politics, as political issues unique to Wales start to emerge. What this process has involved over the last year is charted admirably in Chapter 2 on Scotland, by James Mitchell and members of the Scottish monitoring team, and Chapter 3 on Wales, by John Osmond. Inevitably this involves a great many detailed incidents, some of them apparently only of parochial interest and (in Wales's case) many involving the sensitive and distinctive issues of language and culture. The real importance of such incidents emerges when they are viewed as part of a process of creating a new political community. And with this comes a new political discourse, operating on several levels — whether it be policy development as carried out at the Institute of Welsh Affairs, serious news reporting as carried in the *Western Mail*, or the more light-hearted approach of Patrick Hannan.[10] As John Curtice shows in Chapter 10, this process is also translating itself into public attitudes, which respond to the different political systems involved. None of this would have been conceivable before devolution.

Even here, however, there are serious problems. As John Osmond notes (and is also discussed in Chapters 7 and 8), the legislative arrangements for Wales create a great deal of difficulty — limited by the extent to which devolution to Wales has actually taken place (as the Welsh settlement is effectively re-written with each new Westminster Act), and adding considerably to the work of all those involved in policy-making for Wales. It is clear that many involved in Welsh public life see the key issue as acquiring primary legislative power, and to do so during the life of the second National Assembly, to be elected in May 2003. Whether that would be possible within the framework of the Government of Wales Act 1998 is doubtful; the Act would probably need to be re-written from scratch rather than amended.

---

[10] Hannan 2000. His regular column for BBC Wales is available on the internet at www.news.bbc.co.uk/hi/english/uk/wales/default.stm

To describe Northern Ireland as a success for devolution may seem absurd and would be both premature and optimistic. It is of course impossible to separate devolution in Northern Ireland from the peace process and the implementation of the 1998 Belfast Agreement, of which the devolved institutions constitute only the first of three strands of institutional arrangements to deliver peace. Yet, as Robin Wilson and Rick Wilford show in Chapter 4, the devolved institutions in Northern Ireland have a number of successes to their credit, despite the effects of fits and starts in the peace process. While both Sinn Féin and DUP ministers, in their different ways, have failed to co-operate with each other and ministers from other parties as expected under the Belfast Agreement, ministers from all parties have delivered a number of developments that would not have been conceivable before devolution. The last year has at least seen glimmerings of 'normal' politics in Northern Ireland, even if it is unclear what that may lead to subsequently.

A fourth area of success is probably that of intergovernmental relations – certainly, that is how it is regarded by many of the participants. The system of relations between the four governments that appears to exist a year on is characterised by the use of informal procedures, a great deal of co-operation and information-sharing, and much consensus. It makes limited use of formal mechanisms and institutions, and that use is declining. It operates with strikingly few staff too. In short, it lacks all the hallmarks of pseudo-diplomacy exhibited by intergovernmental relations in established federal systems; perhaps Noreen Burrows is right to use the term '*intra*-governmental relations' instead.[11] The pitfalls that were foreseen in this area, which it was feared would lead to intense political rows or legal disputes between governments, have not happened. However, as Chapter 7 discusses, this success may be less than it appears. The system works so well because of deliberate attempts to avoid confrontation, by both politicians and officials. This involves a good deal of hiding of major issues and so avoiding potential disputes. Issues which could cause a serious fracture in relations are lurking underneath the surface and are likely to emerge later if not sooner. Moreover, the system depends heavily on mutual good-will and a shared commitment to making it work. If that were to change – for example, with the arrival of an administration with a significant nationalist element in Scotland or Wales – the position might be rather different. Intergovernmental relations are better regarded as an area of qualified success, but one which may not hold up if put under serious pressure.

DEVOLUTION'S FAILURES AND THE UNANSWERED QUESTIONS

In the same way as its successes are qualified, so are the areas where devolution has been less successful. One area is the central apparatus of the British

---

[11] Burrows 2000, p114.

state — the courts, the civil service and central executive, and Parliament at Westminster. Chapters 8 and 9 show that the changes made in these areas have been very limited. Each institution has done the minimum to accommodate itself to this changed landscape. That has resulted in a good many detailed adjustments of practice, but little attempt to re-think the role of the central institutions of the state in the light of devolution. The changes to the machinery of government made after the general election have consolidated responsibility for devolution policy, including the English regions, in a new unit within Cabinet Office, responsible to the Deputy Prime Minister John Prescott. However, most front-line Whitehall departments still deal with a patchwork of devolved and reserved matters, relying heavily on the competence of officials to ensure that devolution questions are identified and properly dealt with. Responsibility for the English regions is split between three departments (the Department for Transport, Local Government and the Regions and the Department of Trade and Industry as well as the Cabinet Office). Quite what the territorial offices, particularly the Scotland and Wales Offices, are to do in the longer term remains unclear; their liaison and advisory role looks increasingly redundant as devolution expertise is 'mainstreamed' across Whitehall. In short, Whitehall has made little attempt to re-consider its role or working since devolution, following instead a pattern of incremental and ad hoc adjustment familiar to any observer of British public administration.

At Westminster, the role of Scottish and Welsh MPs and the Select and Grand Committees is no clearer than it was, the more so now that none sit both there and at Holyrood or Cardiff Bay. As Roger Masterman and Robert Hazell point out in Chapter 9, it is especially hard to know what business there is for the Scottish Affairs Select Committee in the Commons to do now that it has looked at poverty in Scotland and the Scottish drinks industry, the two main areas reserved to the UK Government where there is also a distinct Scottish interest. What is happening to the Westminster statute book as a result of devolution is perhaps more interesting (and the point where Westminster and Whitehall intersect), but there is little clear evidence emerging there either. The exception is the courts, where the senior judiciary are now starting to consider matters afresh and to consider how the legal system should deal with the changed situation it faces, but that is a case where a debate has started rather than reached a conclusion.[12]

Policy toward the English regions is an area where change has started to happen, and at a dramatic pace. Despite Labour's commitment in the 1997 manifesto, the issue had sat on the back boiler until early 2001, overshadowed by initiatives to reform local government and particularly to introduce elected mayors. In Chapter 5 John Tomaney shows how a variety of factors, coming from both grass-roots movements and concern from UK-level

---

[12] For an example, see Bingham 2001.

politicians, have given the issue a new prominence. A White Paper is now due in late 2001 or early 2002, but whether that will deliver what proponents of regional government are seeking is doubtful. Yet England remains the big unknown in the institutional arrangements for a devolved United Kingdom. Robert Hazell, who has discussed this theme on a number of occasions, returns to it in the conclusion to this book.[13] The fact that the question is now being seriously addressed can be regarded as a success, but the lack of more tangible progress over Labour's first term in office at UK level, and the lack of any clear timescale for achieving this objective in the second term, are both disappointing.

However, finance is perhaps the single greatest unanswered question in the devolution arrangements. The Barnett Formula, used to allocate funding from the UK Government to the devolved institutions, has been the subject of increasing public discussion since devolution took effect. In Chapter 6 David Bell and Alex Christie assess that debate and look at the workings of the formula and the extent to which it gives the devolved administrations the financial resources they need to develop policies that are different to those of the UK Government. Their answer is not optimistic; for all its virtues, Barnett will not work well in the coming years. Already the devolved administrations are facing a slowing rate of growth in the resources available to them, as a consequence of the 'Barnett squeeze'. The effect of this will be to limit further their room for manoeuvre in policy terms. And that is without considering the claims of the English regions for higher levels of spending, to bring them up to the levels enjoyed by the devolved territories.

This of course comes at a time when policy divergence is starting to become a reality. That too was a goal of devolution. Both Scotland and Wales have started to develop their own home-grown policies, which are discussed in Chapters 2 and 3. Northern Ireland is rather behind the Scottish and Welsh pioneers but has started to develop different approaches too. Whether the new policies relate to free personal and nursing care for the elderly as in Scotland, or free prescriptions for young people as in Wales, these policies start to have an effect on other parts of the UK, and it is here that the logic of devolution becomes hardest for the public to accept and understand. On one hand, in England people still find it hard to understand why policy should be materially different in Scotland or Wales, even though in fact it has been for many years, if only on the administrative level (and what else do local governments do in England?). The larger amounts of public money spent in Scotland, Wales and Northern Ireland under the Barnett Formula aggravates this. On the other hand, spending money on a different policy involves making a choice about the use of that money. When funds are limited, it means not only that Scotland (or Wales, or wherever) has 'more' of one thing, but by implication that it will have less of something else. The issue is not simply whether

---

[13] See Hazell 2000a, the introduction to Hazell 2000b and Hazell 2000c.

Scots have better arrangements for caring for the elderly than the English, but whether they will accept (say) worse arrangements for acute hospital care to pay for that. That is aggravated by the Barnett squeeze; the increases in the funds available to those administrations will continue to slow as overall public spending grows. While people in established federal states are used to such policy divergence as a normal part of life, such an understanding of what has changed has yet to come very readily in the UK, and the financial pressures will worsen it. The ramifications of this are also discussed by Robert Hazell in his conclusion.

How all this plays with the general public is also hard to tell. In Chapter 10 John Curtice has used a great deal of public survey evidence to see what people make of devolution. It appears to be accepted if not embraced with enthusiasm throughout the UK, but much more supported where there are devolved institutions than it is in England. Yet there is still a widespread view that the UK Government remains by far the most important source of power in the UK, even where there are devolved institutions. The material elsewhere in this book suggests that this view remains correct. For all that the landscape has changed, it has not changed enough to deliver what devolution promised. The expectation that there would be a genuine and significant transfer of power to the devolved institutions has not yet been fully realised. Instead, it has become apparent that devolution is a reform half-completed, and the agenda for the next few years will be to complete that process. These issues may not have been prominent in 2000-01 but their importance is growing. Paradoxically, the longer they remain invisible and action to deal with them is deferred, the greater their impact is likely to be when they do break the surface.

Perhaps one way to look at the progress that has been made is a climbing analogy. In 1997, when we were on the valley floor, we set our sights on the vast mountainous bulk of a devolved structure and set out to climb to that height. In 1998-99 we scaled the slopes we saw and thought we were nearing the summit of our ambitions. It is now apparent that in fact we did not reach the peaks, just a plateau. That plateau is high above the valley floor and it is quite an achievement to have got here, especially with the relative ease we have. Despite the dire predictions of figures like John Major, the sky did not fall on our heads as we climbed. But from here we have a clearer perspective. We can now see that we have not reached the real summit, but we can also see more clearly where that summit lies and what we must climb to achieve it. I hope this book gives a clear guide to the achievements made, the objectives that remain and the hurdles in the way of them.

BIBLIOGRAPHY

Lord Bingham of Cornhill (2001). *The Evolving Constitution.* (The *Justice* Annual Lecture), 4 October 2001

Curtice, J. (2001). 'The People's Verdict: Public Attitudes to Devolution and the Union' in Hazell 2000b.

Curtice, J. and Seyd, B. (2001). 'Is devolution strengthening or weakening the UK?', in A. Park, J. Curtice, K. Thomson, L. Jarvis, and C. Bromley (eds.) *British Social Attitudes: the 18th report.* London: Sage.

Electoral Commission (2001). *Election 2001 The official results.* London: Politicos Publishing.

Hannan, P. (2000). *Wales off Message: From Clapham Common to Cardiff Bay* Bridgend: Seren.

Hazell, R. (2000a). 'Regional government in England: Three policies in search of a strategy' in S. Chen and T. Wright (eds) *The English Question.* London: Fabian Society.

Hazell, R. (ed) (2000b). *The State and the Nations.* Exeter: Imprint Academic.

Hazell, R. (2000c). *An Unstable Union: Devolution and the English Question. State of the Union Annual Lecture.* London: Constitution Unit.

McGarvey, N. (2001). *Scotland Quarterly Monitoring report,* August 2001. London: Constitution Unit; available from www.ucl.ac.uk/constitution-unit/

Trench, A. (2001a). *Devolution and the 2001 UK General Election: Devolution Commitments of the Major Parties.* London: Constitution Unit; available from www.ucl.ac.uk/constitution-unit/.

Trench, A. (2001b). *Devolution and the 2001 UK General Election: 'Devolution Literacy' and the Manifestos.* London: Constitution Unit; available from www.ucl.ac.uk/constitution-unit/.

Part I

The Nations

2

In Search of Stability

Coalition Politics in the Second Year of the National Assembly for Wales

John Osmond

LEGITIMACY WITHOUT POWER

The National Assembly was transformed by the creation of a majority coalition government between Labour and the Liberal Democrats in October 2000. At a stroke the Administration was provided with an assured majority and a programme for government, two attributes that had eluded it during the first year of devolution.

Previously there had been instability resulting from Labour's unexpected failure to secure a majority in the first Assembly elections in May 1999. Combined with the provenance, personality and style of administration of the inaugural First Secretary, this led to a series of upheavals culminating in a no confidence vote and the resignation of Alun Michael in February 2000.[1]

Rhodri Morgan's new Administration immediately created a breathing space. However, it was clear from the start that he would have to reach a more formal accommodation with another party to stabilise his government and allow the roots of the devolution settlement in Wales to begin to grow. This was achieved in a matter of months with the partnership agreement with the Welsh Liberal Democrats. Following prolonged negotiations, this was signed on 6 October 2000.[2] However, while the agreement brought about the desired stability for at least the short to medium term, the circumstances in which it was launched contained the seeds of potential destabilisation.

The first intimation was provided by allegations of fraud made against the Welsh Liberal Democrat leader, Michael German, scarcely before there was time for the ink to dry on the agreement, allegations that he strongly refuted. First Minister Rhodri Morgan went ahead with the agreement confident that the allegations would not be made to stick. Nonetheless, the row continued, re-surfacing in the run-up to the UK general election in June 2001, and then again in July when German was forced to stand aside as Deputy First Minister while a police investigation took place.

[1] For an account of this episode see Osmond 2000.
[2] *Putting Wales First: A Partnership for the People of Wales. The First Partnership Agreement of the National Assembly for Wales*, 6 October 2000.

Figure 2.1. Key Events in the National Assembly's second year

2000

19 September	Assembly's Brussels office is officially opened.
6 October	Coalition between Labour and the Liberal Democrats provides a programme for a majority government.
9 October	Tom Middlehurst resigns from Cabinet in protest at the coalition.
10 October	Separate £24m budget voted for the Office of the Presiding Officer.
15 October	Special Welsh Liberal Democrat Conference approves coalition
16 October	Cabinet members assume title of Ministers. Liberal Democrat leader Mike German appointed Deputy First Minister
19 October	Wrexham Labour AM John Marek elected Deputy Presiding Officer.
6 December	Assembly call on the Westminster Government to include a Welsh tick box in the census forms.
19 December	Assembly votes by 29 to 9 against abolition of defendants' right to jury trial in Queen's Speech debate. Plaid Cymru, Liberal Democrat and Conservative members voted against. Nine Labour members voted in favour with 13 abstaining.
19 December	Assembly voted unanimously that a Welsh 'tick box' be included in the 2001 census form.

2001

17 January	Assembly's Operational Review begins.
31 January	Economic Development Committee refuses to endorse the Administration's ten-year National Economic Development Strategy.
2 February	Corus Steel announce 2,500 job redundancies.
2 February	National Health Service Plan for Wales proposes the abolition of the Health Authorities.
1 March	Paul Silk, former House of Commons Clerk, takes up position as Assembly Clerk overseeing Office of the Presiding Officer.
13 March	Assembly debates for the first time the legislative programme it wishes incorporated in the forthcoming Queen's Speech.
1 April	New Assembly policies of free entry to National Museums, abolition of prescription and dental check up charges for the under-25s and over 60s take effect.

8 May	Cabinet Sub-Committees established for Sustainable Development, Children and Young people, Wales in the World, and Corus.
11 May	Administration's Children's Commissioner for Wales Bill passes its final stages at Westminster.
June 7	UK general election produces status quo in Wales with Plaid Cymru and Labour both gaining a seat at each other's expense.
13 June	Education Committee votes to 'disregard' parts of a paper by Dafydd Glyn Jones on the Welsh Language.
5 July	Mike German stands aside from Cabinet as Deputy First Minister while police investigate fraud allegations against him.

A second source of destabilisation began in January when acrimonious debates over the Welsh language invaded the Assembly chamber. This broke a prolonged period of truce between the parties on an issue which some imagined had been taken out of politics. Long-standing worries about the impact of in-migration into fragile Welsh-speaking communities were voiced and soon engulfed Labour and Plaid Cymru (PC) in extravagant charges and counter-charges, variously of racism and using the language as a political football. This continued through the rest of the year, interspersed with an ill-tempered dispute in the Education Committee over evidence it received on the case for a Welsh-medium College within the University of Wales. The overall result was to inject a new tone of acrimony and polarisation into the Assembly's proceedings.

A third source of destabilisation continued to be found in the devolution settlement itself. The Assembly continued to confront constitutional difficulties emanating from its lack of powers over primary legislation and the resultant problems of engaging in a constructive dialogue with Westminster and Whitehall. As Noreen Burrows, Jean Monnet Professor of European Law at the University of Glasgow has put it:

> In Wales there is the anomaly that an Assembly deriving its legitimacy from the will of the people demonstrated in elections lacks the power to carry out the functions associated elsewhere within the United Kingdom with such a body. The National Assembly for Wales therefore has legitimacy but lacks a functional capacity proper to its status whereas prior to devolution the Welsh Office had an extensive functional capacity yet lacked legitimacy. The whole point of devolution was to rectify this position. It has recently turned it upside down.[3]

This underlying destabilising dilemma was addressed during the course of the year by a long-running Operational Review of the Assembly, chaired by

[3] Burrows 2000, p186.

the Presiding Officer. Evidence submitted from all four parties proved remarkably consensual, establishing a common agenda for many improvements. There was no doubt, however, that the Review's main function was to clear the ground in preparation for a more far-reaching independent Commission into the Assembly's powers, to be set in train under the terms of the coalition agreement early in 2002.

THE ADMINISTRATION

The Coalition

Labour's negotiation of a coalition with the Liberal Democrats in October 2000 came with a price tag: two seats in the Cabinet for the Liberal Democrats, with their leader Michael German appointed Deputy First Minister in charge of Economic Development, and Jenny Randerson becoming Minister for Culture, an entirely new portfolio.

These ministerial titles — previously Cabinet members were known as Secretaries — signalled more substantive constitutional developments. The 25-page *Partnership Agreement,* which took more than two months to negotiate, contained a raft of policies across the range of the Assembly's responsibilities. Headline commitments were free school milk for all children under seven, a freezing of prescription charges, and legislation to allow pensioners to travel free on local bus services from 2002. However, of longer-term import so far as the devolution settlement is concerned was a commitment to create an independent Commission to examine the Assembly's powers and electoral arrangements. This will be established early in 2002 but will not report until after the next Assembly election in May 2003. Ron Davies AM, architect of the 1998 Wales Act, was quick to point out that 'any objective review' would conclude that legislative powers were the 'the next logical step'.[4]

The line-up of the coalition Cabinet presented a completely new Executive compared with the first Assembly Cabinet that had taken the reins a little over a year before. Five of the original nine faces had disappeared including Alun Michael as First Secretary. In their place were a group of people more representative of the front ranking politicians available within the Assembly, as Figure 2.2 sets out.

In addition to these appointments Christine Chapman, formerly deputy Minister for Economic Development, took over from Rhodri Morgan as chair of the Monitoring Committee responsible for overseeing implementation of the Objective 1 programme. Karen Sinclair was promoted from Deputy to Chief Whip. In combination these appointments created a 16-strong ministerial team. Add the positions of Presiding and Deputy

[4] Ron Davies, *In Search of Attitude*, paper distributed to AMs, 4 December 2000.

Presiding Officers and this leaves an Assembly with just 42 members from whom the full range of Opposition spokespersons have to be drawn as well as personnel to run an expanding committee system. One inevitable consequence was to push the issue of the Assembly's relatively small membership higher up the constitutional agenda.

Figure 2.2. The coalition cabinet, October 2000

- First Minister: Rhodri Morgan (Lab)
- Deputy First Minister and Minister for Economic Development: Michael German (Lib Dem)
- Business Manager (Trefnydd) and E-Commerce Minister: Andrew Davies (Lab)
- Minister for Finance and Communities: Edwina Hart (Lab)
- Minister for Education and Life-Long Learning: Jane Davidson (Lab)
- Minister for Culture, the Welsh Language and Sport: Jenny Randerson (Lib Dem)
- Minister for Environment, Planning and Transport: Sue Essex (Lab)
- Minister for Rural Affairs: Carwyn Jones (Lab)
- Minister for Health and Social Services: Jane Hutt (Lab)

In addition five Deputy Ministers replaced the previous three:

- Economic Development: Alun Pugh (Lab)
- Local Government: Peter Black (Lib Dem)
- Health: Brian Gibbons (Lab)
- Rural Affairs, Culture and Environment: Delyth Evans (Lab)
- Education and Lifelong Learning: Huw Lewis (Lab)

As the agreement document states, it is closely modelled on the Scottish Parliament's partnership between Labour and Liberal Democrats so far as its working arrangements are concerned.[5] Even so, importing a coalition into Wales was a shock to the system. Little previous groundwork had been undertaken, in contrast to the Scottish experience in which a Convention had preceded the formation of the Scottish Parliament. The Welsh negotiations were undertaken in secrecy over a couple of months by a handful of players on both sides. The first many Labour AMs heard about the deal was the day before it was announced.

From a Labour grassroots perspective the new coalition and most of its detailed policy commitments paled into insignificance when set against the fact that Liberal Democrats were to be brought into the Cabinet. This prompted the resignation of the Cabinet Secretary for Post-16 Education,

---

[5] It was noteworthy that in the first Cabinet following the announcement of the coalition Rhodri Morgan 'encouraged all Cabinet members to establish contact with their counterparts in the Scottish Executive, to learn more about partnership working there' (Cabinet Minutes, 9 October 2000; available on the internet at www.wales.gov.uk/organicabinet/content/CabMeetings/index.htm)

Tom Middlehurst, though it was widely recognised that he 'jumped before being pushed'. Under the agreement Middlehurst's portfolio was merged with Pre-16 Education to create a single Education department.

Labour's concession that proportional representation would be considered for local government elections was also opposed by many Labour local government leaders. Their opposition crystallised in a bitter dispute between the local authority-run, Labour-controlled Welsh Joint Education Committee (WJEC) and the Deputy First Minister, Mike German. This dominated newspaper headlines and television programmes for the first few weeks of the coalition. Before his election to the Assembly the Liberal Democrat leader had worked for the WJEC as European officer responsible for promoting exchanges between Welsh students and those in other European countries. It was alleged that he had left the WJEC with his department running up a large financial deficit due in some measure to extravagant foreign travel and a relaxed approach to expenses, allegations that were strongly denied. There were calls, for example by the Labour leader of Bridgend County Council Jeff Jones, for Mike German to stand aside as Deputy First Minister while the allegations were investigated. However, he claimed in return that the campaign against him was motivated by some local government leaders seeking to destabilise the coalition. In the event, once a police investigation was launched, in July 2001, Mike German was forced to stand aside from the Cabinet.

What the row brought sharply into focus was the coalition's radical departure from the traditional politics of one-party rule that had been experienced in large parts of Wales over the previous two, and sometimes three, generations. In a speech to the Institute of Welsh Politics in Aberstywth Rhodri Morgan declared:

> In moving our democracy forward we need a pluralistic view in which no party or groups of parties on the governmental side have any kind of monopoly on wisdom at all. The structure of the Assembly is very much orientated towards trying to develop a communal 'small-nation psychology' way of working. In pushing the devolution process forward we don't necessarily want to keep the Westminster style for Wales.[6]

The origins of the coalition go back to the fall of the Assembly's inaugural First Secretary Alun Michael, in February 2000. At that point it became clear that the minority Labour Administration would need to find some new accommodation with the opposition parties to provide for greater stability. Indeed, in one television interview at the time the coalition deal was announced, Rhodri Morgan said that when he had taken over from Alun Michael he had received an authorisation from the Welsh Labour Party

---

[6] Rhodri Morgan, *Check Against Delivery*, Address to the Institute of Welsh Politics, Aberystwyth, 13 November 2000.

Executive that, should he judge a coalition was necessary, he could pursue one. That had been a condition under which he undertook the Labour leadership in the Assembly.

It now became clear why Rhodri Morgan refrained from making any substantive changes to his Cabinet when he first took office and, indeed, why he continued to hold on to the Economic Development portfolio. Announcing the new coalition he referred specifically to the difficulties that the minority Administration had experienced because it had been unable to rely on a majority to get its programme through:

> The National Assembly is a new fledgling institution. It is inevitable when people see a lot of political shenanigans and an Administration that is repeatedly hamstrung and deflected from its aims to do its best for Wales that they question its benefits. This positive partnership will provide the unity of purpose to deliver good government and has the wholehearted support of my Cabinet.[7]

What also became clear was that Morgan's Administration had first to deal with the major issue that had precipitated Alun Michael's resignation before it could secure a deal. This was the thorny question of match funding for the west Wales and the Valleys Objective 1 region, whose settlement had to await the Chancellor's Comprehensive Spending Review in July 2000. Once that was out of the way and it was clear that sufficient extra funds would be coming to Wales over the next three years to underpin the Objective 1 programme, the Liberal Democrats could be brought on side. The importance of this sequence of events was underlined by Rhodri Morgan in his speech to the Institute of Welsh Politics:

> We can develop further through having a majority-based government because we have largely lanced the boil of Objective One funding and the wider issue of having a three-year budget via the comprehensive spending review. That allowed us to achieve an agreement with another party to take us to a majority. This is an adequate majority to work on to deliver policies based on the comprehensive spending review. If you have the support of the majority in the Assembly you can push forward a series of objectives, jointly with the Liberal Democrats in this case.[8]

The deficiencies of the creation of the Assembly as a corporate body was much discussed during its first year. This constitutional status, laid down in the Government of Wales Act 1998, meant that the Assembly was a single legal personality. There was no formal distinction between the executive and the legislature, and all members of the Assembly shared responsibility for its decisions. In practice, the establishment of a Cabinet within the Act created a de facto separate Executive. The overall result, however, was some

---

[7] Administration Press Release, 5 October 2000.

[8] Rhodri Morgan, *op. cit.*

confusion and a lack of clarity about where powers lay that the Assembly spent much of its first year attempting to resolve. As the Presiding Officer Lord Elis-Thomas had put it, in a speech looking back on the Assembly's opening months: 'The difficult and complex growth of parliamentary-type government in the National Assembly, from within the body of territorial administrative/executive government in the previous system has provided the main drama of the first year of powers . . . '[9]

In political terms the coalition's creation of a government sure of its majority with a more focused policy programme gave considerable impetus to the momentum towards parliamentary-type government that the Presiding Officer described. Moreover, the creation of a stronger Administration provided a clearer focus for the Opposition in the Assembly. This last dimension was demonstrated within a matter of days when backbench members voted against the coalition government's nominee for Deputy Presiding Officer, former Cabinet member Rosemary Butler. Instead, they supported the Wrexham Labour AM John Marek, albeit by one vote. It was estimated that five Labour and two Liberal Democrat AMs joined with PC and the Conservatives to secure this result in the secret ballot.[10] In practice, such political realities as these were likely to achieve more than any constitutional declarations in establishing a strong executive government within a *de facto* parliamentary system in the remaining three years or so of the Assembly's first term.

The Economy

The coalition faced its first major policy crisis in early 2001 when mounting redundancies in the Welsh manufacturing sector were led by the Corus steel announcement of the loss of more than 2,500 jobs. A sense of beleaguerment was compounded by the onset of Foot-and-Mouth Disease towards the end of February. Efforts to come up with a package of £20 million to persuade Corus to stave off its closure programme was doomed to failure set against the £226 million loss the company made in the first half of the financial year. A leaked internal memo from the Assembly's Director of Economic Affairs, Derek Jones, suggested there would be no additional support from the Treasury: the Assembly would only receive money to deal with the job losses if it agreed to give up other grants that it was entitled to, such as meeting the cost of repairs after recent flood damage.[11]

Meanwhile, the Administration's handwringing at its impotence in the face of the Corus announcement came in for a good deal of criticism. As the

---

[9] Lord Elis-Thomas, *The National Assembly: A year in Power?,* Address to the Institute of Welsh Politics, University of Wales, Aberystwyth, 8 July 2000.

[10] *Western Mail*, 20 October 2000.

[11] The memo, dated 1 February 2001, was leaked as a result of an e-mail accidentally transmitted to Emyr Williams, a Plaid Cymru researcher in the Assembly.

Head of Research in Business and Management at the University of Wales College, Newport, Kath Ringwald, put it: 'What we need from the Assembly now is leadership and vision and direct resources specifically for these problems. We need a strategy for the regeneration of specific areas'.[12]

In light of this it was significant that at the end of January the Economic Development Committee refused by a majority vote to endorse the Administration's Economic Development Strategy. An assault on the document was led by Ron Davies, the Caerphilly Labour AM who, on the eve of the Committee meeting, issued fellow members a 2000-word briefing paper attacking virtually every aspect. This was a key vote and a further defining moment in the early life of the National Assembly. A document that bore all the hallmarks of the previous Welsh Office administration — lacking in research and rigour, unfocused, and undemanding on Whitehall — failed to find democratic endorsement, despite it being sponsored by the new majority coalition. In the plenary debate that followed Ron Davies linked the poverty of thinking with the wider issue of funding, calling for a revision of the Barnett Formula, the basis for the distribution of resources from Whitehall to Wales:

> The issue that we face is not about redistributing slices of the cake but increasing the size of the cake. Whatever the merits of the Barnett Formula over the past years, there is now one inescapable fact: the existing block formula system is disadvantaging Wales. The Barnett block, being historically determined, does not reflect the social and economic difficulties that Wales has experienced over the past 20 years, and is leading to convergence of levels of public expenditure vis-à-vis England, rather than divergence, as our economic and social needs demand. This is not whinging; it is a matter of the basic socialist principles of equity, redistribution and social justice. The present system of financing Welsh public expenditure should be scrapped, and replaced with a needs-based system. That is the single most important issue facing the National Assembly and, until it is resolved, we have no realistic prospects of successfully tackling our economic deficit or our social problems.[13]

A New Structure for the Welsh Health Service

The National Health plan for Wales, *Improving Health in Wales,* published in January 2001, outlined a radical departure in the organisation of the health service with a proposal to abolish the five Health Authorities by April 2003.[14] In their place the 22 existing Local Health Groups, corresponding geographically with the 22 Welsh counties, will become statutory bodies, to be known

[12] *Western Mail,* 20 October 2000.

[13] Assembly *Record,* 13 February 2001; available on the internet at:
www.wales.gov.uk/keypubrecordproceedings/index.htm

[14] See *Improving Health in Wales: a plan for the NHS with its partners* and *Improving Health in Wales — Structural Change in the NHS in Wales; a consultation document.*

as Local Health Boards, responsible for commissioning as well as providing health care. The aim is to create a primary care-led service.

At the same time the new Health Boards will be too small for many specialist functions that need greater critical mass. It is proposed, therefore, that secondary care responsibilities should be carried out by consortia of Local Health Boards based on the three health regions of North, Mid West and South East Wales.

The Administration claims this new structure will result in more account-ability and democracy, providing a direct line of accountability between the Assembly Administration and the Local Health Boards and the NHS Trusts. That is to say, a direct relationship should be established between the Direc-tor of NHS Wales, the Chief Executives of the Trusts, and the General Managers of the Local Health Boards. The line of accountability to the Assembly would no longer pass through the Health Authorities, thereby cutting out a level of administration.

Such are the proposals in outline. However, they leave many questions to be settled. One concern is that having 22 Local Health Groups rather than the five Health Authorities might increase bureaucracy and costs. There are also doubts whether Local Health Groups are ready for the responsibilities that are envisaged for them since they are relatively new bodies. The proposed structure would also bring additional responsibilities to the Assembly Administration whose civil service is already overloaded with work. As Tony Beddow, Director of the Welsh Institute of Health, pointed out: 'It is a massive leap of faith in the existing Local Health Groups. Health Authorities are old and experienced, but now we are moving to two new siblings, Local Health Boards and the Assembly Administration.'[15]

Abolition of the Health Authorities has presented the Administration with the difficult task of coming up with a new structure without being seen to be creating a new level of management and more bureaucracy. At the same time, in its determination to place primary care at the core of health delivery in Wales the Administration has embarked on creating on a structure that will be completely different from the English service.

The Farming Crisis

The Administration's record in handling the Foot-and-Mouth outbreak proved a significant event in the Assembly's development. It consolidated devolution in Wales, providing an opportunity for the Assembly to prove its credibility. In particular, the Administration, led by an authoritative Agricul-ture minister in Carwyn Jones, demonstrated that it was capable of handling complex problems involving multi-level governance in a period of crisis. In turn this reflected on the Assembly more generally, doing something to

---

[15] Interview with Tony Beddow, June 2001.

dispel a widespread view that it was little more than a talking shop. In that process there developed a sense that Cardiff was increasingly replacing London as the main location of political accountability in Wales.

From the start the Administration demonstrated a willingness to take a radically different approach from England if necessary. It rapidly assumed powers from Whitehall by becoming the agent of the Ministry of Agriculture, Fisheries and Food (MAFF) in charge of disease control in Wales. Once Foot-and-Mouth was confirmed in February, the Administration established an operation room to manage, on behalf of MAFF, the culling of infected animals and prevent the spread of the disease. Information points were established across Wales, and emergency powers were rushed through giving local authorities the power to close public footpaths.

On the whole culling decisions were taken quicker and more effectively in Wales since the Welsh Administration was dealing with a much smaller area than the Whitehall-based MAFF. It is arguable that in the process the Welsh Government became clearly visible to the Welsh public as a major decision-maker for the first time. Indeed, when it emerged that Wales had not been included in the remit of a Downing Street task force to assess the impact of the crisis and draw up a rescue plan, it was suggested by a 'source close to the UK Cabinet' that this was because Wales was dealing with the crisis better than England: 'I don't think for a moment that there's any snub to the Assembly. It's just that the UK Government itself is in a mess as to what it's going to do.'[16]

MAFF was keen to use vaccination as a fallback contingency plan in the blackspots of Cumbria and Devon if the disease continued to spread. Carwyn Jones travelled to London in April to tell MAFF that vaccination would not be used in Wales and would not receive the approval it needed from the Assembly. This proactive style showed that the Assembly was capable of exercising the same powers as the Scottish Parliament. As Carwyn Jones put it: 'We can handle the situation. We should have the same powers as Scotland.'[17]

He also asserted that the close interaction between decision-makers in the Assembly Administration and the people affected across Wales would not have occurred during the former days of the Welsh Office regime: 'You're closer to the ground. You meet the farmers. England is too big for that. And officials in the old Welsh Office would never have done it.'[18]

Education

In July 2001 the Administration scrapped secondary school league tables with immediate effect, an initiative which distanced the Welsh from the

[16] *Western Mail,* 14 March 2001.
[17] Interview with Carwyn Jones, 8 May 2001.
[18] *Ibid.*

English education systems. Schools will continue to publish their results in their own prospectuses and governor's annual reports, but the Assembly will now be exploring alternatives to schools tables to be used to compare schools' performances in the future. They will be looking for a more 'value-added' scheme. School tables for primary schools had already been dropped by the Assembly.

In June the Education minister announced that the contract to pilot the new Welsh Baccalaureate post-16 qualification, initiated by the partnership agreement with the Liberal Democrats, had been awarded to the WJEC.[19] The WJEC will now have the task of developing an appropriate curriculum for the pilot which will be undertaken in 18 schools and colleges across Wales for three years from September 2003. However, the Administration has moved away from the commitment made in the October 2000 coalition deal which stated that the new curriculum would be based on the International Baccalaureate. The intent at that time was for the International Baccalaureate to be used as a back-up qualification for those students going through the pilot. Later, however, it was decided that the back-up qualification should be A-Levels. As a result it is difficult to see how a 'baccalaureate approach' can be achieved for the new curriculum now to be piloted.[20]

In September the Education minister unveiled a comprehensive policy statement, *The Learning Country*, published simultaneously with an English Education White Paper. This departed from the English approach in a number of fundamental directions. Proposed was a new Foundation Stage for 3 to 7 year olds with the end of tests for 7 year olds. More generally, reliance on the private sector, a major theme of the English White Paper, was ruled out, as was any programme for specialist schools, another feature of the English approach. As Jane Davidson put it:

> We shall take our own policy direction to get the best for Wales ... In a small country, with relatively small unitary authorities, with so many distinctive features, there would be real risks in a wholesale shift to extensive and untested measures delivered solely through the private or other sectors without the most careful consideration.[21]

The Administration's Legislative Programme 2001-02

In March the Assembly debated for the first time in its history the legislative programme the Administration would like to see incorporated in the next term at Westminster following the UK general election. This will be an annual event in the early Spring, prefiguring the Westminster government's

---

[19] Statement to plenary, Assembly *Record*, 26 June 2001.

[20] See an IWA Paper *The WelshBac Pilot: Will It be Based on a Baccalaureate Approach?*, August 2001, for an in-depth analysis of this issue.

[21] *Wales: The Learning Country*, policy Statement, 5 September 2001.

autumn Queen's Speech. As the First Minister Rhodri Morgan put it in his opening remarks:

> Today's debate is about much more than the Bills in the present Parliamentary session or the next. It goes to the heart of the relationship between the Assembly and the Government of the United Kingdom, in terms of the powers that we have and what we are eager to achieve.[22]

In the inaugural debate the coalition Administration put forward proposals for just four bills, listed in Figure 2.3, it would be pressing to be included in the Westminster government's forthcoming legislative programme.

Figure 2.3. The Administration's four priorities for Welsh legislation in the 2001-02 Westminster parliamentary session

- Promote collaborative working and improve accountability in the NHS in Wales.
- Provide greater cohesion in and between education, training and careers systems in Wales.
- Give the Assembly power to approve the content of census forms in Wales.
- Make St David's Day a bank holiday (sic) in Wales.

PC's leader, Ieuan Wyn Jones, described the Administration's package as 'timid' and not 'a programme for government', while Nick Bourne for the Conservatives spoke of 'a lack of vision across the spectrum of legislative action.'[23] However, Rhodri Morgan took a more robust line:

> We can expect the United Kingdom Government and Parliament to take for what they are, namely proposals drawn up in Wales, to be implemented in Wales. This is proof that the devolution settlement works and provides what Wales needs. [24]

In the event, the Queen's Speech, published in the wake of the June election, contained only one of the Assembly Administration's requests, a Welsh Health Bill to take forward the plans to reorganise the health service structure in Wales. Not only that, a few weeks later even this was removed when it emerged that the Welsh restructuring plans would be incorporated within the English NHS Reform Bill. David Melding, the Welsh Conservative health spokesperson, revealed that members of the Health Committee had been informed of this retreat in an 'unpublicised letter' from the Health minister:

> After all the hype about a special NHS (Wales) Bill, the news that the guts of such a Bill is to be transferred to the English Health Bill is a complete retreat. The Minister has now confirmed that what little remains of the NHS Wales Bill will be

[22] Assembly *Record*, 13 March 2001.
[23] Assembly *Record*, 13 March 2001.
[24] Assembly *Record*, 13 March 2001.

postponed until 2003. It is now possible that the whole of the NHS (Wales) Bill will be scrapped and incorporated into the English Bill.[25]

Consequently the Administration's experience in attempting to promote Welsh primary legislation at Westminster proved less than fruitful. Even on the basis of a relatively unambitious programme, no completely Welsh bill was achieved for the 2001-2002 session. This is likely to contribute to a growing demand for the Assembly to achieve primary legislative powers.

THE ASSEMBLY

Office of the Presiding Officer

A far-reaching constitutional dimension of the coalition partnership agreement was its concern with the role of the Office of the Presiding Officer as the interface between the Assembly and the Administration. Its determination to '. . . secure the independence of the Office of the Presiding Officer and the civil servants that work there'[26] was a decisive move away from the Assembly's status as a corporate body. It put in place a defining characteristic of a parliamentary institution since the Presiding Officer's independence is necessary if a clear separation of powers between the executive and legislature is to apply. Within weeks of the agreement being signed the Assembly overwhelmingly approved a new Standing Order establishing a House Committee to advise the Presiding Officer and to determine a separate budget for his office.

Through the previous summer an ad hoc committee made up of officials from the Office of the Presiding Officer and the Cabinet Office had met to work through the changes. Taken together they are substantial, as Figure 2.4 indicates. All this was agreed by the ad hoc Committee representing what has emerged ever more clearly as the two civil service components within the Assembly. A new set of principles to guide the way the Office of the Presiding Officer should work in future found cross-party support. However, their practical implementation are likely to produce further tension and struggle. For instance, the separate budget has so far proved disappointing to the Office of the Presiding Officer. Every aspect of the Office's expenditure in terms of procurement rules, the involvement of the Assembly Compliance Officer and the Finance Division are still controlled by the Administration.

Equally the new House Committee is not a committee with executive powers, as is the case with its equivalents in the Scottish Parliament and the Northern Ireland Assembly. Instead, it remains an advisory committee. Its remit is essentially Members' services and in respect of these it only advises

---

[25] David Melding AM, Press Release, 27 July 2001.
[26] *Putting Wales First*, para 9.6.

Figure 2.4. Independence for the office of the Presiding Officer

- A separate budget for the Office (£24.3m for 2001-02) out of which is paid Members' and officials' pay and allowances, Assembly accommodation and associated IT and general administration.
- The Clerk to the Assembly, the Office's chief official, becomes an Accounting Officer in addition to the Permanent Secretary. The areas for which he is directly responsible are increased, providing scope for a distinctive approach to staff recruitment and deployment within the Office.
- A House Committee to oversee the Office is established, chaired by the Presiding Officer with representatives from all parties in the chamber.

---

the Clerk as he is the accounting officer and the only person with delegated responsibility to spend money. In turn, the Clerk is bound by executive-governed procedures and by the Permanent Secretary as his line manager.

Nevertheless, the changes marked a highly significant development in the evolving constitutional architecture of the National Assembly. Insofar as the Assembly could act to change its own constitution without achieving an amendment to the Government of Wales Act 1998, it did so. De facto, though not de jure, it put in place a structure that has the potential to ensure the independence of the Office of the Presiding Officer. In turn this has cleared a path towards achieving a separation of powers between the executive and the legislature and the creation of a body more parliamentary than corporate in character. This process was underlined in December when the Presiding Officer, Lord Elis-Thomas, announced the appointment of Paul Silk, a clerk in the House of Commons, as the new Clerk to the Assembly in succession to John Lloyd, a former Welsh Office official, who retired in March 2001.

The Assembly's Operational Review

An extensive review of the Assembly's internal operation and relationship with Westminster and Whitehall took place during the year under the chairmanship of the Presiding Officer. Made up of the party leaders and business managers and supported by officials from the Cabinet Secretariat and the Office of the Presiding Officer the review explored a wide-ranging agenda. By the end of July it had received submissions from 43 organisations and individuals, including each of the political parties. Despite the limitations of its terms of reference, which for example prevented consideration of the Assembly's powers, it was striking how rapidly a consensus was achieved on a range of fundamental propositions, as shown in Figure 2.5.

The contributions from the Liberal Democrats and PC were unsurprising given the determination of these parties to push forward the boundaries of the Assembly's activities. On the other hand, when set against their previous

---

Figure 2.5. Cross-party consensus in the Operational Review

- A stronger identity for the Welsh government and Cabinet combined with a sharper separation between the executive and legislative functions of the Assembly.
- Clearer definition of the scrutiny and policy development roles of the Subject Committees.
- Improved mechanisms for influencing primary legislation at Westminster.
- A more organised approach for dealing with subordinate legislation.
- Sharper plenary sessions with more opportunities for interrogating the administration.
- Extending the Assembly's connections with the European Union and enhancing the role of the European Committee.
- A stronger role for the Regional Committees.

---

hostility to the devolution project, the submission made by the Conservative Group was surprisingly hard-edged, containing a number of on the whole radical ideas for improvement. The views of the Labour Group were more tentative, suggesting as many questions for further consideration as firm recommendations. At the same time there was an acknowledgement that answers to the questions would open up an agenda beyond the brief of the operational review. Indeed, the final section of the Labour submission asked: 'What sort of shape do we want the Assembly to have in ten years?' It then established part of the future agenda by wondering:

> Is there, for example, a consensus that the Assembly should be a strategic/policy making institution with little role in the direct delivery of services or should we take ever more direct responsibility for things currently dealt with by Assembly Sponsored Public Bodies or even by Local Authorities?

Taken together, the submissions of the four parties to the operational review reveal a frank acknowledgement on all sides that there are serious flaws in the basic design of the machine they have to operate. They convey a striking impression of a new institution beginning to find its feet by its Members getting to grips with the devil that lies in the detail of their work. What is also striking is the convergence in many instances of ideas on how to overcome the difficulties. As First Minister Rhodri Morgan put it in a note to the Presiding Officer in July:

> It is now becoming a commonplace belief that the Assembly's status as a corporate body is something of a handicap. It is therefore widely accepted that we should use all the scope available to make a distinction between the governmental and parliamentary side of the corporate body. The suggestions made to the Review that we should formalise this split by the creation of a 'Welsh Executive' or similar reflect frequent comments to the same effect inside and outside the Assembly and elsewhere.

In political terms, the dynamic within Plenary and elsewhere is for Ministers to be held to account for Cabinet policies and Ministers' executive actions. That reflects the realities of government and the nature of delegated power within the Assembly. Debates also take place within that context. I strongly agree that the terminology we use needs to reflect these realities. I also agree that the label 'Assembly' should only be applied to a policy or document if it has been endorsed in Plenary or if it refers to the views or actions of the body of the Kirk.

Whatever term we use, we could not create a Welsh Executive in the Scottish style unless the Government of Wales Act was substantially rewritten. Furthermore, we must be careful not to engender a political culture in which the Cabinet and its officials might start forgetting the nature of their delegated power and exercise executive power in their own right, not on behalf of the Assembly, as it were. Nor do we want to strangulate cross-party policy development in Subject Committees which is unique to the Assembly and a success for the most part.

As regards the terminology, the Cabinet's preference is for 'Government of the Assembly' and that term will be used increasingly in press and other statements which record its decisions. I have no objection to the use of other terms such as the Administration, the Executive or the Cabinet. The only one now used which I think confusing is the 'Government of Wales'. Although I have used it myself from time to time, I believe it allows no recognition of the UK Government *qua* its functions in Wales and its control of 50 per cent of public expenditure in Wales.[27]

The issues raised by the First Minister were relatively easy to resolve when compared with the more intractable questions of the Assembly's relations with Westminster and especially its ability to influence primary legislation. These matters were addressed in some detail in a submission made to the operational review by the Law Society:

It is becoming increasingly difficult for lawyers, voluntary agencies and campaigning organisations advising the public, to gain a clear picture of the National Assembly's powers. As well as the body of powers contained in the Transfer of Functions Orders, there are now the effects of two legislative sessions at Westminster, in which a number of different approaches have been taken to drafting Bills that confer powers on the National Assembly. The result is a rapidly expanding and incoherent mass of statutory powers with no overarching logic to the basis of their devolution to the National Assembly.[28]

THE CIVIL SERVICE

One of the more striking commitments in the partnership agreement, little commented upon at the time, was an undertaking to move the Welsh civil

---

[27] Letter from First Minister Rhodri Morgan to Lord Elis-Thomas, 5 July 2001. The full text is available from the page of the Assembly website dedicated to the operational review,

[28] Law Society of England and Wales Submission to the Review of Procedure of the National Assembly for Wales, May 2001.

service in a more autonomous direction. Given the sensitivity of the matter, the terms in which this aspiration was couched were remarkable:

> We will review the existing structures and workings of Assembly officials to ensure they are in tune with the reality of political devolution. We seek to move towards an increasingly independent and Welsh-based civil service — investigating ways of introducing an Assembly 'fast-track' programme to attract and retain high quality staff.[29]

The need to ensure that Assembly officials should be 'in tune with the reality of political devolution' could only reflect a dissatisfaction with experience hitherto. There was a feeling, certainly on the part of the Liberal Democrats who drafted this clause, that civil servants were continuing the old Welsh Office practice of constantly deferring to Whitehall and being reluctant to countenance Welsh policy initiatives. The outlook was not only confined to the Liberal Democrats. First Minister Rhodri Morgan explored the matter at some length in the speech he gave to the Institute of Welsh Politics in November. Recalling his own time as a civil servant at the Welsh Office in the late 1960s he drew a comparison with the relative autonomy of the Scottish Office:

> In the Scottish Office, which had been around for 100 years, they had developed a tradition of independent policy. The Welsh Office had no capability of policy-making at all in the late 1960s. Likewise you promoted staff in the Scottish Office on the basis that they had put one over Whitehall. You promoted staff in the Welsh Office on the basis of whether they had kept their nose clean with Whitehall. I hope that's not entirely true today but you are still struggling against a very long tradition where there is not an experience of autonomous policy-making. It was made much worse by the policy top-slicing which occurred under the Redwood cutbacks in the civil service in Wales with the loss of 600 jobs in Cardiff. This led to the loss of the people aged 50-plus, people with experience and capability. Policy-making was top sliced just at the time when it needed to be coming up to maximum strength for the incoming Assembly . . . What we need now that we have the devolution settlement is to create a positive problem-solving political culture. We need to generate a policy-making ability in a Welsh context and get rid of the old habits which still inhibit that process.[30]

These perceptions were given concrete expression by a dispute between the Presiding Officer Lord Elis-Thomas and the Permanent Secretary Jon Shortridge in the second part of 2000. It was sparked by a minor amendment to an Assembly resolution on sustainable development, passed by a combination of PC, Liberal Democrat and Conservative votes in September (before the coalition was in place). The amendment required that the civil service Sustainable Development Unit, housed within the Agriculture department of

---

[29] *Putting Wales First: A Partnership for the People of Wales*, section on 'Better Government', para. 6, 6 October 2001.
[30] Rhodri Morgan, *op.cit.*

the Assembly, be relocated to the Central Policy Unit. The objective was to give sustainable development policy greater prominence and enable it to operate within a cross-cutting milieu, to reflect its impact across the range of the Assembly's responsibilities.

However, the Permanent Secretary objected to the move, partly on grounds of cost and lack of consultation but, more fundamentally, because he felt it should be for himself rather than politicians to make operational decisions on how the Assembly's civil servants should carry out their duties.[31] The Permanent Secretary also questioned the legality of the decision but was advised by the Office of the Counsel General that the Assembly had operated within its powers in passing the amendment.There may be an inherent conflict in the Government of Wales Act between the general competence of the Assembly and Section 63 (2) which confers on the Permanent Secretary the right 'to make arrangements as to which member or members is or are to exercise [a delegated] function.'

The issue came to a head in November during a meeting of the party leaders in the Assembly at which both Lord Elis-Thomas and Jon Shortridge were present. There were exchanges between the two men which, the following day, caused the Presiding Officer to send the Permanent Secretary a strongly worded letter, defending his right to uphold Assembly decisions and attacking the civil servant for seeking to circumvent them.[32]

There seems little doubt that this argument was merely the culmination of a succession of disputes between the Administration and the Presiding Officer that reached back the best part of a year. Underpinning them were different perceptions of the Assembly's role and the way it should develop. From the point of view of the Presiding Officer the higher echelons of the civil service in the Administration were endeavouring to operate as though the old Welsh Office was still in existence, with the Assembly itself as merely an add-on, essentially an advisory body. On the other hand, from the point of view of some in the Administration, the Presiding Officer was seeking to push the remit of the Assembly beyond what was laid down or envisaged in the Government of Wales Act.

THE WELSH LANGUAGE INTERVENES

Until well into its second year the survival of the Welsh language, an underlying preoccupation of Welsh politics, did not feature largely in the Assembly's debates. This contributed to a feeling that a 'new politics' was beginning to emerge in Wales with a shared agenda across the party divides, especially between Labour and PC. The widely-used term 'inclusivity',

---

[31] Clive Betts, 'One Battle the Civil Service Cannot Win'. *Western Mail*, 11 November 2000.
[32] The full text is contained in Osmond 2001a.

which featured extensively in the rhetoric of the first 18 months, assumed a consensus around a common national project, including the success of the Assembly itself, together with a new style of politics that included taking the Welsh language out of the cut and thrust of political debate.[33] The Assembly was supposed to provide a forum where difficult issues could be debated without the participants retreating into previously prepared bunkers. It was felt that there were great opportunities for this to be achieved within the subject committees, away from the combative atmosphere of plenary sessions. However, a series of language disputes laid bare the fragility of the so-called new Welsh politics.

In January the question of English immigration into rural Welsh-speaking Wales was articulated by a little-known PC councillor, Seimon Glyn, chairman of Gwynedd County Council's housing committee. This led to a furious row between PC and the Labour Party with accusations of 'racism' flying about in the run-up to the June UK general election.[34] During May and June a heated debate within the Education Committee over proposals for a Welsh–medium College within the University of Wales exposed a sharp gulf between Labour and PC. And in August the language issue was re-ignited once more when a substantial figure in Welsh political and economic life, John Elfed Jones, likened the impact of in-migration into rural Wales to the effects of Foot-and-Mouth Disease.

John Elfed Jones

John Elfed Jones is a man of some stature. He is a former Industrial Director at the Welsh Office (1979-82), Chairman of Welsh Water (1982-93), Chairman of the Welsh Language Board (1988-93), Chairman of HTV Wales (1990-96) and Chairman of the National Assembly Advisory Group (1998-9) that established its Standing Orders. Consequently the words he chose to describe a dilemma central to the future of the Welsh language put the Administration into something of a quandary. Writing in the August 2001 issue of the Welsh-language monthly *Barn* (Opinion) he declared:

> . . . there is another foot-and-mouth disease which is unintentionally changing the way of life of rural Wales — and there is no sign that either the Government or the Assembly is prepared to restrict the increasingly ruinous impact of this particular disease. I'm referring to the migration into rural Wales and the inevitable effect of this type of movement . . .[35]

As undoubtedly was calculated, this intervention lit a smouldering fuse that exploded into a furious debate during the week of the National Eisteddfod in early August. First Minister Rhodri Morgan immediately denounced

---

[33] See, for example, Chaney and Fevre 2001.
[34] See Osmond 2001b.
[35] The *Western Mail* carried a full translation of the article on 8 August 2001.

what he described as a 'misuse of language'. [36] Coincidentally at the Eisteddfod Rhodri Morgan launched a new Welsh Labour consultation document *Culture, Sports and the Welsh Language*. This contained a section that directly addresses the concerns raised by John Elfed Jones:

> We remain sceptical that plans focussing on stopping non-Welsh speakers moving into certain geographical areas will do much to protect far less promote the Welsh language. Welsh Labour believes that a sustainable future for Welsh language communities can only be provided by access to a sound and stable economic future.

Undeterred, a few days later John Elfed Jones returned to the fray. Although apologising for any gratuitous offence his reference to the Foot-and-Mouth outbreak may have caused, writing to the *Western Mail* he observed:

> It is all very well for politicians to proclaim that they are well aware of the problems, but if they take no steps to solve them they are like the captain of the ship that is sinking who declares that he's aware that the ship is going down but does nothing to launch the lifeboats. [37]

Dafydd Glyn Jones

As part of its review of Higher Education the Assembly's Education Committee invited Dafydd Glyn Jones, a long standing campaigner for a Welsh-medium College within the University of Wales, to give evidence. A Reader in Welsh at the University of Wales, Bangor, Dafydd Glyn Jones has a substantial academic reputation. He is co-editor with Bruce Griffiths of *The Welsh Academy English–Welsh Dictionary*, the most comprehensive ever compiled, and is well known as a commentator on Welsh politics.

Dafydd Glyn Jones' submission to the Committee, *The Quality and the Medium*, makes a passionate, heavily ironic and at times idiosyncratic case for attracting more Welsh students to the University of Wales and for the creation of a Welsh-medium college. Glyn Jones has campaigned for decades on these issues, with little effect. For instance, in the last half century only 22 appointments have been made to teach subjects (other than Welsh itself) through the medium of Welsh in a University with more than 4,000 staff. Glyn Jones suggests a critical mass of 200 lecturers would be necessary to address the need — a scholarly community spread between the various institutions of the University of Wales.

However, it was the appendices to the submission, previously published articles, that caught most attention of members of the Committee, in particular one entitled *A University Problem*:

> . . . we ought now to be starting to consider new ways of supporting and financing university education under a Welsh government. The government of Wales

[36] *Daily Post*, 8 August 2001.
[37] *Western Mail*, 14 August 2001.

should, by some means or other, make it possible for the University of Wales to offer especially favourable terms for all who are born and brought up in Wales and who desire to study for a degree in the University and who are suitably qualified. We are not talking about favourable academic terms, and I hope that everyone understands this. Academically, we ought to be raising the requirements, not lowering them. Every student from Wales, Welsh speaking and otherwise, because he is from Wales, should be offered an education in the University of Wales at a very advantageous price . . .

We should accept that Wales's central problem today is the lack of a stable and self-perpetuating native governing class. A Welsh government, at the first available opportunity, should take bold, open and decisive steps towards the resolution of this problem.

In May Dafydd Glyn Jones attended a meeting of the Education Committee to give oral evidence. Following his presentation Huw Lewis, the Labour AM for Merthyr, told the Committee that he had read his submission with 'some degree of growing alarm.'[38] At a later meeting he suggested that if the paper was accepted it would set a precedent that '. . . any Committee must sit and listen to outrageous, sexist, xenophobic, racist, inflammatory, even illegal statements in the future . . .'[39].

At the first meeting Huw Lewis sought to introduce a motion that the paper should be struck from the record. The Chair, Cynog Dafis refused to accept this, and at the following meeting, a fortnight later it was replaced with a motion to the effect that the paper's 'subjective opinions' should be disregarded. Though Dafis felt this still contained 'a whiff of censorship' it was passed by six votes to four, with the Committee dividing on party lines.[40]

Aside from the democratic issue of censorship, there was an equally fundamental ideological and political dimension to the Dafydd Glyn Jones affair. This was provoked by his views on the role of the University of Wales in promoting a Welsh elite which exposed a deep cleavage between the approach of Labour and PC members. Here the key passage in Glyn Jones' paper was the one dealing with University standards:

There are still only two universities in the United Kingdom which can take their pick from among applicants with three or four A's, accept some because they seem to have that rather indefinable 'something extra', and refuse others because they

---

[38] Meeting of the Education Committee, 17 May 2001. Verbatim transcripts of Committee meetings are not normally available, with only tape recordings archived. However, on this occasion the Committee Chair ordered transcripts of the meetings that dealt with the Dafydd Glyn Jones affair to be prepared.

[39] Meeting of the Education Committee, 13 June 2001.

[40] The six Members who voted for the motion were Jane Davidson, Labour, Pontypridd (minister); Alan Pugh, Labour, Clwyd West (deputy minister); Lorraine Barrett Labour, Cardiff South and Penarth; Janice Gregory, Labour, Ogmore; Huw Lewis, Labour, Merthyr; and Eleanor Burnham, Liberal Democrat, North Wales. Those against were Cynog Dafis, Plaid Cymru, Mid and West Wales (Chair); Pauline Jarman, Plaid Cymru, South Wales Central; Gareth Jones, Plaid Cymru, Conwy; and Jonathan Morgan, Conservative, South Wales Central.

do not like their accent or their body-language. That is possible for them because their primary function is still to select and nurture an elite to lead, govern and serve the English nation — although they have other functions as well. The primary function of the University of Wales — I cannot see that it could be otherwise — must be to offer a reasonable education, at a reasonable charge, to a reasonable number of our children; this does not mean that it could not, or should not, at the same time nurture a patriotic Welsh elite, talented, enterprising, faithful people who will stay in Wales, work in Wales and serve Wales — we should never be coy about this function.

Alun Pugh, the Deputy Education minister and Labour Member for Clwyd West, responded:

> . . . it's the offensive anti-English and sneering tone of this document that I find totally unacceptable. We all know that Wales has many problems but the lack of a self-perpetuating, patriotic elite governing class is not one of them in my judgement, and I know that miners' sons like me would be unwelcome at the doors of Mr Jones' proposed college. I wouldn't pass his patriotism exam because I am not Welsh enough for him, but I will console myself with the certain knowledge that he thinks most Welsh people aren't good enough either. This Assembly is for all the people of Wales and bigotry, even bigotry dressed up as an academic paper, is not acceptable here.[41]

Cynog Dafis answered these charges at length in an article for *Barn* (Opinion) later in the year:

> Dafydd Glyn Jones' deepest anxiety is that Wales's most able young people are being constantly drained away from Wales — the very people who should grow to be the leaders of our social, cultural, economic and political life . . . What nation worth mentioning hasn't got a class of people of this kind to serve it and make an effort to improve and develop it? . . . Dafydd Glyn Jones' great sin is that he wants Wales to be a nation . . . The motion that was passed on June 13 (Labour and Liberal Democrats for, PC and the Conservatives against) was an attempt to ensure that the voice of Welsh nationalism should not be heard in our National Assembly. That attempt must of course be defeated, but there is an even more difficult job to be done. The task facing us is to create a nation. Not to protect, but to create. To create it from the raw materials that are at hand — all of the diverse, divided elements and cross currents that inhabit Wales at the beginning of the 21st century. There has to be a greater willingness to listen across the divisions than has been seen on this occasion if this great enterprise is to succeed.[42]

This was an ill-tempered dispute. Undoubtedly it registered deeply with AMs inside the Assembly. What lasting impact it might have outside is more difficult to assess. The row was fuelled to some extent by party rivalries at a time when a British general election was underway. Combined with the

---

[41] Transcript of the Education Committee meeting, 13 June 2001.

[42] Cynog Dafis, *Pechodau Dafydd Glyn Jones* (The Sins of Dafydd Glyn Jones), *Barn* (Opinion — monthly Welsh language current affairs magazine) August 2001.

Seimon Glyn affair followed by the utterances of John Elfed Jones over the impact of incomers on the housing market in Welsh-speaking communities, it projected the Welsh language into the Assembly as a subject of political argument. Previously there had been an impression that the language had been taken out of politics, or at least neutralised in terms of political debate. Henceforth, it would be more difficult to achieve a consensus on these matters. Certainly, one result was an interruption to what some had seen as growing agreement between PC and Labour on a range of policy questions, and not least on the future of the Assembly itself.

THE POLITICAL PARTIES AND THE GENERAL ELECTION

The Political Parties

The advent of the National Assembly has had a substantial impact on the character and strategies of all the political parties in Wales. Each has had to cope with different challenges, not least the onset of coalition government. Whereas in the early months of devolution there was much talk of consensus and an inclusive approach, the emergence of a more clearly focused government and opposition substantially changed the tone and atmosphere of Assembly politics. Similarly the experience of a Westminster general election campaign was much altered by devolution.

The coming of the National Assembly has radically changed the character of PC. For the first time it has a relatively large and cohesive group of full-time, professional politicians within its ranks, the 17 elected Members in the Assembly together with their support staff. These have altered the balance of forces within the party's traditional structure. At the same time the party's focus of attention has shifted decisively from Westminster to Cardiff Bay. For the first time in its history, too, the party has a sense that it could be a party of government. These changes have created new problems of communication and increased the potential for divisions between the leadership and the wider membership, not least over the party's objectives and how they are articulated.

As would be expected PC is further ahead of the other parties in developing its thinking around constitutional change. This is partly because Welsh autonomy is its raison d'être, but also because lack of clarity around its constitutional objectives became an issue during the first election campaign for the Assembly in 1999. In the run-up to the UK general election an internal debate generated by the new leadership under Ieuan Wyn Jones sought to define more clearly the party's aims. As a first step the aim was to achieve parity with the Scottish Parliament, with full legislative powers and some tax-varying powers. This, it said, would involve a reduction in Welsh MPs at Westminster and a corresponding increase in Assembly members in Cardiff.

Developments beyond this stage would depend to a large extent on what happened elsewhere, in particular whether England began to evolve regional government and what progress was made with European integration and enlargement.[43] The document painted two scenarios: a democratic, federal Europe of the Regions with a greatly empowered European Parliament and a written constitution within which Wales could find a role; or, failing that, full national status for Wales as a member-state within a confederal European Union (EU).

However, such options were sketched out only in broad conceptual terms with little detailed or tactical sense of what the party's preference would be, and how it might influence the course of events in that direction. In part this is because the document fails to confront an underlying internal debate that is taking place about what kind of party PC should be: that is to say, one that regards itself as essentially a regionalist movement operating within a British/European framework, or what might be regarded as a more conventional autonomist party seeking independence. In September 2001 the party's annual conference reaffirmed its commitment to seeking 'full national status for Wales within the European Union' at the same time as reiterating its demand for a seat for Wales in the United Nations.

The onset of devolution has also had a profound impact on the Labour Party. In the first place it has changed its name to the *Welsh* Labour Party, from Labour Party Wales (previously the Labour Party in Wales). This registered an important emblematic and tonal shift. There is a recognition by all the parties, but especially Labour, that identifying with the national dimension can bring political rewards in post-devolution Wales. There is now a recognisable nationalist, with a small 'n', wing within the Labour Group in the Assembly that is currently in the ascendant under Rhodri Morgan's leadership. To some extent this Group is defining itself against the policy profile being developed by the Labour Party at Westminster, as set out in successive Queen's Speeches.[44] But so far the Group has not defined a clear developmental path ahead. This is because to do so would open up an unwanted debate, not just within the Assembly Group itself, but more importantly with forces outside — especially within the Welsh Labour Executive, within the Westminster parliamentary party, and elements within the constituency parties and local authority Labour groups. Events are likely to force a debate, however. These include the outcome of the 2001 UK general election, when the party lost some ground to PC and the commitment it has made in the partnership agreement with the Liberal Democrats to establish an independent Commission to examine the Assembly's powers.

The outcome of the devolution process for Welsh Liberal Democrats hangs almost entirely on the progress of the coalition within the Assembly.

[43] *Towards Full National Status: Stages on the Journey* , Plaid Cymru, December 2000.
[44] See Osmond 2000.

They will be judged on the extent to which they are seen to influence policy development, and also on the electoral consequences. The party held its ground in the 2001 UK general election in Wales, but has potentially much to lose in the May 2003 Assembly elections. In this eventuality the party would be presented with an acute identity crisis. Furthermore, its constitutional objective of achieving a federation within the UK creates an inherently weak position, on two counts. First, although Britain may be moving in a quasi-federal direction, given the nature of the British state, devolution is always likely to be asymmetrical. Second, both in terms of participating in the coalition and in its constitutional objectives, the party leadership tends to be out of line with its core support.

Paradoxically, in electoral terms the Conservatives have benefited most from devolution, achieving significant representation in the Assembly through the operation of the regional list proportional system. There is also a determination on the part of the leadership to identify more with Welsh concerns and develop distinctive Welsh policies. The party's identity as an opposition party in the Assembly has also been strengthened by the formation of the majority coalition government. What all this may imply for the party's constitutional thinking has been speculated upon by a number of their AMs in the Assembly. For example David Melding, AM for South Wales Central, declared:

> The party least sympathetic to devolution needs to become its most conspicuous supporter. I believe that we have reached a stage where the British state can only survive with devolution. Commentators should not rule out, therefore, the possibility that the next and most vital advance for devolution in Wales will be instigated by the Conservative Party.[45]

The 2001 General Election

Measured by what most counts in a British election, the seats or scalps that the parties carry home, the results that emerged at the end of the 2001 UK general election in Wales represented a complete status quo: that is to say 34 Labour, four PC, two Liberal Democrats, and again nil for the Conservatives. The immediate interpretation was that Labour retained its iron grip on Welsh politics, PC had fallen back, the Liberal Democrats remained confined to rural mid Wales, while the Conservatives were in free fall. The reality for Welsh politics was that all the parties could claim to have moved forward, though on different fronts, while the real battle is still to come in two years time. Figure 2.6 tells some of the story.

---

[45] David Melding AM, 'Conservatives should finish the job', *Agenda*, IWA, Autumn 2001.

Figure 2.6. All-Wales election results for 2001, 1999 and 1997

	2001 General Election Turn-out: 61.6%		1999 Assembly Election* Turn-out: 48%		1997 General Election Turn-out: 73.6%	
	Votes	%	Votes	%	Votes	%
Labour	666,955	48.6	384,671	37.6	886,935	54.7
Plaid Cymru	195,892	14.3	290,572	28.4	161,030	9.9
Lib Dem	189,434	13.8	137,857	13.5	200,020	12.4
Conservative	288,665	21.0	162,133	15.8	317,127	19.6

*The figures shown are for the constituency vote. The regional lists gave Labour 361,657 votes (35.5%), Plaid Cymru 312,048 (30.6%), Liberal Democrats 128,008 (12.5%), and Conservatives 168,206 (16.5%)

These comparative statistics set against their respective turn-outs are revealing. Comparing the 2001 and 1997 Westminster elections, while Labour maintained a commanding position the number of people actually voting for the party fell by 219,980, or 24.8 per cent. In the case of the Conservatives and the Liberal Democrats, the numbers voting for them also dropped, though to a much lesser extent. On the other hand PC not only saw its relative party position move into third place, but more significantly increased the numbers actually voting for it by 34,862, that is 21.6 per cent, in a situation where the overall turn-out fell by 12 percentage points.

Winning Ynys Môn from PC provided Labour with most satisfaction. It allowed the party's Communications Director, Huw Evans, to point out that in contrast to PC, Labour could now present itself as the 'true party of Wales': 'Not only do we represent all four corners of the country; we represent Welsh and English-speaking areas, urban and rural areas.'[46] Despite this assertion, Labour's loss of Carmarthen East to PC, means it has retreated from the whole of rural central Wales and now represents largely urban areas.

PC's loss of Ynys Môn, together with disappointed expectations of repeating the Assembly election success and winning seats in the Valleys — in particular Rhondda, Caerphilly and Llanelli — created a sense that the party had made no real headway. Yet its share of the vote went up by four points, to 14.3 per cent. Its previous best performance in a Westminster general election was in 1970 when it polled 11.5 per cent (175,016 votes on a 77.4 per cent turnout).

[46] *Western Mail*, 9 June 2001.

Perhaps more significantly, PC's support rose in eastern Wales above the derisory levels it had achieved in the past. Of course, the decisive break was made in the first Assembly elections. But the trend was confirmed in 2001. In the past, for example, the party has regularly lost deposits in Westminster elections in most of the eastern constituencies, 15 in 1997. In 2001, however, it lost deposits in five of the eastern seats.

The Conservatives' repeated failure to win a single seat in Wales, combined with the wider defeat across Britain, contributed to a view that they were withering on the vine as a serious force in Welsh politics. Yet the Conservative performance was far from disastrous. Its overall Welsh vote at 21 per cent, was within the 20 to 30 per cent range it has persistently achieved in Wales over more than a century. In its key target seats — Monmouth (where it came within 400 votes), Brecon and Radnor, Clwyd West, and Preseli — the party performed strongly. Of course, listing these seats also describes an old problem. Historically the party has done well on the peripheral (British) edge of Welsh politics and has been regarded by a majority of Welsh voters as a closet 'English' party. Paradoxically, however, this second large-scale defeat in terms of failing to win a Welsh seat is likely to assist those who are making the case for a stronger Welsh identity for the Conservative Party.

The 2001 election also brought some encouragement for the Welsh Liberal Democrats. It made no substantial advance but did not retreat either. In rural Wales the party fought off a strong Conservative assault in Brecon and Radnor and performed well in Ceredigion. In Cardiff Central, its main target seat, it ran Labour to within a percentage point (659 votes), despite an HTV NOP constituency poll early in the campaign forecasting it would trail by 19 per cent. Before the election Liberal Democrats were worried that their participation in the coalition with Labour in the National Assembly might damage their prospects. There was no sign that this was the case. Neither was there evidence that they were affected by the difficulties of their Assembly leader, Deputy First Minister Mike German, who during the campaign faced renewed allegations of fraud in his previous position with the WJEC's European Unit.

In terms of Welsh politics the decisive election takes place in May 2003. This will be the test of whether Labour's Welsh hegemony will be sustained. In 2003 the second landslide New Labour Government in Westminster will be in mid-term. Welsh Labour will be anxious for it to be seen to be improving the key public services — health, education and transport. The timescale does not augur well. While a week may be a long time in politics, even two years may not be enough to offset decades of under-investment in the public sector. This is a crunch issue for Wales and other Labour heartlands which are characterised by heavy reliance on public expenditure.

THE FUTURE OF WELSH COALITION POLITICS

The independent commission to examine the case for extending the Assembly's powers, being established under the coalition partnership agreement, will report towards the end of 2003 after the next Assembly elections. First Minister Rhodri Morgan has drawn attention to a connection between this event and the forthcoming Intergovernmental Conference (IGC) of the EU:

> The next Inter-governmental Conference will be in 2004 and will aim to define clearly the respective roles of the regional tier — which would include us, the German *Länder*, the Italian Regions and so on — the Member States and the European tier. Therefore there will be an enormous opportunity for the Assembly to play a part in the preparations for that summit. Its timing could not be better, considering that the Partnership Agreement document plans a review of the Assembly's powers, which will report back to the Assembly after the next Assembly elections in May 2003. This will be just in time for the 2004 inter-governmental conference on the respective roles of the Regional, Nation State and European tiers of government.[47]

What Rhodri Morgan plainly has in mind is that separate arguments made at the Welsh and EU levels will reinforce one another in helping persuade a Westminster government to give ground on extending primary legislative powers to the National Assembly. The timetable he has in mind would require a commitment in Labour's manifesto prior to the next Westminster election.

Certainly opinion polls carried out during 2000 and 2001 suggest that a significant shift in attitudes is taking place. In July 2000 an NOP poll carried out for HTV elicited a 43 per cent response to the proposition that the Assembly should have law-making powers. A little under a year later this had risen to 54 per cent, as Figure 2.7 shows.[48]

When tracked against how electors voted at the Assembly election in 1999, only Conservative supporters would appear to be reluctant to progress devolution further. A surprising number of Liberal Democrats appear to want to turn the clock back, but this is countered by just under half who would wish to see Wales with a more powerful elected Parliament. The key finding however, is the proportion of Labour supporters who would strengthen the Welsh constitutional position. Given the level of defection to PC at the last Assembly elections, the Labour Party will be under considerable pressure to adopt a pro-active programme to enhance devolution or risk further electoral losses.

---

[47] Assembly *Record*, 19 December 2000.

[48] The 52 per cent in the 2001 poll is attained by combining the percentages of those opting for independence and law-making powers for the Assembly.

Figure 2.7. NOP poll for BBC Wales June 2001

	Recalled 1997 vote (%)				
	ALL	Lab	Con	Lib Dem	Plaid
Wales should become independent	8	7	11	–	12
Wales should have its own elected Parliament like Scotland with law-making and taxation powers	44	42	14	47	66
Wales should continue to have an Assembly with limited law-making Powers	24	29	31	13	14
Wales should have no elected Assembly or Parliament	18	17	43	32	7
Don't Know/No answer	5	5	–	7	1

Having said that, the coalition may be under less pressure in the run-up to the May 2003 election because of internal divisions over the leadership of PC. These were sparked by the party's difficulties in dealing with the in-migration issue and the intervention of its own councillor, Gwynedd Housing Chairman Seimon Glyn. Matters came to a head when BBC Television's *Question Time* came to Caernarfon in February. During the programme PC leader Ieuan Wyn Jones came under pressure from Glenys Kinnock, a Labour Member of the European Parliament. She challenged him to expel Seimon Glyn from PC and to state whether he disapproved of his comments or not. Ieuan Wyn Jones refused to denounce Seimon Glyn, claiming that 'Labour spin' had resulted in his being misquoted. However, this backfired when David Dimbleby, *Question Time's* presenter, held up a BBC transcript of Glyn's comments for him to read. The *Western Mail* was in no doubt as to who had won the battle on the programme which, it said, had 'brought seri-ous questions about his leadership and whether unfavourable comparisons with Dafydd Wigley's statesman-like leadership will cost Plaid at the UK general election.'[49]

In the wake of PC's loss of Ynys Môn in the UK general election the lead-ership issue returned, with the *Western Mail* leading a damaging campaign against Ieuan Wyn Jones. This was countered by strong support he received at the party's annual conference in September.

There is no doubt that during the second year of the Assembly the emer-gence of the coalition wrongfooted the opposition. The ability of both PC and the Conservatives to dictate events, as had happened at key moments during

[49] *Ibid.*

the first year, sharply diminished. Both became preoccupied with internal debates, PC with its leadership and the Welsh Conservatives with their relative autonomy within a British party also riven by a divisive leadership struggle.

A consequence was that on a range of issues the coalition Administration was let off the hook by a less-than-vigilant opposition during the second year. Examples where the Administration was vulnerable included failure to influence the Westminster government's legislative programme, a lack of focus around the development of its economic development strategy, a lack of vision in relation to aspects of education policy, and a sense of confusion around its plans to reorganise the health service in Wales. It is unlikely that the Administration will have such an easy time during the forthcoming period. Its difficulties arising from the police inquiry into the activities of the Deputy First Minister may accentuate. And the run-up to the next Assembly elections in May 2003 will inevitably bring further strains on the partnership between Labour and the Liberal Democrats.

The experience of coalition politics in the National Assembly's second year certainly provided a much needed stability allowing the Administration to set in train a policy programme stretching forward to the next election. At the same time the Administration was subject to a great deal of buffeting that reproduced some of the destabilisation that characterised the first year of devolution.

The coalition experience coupled with the Assembly's operational review that was largely completed during the year were also part of a process of developing the intellectual case for primary legislative powers. They demonstrated that without a coherent constitutional base it is difficult for any government — coalition or otherwise — to achieve the equilibrium that stability requires.

BIBLIOGRAPHY

Official Documents

Putting Wales First: A Partnership for the People of Wales The First Partnership Agreement of the National Assembly for Wales, 6 October 2000, available on the internet at www.wales.gov.uk/organicabinet/content/putting.html

Improving Health in Wales: a plan for the NHS with its partners (National Assembly for Wales, Cardiff): available on the internet at www.wales.gov.uk /healthplanonline/health_plan/index.htm

Improving Health in Wales — Structural Change in the NHS in Wales; a consultation document: available on the internet at www.wales.gov.uk/healthplanonline/health_plan/index.htm

Secondary Sources

Burrows, N. (2000). *Devolution*. London: Sweet and Maxwell.

Chaney, P., Hall, T., and Pithouse, A. (eds) (2001). *New Governance, New Democracy? Post-Devolution Wales*. Cardiff: University of Wales Press.

Chaney, P., and Fevre, R. (2001). 'Ron Davies and the Cult of 'Inclusiveness': Devolution and Participation in Wales', *Contemporary Wales,* Vol. 14. (Cardiff: University of Wales Press).

Davies, I. (2001). 'The Challenge of Legal Wales', Law Society Eisteddfod Lecture.

Jones, J. B. and Osmond, J. (eds) (2001). *Inclusive Government and Party Management: The National Assembly for Wales and the Work of its Committees*. Cardiff: IWA and Welsh Governance Centre, Cardiff University, IWA.

Law Society (2001). *The Law Making Powers of the National Assembly for Wales*, Papers from a Seminar held at the Temple of Peace, Cardiff.

Osmond, J. (2000). 'A Constitutional Convention By Other Means: The First year of the National Assembly for Wales' in Robert Hazell (Ed) *The State and the Nations*, (Exeter: Imprint Academic).

Osmond, J. (ed.) (2001*a*). *Coalition Politics Come to Wales: Monitoring the National Assembly September to December 2000*. Cardiff: IWA.

Osmond, J. (ed.) (2001*b*). *The Economy Takes Centre State: Monitoring the National Assembly December 2000 to March 2001*. Cardiff: IWA.

Osmond, J. (ed.) (2001*c*). *Farming Crisis Consolidates Assembly's Role: Monitoring the National Assembly March to May 2001*. Cardiff: IWA.

Osmond, J. (ed.) (2001*d*). *A Period of De-Stabilisation: Monitoring the National Assembly May to August 2001*. Cardiff: IWA.

3

Scotland: Maturing Devolution

James Mitchell and the Scottish Monitoring Team[1]

INTRODUCTION

Any review of the politics of Scottish devolution in its second year must almost be apologetic. Those who have followed debates on Scottish politics and recollect the high excitement of debates leading up to 1997 with that year's general election, devolution referendum and then the subsequent first elections to the Scottish Parliament might feel a sense of disappointment in the unexceptional nature of Scottish politics over the last year. That may be true for those who equate politics with party politics and the theatre of elections. To those interested in public policy and institutional politics, the Parliament's second year has been an exceptionally interesting and important one. The outline of Scottish politics is becoming clearer. In order to understand how Scottish politics is settling down, maturing even, it is necessary to appreciate the importance that substantive matters, policy-making and policies, have attained post-devolution. This chapter offers an overview of the year but also the necessary detail to justify our claim that devolution continues to be normal politics: it is about who gets, what, when, how.[2]

The high hopes attendant on the creation of the Scottish Parliament have given way to a more realistic assessment of its potential over the last the two years. For some supporters of the Parliament, the expectations have sunk low indeed. The late Cardinal Winning, an enthusiastic supporter of the establishment of the Parliament remarked that it had been an 'utter failure' and that he had been enthusiastic but 'I almost feel ashamed of our politicians'.[3] This, of course, reflected his hostility to proposals to abolish Section 28. But whether supported or opposed, the Section 28 debate demonstrated that the Parliament could make a difference or, at least, provoke a reaction.[4] More typical

---

[1] The members of the team are James Mitchell, Professor of Politics, University of Strathclyde; Barry Winetrobe, independent parliamentary and constitutional consultant; Mark Shephard, Lecturer in Politics, University of Strathclyde; Philip Schlesinger, Professor and Director, Stirling Media Research Institute, University of Stirling; John Curtice, Professor of Politics, University of Strathclyde; Alex Wright, Lecturer in Politics, University of Dundee; Neil McGarvey, Lecturer in Politics, University of Strathclyde; and David Bell, Professor of Economics, University of Stirling.

[2] Lasswell 1936.

[3] *Scottish Catholic Observer*, 2 June 2000.

[4] Section 28 of the Local Government Act 1988 amended the 1986 Act so as to ban local authorities in Great Britain from promoting homosexuality or its acceptability as 'a pretended family relationship' in schools, or publishing material promoting homosexuality.

Figure 3.1. Key events in the second year of the Scottish Parliament

30 May 2000	Results of 'Keep the Clause' campaign referendum announced. 34.5 per cent responded to postal ballot with 87 per cent voting in favour of retaining Section 28 and 13 percent for repeal.
21 June 2000	Scottish Parliament votes to repeal Section 28 by 99 votes to 17 with 2 abstentions.
17 July 2000	Alex Salmond announces his decision to stand down as leader of the Scottish National Party (SNP) with effect from annual conference in September.
9 August 2000	First reports of a crisis at Scottish Qualifications Agency (SQA). *Daily Record* reports that 'thousands of pupils' were 'facing a week of chaos' as universities were still waiting for exam results from SQA.
10 August 2000	'Higher' exam results due to be issued.
11 August 2000	SQA admits that it could not guarantee the integrity of any exam results.
12 August 2000	Ron Tuck, SQA chief executive resigns.
14 August 2000	Donald Dewar returns to work following heart operation.
4 Sept. 2000	Scottish Parliament returns from summer recess.
23 Sept. 2000	Election of John Swinney MSP as leader of SNP with 67 percent support at annual conference in Inverness over Alex Neil MSP.
5 October 2000	Susan Deacon, Health minister responds to Sutherland cby rejecting key recommendations and conforms with policy for England and Wales.
11 October 2000	Death of First Minister Donald Dewar.
21 October 2000	Election of Henry McLeish MSP as Leader of Scottish Labour Party by 44 votes to Jack McConnell's 36.
26 October 2000	Scottish Parliament elects Henry McLeish as First Minister.
27 October 2000	Henry McLeish formally appointed First Minister by the Queen.
29 October 2000	Henry McLeish announces make-up of new Cabinet.
1 November 2000	Henry McLeish calls for a policy review, hinting that Government might change its position on Sutherland.
1 November 2000	Parliament agrees an Executive resolution on Parliamentary scrutiny of Executive.
3 November 2000	Entire board of SQA resigns.
5 November 2000	Henry McLeish announces U-turn on care for the elderly in newspaper interview.

28 Nov 2000	Parliament's Health and Community Care Committee publishes report calling for full implementation of Sutherland.
30 Nov. 2000	Enterprise and Learning Report of Parliament criticises SQA as 'fundamentally negligent'. Ministers cleared of direct blame.
8 December 2000	Education, Culture and Sport Committee of Parliament criticised 'serious failures at board and management level' in SQA.
9 December 2000	Scottish Labour Party endorses Henry McLeish as leader and CathyJamieson MSP as deputy leader.
8 January 2001	Changes to committee structure came into effect reducing maximum numbers on committees; splitting Justice and Home Affairs Committee into two; renaming and changing remits of some committees; and providing for nomination of substitute members with voting rights.
9 January 2001	Tom McCabe, Parliament Minister, suggests that Executive should be called 'Scottish Government'. Meets with immediate hostile response from London ministers.
17 January 2001	Tommy Sheridan's Abolition of Warrant Sales Bill receives Royal Assent.
18 January 2001	George Reid, deputy Presiding Officer ruled that a ministerial statement widely reported in advance of its Parliamentary announcement be 'taken as read'.
24 January 2001	Resignation of Peter Mandelson as Secretary of State for Northern Ireland and appointment of John Reid in his place. Helen Liddell takes Reid's place as Secretary of State for Scotland.
24 January 2001	Susan Deacon announces change of policy on care for the elderly and announces establishment of a committee under Malcolm Chisholm, Deputy Minister for Health and Community Care, to report in August 2001.
24 January 2001	Keith Raffan resigns as Liberal Democrat Health spokesman disagreeing with Executive policy on care for the elderly.
25 January 2001	Tom McCabe, Parliament Minister, tables emergency motion supporting implementation of Sutherland recommendations to avert an Executive defeat in Parliament.
1 March 2001	First cases of Foot-and-Mouth Disease in Scotland reported.
8 March 2001	Executive suffers first defeat — on opposition motion on fishing in which David Steel, as Presiding Officer, cast his vote with the opposition after a tied vote.
8 March 2001	Tavish Scott, Liberal Democrat MSP for Shetland, resigns as deputy Parliament Minister because of difference with Executive on fisheries policy. Scott replaced by fellow Liberal Democrat Euan Robson.

20 March 2001	Sam Galbraith resigns as Environment Minister and announces his decision to stand down from Scottish Parliament and House of Commons at the UK general election.
23 April 2001	Executive withdraws invitation to Rod Lynch to head *visitscotland*, the Scottish tourist industry quango.
21 May 2001	Letter from twelve prominent economists to *The Scotsman* urging full fiscal autonomy for Scottish Parliament.
7 June 2001	UK general election.

of commentators has been the evolution in the thinking of Iain MacWhirter, one of Scotland's most respected commentators. MacWhirter expressed his disillusionment with the 'new Scottish politics' a year after the Parliament's establishment provoking a heated exchange with David McCrone, one of the leading proponents of 'new politics'.[5] On the second anniversary of the Parliament's election, MacWhirter argued that the Parliament had made a difference. In particular, it had achieved four things that it was designed to do: redress a perceived democratic deficit; bring government closer to the people; improve accountability; and resolve the constitutional issue which had dominated Scottish politics for 30 years.[6] Some might quibble with one or two of these items but few would challenge all of these claims.

These attitudes amongst pundits appear to be shared by the electorate. The 'expectations gap' that existed prior to devolution and for a period immediately afterwards was a potential source of trouble. As Figure 3.2 below shows, pre-devolution the expectations of the Scottish electorate were very high. The Parliament simply did not have the powers to meet the expectations that Scots had of it. Public expectations were that devolution was going to be the panacea for Scotland's ills. It could be that the campaigns for home rule and the talking up of the capabilities of the Parliament is directly linked to the largely negative media and public assessment of its initial performance. James Kellas, doyen of Scottish political commentators, has warned that the system that has emerged is 'unstable'.[7] The gap has not been closed but it has been narrowed. As the Scottish Attitudes Survey research has shown, Scots now have a more realistic expectation of their Parliament.[8] Whereas early in its life, the Scottish Parliament was thought to be more powerful than Westminster, they now recognise that power has not shifted so dramatically northwards.

---

[5] *Sunday Herald*, 3 and 10 September 2000.
[6] *Sunday Herald*, 1 July 2001.
[7] Kellas 2000, p30.
[8] *The Scotsman*, 26 June 2001.

Figure 3.2. Expectations of the Scottish Parliament

	A lot (%)	A little (%)	Total (%)
The Scottish Parliament would:			
Increase unemployment	2	9	11
Increase taxes	2	68	70
Improve the economy	26	60	86
Improve the standard of the NHS	36	46	82
Improve the quality of education	39	50	89
Improve the standard of social welfare	19	53	71

Source: Denver *et. al* 2000, *Scotland Decides: The Devolution Issue and the Scottish Referendum,* p.200

In some ways, the excitement has gone out of devolution. In its place, Scottish politics has 'normalised'. This is not to suggest that the drama has gone out of Scottish politics, nor that territorial conflicts have disappeared but that Scottish politics, as evident during the 2001 general election campaign, is no longer defined almost exclusively as being concerned with constitutional issues. As scholars of public policy frequently remind us, issues that affect the lives of the public may often appear humdrum, even boring, to commentators and journalists but these are the essence of normal politics.

The events that shape politics, often unforeseen, sometimes dramatic, and the process of making policy are the focus of this chapter. The most significant event of the last year was the death of Donald Dewar, First Minister, on 11 October 2000. Dewar had been a long-standing supporter of devolution. In retrospect, we can see that his death marked a significant watershed in Scottish politics. Even before the illness preceding his passing, Dewar appeared to be a caretaker — with constant jostling for position amongst some of his senior ministers for the succession. He was both a senior British and Scottish politician with authority in London and Edinburgh and he personified the transition to devolution. Devolution would only really be tested after he had gone. In some respects, Dewar personified the idea of devolution as an event rather than a process, the idea that devolution was just one more policy on New Labour's constitutional reform list to be ticked-off as 'delivered'. Donald Dewar's First Ministership was seen, and probably even by himself, as more a fitting culmination of his career, that is an essentially static view, rather than a new and radical phase of political activity, a more dynamic phase. The Dewar Administration, from May 1999 to October

2000 was an 'ending' rather a 'beginning'. Henry McLeish appears to have viewed his succession differently and has set out to be seen not as a continuation of this, rather conservative, form of devolution but as a kick-start of a new, more distinctive devolution era. This interpretation of McLeish's Administration is not shared by all, even all within it.

The notion of a transition in Scottish politics was emphasised with Alex Salmond's decision to stand down as leader of the Scottish National Party (SNP) after ten years in the post. Commentators whose interest in Scottish politics started with devolution were shocked and looked for a conspiracy behind the resignation while those with a deeper knowledge of Scottish politics set the bruising experience of serving a ten year stretch alongside Salmond's private declarations made early in his leadership that he had no intention to serve more than a decade.

Relations between the different institutions – the Executive and Parliament, London and Edinburgh – became the focus of media attention when conflict or its likelihood emerged. For the most part, the operation of inter-governmental relations operated smoothly. This was partly due to the effort the UK Government and Scottish Executive invested in avoiding any potential conflicts (see Chapter 7 for a more detailed discussion). There were some significant developments — especially in the relations between the Executive and Parliament. However, the most significant aspect of post-devolutionary Scottish politics over the last year has been the emphasis on public policy matters. Dealing with crises or developing policies, the Executive has been scrutinised in a manner and to an extent unknown before in Scottish history.

Scottish policymaking capacity for issues such as health and education are not newly 'devolved', as they were generally Scottish Office matters pre-devolution. However, the creation of devolved institutions has dramatically increased their visibility and transparency, especially in terms of spotlighting the focus of true ministerial accountability and responsibility for much Scottish domestic policy.

There are weaknesses in the system and the Parliament is concerned that the four principles — the sharing of power, accountability, participation and equal opportunities — that informed the Consultative Steering Group's (CSG) deliberations when it was drawing up plans for the operation of the Parliament may have been lost sight of. [9] Nonetheless, by Westminster standards the Scottish Parliament can claim to have maintained relatively high standards. It has begun to establish its own identity and carve its place within the new structure of devolved government, even if (or perhaps because) that place was not exactly as that envisaged but the CSG. Changes are likely but procedures established early in the life of an institution are likely to persist, more or less, over time.

[9] CSG 1998.

THE EXECUTIVE

The year 2000–1 saw significant changes in the Executive. These came from two sources: the fact that leadership changed as Henry McLeish became First Minister and composed a Cabinet in his own image, and the development of a more distinctively Scottish approach to policy.

The Labour Leadership: McLeish's Succession

The extraordinary reaction to Donald Dewar's death in October 2000 suggested more than the passing of a senior politician. Dewar had been fiercely criticised in sections of the press during his period as First Minister. His standing in the polls did not sit easily with the politician who appeared in the obituaries. When asked whether he had done a good or bad job, attitudes had swung against Dewar from just after elections to the Scottish Parliament in 1999 when the gap between his positive and negative rating was 46 points to 10 in September 2000. Dewar had been a more successful politician in opposition. He had been unable to stop the constant infighting in his Cabinet. The misreading of public opinion, failure to provide clear leadership and deal with deep divisions over Section 28 may not have been typical of his leadership, but it was symptomatic of a party that had a culture of opposition instilled into it over eighteen years in opposition. Dewar had been a conservative politician. The Section 28 debate was untypical not least because it was a bold measure that challenged the enduring illiberalism in Scottish society. Though time may have prevented him from pursuing more adventurous policies, Dewar's 'safety first' approach and unwillingness to rock the boat in relations with London ensured that no single innovative policy became attached to his name. To fill the gap, the obituaries made too much of his contribution to the home rule cause. The hagiographic reports were not only hypocritical given the press criticisms before but were also symbolic. Dewar's death marked the end of the transition to devolution. Whoever succeeded him would be a more 'home grown' politician, one less significant in the Westminster village.

Speculation as to Dewar's successor had been a persistent theme from before the Parliament met. In September 2000, a *Scotsman*/ICM poll asked who should replace the First Minster after he retired, the assumption being that he would not serve beyond the end of the Parliament, especially following illness at the start of the Summer. The clear leader was Henry McLeish. He commanded the support of 29 per cent of Labour supporters and 24 per cent of the public as a whole. Susan Deacon, the Health minister, had the support of 11 per cent of Labour voters and 10 per cent of all voters. Finance minister Jack McConnell had the support of 15 per cent of Labour voters but only 7 per cent of all voters while Wendy Alexander, Communities minister trailed behind with 5 per cent support amongst Labour voters and 7 per cent of all voters.[10]

However, the public would have no role in the choice of Scotland's second First Minister. Indeed, one of the unforeseen problems caused by Dewar's death was that the provisions of the devolution legislation collided with the Scottish Labour Party's rules on electing a leader. The Scotland Act 1998 (section 46) stipulated that an election had to be called if the Parliament failed to choose a First Minister within 28 days of a vacancy. The logic behind this was that a hung Parliament was likely, given the electoral system, and this provision would concentrate minds, preventing stalemate leading to a long period without an Executive. Labour's rules for electing a Scottish leader involved a long drawn-out process that would have been difficult to compress into the time available, especially given that decency demanded that the process could only begin after Dewar's funeral. In the event, an electoral college consisting of all MSPs plus members of Scottish Labour's executive met ten days after the First Minister's death to choose the new leader. This was later endorsed formally by the party on 9 December 2000.

Two candidates stood for the leadership. The favourite, Henry McLeish, had the support of all members of the Scottish front bench, including one member who had initially supported Jack McConnell. McLeish was also the leadership's candidate, though London was careful not to be seen to be too involved in the contest. Gordon Brown, using his position as a Scottish MP, was involved in lobbying on McLeish's behalf. Mistakes made in the contests for the London mayor and leadership of Labour in Wales were successfully avoided. McConnell had been a young, radical leader of Stirling District Council before becoming general secretary of the Scottish party. Not only had he been a member of Scottish Labour Action, the home rule pressure group, but he had argued for a more radical home rule package and had been a thorn in the side of Labour's more conservative Scottish leadership.

The shortened campaign ensured that Labour was spared a deeply divisive and bitter contest. It also meant that there was little time for detailed scrutiny of the candidates, something that in retrospect can be seen to have benefited Henry McLeish, given his frequent public gaffes. In the event McLeish won 44 votes to McConnell's 36. The ballot was secret but the interpretation that came to be accepted was that if the front bench had voted for McLeish, as they had publicly stated they would, and members of Scottish Labour's executive had voted similarly, given its reputation for doing what it is told by the leadership, then McConnell had done remarkably well amongst Labour backbenchers, winning a clear majority there.

McConnell's strong showing and his remarkably loyal approach, failing to complain about procedures that disadvantaged him, placed him in a strong position following the vote. Entering the contest did McConnell no damage

---

[10] See the discussion of Dewar's possible successor in Leicester (ed.) 2000.

at all. On the other hand, Wendy Alexander's position, after the mishandling of the Section 28 policy and failure to enter the contest ensured that her position has been weakened, at least amongst pundits, as compared to the year before. Alexander's personal political position mirrors that of devolution; high expectations had been allowed to be built up that simply could not be sustained.

The formal endorsement of Henry McLeish by the Scottish Labour Party in December was accompanied by the unopposed election of Cathy Jamieson, Ayrshire MSP, as deputy leader. The formality of the procedure meant that only 62 of the 81 electors bothered to turn up to vote. Jamieson's election surprised some, given her left-wing past, though the post carries little power and was more a sop to old Labour in much the same way as John Prescott's position is within the party in Britain.

'Team McLeish'

Within a short period of time, Henry McLeish gained a reputation as prone to gaffes and verbal infelicities, known as 'McLeishies'. While there is some truth in this, many of his 'gaffes' were attempts to assert his presence and stamp his authority on Scottish devolution. His gaffes became a convenient way in which unwelcome ideas and pronouncements could be written-off by his opponents, especially inside Labour. McLeish let it be known that one of his political heroes was Mario Cuomo. Many more likely figures than the former Governor of New York State can be imagined. The one term borrowed from American politics adopted by his spin doctor Peter McMahon, former *Scotsman* and *Mirror* political editor, was the notion of 'Team McLeish' (Figure 3.3 below outlines full details of 'Team McLeish'). It proved a team at war with itself. Dewar's death and the election of McLeish did not end the jostling for position within the Executive, something the new First Minister has proved incapable of containing, far less ending.

McLeish's authority was seriously undermined after a dispute concerning responsibility within the Executive for water after Sam Galbraith resigned as Environment minister for health reasons in March 2001. Initially, it was reported that Wendy Alexander, Minister for Enterprise and Lifelong Learning, would assume responsibility for water. This was followed by reports that Alexander had refused this and had 'thrown a tantrum', a sexist phrase reproduced uncritically throughout the press, a sure sign of a quack spin doctor at work. Water was ultimately allocated to Ross Finnie, Rural Affairs minister (already dealing with the Foot-and-Mouth crisis) in a defeat for the First Minister. Alexander was criticised for being unable to accept the position because of her duties as a senior figure in Labour's general election campaign in Scotland. Reports suggested that Chancellor of the Exchequer Gordon Brown had intervened to protect Alexander.

Figure 3.3. Team McLeish: the Scottish Cabinet, March 2001

First Minister	Henry McLeish
Deputy First Minister and Minister for Justice	Jim Wallace
Minister for Education, Europe and External Affairs	Jack McConnell
Minister for Enterprise and Lifelong Learning	Wendy Alexander
Minister for Environment and Rural Affairs	Ross Finnie
Minister for Finance and Local Government	Angus MacKay
Minister for Health and Community Care	Susan Deacon
Minister for Parliament	Tom McCabe
Minister for Social Justice	Jackie Baillie
Minister for Transport and Planning	Sarah Boyack

Since becoming First Minister, McLeish has attempted to assert himself in three ways:

* institutional innovation;
* policy innovation
* symbolic politics.

In each way he has encountered difficulties and been forced into a U-turn. In each case, the First Minister's initial proposal appears to have been wanting in preparation and execution. In trying to cut out a distinct role for the Executive, he has found himself at odds with London and has had to back off embarrassingly.

Institutional Innovation

Within days of winning, in an effort to win support amongst Labour back-benchers, amongst whom he reputedly had little support, McLeish promised a more inclusive style, suggesting that Labour MSPs would have access to civil servants. This provoked strong criticisms. Opposition politicians and civil servants took from McLeish's statement that civil servants would be at the disposal of Labour members. McLeish's notion appeared to be based on a local government rather than a British parliamentary model. This may have derived from the common view that existed in the Constitutional Convention and which lingered thereafter, even amongst some MSPs in the Parliament's early days, of a Parliament–Executive unitary body which would give MSPs direct access to Executive officials. Having to spin his way out of this ensured that McLeish's statement had the opposite effect of that intended. Instead of asserting his authority, he had undermined it.

Institutionally, greater emphasis was placed on the European and wider overseas dimension. While European Union (EU) and foreign affairs were retained matters, explicitly not devolved, there was much that the Scottish Parliament had responsibility for that had a significant EU dimension. Donald Dewar had been wary of treading on London's toes but McLeish determined to give greater prominence to the European dimension. This took institutional form in the shape of appointing his challenger, Jack McConnell, to the new post of Minister for Education, Europe and External Affairs. Coupling education with foreign affairs was a highly unusual, probably unique way to organise a government department. Statements made by the new minister and his deputy make clear the view that engagement with Europe cannot be avoided because it permeates so many areas of policy. The External Relations division within the Executive has three priorities in relation to the EU:

- to monitor and, where necessary, influence the UK line on the forthcoming enlargement;
- to raise Scotland's profile within the EU in relation to the smaller member states, other territorial governments and the EU's institutions;
- to exchange ideas with other territorial governments on policy.[11]

In a news release in December 2000, headed 'Scotland must increase links with Europe', McConnell, the Minister for European Affairs pointed out that for the first time the Executive had a minister for Europe demonstrating that it is a 'top priority' and that having created links with other nations and regions, 'we need to move our engagement up a gear or two.'[12]

However, while Robin Cook had been Foreign Secretary the relations between London and Edinburgh in the area of European affairs had been fairly relaxed. Commentators have suggested that a less pluralist approach might develop with the appointment of Jack Straw as Foreign Secretary in London. McLeish took his European policy a stage further in late May 2001 when he signed the Flanders Declaration, along with other 'constitutional regions' in Europe, calling for Europe's devolved governments to be involved in preparations for the next EU Intergovernmental Conference (IGC). Notably, Wales had been involved as an observer in earlier discussions leading up to the declaration but was not involved in the final declaration. McLeish had been involved in discussions with Foreign Secretary Robin Cook prior to signing up. After the election, however, the SNP maintained that under Jack Straw, McLeish had been forced to back down in his efforts to gain Scottish involvement in discussions on the forthcoming IGC.

[11] See discussion in Mitchell 2001c pp. 35-48.
[12] New Release SE 3124/2000, 4 December 2000.

All Change at Dover House

Another significant development in intergovernmental relations occurred following Peter Mandelson's resignation as Secretary of State for Northern Ireland in January 2001. John Reid, who had replaced Dewar as Scottish Secretary, took Mandelson's place in Northern Ireland, vacating the Scotland Office. Reid and Dewar had been engaged in bitter turf wars that were never properly resolved. Each saw himself as the key figure in Scottish politics. Dewar was certainly perceived as the key figure by commentators and the public and though he did not win each skirmish, his position as a senior British politician placed him in a strong position. However, there was little doubt that the Scottish Secretary assumed a relatively more significant position following Dewar's death. The poor relations between Reid and McLeish, though little commented upon, was well known to many following Scottish politics. Hostilities between the two never produced the headlines that had marked the relationship between Dewar and Reid, partly because Reid moved on soon after McLeish became First Minister. However, on the day after the general election, McLeish's unguarded comments about Reid and junior Scotland Office minister Brian Wilson caught on tape by a radio journalist — describing Reid as a 'patronising bastard' and Brian Wilson as a 'liability' — suggest that the poor relations between the First Minister and Scottish Secretary under Dewar and Reid continued under McLeish.

Helen Liddell, Reid's replacement, appears in no doubt about her position vis-a-vis the Scottish Executive with various reports, obviously spun by her supporters, that she had knocked a few heads together when internal conflict hit the Scottish Cabinet prior to the UK general election. In April 2001, Liddell was reported to have reprimanded members of the Scottish Executive for the poisonous atmosphere created by infighting.[13] It might have been assumed that it was the job of the First Minister to deal with internal Cabinet conflicts but McLeish's position appeared to have been undermined by the Scottish Secretary. Suggestions that the office of Scottish Secretary should be abolished or in some way combined with other offices may have been logical, but there are inconsistent messages coming out of London on this. Ultimately, London still needed a Scottish minister to 'quell those turbulent Scots', as Churchill had instructed Lord Home on appointing him Minister of State at the Scottish Office in 1951.[14]

On becoming First Minister, McLeish made it clear that there would be a shake-up in policy. As he told the BBC, 'Policies that might have been attractive two years ago might not be attractive now. I want an administration that is sensitive to the people that elected it. It's not a matter of political correctness or anything else. I am concerned that we do have policies that are in tune

---

[13] See press 28 March, 1 April, 10 April especially (*Sunday*) *Herald*.
[14] Lord Home 1978, p101.

with the Scottish people.'[15] These comments were in part a reaction to the Section 28 debates of the previous year. McLeish, along with McConnell and Tom McCabe (Parliament minister), had been a critic of the policy to remove the Section. It was, therefore, seen as a criticism of Wendy Alexander. But it was more than that. McLeish was striking out with a more populist message.

THE SCOTTISH PARLIAMENT AND THE PARTIES

The second year of devolution has seen the Parliament start to grow into its role, and to begin to assert itself against the Executive on occasion. It has also been increasingly the forum for differences between the parties, shaped in part by a new approach from the Scottish National Party (SNP) following its change of leadership.

Executive–Parliament Relations

Relations between the Scottish Parliament and Executive became more complex during the second year. In April 2000, Scottish Socialist Party MSP Tommy Sheridan had scored a remarkable victory for the Parliament over the Executive. His Abolition of Poindings and Warrant Sales Bill won majority support. The Executive had then backed down after it became clear that even its most loyal, ambitious backbenchers were willing to vote against it partly because they felt committed, having supported it in three different commit-tees. During the last year, the Executive has had difficult relations with the Parliament on a number of occasions. There are a number of explanations for this. The make-up of the Parliament, with no built-in majority for Labour, is one. The bizarre nature of the coalition, in which the Liberal Democrats appear on occasion to be part of the opposition rather than in the coalition, is another. But poor management of Parliamentary business on the part of the Executive played its part, though ministers are gradually learning that they cannot dominate the running of the Parliament in the same way that their UK counterparts can in the House of Commons.

Significantly, the Executive has rarely been the subject of a defeat on account of rebellions from Labour backbenchers. The Warrant Sales and Poindings Bill was the exception not the rule during the first year, but over the last year the Parliament has asserted itself. In two areas, a combination of factors resulted in embarrassing reverses for the Executive. The debates on the Sutherland Report on care for the elderly witnessed the Executive being forced to alter course. As discussed in detail below, a row followed the announcement by Susan Deacon, Health minister, on 24 January watering down McLeish's earlier support for free personal care. The public criticisms stung the Liberal Democrats, Labour's coalition partners. An SNP motion

---

[15] news6.thdo.bbc.co.uk/hi/english/uk/scotland/newsid%5F997000/997445.stm

tabled for the next day cheekily noted that it was the policy of the 'Liberal Democrats, SNP and Conservatives and others to introduce free personal care for the elderly'. Labour managers were concerned that some 'flaky' Liberal Democrats would join with the opposition and an emergency amendment was cobbled together which supported Sutherland in full, a reversal of the position Deacon had announced the previous day. Though the decision taken in January may yet be reversed (again) the Parliament played a role in this long-drawn-out process.

Another example occurred over fisheries policy. On 8 March the Executive suffered a defeat. On a tied vote (55 for and 55 against) on an amended Opposition motion, the Presiding Officer, Sir David Steel, used his casting vote for the Opposition motion. The Executive decided to ignore this, claiming that the resolution was only advisory and not binding on it. There were two explanations for this result. First, a number of Labour MSPs had been given permission by Tom McCabe, Parliament minister, to go to Inverness to hear Prime Minister Tony Blair address Labour's Scottish conference. Thirteen Labour MSPs were marked absent. In addition, four Liberal Democrats voted against the Executive. Tavish Scott, McCabe's deputy and Liberal Democrat MSP for Shetland resigned following the vote though he had voted with the Executive. The explanation he gave for his resignation was that his constituency interest forced him into this position. He was replaced by Euan Robson, who had abstained in the vote.

Steel's decision to vote with the Opposition raised a few eyebrows. Though there are no rules as to how a Presiding Officer's casting vote should be used, the Executive had assumed that in a tied vote he would have backed the Executive. Steel, however, had earlier asserted himself as Presiding Officer when he supported George Reid, one of his deputies, in a dispute with the Executive. In January 2001 a statement to be made in the Parliament by Angus MacKay, the Finance minister, was extensively reported in the Scottish media in advance of the official announcement. Reid refused to permit Mackay to make the statement and ruled that the speech should be 'taken as read'.

The Parliament has been asserting itself in other ways. In June 2001 Alasdair Morgan introduced the Protection from Abuse (Scotland) Bill on behalf of the Justice 1 Committee. The Protection from Abuse (Scotland) Bill is the first bill ever to be introduced by a subject committee in the Parliament.

The Work of the Parliament's Committees

The Parliament's second year saw its committees grappling with the operational pressures that had arisen in the first twelve months, especially those of overwork and the imbalance between legislative and inquiry work. These problems had limited the degree to which the committees could operate fully in the innovative and participative spirit desired by the CSG and others, and even when not in legislative mode, they tended to work in familiar evidence-gathering ways. The balance in practice between the committees and the plenary was not what was originally envisaged, as the media and the public tended to focus on the Chamber, especially once First Minister's Question Time was created in January 2000.

From mid-2000 there was much discussion within the Parliament about a restructuring of the committees to cope with the overall workload, and the disproportionate pressures on committees such as Justice and Home Affairs. Sadly, these negotiations took place through the usual channels, rather than openly and transparently, such as through a Procedures Committee inquiry. Rumours abounded during these six months, especially that the very commit-tees that symbolise the Parliament's unique ethos, such as Public Petitions and Equal Opportunities, were to be sacrificed in favour of the more 'produc-tive' (especially in the Executive's view) subject committees. Eventually a messy compromise, including the de facto splitting of Justice and Home Affairs into two identical committees unimaginatively called Justice 1 and Justice 2, was agreed, and was endorsed by the Parliament at the end of 2000.

Another instance of the Executive's concern at the committees' potential was its reaction to the attempts by several committees to dig deeply into the SQA school exams fiasco. Its response in the autumn of 2000 was to draft a resolution limiting how the committees would exercise their statutory evidence-gathering powers against Executive departments, much in line with Westminster practice. Despite promises from both the original First Minister and the Presiding Officer the previous November that no UK-style 'MacOsmotherly Rules', on the operation of Executive's accountability to the Parliament and its committees, would be imposed unilaterally by the Executive, this resolution was presented to the Parliament for endorsement, without any prior detailed examination of this fundamental issue.[16] The Parliament's agreement to this resolution on 1 November, after a lively debate, must be regarded as the nadir of its relationship with the Executive.

Members' bills continued to test the robustness of the committee system. Mike Watson's anti-hunting bill was the subject of prolonged scrutiny, espe-cially by the Rural Affairs Committee. Eventually, and not until after some internal acrimony, that Committee recommended in July 2001 that the Parliament reject the bill at Stage 1.[17] Committees have also begun to initiate their own legislation. *The Protection from Abuse (Scotland) Bill* was pro-posed by the Justice and Home Affairs Committee in late 2000, and is, at the

[16] A protocol on certain operational issues had already been concluded between committee clerks and the Executive in September 2000, without any public parliamentary discussion or endorsement. The compromise proposed for dealing with the particular SQA inquiries was a form of limited access to sensitive official material, eerily reminiscent of the 'Crown Jewels' procedure adopted at Westminster for the Belgrano/Falklands inquiries of the mid-1980s.

[17] This was the first such recommendation by a committee, and was rejected by the Parliament when it debated the bill in September 2001.

time of writing, well into its legislative scrutiny. The Standards Committee's proposal for a Standards Committee Bill has also been considered by the Parliament.

The formal establishment under Standing Orders of the Conveners' Liaison Group, agreed in principle in September 2000 after long negotiation behind the scenes and after Procedures Committee scrutiny, but not yet implemented, should assist in raising the committees' profile and influence within the Parliament. In particular, it should dilute the de facto control of the Executive-dominated Parliamentary Bureau over the constitution and operation of committees, which must be welcomed.

The SNP and its New Leadership

The election of John Swinney as SNP leader did not involve a major shift in strategy so much as a change of style. Traditionally, as outlined in the party's constitution, the SNP leader convenes the party rather than leads it. Salmond was the first clear leader of the party since Robert McIntyre had provided firm leadership in the late 1940s and the first to have a level of public recognition compared with counterparts in other parties. The contest for the leadership between Swinney and Alex Neil involved a test of the respective strengths of the two tendencies, pragmatists and fundamentalists, that have dominated internal SNP politics since it came into existence.

The hardliners were in the difficult position of having been staunch critics of devolution and those who supported it within the SNP, but were now having to come to terms with it. Alex Neil, standard bearer for the fundamentalists in the contest, was himself a Member of the Scottish Parliament and acting like any other well-behaved MSP. Neil had joined the SNP after the 1987 general election and had previously been a senior Scottish Labour official, drafting Labour's October 1974 manifesto around the time the party reversed its devolution policy. He had been an 'important member of the group which conceived and launched' Jim Sillars' breakaway Scottish Labour Party[18] and became its general secretary. He was to follow Sillars into the SNP and, still later, follow him from pragmatist to hard-liner.

Swinney's was an altogether different political background, rising up through the SNP from his days as a student. Serving as a young National Secretary had done little to raise his profile with the voters but made him well-known as a administratively competent official to SNP activists and provided him with an understanding of his party that Neil has never gained. Later, as deputy to Alex Salmond, he became firmly associated with the strategy adopted by Salmond. Short of some catastrophe, there was never much doubt that Swinney would win. The two key questions in the contest were the size of his victory and the results of other elections to other national offices. The SNP's remarkably non-modernised structure includes a very large

[18] Drucker 1978, p20.

number of elected posts, considerable power vested in its national conference and quarterly national councils. One of Salmond's difficulties had been
that he was always having to contest battles over and over again and operate
with a sizeable minority of senior figures who were at odds with him.

In the event, Swinney's victory was emphatic, even more so than had been
Salmond's a decade before. With 67 per cent of the vote and Swinney
supporters winning all of the other posts, Swinney was in a remarkably
powerful position, at least for the next year. The challenge for Swinney was
that challenges could emerge very easily annually at conference and
quarterly at national council. His national executive was overwhelmingly
supportive but some tensions emerged within the leadership during the
general election campaign. Whether this signals the decline in importance of
the fundamentalist-pragmatist tension or a fissure within the pragmatist
camp that might be exploited by the hardliners will become clearer in time.

The Parliament as a New Model of Assembly

In a recent review of the first two years of the Parliament and devolution
McLeish argued that what it had achieved was 'world away from the
Westminster–Scottish Office model'.[19] In a speech to the Oxford Union Sir
David Steel, the Presiding Officer, made similar claims of how the Parlia-
ment had 'proved effective in delivering greater speed and degree of legisla-
tion for Scotland than was ever possible in the crowded agenda at
Westminster'.[20] Scottish public opinion also appears to be moving in favour
of the Parliament as Figure 3.4 below highlights.

Figure 3.4. The Scottish Parliament & public opinion

From what you have seen or heard do you think the Scottish Parliament has achieved a lot, a little or nothing at all? (figures in percentages)			
	Feb 01	Sep 00	Feb 00
A Lot	25	11	5
A Little	56	56	64
Nothing at all	14	29	27

Source: www.icmresearch.co.uk

As a maturing institution the Parliament has begun to gain attention from
would be reformers of the House of Commons. Robin Cook, the Leader of
the Commons, is reported to be interested in adopting many of the practices

[19] 'McLeish lays it on the line for public services', *The Herald,* 21 August 2001.

[20] Sir David Steel, 'A dozen differences of devolution', Speech to the Oxford Union, 4 June 2001.
Available at www.scottish.parliament.uk/whats_happening/news-01/pa01-031.htm.

of the Scottish Parliament. He visited the Parliament in September, meeting Sir David Steel, the Presiding Officer, Murray Tosh, the convener of the procedures committee, Tom McCabe, the Parliament minister, and Henry McLeish, the First Minister. He is likely to have noted numerous innovations such as the more family-friendly working hours, the significant representation of women, the public petitions committee and the more informal nature of proceedings. It could be that such practices will influence any House of Commons reform agenda.[21]

Cost will, as always, be a significant influence on this agenda, as Cook will no doubt have noted in the ongoing and seemingly never-ending controversy over the cost of the new Scottish Parliament building. The May 2001 Parliament debate on the subject, called by the Conservatives, followed claims that the new parliament building is likely to be six times more than the original estimate of £50 million. A motion by Scottish Conservative leader David McLetchie asking the Executive to reconfirm the cash limit of £195 million on the project was watered down by a further amendment from Labour MSP John Home Robertson. The SNP argued that 'It was the wrong design in the wrong place' and the root problem was in the way it was conceived and brought forward by Westminster and Westminster ministers.[22] It is unlikely that we have heard the end of this long-lasting political controversy.

Positive assessments of the Parliament's first two years have also been tempered with widespread criticism of the Scottish Executive's performance. Devolution was always a means to an end, the end being an improvement in the lives of Scottish people through things like better education, health care, housing and transport and the like. Its actual impact to date in these areas is negligible. It is the performance on these issues in the next two years that his Executive is likely to be judged in the May 2003 Scottish elections.

It is not only the Executive's performance that will affect the incumbency prospects of many of Scotland's parliamentarians. The number of Scottish MPs is expected to be cut to 57–60 by the next general election in 2005. Under the Scotland Act 1998 this would also result in a reduction in the number of MSPs at Holyrood from 129 to between 102 and 106 because the constituencies are the same for both parliaments. It is likely such a reduction would present difficulty for the Parliament as it works mainly through committees, which have a legislative as well as a scrutinising role. With its current 129 MSPs it has difficulty filling its committees even as things stand. Indeed this year Holyrood business managers cut the size of the committees so that MSPs could cope. The likely outcome is an amendment to the

---

[21] See 'Cook seeks to emulate Holyrood', *The Scotsman,* 10 September 2001, and Miller 2000.
[22] See SNP press release at www.snp.org.uk/press/news/pr10510970ww.htm.

Scotland Act and a decoupling of the Westminster and Holyrood Parliamentary boundaries. [23]

POLICY DEVELOPMENT AND DIVERGENCE

This second year has seen the emergence of an increasingly distinctive approach to public policy in Scotland. This section will try to draw some of the rather disparate threads of this together.

Legislation

The Parliament's legislative output is impressive; in its two years it has passed 24 bills. In the two years preceding devolution Westminster managed only four Scottish bills. The Parliament has passed the first Scottish Housing Bill in 13 years and has dealt with other legislation that would never have been considered in Westminster.[24] Figure 3.5 below outlines the bills passed this year.

Figure 3.5. Bills passed in Scottish Parliament December 2000-August 2001

- Abolition of Poindings and Warrant Sales Bill
- Salmon Conservation (Scotland) Bill
- Budget (Scotland) (No. 2) Bill
- Leasehold Casualties (Scotland) Bill
- Education (Graduate Endowment and Student Support) Scotland (No. 2) Bill
- Convention Rights (Compliance) (Scotland) Bill
- Education (Graduate Endowment and Student Support) (Scotland) (No. 2) Bill
- Housing (Scotland) Bill
- Regulation of Care (Scotland) Bill
- Scottish Local Authorities (Tendering) Bill
- Mortgage Rights (Scotland) Bill

Care for the Elderly

McLeish's new populist message took concrete form in the reversal of previous policy on care for the elderly. In December 1997, a Royal Commission on Long Term Care under Sir Stewart Sutherland was set up by the UK Government in London. Its majority report was published in March 1999, recommending that all nursing and personal care should be met by the state. The Scottish Executive, responsible for these matters in Scotland, formally responded in October 2000 against the full implementation of Sutherland. Under Dewar, the Scottish Executive had accepted London's lead. In an

---

[23] See 'Parliaments on collision course over numbers', *The Scotsman,* 22 August 2001, 'Scotland may face another referendum', *The Scotsman,* 27 August 2001, 'SNP hits at 'wreckers' on plan to cut MSPs', *The Herald,* 31 September 2001.

[24] For example, the abolition of feudal tenure see, 'Politicians under the spotlight', *BBC News Online,* 30 June 2001, available at news.bbc.co.uk/hi/english/uk/scotland/newsid_1414000/1414853.stm.

interview in early November, McLeish argued, in line with his earlier state-ment, for a change of policy,

> If you are rooted in public concern then you will know that [if] every organisation you talk to, every medical group, local authority, the Sutherland people themselves, the Parliamentary Labour Party, the opposition [are agreed] then sometimes you just have to say to yourselves: 'Well, look. There is a firm body of opinion. Is what we have as a policy the right thing to do?'[25]

McLeish reiterated his support for the full implementation of Sutherland in a later interview with the BBC.[26] Both his general statement on the need for new policies and the specific comment on Sutherland pointed to some problems ahead. Driven by popular demands, public policy has a habit of becoming costly and ineffective. The First Minister's lack of self-confidence was all too obvious.

Later in November the Scottish Parliament's Health and Community Care Committee published its report on Community Care Services and called for full implementation of Sutherland. However, pressure from London was built up against full implementation and Lord Lipsey, New Labour peer and a member of the Royal Commission who was a signatory of the minority report that opposed full state support for nursing and personal care, was sent north to make the case against Sutherland. Lipsey made the less than convincing claim that the more generous policy being pursued by the First Minister would encourage elderly people living in England to move to Scotland. The more fundamental issue for the Executive was, however, financial. The costs of the policy might prove prohibitive — especially significant given the lack of revenue raising powers of the Parliament.

Divisions within the Executive and pressure from London added to McLeish's problems. The Liberal Democrats were supporters of the full implementation of Sutherland, keen to take credit for forcing the Executive to adopt a more generous policy. A formulation that would allow McLeish to save face while significantly backing down in the policy had to be found. Susan Deacon, Health minister, had opposed full implementation of Suther-land from the start and saw difficulties with the policy not least that free care would advantage wealthier pensioners and that limited resources would not be targeted according to need. Her statement in the Scottish Parliament on the subject in January 2001 emphasised targeting and did not commit the Executive to full implementation of Sutherland. Amongst its provisions was a commitment to establish a development group to report in August 2001, led by Malcolm Chisholm, Deputy Minister for Health and Community Care. The following day an SNP motion demanding 'unequivocal commitment' to free personal care was debated in the chamber. The delicate compromise that

---

[25] *Sunday Times*, 5 November 2000.
[26] BBC *News Scotland*, 14 November 2000.

Deacon had outlined might have satisfied Labour members but Liberal Democrats created problems.

The most extraordinary aspect of the development of the policy at this stage was that the coalition partners were either not fully involved in agreeing the position on this highly-contentious policy that Deacon announced or decided to renege on this in anticipation of criticism from the opposition benches. A last-minute deal was agreed and an amendment to the SNP motion was won for the Executive. It was a classic fudge and bought time rather than resolved the matter. Keith Raffan, the Liberal Democrat health spokesman resigned because of the ambiguity while his leader, Jim Wallace, Deputy First Minister, maintained that free personal care was now government policy. To add to the confusion, McLeish announced a few days later that the Executive was fully committed to the principles of Sutherland and would begin introducing free personal care soon after April 2002. The development group under Chisholm would still meet and 'bring forward proposals for personal care for all, its costs and implications' to consider in August 2001. The Executive have found themselves in the highly unusual, indeed utterly implausible, position of investigating the implications and costs of a policy after it has been agreed. Following the incompetence surrounding care for the elderly, it is little surprise that there have been few other major examples of policy innovation initiated by the First Minister. As was predicted prior to the establishment of the Scottish Parliament, policy innovation involving increased costs was something the Parliament and Executive would be unlikely to undertake. The best hope lay in regulatory policies and symbolic policies, essentially those that did not involve incurring financial costs to the Executive.[27]

Finance

One of the most contentious issues in debates leading up to devolution had concerned how a Scottish Parliament should be financed. The issue of Scotland's share of public spending and contributions to the Exchequer had, in fact, been a periodic cause for complaint throughout the twentieth century and there was little reason to believe that devolution would change this. Indeed, if anything it might be expected to highlight existing tensions. The issue of finance emerged during the last year in a number of forms and its technical aspects are discussed in detail in Chapter 6. The discussion here focuses on two aspects. First, the perennial issue of how much Scotland should receive and the operation of the Barnett Formula which came to prominence in the lead up to and during the general election. Second, an accumulating list of spending commitments on the part of the Executive called into question whether the Executive might have to either make use of its powers to raise tax (breaking an election pledge made by Labour during

[27] Mitchell 1998*a*.

the 1999 Scottish elections) or plead for additional support from the Treasury. In fact, these two matters were, of course, inter-related.

Barnett and the UK General Election

During the general election campaign, a group of twelve Scottish economists wrote a letter to *The Scotsman* arguing that the mechanism used for determining the Scottish Executive's budget, the Barnett Formula, ought to be prominent amongst issues addressed by the political parties during the election campaign.[28] Accusations that the economists had been put up to writing the letter by Andrew Wilson, the SNP's energetic, young finance spokesman, were denied, but the SNP's involvement was evident though only a minority of the twelve had connections with the party. *The Scotsman* gave prominence and editorial support to the call for 'fiscal autonomy', but the policy was given far less coverage in other papers.

However, the letter appeared early in the campaign and the SNP failed to keep the issue alive for the duration of the campaign and seemed unable to link it to issues concerning health or education, despite the obvious implications that funding has for these matters. In part, this reflected media bias against the SNP but also pointed towards some failings in the SNP's campaign. First, as in all previous general elections, the SNP was squeezed out of the picture in the closing stages and while it gained a few days of useful coverage at the start, its real need for such coverage was towards the end. Second, and more fundamentally, a tension appeared within the SNP's leadership between those such as Wilson who sought to push the issue of fiscal autonomy hard and others who preferred to focus on health and education but without making the obvious connections. This tension was notably within the leadership, amongst the SNP's pragmatic wing, and not between it and the fundamentalists. The last, as ever, merely wanted to repeat the word 'Independence' ever louder.

Barnett had caused Labour some difficulties in the lead-up to the UK general election when John Prescott, Deputy Prime Minister, was reported to favour a review of the funding arrangements. In an unusual alliance, Peter Mandelson also gave strong support to a review. Barnett was a topic Labour wished to avoid. During the campaign, Prime Minister Blair proved less than adept in handling some questions on the subject in a *Radio Scotland* interview. Blair left the impression that he had not been well briefed on this most contentious issue. Sections of the Scottish media pursued Blair on the issue of Barnett during the election campaign but mainly *The Scotsman*, a paper that is less significant than it used to be. Barnett may not have come alive during the election campaign but there is little doubt that this will continue to be a problem and has all the characteristics of an issue likely to explode on to the political agenda at some stage.

[28] *The Scotsman*, 18 May 2001.

Local Government Finance and the CoSLA Crisis

A series of commitments made by the Executive proved costly and put the Executive's resources under strain. The package agreed with the Convention of Scottish Local Authorities (CoSLA) for local government amounted to a relatively generous total commitment. An increase in the total budget for Scottish local government amounted from £5.5 billion in 2000-01 to £6.5 billion in 2003-04, an overall increase of 15.6 per cent amounting to £876 million. It was, however, not without its critics in local government. Some authorities, led by Glasgow City Council, argued that the settlement agreed through CoSLA favoured a number of east of Scotland local authorities. While Scottish local authorities during the Conservative years had found common cause complaining about central–local financial relations, successive Conservative Scottish Secretaries had been careful not to antagonise west coast Labour authorities, in particular the massive Strathclyde Regional and Glasgow District Councils. This was most notable in the early 1980s when a number of relatively radical Labour administrations were elected in places such as Edinburgh, Lothian Region and Stirling (the last included a young radical Jack McConnell). George Younger's strategy had been to ensure that the distribution of total grant favoured large west coast authorities.

The Scottish Executive altered the distribution provoking criticisms from the west that they were being discriminated against. This contributed to increasing tensions within CoSLA and between Glasgow City Council and the Executive. Glasgow led the way in voting to leave CoSLA, creating the most serious crisis in the organisation's history. Thus, a settlement that in total was relatively generous to local authorities contributed to the Executive's problems, and proved highly controversial and caused a serious breach in CoSLA.

Tuition Fees, Care for Elderly and NHS Salaries

Other spending commitments during the year, along with previous commitments that had lasting implications, added to growing pressure. The Comprehensive Spending Review (CSR) of Summer 2000 had allocated spending limits to UK departments and was the basis for the Scottish Executive's spending limits under Barnett. While the allocation for the UK as a whole had been generous, the amount allocated to Scotland was relatively less generous. In other words, there was a move towards convergence across the UK. Though the total amount allocated had been increased, there was more to observe behind these aggregate figures. Scotland's position resembled that of Glasgow City Council. Both saw an increase in its allocation but this was not as great as other areas. Scotland, of course, was not alone in this (see Chapter 6 on Finance).

Other commitments added up. The abolition of tuition fees recommended by the Cubie Committee is estimated to cost around £50 million by 2004. An enquiry into teachers' pay and conditions, the McCrone Enquiry, established by the Executive recommended that there should be a 23 per cent pay increase for teachers over three years as well as employing an additional 4000 new teachers. The estimated cost over three years at £816 million amounted to one quarter of the annual increase to Scotland provided by the Comprehensive Spending Review. The care for the elderly policy remains an uncertain commitment but it seems likely that the Executive will have to find funds for some level of additional support though the precise amount will remain unclear until a policy is clarified. The costs of funding NHS salaries will also have an impact. This area exemplifies the problems inherent in the current funding arrangements. NHS salaries are largely determined through collective bargaining on a UK basis. The (UK) Department of Health had won a substantial increase in its budget under the CSR but the Barnett Formula provided a less substantial increase for Scotland. Consequently, a pay increase awarded across the UK on the basis of a relatively generous allocation in England would eat into the Scottish Executive's budget.

Taken individually, each commitment might have been accommodated within the Executive's plans but taken together and combined with the possibility of other unforeseen demands and the prospect of care for the elderly proving expensive, indeed a rather open-ended commitment, the Executive have created some problems for themselves. All of this was identified in work by David Bell published in early 2001[29] but was only taken up in the Scottish media some time after the general election.

Symbolic Politics

Symbolic politics are not without costs but these are often political rather than financial. The most significant example of McLeish's determination to be different took the form of his desire to change the name of the 'Scottish Executive' to 'Scottish Government'. The First Minister had referred to the Scottish Government in interviews immediately on assuming office but this was hardly noticed in the media, widely thought to be one of his frequent 'slips'. In early January 2001, however, Tom McCabe, Parliament minister, let it be known that there was a preference for 'Government' within the Executive, suggesting that this should be the term adopted officially. The hostile reaction from London ministers was as swift as it was un-compromising.

Symbolic name changes while a policy otherwise remains intact had occurred in Labour's devolution policy-making before. Labour committed itself to a Scottish Parliament, rather than an Assembly, in the 1980s in an effort to underline the strength of its commitment while the substantive measure supported had hardly changed. This engagement in symbolic

[29] See David Bell's contribution to Mitchell 2001c.

politics was a response to Nationalist electoral pressure. On this latter occasion, the proposed change appears to have had more to do with McLeish asserting his leadership on the Scottish Labour Party and in the Parliament. The thinly veiled rebuke from No. 10 killed off the idea. Significantly, a line fed to various journalists was that a 'senior' London minister had described McLeish as 'thick'.[30]

Scotland Abroad: Europe and the Wider World

Symbolic politics were also evident in the emphasis placed on Europe by the new First Minister. The appointment of a designated Minister for European Affairs, albeit one also responsible for education, was more about presentation than substance. As discussed above, the Executive promised that engagement with Europe would 'move up a gear or two'. The actual role of the External Relations division within the Executive, however, hardly amounted to a major shift in approach to European affairs. Each of the three 'priorities' that were outlined above were adopted by the Scottish Office some years before and indeed by many large local authorities. Junior European minister Nicol Stephen's news release in December 2000 entitled 'Scotland should develop direct links with Europe'[31] implied a more direct relationship than the devolution legislation allowed or London would be willing to contemplate.

Another significant element of symbolic politics was the First Minister's visit to the United States to celebrate 'Tartan Day' in April 2001. In an effort to emulate St Patrick's Day in the USA, a group of Americans with Scottish ancestors had decided to adopt a Scottish Day. McLeish met with President Bush at the White House and took evident pride in the meeting. As he reported in the *Holyrood Magazine*,

> As our car drove up to the real West Wing with myself and the British Ambassador, I did reflect on the fact that this was no small honour for our small nation. It became very apparent very quickly however that the President does have a special fondness for Scotland, stemming in part from time spent here in his youth.[32]

However, McLeish was not alone in visiting the US for 'Tartan Day'. A contingent of Nationalists, including Sean Connery, turned up and the veteran film star — with his call for devolution to move on to independence — attracted far more attention than the unknown First Minister. Symbolic politics has a habit of rebounding.

The visit was linked by the Executive to trade issues and shortly after the visit it was announced that a Scottish official would be based at the UK

---

[30] See press, 11 January 2001.
[31] News release: SE31222/20000, 4 December 2000.
[32] *Holyrood Magazine*, 23 April 2001.

Embassy in Washington provoking unwelcome headlines for the First Minister. 'Scotland to have own envoy in US', declared the *Sunday Herald*.[33] Even more worryingly, *Holyrood Magazine* suggested 'McLeish sets up worldwide Scottish diplomatic corps'.[34] McLeish was determined not to be seen to be undermining the UK Government:

> I am determined to make sure that we pursue Scotland's European and international interests energetically, working with the UK Government to obtain the greatest benefit we can for the people of Scotland.[35]

In some respects, this development was little different from what had gone before. There has long existed a Scottish international presence for trade purposes, supported in the past by the Scottish Office. Some of the media reaction was hostile and suggested that McLeish was set on undermining the integrity of the state. To seasoned observers of Scottish politics, it was all very familiar. A similar reaction had met Ian Lang's proposals to back the Scotland Europa office in Brussels a decade before. As the leaked correspondence between ministers and civil servants from that time showed, there were fears that such an office would simply have a symbolic function, might encourage more demands, could undermine UK efforts to present a united front and be used for junkets. Though presented as a major innovation, it was not. The proposal to base someone in Washington was seen by the First Minister as operating within the parameters of para-diplomacy, in which sub-state actors work in parallel with central governments, rather than proto-diplomacy, when sub-state actors have quite different, even contradictory and undermining strategies, in international dealings.[36]

Symbolic politics are double-edged. On the one hand, it can satisfy demands for a more imaginative or radical approach. On the other hand, it can create unrealistic expectations that might in the long run lead to disillusionment. So far, the largely symbolic nature of the Executive's 'European policy' has had only a limited impact on the public at large but has served the Executive well amongst local government elites and sections of business with an interest in European affairs.

Normalisation

As noted at the outset of this chapter, Scottish devolution in its second year highlighted a normalisation of Scottish politics. Everyday issues, matters that affect the lives of people have come to the fore. There have not only been policies planned by the Scottish Executive but also dealing with crises and unexpected events. Of these, five of the most significant of the last year have been the problems at the Scottish Qualifications Agency SQA, the

---

[33] *Sunday Herald*, 8 April 2001.
[34] *Holyrood Magazine*, 23 April 2001.
[35] *Ibid.*
[36] Mitchell 1995.

Foot-and-Mouth crisis, the shambles surrounding the tourism industry — especially the appointment of the head of *visitscotland*, the downturn in the electronics industry and the UK general election. In each case, these episodes illustrate something about how devolution is bedding down.

Foot-and-Mouth Disease

The Foot-and-Mouth crisis particularly hit the Scottish Borders and amongst other things became a test of the ability of the centre to co-ordinate policy post-devolution. Though the initial outbreak was in Essex, within a week there were confirmed outbreaks of the disease in Scotland. By late Summer, there was general agreement that the handling of the crisis in Scotland had been good. Notably, compensation payments to farmers did not come from the Scottish Executive but rather from contingency funds from the UK Treasury. This was a case in which the general policy was decided on a UK-basis and funded through the Treasury, while implementation was achieved through the Scottish Executive. Inevitably, Scottish Executive ministers, notably Rural Affairs minister Ross Finnie, and Secretary of State for Scotland Helen Liddell played a prominent public role in the crisis.[37]

The Scottish Qualifications Agency Fiasco and Aftermath

In Summer 2000, the greatest crisis in Scottish educational history unfolded when Scottish school students received inaccurate exam results. The Scottish Qualifications Agency (SQA) came under scrutiny for this extraordinary policy failure. A catalogue of management failures was uncovered by an independent consultant's enquiry which provoked the resignation of the SQA chairman and entire board. Calls were made for the resignation of Sam Galbraith, the Education minister but these were ignored. In the event, on becoming First Minister, McLeish replaced Galbraith with Jack McConnell. This appeared to be a 'poisoned chalice' but McConnell appeared to relish the opportunity to ensure that there would be no repeat the next year. A much tighter administration, under far more scrutiny, ensured that school students received accurate exam results in summer 2001.

Though there were opposition calls for the resignation of the minister, there was far less than might have been expected, given past experience under the old Scottish Office. It would have appeared extremely arrogant of any Conservative Scottish minister to have clung onto power in such circumstances, and probably unlikely. The emphasis on examining the nature of the problem and identifying the weaknesses that had resulted in the crisis can be interpreted as a maturing of Scottish politics that would have been difficult to imagine before devolution. It also raises questions about the nature of accountability after devolution, when so much public policy is determined indirectly through agencies.

---

[37] See also 'IGR in crisis: Foot-and-Mouth' in Chapter 7.

VisitScotland

Scottish tourism had been hit by the Foot-and-Mouth crisis as tourists kept away from Scotland in the belief that it was 'closed down'. Strenuous efforts were made by the Executive, including using the platform offered by 'Tartan Day' in the USA, to push the message that it was business as usual. Tourism had been having difficulties without Foot-and-Mouth and these were only compounded when a new head of a re-launched tourism quango, *visitscotland*, had to resign within a week of his appointment. There had been some embarrassment when it turned out that Rod Lynch had planned a holiday in America, political correctness dictated that public figures — especially those associated with tourism — should not go abroad on holiday. The Executive could have weathered this minor squall but had serious problems when it turned out that Lynch had a major conflict of interest, being chief executive of a small cargo airline. Wendy Alexander, Enterprise minister, had been involved in Lynch's appointment and participated prominently in the public announcement and came in for criticism. It had not been a good year for her.

The episode was another that underlined the difficulties that these very inexperienced ministers are discovering when governing through agencies. It also highlighted the importance in modern politics of political spin. So much effort had gone into the relaunch of the tourist agency and its new head that ministerial reputations were damaged.

The Electronics Industry

The downturn in the global electronics industry affected Scotland. Though this covered a matter that was not devolved, there was never any doubt that the Scottish Executive would be expected to play some part in tackling the consequences of the closure of the Motorola plant in West Lothian at a cost of 3000 jobs. As Scottish Secretaries in the past discovered, there is no issue that a Scottish minister could brush aside as beyond his or her responsibility. Little had changed. A role that the Scottish Parliament and Executive had inherited from the Scottish Office was that of acting even where it had no formal power.

THE UK GENERAL ELECTION IN SCOTLAND

The UK general election campaign and its aftermath dominated the Scottish political agenda during May and June. In historical terms it is likely to be seen as a transitional election with all parties learning on their feet about the dynamics of campaigning for a UK election in a devolved environment. In terms of seats won and lost in Scotland little changed. Labour retained all of its seats; the only change was a Conservative gain in Galloway and Upper

Nithsdale at the expense of the SNP. Turnout in Scotland fell by 13.2 per cent — even higher than the fall at the UK level (12.3 per cent).

This low turnout might contradict suggestions that turnout at the 1999 Scottish Parliament Elections reflected its status as a second-order election. Placed in the context of the 2001 election it looks as if it marked the beginning of a downward trend. The election also signalled the end of dual-mandate MSPs — of the thirteen remaining , twelve resigned their Westminster seats, while the former SNP leader resigned his Holyrood seat to remain as leader of the SNP group in Westminster. As Figure 3.6 shows, the Labour vote was down 2.4 per cent to 43.2 per cent but the party held all 55 of its Westminster seats (one is now held by the Speaker). The SNP's vote was down 2 per cent to 20.1 per cent, but they held 5 of their 6 seats. The Liberal Democrat vote was up by 3.4 per cent to 16 4. per cent, retaining all 10 seats and the Conservative vote was down 1.9 per cent to 15.6 per cent but making a gain to give them Commons representation from Scotland. For further discussion of dual-mandate MPs, see Chapter 9; and Chapter 10 for further discussion of the general election result.

Figure 3.6. Votes and seats in Scotland in the 2001 (1997) general elections

	Conservative	Labour	Lib Dem	SNP	SSP/other
Vote (%)	15.6 (17.5)	43.2 (45.6)	16.4 (13.0)	20.1 (22.1)	3.1 (1.9)
Seats	1 (0)	55* (56)	10 (10)	5 (6)	1* (0)

* The Speaker holds Glasgow Springburn

CONCLUSION

Despite the fact that the boom in Scottish politics publications continues unabated (see the Bibliography below for an incomplete selection), in its second year it is possible to detect that a less excitable atmosphere surrounding devolution exists than was evident when the Parliament first met. This is hardly surprising — public opinion appears to be settling down to accept that the Parliament cannot do many of those thing they had hoped for. Some have chosen to interpret this as a growing disillusionment. Another interpretation is that optimism still exists but that it is tempered by a better understanding of the true nature of devolution. Two-year anniversary evaluations and report cards have tended to be kinder to the Parliament than the Executive. The Parliament is receiving more praise reflecting its growing maturity as an institution. The Executive, on the other hand, is being routinely criticised for its lack of impact on substantive policy outputs and outcomes to date.

Much that has happened in the last year would appear unexceptional to students looking at Scotland from outside: battles over resources, arguments over public policy, party political intrigues (both within and between parties) and handling crises often created by being part of an interdependent world. This has been normal liberal democratic politics in action. There remain debates on Scotland's constitutional future. But that debate takes place in the context of having a settlement that Scots voted for, providing it with a legitimacy that had seriously eroded in the pre-devolution years.

In its second year of operation, the Parliament has seen a greater focus on substantive matters of public policy. Civil servants, ministers, interest groups and lobbyist continue to make policy but there is a much more significant role for elected representatives in each stage of the policy making process. The opportunities for ordinary, including opposition, politicians to make a difference exist. It would be mistaken to claim that the Parliament has the kind of transformatory role that is to be found in systems such as the United States. Equally, it would be wrong to suggest that Parliamentarians are mere rubber stamps.

The emphasis of this second review has been on much that might appear tedious to those looking for the excitement of territorial political conflict. In politics as in people, maturity tends to bring with it less excitement but more reasoned behaviour. The excitement has not gone out of Scottish politics and issues of significance, including constitutional issues, remain unresolved.

BIBLIOGRAPHY

Publishing on Scottish politics has been a major growth industry in the last year. This list is an attempt to cover those publications, some but not all of which are referred to in this chapter.

Official Documents

Consultative Steering Group (1998). *Shaping Scotland's Parliament.* Scotland Office

Secondary Sources

Bennie, L., Denver, D., Mitchell, J. and Bradbury, J (2001). 'Harbingers of New Politics? The Characteristics and Attitudes of Candidates in the Scottish Parliament Elections', *British Elections and Parties Review 11.* London: Cass.

Bennie, L., Denver, D., Mitchell, J. and Bradbury, J (2001). 'Harbingers of New Politics? The Characteristics and Attitudes of Candidates in the Scottish Parliament Elections', *British Elections and Parties Review 11.* London: Cass.

Black, D. (2001). *All the First Minister's Men: The Truth Behind Holyrood.* Edinburgh: Birlinn.

Bradbury, J. and Mitchell, J. (2001). 'Devolution: New Politics for Old?' *Parliamentary Affairs* 54(2): 257-75.

Bradbury, J., Denver, D., Mitchell, J., Bennie, L. (2000). 'Devolution and Party Change: Candidate Selection for the 1999 Scottish Parliament and Welsh Assembly Elections', *Journal of Legislative Studies*, 6 (3), 2000, pp.51-72.

Bradbury, J., Mitchell, J., Bennie, L. and Denver, D. (2000). 'Candidate Selection, Devolution and Modernisation: The Selection of Labour Party Candidates for the 1999 Scottish Parliament and Welsh Assembly Elections', *British Parties and Elections Yearbook, 2000,* vol.10, pp.151-172.

Brown, A., Curtice, J., Hinds K., McCrone D., Park A., Paterson L. and Surridge P. (2001). *New Scotland, New Politics.* Edinburgh: Edinburgh UP.

Brown, A. (2000). 'Designing the New Scottish Parliament' *Parliamentary Affairs* 53(3): 542-556.

Cavanagh, M., McGarvey, N., and Shephard, M. (2000). 'Closing the Democratic Deficit? The First Year of the Public Petitions Committee of the Scottish Parliament' *Public Policy & Administration* 15(2): 67-80.

Denver, D., Mitchell J., Pattie C., and Bochel, H. (2000). *Scotland Decides: The Devolution Issue and the Scottish Referendum.* London: Cass.

Drucker, H. (1978). *Breakaway: The Scottish Labour Party.* Edinburgh: EUSPB.

Dyer, M. (2001). 'The Evolution of the Centre-right and the State of Scottish Conservatism' *Political Studies* 49(1): 30-50.

Governance of Scotland Forum Nations and Regions Interim Results January 2001 www.ed.ac.uk/usgs/forum/Leverhulme/interimreportjan2001.html

Hassan, G. and Warhurst, C. (2001). 'New Scotland? Policy, Parties and Institutions' *Political Quarterly* 72(2): 213-226.

Hassan, G. and Warhurst, C. (eds.) (2000). *The New Scottish Politics: The First Year of the Scottish Parliament.* Edinburgh: The Stationery Office.

Hassan, G. and Warhurst, C. (eds.) (2000). *A Different Future: A Modernisers' Guide to Scotland.* Glasgow: The Big Issue/Centre for Scottish Public Policy.

Hearn, J. (2000). *Claiming Scotland: National Identity and Liberal Culture.* Edinburgh: Polygon.

Lord Home (1978). *The Way the Wind Blows.* London: Fontana.

Hutchison, I. G. C. (2001). *Scottish Politics in the Twentieth Century.* Basingstoke: Palgrave.

Kellas, J. (2000). 'Some Constitutional Aspects of Devolution', in A. Wright (ed.) *Scotland: the Challenge of Devolution.* Aldershot: Ashgate.

Laswell, H. (1936). *Politics: Who gets What, When, How.* Cleveland, Ohio: Meridian.

Leicester, G. (ed.) (2000). *Scotland: Monitoring Report November 2000.* London: Constitution Unit.

Lindsay, I. (2000). 'The New Civic Forums' *Political Quarterly* 71(4): 404-11.

Lynch, P. (2001). *Scottish Government and Politics.* Edinburgh: Edinburgh UP.

Marr, A. (2000). *The Day Britain Died.* London: Profile Books.

MacCormick, N. (2000). 'Is there a constitutional path to Scottish independence?' *Parliamentary Affairs* 53(4): 721-36.

McCrone, D. (2000). 'Scottish Opinion Polls May 1999 – June 2000' *Scottish Affairs* 32: 86-94.

McCrone, D. (2001). *Understanding Scotland - The sociology of a stateless nation* 2nd Ed. London: Routledge.

McGarvey, N. (2001). 'New Scottish Politics, New Texts Required' *British Journal of Politics and International Relations* 3(3): 427-444.

Midwinter, A. and McGarvey, N (2001). 'In Search of the Regulatory State: Evidence from Scotland' *Public Administration* 79(4): 825-849.

Miller, D. (2000). 'Scotland's Parliament: A Mini-Westminster, or a Model of Democracy?' in A. Wright (ed.) *Scotland: The Challenge of Devolution.* Aldershot: Ashgate.

Mitchell, J. (1995). 'Lobbying Brussels', *European Journal of Urban and Regional Studies,* vol.2 (4).

Mitchell, J. (1998a). 'What could a Scottish Parliament do?' *Regional and Federal Studies,* 8 (1).

Mitchell, J. (2000). 'Conceptual Lenses and Territorial Government in Britain', in P. Catterall, W. Kaiser and U. Walton-Jordan (eds.), *Reforming The Constitution: Debates in Twentieth-Century Britain.* Ilford: Cass.

Mitchell, J. (2000a). 'Devolution and the End of Britain?', *Contemporary British History,* 14(3): 61-82.

Mitchell, J. (2000b). 'New Parliament, New Politics' *Parliamentary Affairs* 53(3): 605-621.

Mitchell, J. (2001a). 'The Study of Scottish Politics Post-Devolution: New Evidence, New Analysis and New Methods? *West European Politics* 24(4): 216-223.

Mitchell, J. (2001b). 'Towards a New Constitutional Settlement' in C.Hay (ed) *British Politics Today.* Cambridge: Polity.

Mitchell, J. (ed.) (2001c). *Scotland: Monitoring Report February 2001.* London: Constitution Unit.

Nairn, T. (2000). *After Britain: New Labour and the Return of Scotland.* London: Granta.

Parry, R. and Jones, A. (2000). 'The Transition from the Scottish Office to the Scottish Executive' *Public Policy & Administration* 15(2): 53-66.

Paterson, L. (2000a). *Crisis in the Classroom.* Edinburgh: Mainstream.

Paterson, L. (2000b). 'Social Inclusion and the Scottish Parliament' *Scottish Affairs* 30: 68-77.

Ritchie, M. (2000). *Scotland Reclaimed: The Inside Story of Scotland's First Democratic Parliamentary Elections.* Edinburgh: Saltire Society.

Schlesinger, P (2001). *Open Scotland? Journalists, Spin Doctors and Lobbyists.* Edinburgh: Polygon.

Sheridan, T. and McCombes, A. (2000). *Imagine: A Socialist Vision for the 21st Century.* Edinburgh: Rebel Inc.

Watson, M. (2001). *Year Zero: An Inside View of the Scottish Parliament.* Edinburgh: Polygon/Edinburgh University Press.

Webster, D. (2000). 'Scottish Social Inclusion Policy: A Critical Assessment' *Scottish Affairs* 30: 28-50.

Wright, A. (ed.) (2000). *Scotland: The Challenge of Devolution.* Aldershot: Ashgate.

4

Northern Ireland: Endgame

Robin Wilson and Rick Wilford

OVERVIEW

At the conclusion of the comparable chapter in last year's volume,[1] we warned of the fragility of the devolved institutions in Northern Ireland:

> The malign scenario is not hard to outline. Continuing battles over proxy-sovereignty issues — policing, flags, decommissioning — bedevil the Executive Committee and fuel popular cynicism and support for 'no' unionists, against a background of continuing paramilitary violence. Meanwhile, the self-presentation of SF as not just nationalists but nationalists 'with attitude' favours its growth as against the SDLP in this mistrustful context. Eventually, Mr Trimble's enemies secure 50 per cent plus one and that is that.

And, with the exception of the last point, so it was. A very 'hot' summer on, Belfast was once more synonymous with sectarian riots and burning vehicles: 'Remember the peace process . . . ?' began one BBC reporter's piece to camera from amidst the debris. The June elections had revealed a lurch to extremism, and David Trimble had secured his survival as Ulster Unionist Party (UUP) leader only by the unusual device of resigning as First Minister.

In the sort of coincidence that can embarrass programme schedulers, amidst these alarums and excursions the BBC broadcast a major series on the 'peace process', confidently entitled *Endgame in Ireland*. With a developed Irish sense of irony, the Republic of Ireland's state broadcaster, RTE, transmitted the same series with a question mark at the end. Indeed, a terminal crisis for the Belfast Agreement in mid-August was only averted by the Northern Ireland Secretary, John Reid, suspending for one day the post-Agreement institutions.

Last year's chapter, however, also pointed to an alternative, more benign scenario, where the Office of the First Minister and Deputy First Minister (OFMDFM) provided a more manageable 'government within a government', the political centre strengthened and the Executive Committee delivered tangible benefits. And elements — though not enough — of that scenario were evident during the period.

[1] Wilford and Wilson 2000, pp. 114-5.

The most notable achievement of the devolved administration was the first Programme for Government, prepared by the OFMDFM and eventually agreed by the Assembly in March 2001. Tellingly, it was called *Making a Difference*.[2] Also of import was the first 'home-grown' budget drafted by the Finance minister, Mark Durkan (SDLP), agreed in revised form by the Assembly in December 2000. Moreover, within the Assembly itself, solid if unspectacular work by the committees was associated with more amicable relationships between the parties.

There was no doubt that Northern Ireland's new democratic structures were popular on the ground, But 'swing' Protestant attitudes were hardening, as the price of sustaining the inclusion of republicans in the new democratic structures appeared, in Northern Ireland's culture of 'protest and demand',[3] to ratchet ever higher. Only a major gesture by the IRA on arms decommissioning was capable of arresting that haemorrhage of Protestant opinion towards Agreement-scepticism.

THE 'PEACE PROCESS'

In October 2000, the First Minister, Mr Trimble, began to refuse to authorise the attendance of the two Sinn Féin (SF) ministers at meetings of the North–South Ministerial Council (NSMC). SF correspondingly boycotted meetings of the British–Irish Council (BIC). The Democratic Unionist Party (DUP) had already disdained both, while its two ministers refused to sit at the Executive Committee table.

Thus the post-Agreement institutions inhabited a political *demi-monde* during the course of the year, with just two of the Executive's four parties, the UUP and the SDLP, playing a full role in each. As so often with Northern Ireland politics, 'asymmetric devolution' acquired a whole new meaning.

Mr Trimble's attempt to shore up his party and its electoral support, by excluding SF from the NSMC, followed in the wake of the loss of the UUP's second safest Westminster seat, South Antrim, to the DUP at a by-election in September 2000.[4] The result weakened the already embattled *Trimblista*

---

[2] Northern Ireland Executive 2001.

[3] A phrase coined by a minister in the current administration, warning at a Democratic Dialogue round table in the wake of the Agreement that this would have to change.

[4] The by-election was caused by the death of the incumbent, Clifford Forsythe (UUP), in May 2000. At the 1997 general election he had been unopposed by the DUP and taken 57 per cent of the vote — beating the runner-up, Donovan McClelland (SDLP), by a majority of 16,601. At the 1998 Assembly election, the constituency had returned four unionist MLAs, two of whom were anti-Agreement, as was the non-contesting Mr Forsythe; the balance of pro- and anti-Agreement first-preference votes, 14,721 and 13,310 respectively, was tight. The selection of David Burnside as the UUP by-election candidate — he had voted for the Agreement though was now making sceptical noises — set the context for a battle royal with the DUP, which fielded Rev William McCrea. On a turnout of 43 per cent, the DUP won the seat for the first time, with a majority of 822 over the UUP. Even the authors of this chapter were surprised: in last year's chapter we had described it as 'safe'.

Figure 4.1. Key events in Northern Ireland

21 Sept. 2000   The Ulster Unionist Party (UUP) loses its second safest Westminster seat to the Democratic Unionist Party (DUP) in a by-election occasioned by the death of the incumbent. The loss is linked to Protestant disenchantment with the Belfast Agreement and particularly the Police (Northern Ireland) Bill, the outworking of the report of the policing commission chaired by the former Hong Kong governor Chris Patten and published a year earlier.

9 October 2000   The inaugural meeting takes place in Belfast of the Civic Forum established by the Agreement.

17 October 2000   The Finance minister, Mark Durkan (SDLP), presents his first 'home-grown' budget to the Assembly.

24 October 2000   The Northern Ireland Executive Committee's first draft Programme for Government is launched.

28 October 2000   The UUP leader, David Trimble, staves off pressure for withdrawal from the Executive Committee, by securing the support of his party's ruling Ulster Unionist Council for a motion banning Sinn Féin (SF) ministers from the North/South Ministerial Council (NSMC) in the absence of substantial IRA re-engagement with the Independent International Commission on Decommissioning (IICD).

23 Nov. 2000   The Police (Northern Ireland) Bill receives royal assent. It effectively replaces the Royal Ulster Constabulary (RUC) by a Police Service of Northern Ireland — the main source of unionist antagonism — but Northern Ireland nationalist parties and the Republic of Ireland's government remain dissatisfied with its substantive provisions.

12 Dec. 2000   The Finance minister, Mr Durkan, presents his revised budget to the Assembly.

13 Dec. 2000   A visit to Belfast by the US President, Bill Clinton, before the expiry of his second term, in the company of the UK Prime Minister, Tony Blair, fails to break the political deadlock between the Northern Ireland parties over arms decommissioning, policing and security normalisation.

24 January 2001   Domestic developments bringing an end to the ministerial career of Peter Mandelson lead to his replacement as Northern Ireland Secretary by the Scottish Secretary, John Reid.

29 January 2001   The High Court declares unlawful the decision by Mr Trimble to ban SF ministers from NSMC attendance. The First Minister however elects to appeal the ruling and the ban remains.

6 March 2001	After a two-day debate, the Assembly approves the Executive's revised Programme for Government.
8 March 2001	After weeks of talks between the London and Dublin governments and the Northern Ireland pro-agreement parties since the turn of the year, a final pre-election effort at Hillsborough Castle — involving the Prime Minister, Mr Blair, and the Taoiseach, Bertie Ahern — fails as SF rejects a paper acceptable to the other parties. The IRA meanwhile says it will renew contact with the decommissioning commission.
8 May 2001	The UUP leader, Mr Trimble, delivers to the Speaker of the Assembly a post-dated resignation letter promising he will resign as First Minister on 1 July in the absence of substantive IRA decommissioning.
7 June 2001	Polling for local and UK general elections in Northern Ireland is marked by setbacks for the UUP and SDLP and gains for the DUP and SF, amid highly charged scenes at the counts including a mob assault on David and Daphne Trimble.
1 July 2001	Mr Trimble's resignation is effected. The Deputy First Minister, Séamus Mallon (SDLP), automatically loses his position simultaneously. Mr Trimble designates Sir Reg Empey (UUP), the Enterprise, Trade and Investment minister, to execute his functions.
9 July 2001	A week of talks begins at Weston Park in Shropshire to try to save the Belfast Agreement, involving the London and Dublin governments and the pro-Agreement parties. Mr Trimble tries to confine the discussions to arms decommissioning but the agenda includes policing, security normalisation and ensuring the stability of the post-Agreement institutions. During the talks, the largest loyalist paramilitary organisation, the Ulster Defence Association (UDA), indicates it has moved against the Agreement. The Progressive Unionist Party, political vehicle for the Ulster Volunteer Force, announces its withdrawal from the post-Agreement process. Meanwhile there are intense clashes in Belfast.
14 July 2001	The Prime Minister, Mr Blair, and the Taoiseach, Mr Ahern, announce at the end of the Weston Park talks that they will prepare a 'take it or leave it' document for the parties.
1 August 2001	The intergovernmental package is presented. There are detailed proposals on policing and security normalisation, as well as an end to the ban on SF ministers attending NSMC meetings, an amnesty for on-the-run paramilitaries and inquiries into disputed killings, but only a paragraph on decommissioning, said to be 'indispensable'.

6 August 2001	The decommissioning commission reports that the IRA has proposed a method for putting arms 'beyond use' which the commission is 'satisfied' complies with a new decommissioning scheme published that day by the UK government; the commission thereby concludes that this 'initiates a process' that will put arms 'beyond use'. The 'deadline' for party responses to the London-Dublin paper passes with only the Women's Coalition meeting it.
7 August 2001	The UUP leader, Mr Trimble, says the IRA proposal on decommissioning does not go far enough as it only addresses the 'modalities', as had loyalists some months earlier, and does not indicate when arms will be decommissioned.
11 August 2001	The Northern Ireland Secretary, Dr Reid, suspends devolution for one day, to allow a new six-week breathing space to save the institutions.
14 August 2001	The IRA withdraws its proposal of the previous week. It emerges that three IRA suspects have been detained in Colombia, having been allegedly engaged with FARC guerrillas in the 'demilitarised zone'.

tendency in the UUP, to be further enervated by the local and general elections in June 2001 (see below).

Before the latter, Mr Trimble sought to steady the nerves of Protestant voters by signalling his intention to stand down as First Minister unless there was a palpable start to IRA decommissioning by the end of the month. Resign he duly did — on the symbolic date of 1 July, 85th anniversary of the Battle of the Somme — thereby precipitating a crisis over what he deemed the failure of the IRA to fulfil its 'promise' of decommissioning in its statement of 6 May 2000.[5]

The prolonged consequent talks at Weston Park, co-hosted by the London and Dublin governments, yielded no agreement, but an apparent determination by the Prime Minister and the Taoiseach to produce a non-negotiable, 'take-it-or-leave-it' package to secure the 'full implementation' of the Agreement. This show of prime-ministerial virility convinced no one, however, and the time-limit for acceptance or rejection slipped by without any of the major pro-Agreement parties reaching a definitive conclusion about the proposals, which were heavily skewed towards republican concerns about policing and 'demilitarisation' and contained just a

---

[5] The statement was in fact heavily contextualised and no timescale was attached, whereas a statement by the Prime Minister, Tony Blair, and the Taoiseach, Bertie Ahern, the previous night had set a timetable of one further year (decommissioning was to have been completed by all paramilitaries by May 2000).

paragraph on decommissioning. Republicans said the former were insufficient and unionists found the latter derisory.

The impasse was apparently broken when, on 6 August, the International Commission on Decommissioning (IICD) declared itself 'satisfied' that a method for disposal of arms proposed by the IRA at a 'recent' meeting complied with a new government decommissioning scheme. The proposal was not released, and the publication of the revised scheme by the UK government that day did not elucidate the ways and means by which arms would be dealt with. Nevertheless, the commission concluded: 'Based on our discussions with the IRA representative,[6] we believe that this proposal initiates a process that will put IRA arms completely and verifiably beyond use.'[7]

The absence of detail about the 'modalities' was of less concern to Mr Trimble, the by-now-former First Minister, than the omission of a start date and subsequent timetable. The UUP leader welcomed the statement from the commission as a 'significant step forward' but reiterated that he needed 'more than words'. He continued: 'In the absence of real, tangible movement to put the IRA's arms completely and verifiably beyond use, it will not be possible for the Assembly to elect a First Minister and a Deputy First Minister.'[8] In effect, Mr Trimble regarded the statement as a necessary but insufficient means of restoring the (already imperfect) status quo prior to his resignation on 1 July.

In the event of resignation, death or incapacity of one or other of the incumbents, under section 16 (8) of the Northern Ireland Act 1998 there is a maximum of six weeks before a fresh, joint election of the First and Deputy First Ministers has to occur. The period was scheduled to end at midnight on 11 August and, if the situation remained unresolved, the Northern Ireland Secretary, John Reid, had to make a difficult choice.

He could suspend devolution temporarily, thereby creating a further six-week breathing space, during which another attempt at resolving the difficulties would be made; or, more dramatically, he could dissolve the Assembly and announce a fresh Assembly election — which would be the seventh time in four years that the Northern Ireland electorate had been summoned to the polls. He chose the former, less risky, alternative, suspending devolution for 24 hours at midnight on 11 August. The clock started running down again just after midnight on 13 August, with the next deadline 23 September.

---

[6] Widely believed to be the Army Council member Brian Keenan.
[7] IICD press release, Belfast, 5 August 2001.
[8] *Belfast Telegraph*, 9 August 2001.

The constitutional and legislative basis for such a brief, if imaginative, hiatus — an apparent loophole in the Northern Ireland Act 2000 — may have been questionable. In any event, suspension was not cost-free. It incensed republicans, who interpreted the decision as a capitulation to the UUP by London and, by implication, Dublin — which, in contrast to the first suspension in February 2000, endorsed the move.

In an anticipated riposte, on 14 August the IRA withdrew its proposal of a week earlier. 'P O'Neill' asserted that 'the outright rejection of the IICD statement by the UUP leadership . . . is totally unacceptable. The subsequent actions of the British Government, including their failure to fulfil their commitments, is [sic] also totally unacceptable. The conditions do not therefore exist for progressing our proposition. We are withdrawing our proposal.'[9]

That day, however, it began to emerge that three suspected IRA members had been detained in Colombia, allegedly having been involved with the FARC guerrilla group in the huge 'demilitarised zone' it controls in the south. This renewed questions, north and south of the border in Ireland — but particularly in Washington — as to the bona fides of the republican movement.

On a wider canvas, the Northern Ireland Executive Committee sought to administer devolved government in a society scarred by pipe-bomb attacks by loyalists on Catholic homes, 'punishment' shootings and beatings (organised thuggery is a more accurate description) and sectarian street confrontations, notably in north Belfast. The guns, whether republican or loyalist, were far from 'silent' and during the summer of 2001 they claimed the lives of two young men — one Catholic, the other Protestant — each killed in a 'drive-by' shooting by loyalist paramilitaries.

The murderers masqueraded under the *nomme de guerre* of the 'Red Hand Defenders', a label of convenience employed by loyalists ostensibly 'on ceasefire'. The UDA, the largest paramilitary group, is nominally run by a six-man 'inner council' which, during the summer, announced it was withdrawing support for the Agreement. Shortly afterwards, it claimed — to an incredulous population — that the UDA ceasefire was intact.

A further depressing reminder of an alternative future was provided by the car bomb detonated by the splinter 'Real IRA' in west London in early August. This was the latest of a sequence of attacks in the capital.

---

[9] *An Phoblacht*, 14 August 2001.

THE EXECUTIVE

The Absence of Trust

What these events, among others, confirmed was the fragility of the Agreement. In key respects, the Agreement left much unresolved. The volume and complexity of the unfinished business meant that political life in Northern Ireland proved a continuous process of negotiation, and renegotiation, among the three pro-Agreement parties to the Executive — the UUP, SDLP and SF — constantly assailed by their theoretical partner in government, the DUP. The measures of the deterioration of relations since the election in June 1998 turned on decommissioning, the accelerated release on licence of paramilitary prisoners, the reform of the police and the criminal justice system and the scaling-down of the army presence.

Such was the gravity of these issues, especially decommissioning and reform of the RUC, that they occasioned the gradual erosion of support among unionists for the Agreement (see below). On the other flank, the leakage of personnel and *matériel* from the Provisional IRA into, primarily, the Real IRA demonstrated the tenacity of the 'long war' tradition within republicanism.

With the exception of prisoner releases — though two loyalists[10] were reimprisoned for breaching their licences — none of these issues had been resolved at the time of writing, with detrimental effects on the political institutions essayed in the Agreement's three 'strands'.[11] Indeed, since the formal transfer of devolved powers on 2 December 1999, there had never been a time when at least one of the institutions has not operated as intended. By the summer of 2001, the only fully functioning institution was the advisory Civic Forum, which itself did not meet until the previous October, two and a half years after the Agreement was endorsed.

The risks involved in establishing an inclusive and ostensibly involuntary 'coalition' were foreseeable. The hazards, including the absence of collective responsibility within the Executive Committee, were circumvented by means of the D'Hondt mechanism — through which the eligible parties nominated *their* individual ministers.

The adoption of D'Hondt did nothing to subvert the ethnic ties that bind political leaders to their discrete electorates. Rather, it reinforced them—as did the requirement that Assembly Members designate themselves as 'unionist', 'nationalist' or 'other'. Any lingering assumption that there would be a sense of joint 'ownership' of the Executive was swiftly dismissed as ministers took up residence in their respective departmental 'fiefdoms',[12] there to

---

[10] Johnny Adair and Gary Smith of the UDA.

[11] Internal to Northern Ireland, north-south in Ireland and 'east-west' involving Ireland and Britain.

[12] Laver 2000.

exercise their relative autonomy — though some ministers behaved in a co-operative fashion, such as Sean Farren at Education and Employment and the Economy minister, Sir Reg Empey.

True, each minister had to affirm a pledge of office committing them, among other things, to exclusively peaceful and democratic means. Equally true was the requirement that ministers agree on 'key decisions', including the Programme for Government and annual budgets — yet, in relation to both, the unanimity 'rule' has been breached, and now approximates more to a voluntary code.

Consociationalism has been criticised by many academic observers, not least its inherent capacity to consolidate ethnic divisions. Although its progenitor, Arend Lijphart, believed that in divided societies high fences made for good neighbours, he also believed that, over time — as mutual understanding, tolerance, respect and, particularly, trust were nourished — the rationales for such fences would diminish. Indeed they could, ultimately, be removed as citizens began to coalesce around other, less divisive, sources of political identity. Along with these cross-cutting cleavages, a sense of political normalcy could eventually emerge.

The key to such a realignment is the extent to which the conditions apply that enable trust to flourish among ethnically divided 'communities' and their respective political leaders. It also implies that ethnic rivals should relinquish their preferred and exclusive futures for one that can be commonly agreed.

None of these conditions has, however, prevailed. The very open-endedness of the Agreement sustained mutually exclusive futures and suggested the long-term impermanence of the devolved structures. The lack of trust that envelops Northern Ireland has turned the fleeting phase of positive-sum politics into a zero-sum game. The earlier discourse of pluralism, equality and human rights has been transformed more recently into the harsher language of demands and concessions—and a sense of loss, especially apparent among unionists.

On the critical matter of trust, for its part the DUP has, at least, been consistent. Ever since SF was permitted in 1997 to participate in the talks that led to the Agreement, it has voiced its distrust of the republican movement and resolutely opposed its inclusion in government — seeking, on a number of occasions, to exclude it through Assembly motions. Indeed, when it tabled such a motion in July 2000 most unionist-designated MLAs (32 out of 58) supported it, including four UUP members.[13]

Though not opposed to devolution per se, the DUP's opposition to 'Sinn Féin/IRA' participation in the Executive — though not the Assembly — rests on its perception of the republican movement as an immutable body of unreconstructed terrorists and fellow travellers. It is a political expression of the party's Old Testament belief in original sin.

[13] See the Assembly's *Official Report*, 4 July 2000.

Mr Trimble's leadership of the UUP, in contrast, owes more to New Testament thinking. Not only has he acknowledged the imperfections of the old-Stormont unionism that built a 'cold house for Catholics',[14] but he has readily accepted the capacity for redemption among even paramilitaries:

> We are not saying, and we have never said, that the fact that someone has a certain past means he cannot have a future. We have always acknowledged that it is possible for people to change.[15]

It was on this forgiving ground that in his Nobel acceptance speech Mr Trimble envisaged the construction of 'a pluralist Parliament for a pluralist people',[16] an inclusive, democratic structure that brought benefits for all. Absent any tangible beginning to decommissioning, he 'jumped first' into the Executive, in November 1999 and May 2000, in the expectation that the republican arsenal would, progressively, be dumped in the dustbin of history and that the process would begin within weeks of the transfer of devolved powers. But, twice bitten, he was thrice very shy.

Rubbing Along

The hallmark of consociational democracy is, however, the 'politics of accommodation'. And during the period, behind the high-political blame game, there was a degree of rubbing along.

Indeed, the four Executive parties proved surprisingly pliant in improvising operating procedures. The discipline of unanimity in relation to key decisions helped to facilitate the conduct of business — at least up to a point — as did the considerable autonomy enjoyed by ministers. Avoidance of conflict enabled the centre to hold. As one (straight-faced) senior official in the OFMDFM put it, ascribing a disposition to technocracy at the top table, ministers had tried to 'keep politics out' of the Executive.[17]

The most obvious accommodation was in relation to the DUP's two ministers, latterly Gregory Campbell (regional development) and Maurice Morrow (social development). They, and their predecessors,[18] boycotted all meetings of the Executive because of the inclusion of SF colleagues. They similarly boycotted sub-Executive ministerial meetings — delegating

---

[14] Trimble 2001, p62.

[15] New Northern Ireland Assembly, *Official Report*, 1 July 1998.

[16] Trimble 2001, p79 — the reference is to the boast by the first Northern Ireland premier, Sir James Craig, that Stormont epitomised 'a Protestant parliament and a Protestant state'.

[17] Wilford and Wilson 2001, p66.

[18] Respectively, Peter Robinson and Nigel Dodds, who resigned their ministerial posts on 27 July 2000.

officials to discuss cross-departmental policy initiatives — and refused to attend sectoral and plenary meetings of the NSMC and the BIC.

In the latter two cases, the other members of the Executive, through the OFMDFM, made proxy arrangements to enable business to be conducted. This was of particular significance in relation to the BIC, as Northern Ireland has the lead responsibility for transport, which falls within the remit of the Department for Regional Development. No attempt was made by any other parties to exclude the DUP from the Executive, although its boycotts could be construed as a breach of the ministerial pledge of office.

A degree of accommodation — more a non-decision — also attended events following Mr Trimble's refusal to authorise the attendance of SF ministers at meetings of the NSMC. All sectoral NSMC meetings have involved the participation of a unionist and a nationalist minister: the convention has been the lead minister would be accompanied, as appropriate, by one from the other 'side'. Their attendance required the authorisation of both the First and Deputy First ministers. Once Mr Trimble imposed his ban, the possibility arose that his co-equal, Mr Mallon, would establish a reciprocal curb on unionist ministers. Mr Mallon did not, however, take this action, enabling most north-south meetings to take place unhindered. Moreover, meetings of all north-south bodies continued at official level after the ban, including those in which SF ministers had a departmental interest.

While the DUP maintained its aloofness from the full Executive, its ministers did not operate entirely in isolation. Meetings with their peers, other than SF's Health and Education ministers, did take place on a bilateral or multilateral basis—not least in relation to budgetary matters and the Programme for Government, which (as 'key decisions') were meant to command agreement within the Executive itself.

As implied earlier, however, when each of these items came to the floor of the Assembly for cross-community legitimation, as required by the Northern Ireland Act 1998, the DUP voted against. Its actions thereby made something of a mockery of the unanimity rule that applies to key decisions, as did SF's decision to put down an unsuccessful amendment to the budget (although its members did support the main motion thereafter).

While a great deal of latitude was accorded to the DUP ministers, their semi-detachment was not without consequence. Shortly after the lifting of the first suspension, the DUP announced it would henceforth rotate its ministers 'on a frequent basis' and that it would 'uncover and reveal what is going on at the heart of Government'.[19] After the next Executive meeting, on behalf of the Executive Messrs Trimble and Mallon indicated that 'pending the receipt of satisfactory assurances from DUP ministers about the

---

[19] DUP press release, 31 May 2000.

confidentiality and integrity of Executive Committee business, the Minister for Social Development and the Minister for Regional Development will not receive Executive Committee papers as a matter of course'.[20]

No such assurances were forthcoming. Instead the DUP ministers sought a judicial review. In March 2001 the High Court ruled that the Executive's action had not been unlawful. The First and Deputy First Minister commented: 'The judgement has made it clear that we are within our rights not to circulate Executive papers to ministers who refuse to attend its meetings.'[21]

This was not the only instance of judicial review during the period. In November 2000 opponents of the decision by the Health minister, Bairbre de Brún (SF), to centralise Belfast's maternity services at the Royal Victoria Hospital (in her west Belfast constituency) succeeded in such a review (the second in this long-running saga), in which the minister was found to have acted precipitately.[22] She initiated a fresh consultation exercise — though the alternative maternity hospital building, located in the south of the city, was demolished by ministerial order.

Moreover, in January 2001, the SF ministers themselves prevailed in a judicial review of Mr Trimble's ban on their attendance at NSMC meetings.[23] But the (former) First Minister retained the ban while appealing the ruling.

As these see-you-in-court episodes indicated, inter-party relations within the Executive were undeniably strained, but not — at least until the summer of 2001 — to the point of immobilism. The possibility of further disruption posed by the DUP's threatened 'frequent' rotation of ministers was not realised. By the time of writing, only one rotation had occurred, in July 2000, representing the only change in the composition of the Executive over the past year.

Though collective 'cabinet' responsibility did not materialise, through a mixture of accommodation and improvisation the major items of business were transacted, including the conclusion of the Programme for Government. Mr Trimble's resignation as First Minister on 1 July 2001 created the need for a new bout of invention.

Following his departure from the top table — and the associated, enforced exit of the Deputy First Minister — the functions of the OFMDFM were fulfilled by Mr Trimble's fellow minister Sir Reg Empey (UUP) and Mr Mallon, even though the roles of First and Deputy First Minister were no longer occupied. This enabled the machinery of government to continue to tick over.

---

[20] Northern Ireland Executive Committee press release, 8 June 2000.
[21] Northern Ireland Executive Committee press release, 30 March 2001.
[22] *Irish Times*, 30 November 2000.
[23] *Irish Times*, 30 January 2001.

Figure 4.2. Northern Ireland Executive Committee at 31 July 2001

- Reg Empey (UUP): Minister of Enterprise, Trade and Investment and *acting as if* First Minister*
- Séamus Mallon (SDLP): *acting as if* Deputy First Minister*
- Michael McGimpsey (UUP): Minister of Culture, Arts and Leisure
- Sam Foster (UUP): Minister of Environment
- Sean Farren (SDLP): Minister for Employment and Learning**
- Mark Durkan (SDLP): Minister of Finance and Personnel
- Bríd Rodgers (SDLP): Minister of Agriculture and Rural Development
- Gregory Campbell (DUP): Minister for Regional Development***
- Maurice Morrow (DUP): Minister for Social Development***
- Martin Mcguinness (SF): Minister of Education
- Bairbre de Brún (SF): Minister of Health, Social Services and Public Safety

* Sir Reg and Mr Mallon were only executing the functions of FM and DFM: they could not so describe themselves.

** Redesignated during the year. Formerly the department was called Higher and Further Education, Training and Employment.

*** Messrs Campbell and Morrow replaced Peter Robinson and Nigel Dodds respectively when the DUP 'rotated' its ministers.

Though the situation was difficult, it might have been rendered impossible had Mr Trimble's resignation been coupled with that of his three party colleagues with ministerial posts, as was threatened at the time of the first suspension on 11 February 2000. Had all four ministers gone — along with the UUP junior minister, Dermot Nesbitt, in OFMDFM — that would, it seems, have triggered the resignation of the DUP's two ministers.

On 25 June, Mr Campbell made a statement to the Assembly — on behalf of himself and his fellow DUP minister, Mr Morrow — informing the house that a letter of resignation had been tendered to the Speaker 'effective on the resignation of all the First Minister's party colleagues from the Executive'.[24] This 'offer' — described as a 'shadow stunt' by the Finance minister, Mr Durkan, and an act of 'political cowardice' by Mr Trimble, would, if effected, have rendered the Executive Committee inoperable: the Assembly's Standing Orders stipulate that it must contain at least three unionists.

By omitting his colleagues from his action, Mr Trimble signalled his desire to keep the wheels of the administration moving, with a view to restoring momentum if the impasse over decommissioning was resolved.

THE ASSEMBLY

Despite the difficulties besetting the Executive, the Assembly was not unduly disrupted in conducting its business. Indeed, while inter-party

[24] Northern Ireland Assembly, *Official Report*, 25 June 2001.

relations within the 'cabinet' grew increasingly strained, those within the legislature were marginally better, particularly in the statutory and standing committees. Over the year, there was evidence of a fledgling committee *system* emerging.

The skewing of legislation towards 'parity' (see below) has meant the Assembly has not exerted a discrete *legislative* impact in Northern Ireland. The paucity of 'home-made' law has arrested any clear sense that MLAs have made a significant difference in these terms to the everyday lives of the region's inhabitants. There are, however, exceptions.

For instance, the health, social services and public safety (statutory) committee put down an amendment to the Health and Personal Social Services Bill (NIA Bill 3/00), seeking to extend GP fundholding until 31 March 2002, a year longer than envisaged. What exercised the majority of the committee was the absence of a viable scheme to replace GP fundholding at the end of March 2001. Despite the opposition of the minister and SF MLAs, including two who sit on the committee, the amendment was carried by 52 votes to 32.[25]

Such instances of committee–minister clashes over legislation have, however, been rare. While committees have routinely appointed special advisers to assist their inquiries, briefing on the technical aspects of primary legislation has been provided by officials drawn from the relevant department.

In part, the tendency to defer to departments on primary bills has stemmed from the hybrid nature of the statutory committees. To draw a rough parallel with Westminster, they are a mix of their distant cousins: select committees and standing committees. Unlike standing committees at Westminster, however, the statutory committees do not contain a critical mass of members with relevant expertise. Not only are the Assembly's statutory committees, and the committee of the centre, smaller (11 members in the former case and 17 in the latter), but their members are for the most part generalists and make-weights—rather than, as at Westminster, a nucleus of specialists complemented by lobby fodder.

The, in some cases, extensive and untidy sprawl of departmental responsibilities has left many MLAs floundering in coming to terms with their associated departments. Most of the early sessions held by committees were concerned with getting a purchase on the remits of the departments, their resources and personnel and the policies the newly wrought ministries had inherited.

Unlike their counterparts in Scotland and Wales — who, from the first, held the vast majority of their meetings in public — MLAs displayed a preference for closed sessions. In reply to a written question from Ian Paisley Snr (DUP), Ian Adamson (UUP), a member of the Assembly Commission,

---

[25] Northern Ireland Assembly, *Official Report*, 30 January 2001..

disclosed that from 2 December 1999 to 8 September 2000, 55 per cent of all committee meetings were held completely in private, 38 per cent were in part held in private and only 6 per cent were fully open.[26]

More recent findings by Liz Fawcett[27] show some improvement, but also considerable variation across committees. She found that almost one-third (31 per cent) of statutory committee meetings were still held in private, 48 per cent in public and the remainder part closed. Yet while the finance and personnel committee was almost fully open (just 10 per cent of its meetings were in closed session), the education committee held only 14 per cent of its meetings wholly in public with 62 per cent *in camera*.

The requirement that statutory committees (and the committee of the centre) take the committee stage of primary bills, allied to their undue reliance on officials for briefings, has tilted the balance of advantage on legislative matters towards the departments. Yet the significant workload this has placed on members has meant that of the total of 39 committee reports to the time of writing, almost half (17) arose from the committee stage of bills. Rather than the partnership principle that underpinned the thinking behind 'strand one', this suggests Executive predominance.

The remaining committee outputs have stemmed from freely chosen inquiries (16) and policy initiatives referred by departments (6). Juggling the legislative role, scrutiny of the associated departments, advising and assisting in policy formulation and undertaking freely chosen inquiries has overloaded the committees. Give their extensive repertoire of roles it is no surprise that, as yet, no statutory committee has made use of its considerable power to initiate primary legislation. Moreover, only one private member's bill has been tabled.

'All the committees are absolutely snowed under,' one MLA told the authors.[28] The claim of overload may seem gratuitous given the size of the Assembly. There are 108 MLAs,[29] which could be construed as generous — if not extravagant — representation, easily sufficient to 'man' the committees, especially when compared with the 129-member Scottish Parliament catering for a population three times as large. The committees comprise ten statutory, six standing and the Assembly Commission (besides the occasional ad hoc committee[30] created to advise the Northern Ireland Secretary on reserved matters).

---

[26] Northern Ireland Assembly, *Written Answers Booklet*, 29 September 2000.

[27] Fawcett 2001.

[28] Wilford and Wilson 2001, p37.

[29] Eighteen of these MLAs arose simply because loyalist paramilitary representatives at the talks in the final days before the Agreement demanded six- rather than five-seat STV constituencies to maximise their representation in the Assembly (to little avail).

[30] Four ad hoc committees have produced reports on reserved matters. These were (date of report in brackets): the Flags Order (10/10/00); the Financial Investigations Order (06/02/01); the Life Sentences Order (12/03/01); and the Proceeds of Crime Bill (29/05/01). The full list of committee reports can be found on the committee page of the Assembly's web site: www.ni-assembly.gov.uk.

But the ineligibility of the Speaker and the 14 ministers (including the two juniors), the committee boycott by the three-member Northern Ireland Unionist Party (NIUP) and the one-man UK Unionist band, and the fact that Mr Adams (SF) and John Taylor (UUP) have declined a committee role leaves 87 members available in practice to fill 183 committee places. Thus 20 MLAs sit on one committee, 46 serve on two, 19 on three, and John Dallat (SDLP) and Roy Beggs Jr (UUP) each manage four.

Initially, the committees did not sit on plenary Assembly days — Mondays and Tuesdays — but, increasingly, as their volume of work mounted, this convention was abandoned. Moreover, such was the press of business that the committees were largely Stormont-based, rarely venturing beyond the precincts of Parliament Buildings. Up to March 2001, of a total of 401 statutory meetings, only 12 were held elsewhere.

In that respect, the committees have done little to reach out to the wider community. Other than issuing general invitations via the press to those with an interest in the relevant policy area to submit evidence, and exploiting the consultation lists administered by departments for the same purpose, they have not been noticeably proactive. Indeed, the Assembly as a whole has done little to address the citizenry. By September 2001, it had yet, for instance, to publish its *first* annual report.

Measuring the outputs of the committees is relatively straightforward, as compared with assessing the outcomes of their activities. There have been few instances where substantive amendments to primary bills have been moved successfully by committees (GP fundholding being a notable exception). Clashes over statutory rules have been even rarer: these have gone through the statutory committees more or less 'on the nod'. The fact that members of the four governing parties supply a majority on the committees also allows the Executive considerable leverage, and underscores the absence of a formal opposition capable of forming an alternative government.

When committee reports have been debated on the floor of the chamber — as all have, irrespective of their provenance — it has been the chair of the committee who has moved the report and who has invariably responded first to all ministerial statements. This convention has evolved because the D'Hondt rule employed to nominate chairs and deputy chairs, as well as ministers, was applied to ensure that the incumbents were drawn from parties other than that of the minister, lending a potentially oppositional character to the relationship.

A clear instance of such adversarialism emerged in the debate over the higher education committee's ostensibly unanimous report on student finance (1/00/R 12 October 2000). The committee had opted for a model closely resembling that adopted in Scotland and called on the minister, Sean Farren (SDLP), to implement its recommendations at the 'earliest feasible opportunity'.[31] Dr Farren, however, was not content to accept the report in its entirety — believing it would not widen access as effectively as his own thinking — and moved an amendment that would have required him merely to 'consider' its recommendations.

The amendment was lost, much to the annoyance of the minister, who vented his anger in an article in a nationalist daily newspaper castigating the report and the reasoning of the committee's members, though the two SDLP members escaped his wrath.[32] They had signed up to the report but, under pressure from their party whip, when the vote was taken they supported 'their' minister, thereby breaching the committee's unanimity.

In the wake of the debate, the committee chair, Esmond Birnie (UUP), sought an early meeting with Dr Farren to heal the rift. Instructively, while prepared to challenge the minister, the committee did not wish its relationship to deteriorate to the point of antagonism, a situation that would be contrary to the partnership principle mentioned above. The other lesson of this affair was that party loyalty had prevailed over committee cohesiveness.

A golden rule for parliamentary committees that seek to influence their associated departments is the need for consensus. In the troubled context of Northern Ireland, a divided committee can be a boon to an otherwise beleaguered minister who can exploit such divisions to advantage, especially if the intra-committee rift occurs along sectarian or pro- versus anti-Agreement lines. Remarkably, perhaps, such instances have been rare (aided, in some measure, by the NIUP/UKUP boycott).

Recent research indicates that inter-party relations within the committees have generally become cordial and have led overwhelmingly to the production of unanimous reports.[33] Apart from the above example, and the support for Ms de Brún from the health committee's SF members over GP fundholding, the only other occasion of intra-community dissent involved the same two members (and the committee chair, Joe Hendron (SDLP)) supporting her decision in favour of the Royal Victoria Hospital on maternity provision.

Over the last year the committee chairs established a liaison committee modelled along the lines of the equivalent committee of select committee chairs at Westminster, though it had yet to publish any report at the time of writing. Nevertheless, its creation indicated its utility for the chairs, supplying the opportunity for improved co-ordination and co-operation and was one index of the growth of a committee system.

Increasingly, committees co-operated in relation to policy and legislation cutting across the remits of their associated departments. In some cases, committees held joint meetings to take evidence from witnesses in pursuit of

[31] Northern Ireland Assembly, *Official Report*, 21 November 2000.
[32] *Irish News*, 12 December 2000.
[33] Wilford and Wilson 2001.

particular inquiries. For instance the finance and personnel, and enterprise, trade and investment committees sat jointly to hear evidence on relief for businesses affected by Foot-and-Mouth Disease. Similarly, two standing committees, procedures and audit, sat together during a fact-finding session on the role of the Comptroller and Auditor-General. In addition, the higher education and enterprise, trade and investment committees co-operated closely on the cross-cutting issues raised by the major report on economic development *Strategy 2010*.[34]

While 'joined-up' government has proved especially tricky in Northern Ireland, joined-up scrutiny was more evident. The statutory committees began to devise means by which they could keep abreast of one another's activities, particularly in relation to the strategic policies adopted by the Executive Committee. While specific departments took the policy lead on, for instance, the public-health, regional-development and rural-development strategies, the associated committees routinely sought the views of their sister committees. The same was true of some legislative proposals: where a bill was understood to have relevance for not just the lead department but others, the statutory committees ensured that the relevant committees were kept informed of its progress, especially during the committee stage.

The need for a more systematic approach to the scrutiny of policy, legislation and, particularly, expenditure was of special concern to the finance and personnel committee. It has the task, inter alia, of co-ordinating the views of the other statutory committees on budgetary matters, including departmental bids, and reporting them to the Assembly. In marshalling the views of its sister committees on the budget proposals and the dovetailing of Departmental spending plans with the Programme for Government, it proved a persistent — and unified — critic of its 'target' department. It was especially critical of the time constraints under which the committees laboured in responding to budget proposals and the inadequacy of the information supplied.

So tight was the timetable in relation to the Executive's first draft budget that two of the committees — health and social development — did not have time to submit a written response to finance and personnel.[35] Partly as a response to this unhealthy state of affairs, the latter committee — with the support, not only of its members, but of all statutory committees — succeeded in changing the timetable for debating spending proposals in the future, thereby providing more time for MLAs to subject them to scrutiny.[36]

The finance and personnel committee also issued a highly cautious and admonitory report on the adoption of Public-Private Partnerships (PPPs) by

---

[34] Strategy Steering Group 1999.
[35] Northern Ireland Assembly, *Official Report*, 18 December 2000.
[36] See *Official Report* for 29 May 2001 and 18-19 June 2001.

the Executive, debated on the day of its publication.[37] The Executive has established a working group on PPPs, expected to report next spring, but — judging by the remarks of the Finance minister during the debate — was in principle in favour of their growing introduction as a means of financing public services. Mr Durkan's rather sanguine attitude to PPPs was not shared by the finance committee and, were devolution to be sustained, would likely issue in a clash between its members and the Executive.

The occasionally fractious debates[38] on the floor of the Assembly were largely absent from the committee rooms, where members generally enjoyed at least business-like, if not entirely cordial, relations. Even the committee of the centre, charged with scrutinising around half the 26 functions of the OFMDFM—which endured a decidedly ill-tempered and unproductive early life — developed a certain *esprit* under its new chair, Edwin Poots (DUP).

Among the several accomplishments of the committees, its report on the creation of a children's commissioner for Northern Ireland should be noted, as should that produced by the standing committee on standards and privileges on the appointment of a commissioner for standards, by the finance committee on budgetary reform and PPPs, and the higher education committee on student finance. Increasingly, too, the committees extended their links with their counterparts in not only the Scottish Parliament and National Assembly for Wales, but also the Irish Dáil.

Weaknesses remained, though. The Assembly operated under the shadow of Executive dominance, and there were lacunae in the accountability of the OFMDFM, north-south bodies and the European dimension of the institutional architecture. The lack of a concerted, 'loyal' opposition within the Assembly and the existence of fissiparous forces within the Executive trammelled the operation of the institutions — as did, of course, the persistence of the more intractable issues, chiefly decommissioning.

Over the period, the institutions managed to function, albeit increasingly imperfectly. It would be miserly to suggest that the greatest achievement of devolution until the time of writing was its survival: though the accomplishments were modest, they were real. Yet it was clear there was scope for reform in the institutional outworking of devolution—but wider political conditions could overwhelm the opportunity for such change to occur.

---

[37] *Report on the Inquiry into the use of Public Private Partnerships*, 7/00, 3 July 2001.

[38] See for example the debates on the display of Easter lilies in Parliament Buildings (10 April 2001), those following the announcement of Mr Trimble's resignation (8 May 2001) and its implementation (2 July 2001), on 'punishment' beatings (23 January 2001) and electoral fraud (20 February 2001). In addition, when SF ministers appear at the despatch box to take oral questions, anti-Agreement unionists rarely missed the opportunity to turn the occasions into ritual ministerial abuse.

POLICY-MAKING AND LEGISLATION

The highlight of the year in policy terms was undoubtedly the Executive Committee's first Programme for Government, endorsed by the Assembly in March 2001.[39] In an interesting devolution cross-over, the programme followed the advice of the Scottish Council Foundation report on 'holistic government'[40] by being organised around policy goals — even though the Scottish Executive had adopted a more conventional departmental approach.[41]

These five goals, or 'priorities', were:

- growing as a community,
- working for a healthier people,
- investing in education and skills,
- securing a competitive economy, and
- developing north/south, east/west and international relations.[42]

Each priority headed a chapter of the programme, with a series of sub-headings leading in each case to bullet-point action lists. All told, some 250 actions were included.

Perhaps the weakest of the priorities was the first. What clearly scars Northern Ireland is its vertical politico-cultural division into religious 'communities' and its horizontal socio-economic inequalities. Together they give the region its distinctive appearance of ghettoisation — with the imaginary response to both problems that paramilitaries offer. 'Growing as a community' was a rather bland response to this twin challenge.

This priority did include a range of commitments on 'the promotion of equality and human rights' and 'tackling poverty and social disadvantage'. But these were inevitably limited by the absence of macro-economic or welfare-model levers from the devolved administration's policy tool-kit, in the context of very modest revenue-raising capacity and broad 'parity' on benefits with the rest of the UK. And on the even bigger challenge of intercommunal division — widening as the year progressed — the principal commitments were to the subsequent publication of strategies on 'community relations' and 'victims'.

The fact that these two areas — and more-victimised-than-you debates make the second as fraught as the first — were not the subject of more substantive proposals in the programme reflected the great difficulty the four Executive parties have had in handling them. They go to the heart of the

---

[39] Northern Ireland Executive 2001.

[40] Leicester and Mackay 1998.

[41] Presentation by the SCF director, Graham Leicester, to Democratic Dialogue round table on the Programme for Government, Belfast, September 2000.

[42] Northern Ireland Executive 2001, p11.

legitimacy of ethno-nationalist protagonism, prior 'armed struggle' and how the 'security forces' dealt with it. Addressing them substantively would require Northern Ireland politicians to find a language of multi-ethnicity and civic responsibility, absent to date except among the small non-confessional parties (Alliance and the Women's Coalition) unrepresented in the Executive.

A consultation paper on victims strategy appeared at the conclusion of the period, in early August 2001.[43] On 'community relations', senior officials in the OFMDFM admitted they were somewhat at a loss but one of the most respected Northern Ireland civil servants, Jeremy Harbison, on the point of retirement, was given responsibility for the task.

An odd feature of the Programme for Government was the inclusion of 'public service agreements' (PSAs) with departments. Odd in the sense that UK government PSAs are widely understood to have stemmed from the Chancellor's desire to extend influence into other departments. The Northern Ireland Finance minister, Mr Durkan, is mild-mannered and unassuming. It appears that the notion of PSAs was simply carried over without a clear understanding of its political — as against ostensible policy — context.

Much the same problem has bedevilled the issue of public finance. The programme, and the subsequent 'position report' on its first iteration,[44] betrayed a strong commitment to the Private Finance Initiative, which in Northern Ireland's largely policy-free public political debate has not been subject to any argument—apart from the important contribution by the Assembly's finance and personnel committee (see above).

The difficulty for the Executive has been the reinforcing financial pressures of an infrastructure deficit inherited from negligent direct-rule administrations, costly duplication of services arising from communal division and the prospect of a tightening 'Barnett squeeze' (see Chapter 6). Mr Durkan referred to the first and third — though, notably, not the second — of these in presenting his revised budget to the Assembly.[45]

The only revenue-raising instrument at the Executive's disposal, in the absence of tax-varying powers, has been the 'regional rate' arising from Northern Ireland's odd local government system. But Mr Durkan had to row back somewhat from his initial budget proposal in October, to raise the rate by 8 per cent, when he presented his revised budget in December. He subsequently indicated his intense displeasure at the lack of loyalty of ministerial colleagues from other parties in this regard.[46]

The big winners in the first 'home-grown' budget published in October 2000 were education and health, the departments respectively securing £1.33

[43] OFMDFM 2001.
[44] Northern Ireland Executive 2001a.
[45] Northern Ireland Assembly, *Official Report*, 12 December 2000.
[46] *Belfast Telegraph*, 31 May 2001.

billion and £2.28 billion (increased to £2.29 billion in December) out of a departmental expenditure limit of £5.84 billion.[47] SF had exploited the D'Hondt rule more strategically than any other party in taking the two departments with the greatest scope for public-expenditure patronage when the mechanism was operated at the end of November 1999.

The most novel aspect of the budget was the cross-departmental Executive Programme Funds (EPFs), of which there were five:

- social inclusion/community regeneration,
- service modernisation,
- new directions,
- infrastructure/capital renewal, and
- children.

The aim was to enhance 'joined-up' government by creating a financial incentive for cross-departmental co-operation. Unfortunately, the absence of a real sense of mutuality in the Executive undermined this initiative. Remarkably, by the end of the survey period the Executive had still not established any sub-committees, and 57 of 62 successful bids for the funds in the first tranche of EPF expenditure announced by the minister (totalling £146 million) were from single departments.[48]

By contrast with the innovative character of the Programme for Government, legislative activity during the period was relatively pedestrian. Eighteen pieces of primary legislation received royal assent and a further four were at various stages of the legislative process.

Figure 4.3: Primary bills enacted in the 2000-01 session
(date of royal assent in brackets):

- Child Support, Pensions and Social Security Bill (20 November 2000)
- Weights and Measures (Amendment) Bill (20 December 2000)
- Dogs (Amendment) Bill (29 January 2001)
- Ground Rents Bill (20 March 2001)
- Fisheries (Amendment) Bill (20 March 2001)
- Health and Personal Social Services Bill (20 March 2001)
- Planning (Compensation etc) Bill (20 March 2001)
- Government Resources and Accounts Bill (22 March 2001)
- Budget Bill (22 March 2001)
- Street Trading Bill (5 April 2001)
- Electronic Communications Bill (5 April 2001)
- Defective Premises (Landlord's Liability) Bill (2 July 2001)
- Adoption (Intercountry Aspects) Bill (2 July 2001)
- Trustee Bill (20 July 2001)
- Department for Employment and Learning Bill (20 July 2001)
- Product Liability (Amendment) Bill (20 July 2001)

---

[47] Executive Information Service, 17 October 2000.
[48] Executive Information Service, 2 April 2001.

Two further bills — the Industrial Development Bill and the Local Government (Best Value) Bill — had reached their second and first stages, respectively, at the end of the session.

Most legislation was of a 'parity' nature — introduced to achieve conformity with laws passed at Westminster. But because the committee stage of all bills is taken by the statutory committees and, in the case of the OFMDFM, by the standing committee of the centre, the autonomy of these committees was consequently constrained (see above).

One interesting issue arising from devolution has been the reaction of the civil service to a situation where it has regional, and perhaps more demanding, hands on the political tiller. One Assembly official, for instance, claimed that the departments had 'done their damnedest'[49] to make the lives of the committees difficult, while an official in OFMDFM described the reaction of the departmental civil servants at devolution as akin 'to a clam closing up'.[50]

The most revealing insight into officials' discomfiture with the new institutions surfaced in February 2001, in the form of a leaked memorandum prepared by Ronnie Spence, then Permanent Secretary of the Department for Regional Development, and circulated to five of his colleagues. The memo, which carried the *imprimatur* of the Head of the Northern Ireland Civil Service, Gerry Loughran, disclosed that senior officials had been discussing 'the emerging difficulties under devolution of the absence of the sorts of conventions about the roles of ministers, officials, the Assembly, Committees, etc, which have been evolved over centuries at Westminster'.[51]

Among other things, senior civil servants were distracted by the environment committee's request to 'see discussion papers at a draft stage'. In the mandarin manner the memo argued that while committee members had a right of access to all papers, a Westminster committee, by convention, would not seek to exercise it. Clearly officials saw Westminster as the yardstick for the modus operandi of the committees, although the memo did say that Mr Loughran wanted to 'work with the Executive Committee and the Assembly to gradually establish conventions which are appropriate to the NI circumstances probably on a case by case basis'.

Shortly after the leak, which caused a furore in the Assembly and the media, Mr Loughran met committee chairs on two occasions. At the second meeting he furnished a list of 15 categories of material that might be deemed 'difficult' in terms of disclosure, including policy papers not yet published. This goes to the heart of the controversy aroused by the UK government's decision not to provide for the release of policy advice into the public domain under its new freedom of information regime.

[49] Personal communication.
[50] Wilford and Wilson 2001, p27.
[51] *Belfast Telegraph*, 2 February 2001.

The Executive Committee — or at least the OFMDFM, which has lead responsibility in this area — has been complicit in this view. It has no plans to depart from the Whitehall view on policy advice, proposing to implement the Freedom of Information (FoI) legislation in Northern Ireland in unamended form, with the proviso of a promised consultation on the need for amendment in 2002.

PUBLIC OPINION

Three years ago the Agreement was presented by its disparate advocates as a political bargain in which they had respectively prevailed — with Mr Trimble claiming the Union was secure but the SF leader, Mr Adams, detecting a transition to a united Ireland. They were both right — or wrong — in the sense that the Agreement was not in itself a final settlement, since the constitutional status of Northern Ireland was to rest, ultimately, on the consent of its electorate.[52]

This open-endedness facilitated the coalescence of eight political parties — flanked by a variety of civic groups, churches, business organisations and trades unions — sufficient to carry majorities of both main religious 'communities' at the ensuing referendum and a massive pro-Agreement majority in the duly elected Assembly. But the weight of opinion among Protestants was finely balanced.

Northern Ireland benefits from a rolling attitude survey, the *Northern Ireland Life and Times Survey* (NILTS). And during the year what every politician and analyst knew to be true was revealed in the NILTS data: Protestant opinion was moving against the Agreement. Bernadette Hayes and Lizanne Dowds of Queen's University presented the end-2000 data at a round table on the third anniversary of the Agreement in April 2001.[53]

Superficially, the results were not too serious. Protestant support for the Agreement appeared to have fallen from 59 per cent to 46 per cent. Given Catholic support had only shifted from 99 to 98 per cent in the same period, there would still be a healthy majority in favour of the Agreement in a rerun referendum (see figure 4.4).

What was perhaps more serious, however, was the underlying disposition of Protestant opinion and its implications for the sustainability of a critical mass of Ulster Unionist support for the institutions. First, it was clear that it was among UUP voters that the shift had primarily occurred, falling from 71 per cent 'yes' in 1998 to 56 per cent backing in 2000.

Secondly, the data showed serious erosion of support for the power-sharing Executive — down among Protestant respondents from 65 to 40 per cent over the period; there were smaller but also substantial drops in

---

[52] See McGinty and Wilford forthcoming.
[53] Hayes and Dowds 2001.

Figure 4.4. Religion and the referendum vote

	Protestant	Catholic	Other/ Independent	Total
Vote choice in 1998*				
Yes (%)	59.4	99.1	69.7	74.2**
No (%)	40.6	0.9	30.3	25.8
Vote choice today*				
Yes (%)	45.5	97.8	63.9	65.7
No (%)	54.5	2.2	36.1	34.3

* Voting respondents only   ** The actual figure in 1998 was 71.2 per cent

Source: *Northern Ireland Life & Times Survey*, 2000

endorsement for the Assembly and the north–south bodies. Little over a quarter supported the Patten policing commission (now its results were known) and just 3 per cent of Protestants the early release of prisoners (now complete). Decommissioning, meanwhile, was demanded by 94 per cent of Protestant respondents.

Perhaps the most telling answer was in response to the key 'who won?' question about the Agreement. In the 1998 *Northern Ireland Referendum and Election Survey*, 66 per cent of Protestants had said the Agreement had benefited 'unionists' and 'nationalists' equally. By 2000, however, 53 per cent of Protestants said it had benefited nationalists a little or a lot more — and 43 per cent said the latter. This was just the 'all pain and no gain' message the DUP pressed in its electoral assaults on its UUP rival in June.

And there was an even more sinister result. When Hayes and Dowds broke down the data on respondents who had shifted from the 'yes' to the 'no' camp since 1998, three variables proved the best predictors: Protestant, obviously, but also male and of low education — just the people, they pointed out, most amenable to loyalist paramilitary recruitment.

The NILTS time-series are one thing, but the UUP leader, Mr Trimble, was unfortunately swayed by other, more ephemeral, polling data. Throughout the election campaign he made oblique references to UUP private polling which suggested his party would do well. He was doubtless also buoyed up by a rogue poll in the *Belfast Telegraph* which suggested Protestants were *more likely* to vote for the Agreement than in 1998.

THE MEDIA

Earlier in this chapter we addressed the issues of Executive policy towards freedom of information and Assembly committee transparency. But what of the role of the media themselves after a year of continuous devolved government? Had they changed their ways from the round-up-the-usual-suspects routinism of the 'troubles' years?[54]

MLAs we talked to in the spring felt coverage of the Assembly to be adequate in quantitative terms.[55] BBC Northern Ireland, for example, has invested substantially, with a large number of additional correspondents recruited. The Assembly Commission arranged the establishment of a media unit in Parliament Buildings, with facilities for press conferences and interviews, and a studio from which BBC NI could transmit its weekly *Assembly Live* (albeit on BBC2). A liaison panel between the commission and the regional media has been meeting roughly every quarter.

There has, however, been some disquiet about the quality of the reportage. This is partly the complaint of parliamentarians everywhere — that media organisations seek only to highlight, indeed exaggerate, the sensational or controversial, at the expense of the bulk of worthy, but dull, activity in which any such assembly engages.

This media preoccupation carries a particular charge in Northern Ireland, however, for two reasons. First, the tendency to focus on issues on which parties adopt antagonistic stances has meant an emphasis on those concerns — such as the plight of 'victims' — that expose the bitter sectarian divisions the Agreement has not assuaged. Secondly, and relatedly, what political correspondents in the region deem to be 'political' (as with the politicians from whom they take their cue) is in fact a relatively narrow agenda of issues revolving around sectarianism and violence inherited from the long struggle over the region's constitutional future. The nature of the coverage may thus unwittingly have modestly contributed to the weakening of confidence in the Agreement's future.

One MLA complained that political correspondents only turned up at the Assembly in anticipation of 'a row'. In particular, he suggested, the promulgation of the Programme for Government had been 'very ill served'. He said: 'The media are not geared to concentrating on serious, detailed policies.' Indeed, while most committee meetings had now been rendered public, another MLA said, the media still rarely covered them — somewhat defeating the object.[56]

---

[54] Wilson 1997.

[55] Wilford and Wilson, 2001.

[56] *Ibid*, p18-19.

THE ELECTIONS

On 8 May, the day the Prime Minister, Tony Blair, announced the date of the general election, Mr Trimble made his statement to the Assembly disclosing that he had submitted a post-dated resignation letter to the Speaker of the Assembly, take effect on 1 July. Mr Trimble's action thereby ensured that the election campaigns became a litmus test of unionist support for the model of devolution so painstakingly crafted on 10 April 1998.

Figure 4.5. 2001 UK general election results

Party	Total vote	Vote share (%)	+/− 1997 vote share (%)	Number of Seats*
UUP**	216,839	26.8	−5.9	6 (10)
DUP	181,999	22.5	+8.9	5 (2)
SDLP	169,874	21.0	−3.1	3 (3)
SF	175,933	21.7	+5.6	4 (2)
Other	65,738	8.0	−5.5	0 (1)***

* Seats won in 1997 in brackets.
** The UUP lost its South Antrim seat at the by-election in September 2000.
*** Robert McCartney UKUP, North Down.

Figure 4.6. 2001 Northern Ireland local election results

Party	Vote (N)	Vote share (%)	+/− 1997 vote share (%)	Seats (N)*
UUP	181,336	22.9	−5.0	154 (187)
DUP	169,477	21.4	+5.6	131 (91)
SDLP	153,434	19.4	−1.2	117 (120)
SF	163,269	20.7	+3.8	108 (74)
Others	64,416	15.6	−3.2	72 (112)

* 1997 figures in brackets.

The outcomes of the elections were dramatic, signalling shifts in both Protestant and Catholic electorates.[57] Overall, the UUP suffered a net loss of four Westminster seats since the 1997 general election — gaining North Down from the UKUP, but losing East Londonderry, North Belfast and Strangford to the DUP and Fermanagh/South Tyrone and West Tyrone to SF. The DUP and SF each gained two and the SDLP maintained its three seats.

[57] Ruohomaki 2001.

The UUP's losses, while significant, were not however as damaging as some had feared — and others, including some of Mr Trimble's internal party critics, had hoped.

The movement within unionist electoral opinion was more than matched among nationalists. The final declaration of the general election came from Fermanagh and South Tyrone where Michelle Gildernew picked up SF's fourth Westminster seat at the expense of the UUP, though her wafer-thin victory was subjected to a legal challenge by the defeated candidate, claiming electoral malpractice. From a republican perspective, whatever Churchill may have mused, never had the constituency's steeples seemed less dreary.

The overall result of the general election confirmed the SDLP's fears: it was overhauled by a jubilant SF which, for the first time, took the larger share of the nationalist vote in any SF/SDLP Westminster contest. While winning nine fewer council seats, SF also took a larger local-election vote share than the SDLP, while the DUP closed the gap in vote share with the UUP, from 12.1 per cent in 1997 to 1.5 per cent.

The electoral landscape changed dramatically on 7 June, especially at Westminster level where, west of the River Bann, Northern Ireland is now electorally 'green'. In the minds of some, these outcomes appeared to make an already difficult political situation seemingly impossible.

CONCLUSION

A visiting Martian (or, perhaps, a visiting anybody) would have found it hard to fathom what was going on at Stormont this past year.

If they had dropped in on an Assembly committee meeting, they might have been impressed by diligent, if not always inspired, endeavour, and in particular by cross-party co-operation — first names all round (if they understood the language). If, however, they had observed a riot in north Belfast, they might have left with the impression that these strange human sub-species could never live as neighbours. Pragmatism and pugilism vied throughout the year.

Few doubted that devolution was 'making a difference'. Ministers with regional dialects and full-time commitment to their departments were accountable to an Assembly which had in its short life banished bad memories of the unionist *ancien régime* (even if Lord Carson still looked down the avenue at Stormont with his brooding gaze).

And yet. The mistrust that the architects of the Belfast Agreement thought they could obviate via such fancy footwork as forming a government by D'Hondt appeared more visceral than ever. And the violence on the streets told its own story of how a 'peace process' cannot avoid the challenge of reconciliation.

BIBLIOGRAPHY

Official Documents

Northern Ireland Executive, (2001). *Programme for Government 2001/2004: Making a Difference*. Belfast: Economic Policy Unit, OFMDFM.

Northern Ireland Executive, (2001). *Preparing for 2002-03: The Executive's Position Report to the Assembly*. Belfast: Economic Policy Unit, OFMDFM.

OFMDFM (2001). *Consultation Paper on a Victims' Strategy*. Belfast: Victims Unit.

Strategy Steering Group (1999). *Strategy 2010: Report by the Economic Development Strategy Steering Group*. Belfast: Department of Economic Development (now DETI).

Secondary Documents

Fawcett, L. (2001). 'Political communication and devolution', unpublished conference paper, Belfast.

Hayes, B. and Dowds, L. (2001). 'Underpinning opinions: declining levels of support among Protestants for the Good Friday Agreement', paper presented at Democratic Dialogue round table in Belfast on The Belfast Agreement Three Years On.

Laver, M. (2000). 'Coalitions in Northern Ireland: preliminary thoughts', paper presented at Democratic Dialogue round table in Belfast, Governing with Consensus? The Programme for Government, 20 September 2000.

Leicester, G. and Mackay, P. (1998). *Holistic Government: Options for a Devolved Scotland*. Edinburgh: Scotland Council Foundation.

McGinty, R. and Wilford, R. (forthcoming). 'Consenting adults: the principle of consent and Northern Ireland's constitutional future', *Government and Opposition*.

Ruohomaki, J. (2001). *Two Elections, Two Contests: the June 2001 Elections in Northern Ireland*. Belfast: Democratic Dialogue.

Trimble, D. (2001). *To Raise up a New Northern Ireland*. Belfast: Blackstaff Press.

Wilford, R. and Wilson, R. (2000). 'A "bare knuckle ride": Northern Ireland', in Hazell, R. (ed), *The State and the Nations: The First Year of Devolution in the United Kingdom*. Exeter: Imprint Academic.

Wilford, R. and Wilson, R. (2001). *A Democratic Design? The Political Style of the Northern Ireland Assembly*. London: The Constitution Unit.

Wilson, R. (1997). *Media and Intra-state Conflict in Northern Ireland*. Düsseldorf: European Institute for the Media.

5

Reshaping the English Regions

John Tomaney

INTRODUCTION

The period since July 2000 has seen the question of the English regions begin to re-emerge on the political agenda. In Labour's first term its action in the regional field was restricted to the establishment of Regional Development Agencies (RDAs) in 1999 and the promotion of voluntary Regional Chambers. However, Labour did not move on the promise, contained in its 1997 manifesto, to introduce directly elected Regional Assemblies, where there was demonstrable demand.[1] The period before the UK general election saw the Government act to strengthen the main regional institutions within England. These included additional resources and the promise of increased financial flexibility for RDAs and new central government resources for Regional Chambers. Labour's deepening engagement with the issue culminated in the commitment to publish a White Paper on English regional government. However, the first Queen's Speech after the election failed to mention the English regions. Moreover, in the aftermath of the election, significant changes in Whitehall departmental responsibilities occurred which have implications for the governance of the English regions. New Labour's engagement with the English regions reveals its continuing ambivalence about devolution in general and English regionalism in particular.

This chapter outlines the evolution of the new thinking emerging within the government as far as the English regions are concerned and reports on the development of RDAs, Regional Chambers and the various civic campaigns for devolution that have sprung up in parts of England. The chapter also examines the ways in which the concerns of the English regions have been addressed in Westminster and Whitehall. Although the space for regionalism may have expanded within England, its shape and progress remain uneven and hotly contested. London is the only part of England with a tier of regional government. The chapter very briefly reviews the performance of the Greater London Authority in the period since July 2000, especially in light of its potential as a model for the governance of the English regions. The chapter concludes by assessing the issues that confronted the UK Government as far as the English regions are concerned.

[1] Tomaney 2000.

THE REGIONAL DEBATE

The evolution of the regional debate was punctuated by a series of interventions by senior Labour figures in the period after July 2000. These interventions followed a call by the Party's National Policy Forum for the Government to bring forward a White Paper on regional government.[2] A series of ministerial statements also prepared the way for new resources and responsibilities for RDAs and for Regional Chambers. Ministers' statements also helped to stake out the territory upon which the Government's White Paper on regional government will be produced.

The leading Government figure in the promotion of regional policy and regional government during this period was — and remains — the Deputy Prime Minister (DPM), John Prescott. A significant development in the run-up to the UK general election of 2001 though, was the sound of new voices in the debate. Chief among these was that of the Chancellor of the Exchequer, Gordon Brown, who in a number of speeches began to make the case for greater action at the regional level to alleviate socio-economic disparities. Gordon Brown's interventions were prefigured by those of his Chief Economic Advisor, Ed Balls, who began to sketch out arguments in favour of greater regional autonomy in the field of economic development policy. Balls contributed to a pamphlet in which he made the case for a 'new approach' to regional policy:

> Our new regional policy is based on two principles — it aims to strengthen the essential building blocks of growth — innovation, skills, the development of enterprise — by exploiting the indigenous strengths in each region and city. And it is bottom-up not top-down, with national government enabling powerful regional and local initiatives to work by providing the necessary flexibility and resources.[3]

This new approach of promoting regional initiative raises questions of accountability:

> . . . the new resources and flexibilities for RDAs will require greater regional and local accountability and public scrutiny — to ensure the regional strategies are responding to the needs and helping to ensure that decisions of RDA boards are consistent with regional and local strategies.[4]

The Chancellor echoed these themes in a speech made in Manchester at the end of January 2001. In the speech he called for a regional policy based on local initiative and focused on the promotion of 'indigenous measures' aimed at the promotion of enterprise, skills, technological change and job

---

[2] See Tomaney 2000.
[3] Balls 2000, p12-13.
[4] Balls 2000, p15.

creation.[5] This would provide the basis for 'a Britain of nation and regions'. The Chancellor argued that stronger regional initiative requires greater local accountability based both on strengthened Regional Chambers and changes to the House of Commons.

> By extending the scope for region by region initiatives and by complementing these with greater accountability at a regional level and through the select committee system in the Commons, we are proving our ability to ensure that regionally set objectives are met.

The Chancellor connected his approach to a wider set of constitutional concerns:

> We are moving away from the old Britain of subjects where people had to look upwards to a Whitehall bureaucracy for their solutions — to a Britain of citizens where region to region, locality to locality we are ourselves in charge and where it is up to us.

Although Mr Brown stopped short of raising the issue of directly elected assemblies, the press coverage of the speech suggested it was the first step to the Chancellor's endorsement of an idea hitherto associated with John Prescott. A report in the London *Evening Standard* noted that the content of the Chancellor's remarks had little or no connection with his Treasury responsibilities: [6]

> Instead, it outlined plans to increase the accountability of regional development agencies as *a first step toward elected assemblies* for the English regions. The policy has its keenest supporter in Deputy Prime Minister John Prescott, into whose turf it falls. There is little suggestion, however, of Mr Brown's choice of subject sparking protests from Prescott. Instead there were claims that the two men are forging new links with polling day rapidly approaching (emphasis added).

The *Financial Times* also claimed that talk of increased accountability of RDAs was 'an interim measure before elected assemblies are created in English regions'.[7] The more immediate effects of the Chancellor's new-found interest though were increased funds and flexibility for RDAs and central government resources for Regional Chambers.

Other developments during early 2001 also suggested that a space for regionalism was opening up. For instance, Department for Environment, Transport and the Regions (DETR) ministers implied that they had dropped Labour's previous stipulation that unitary local government was a pre-requisite of moves to regional government. In the House of Commons in

---

[5] Brown 2001; see also Tomaney and Hetherington 2001b for further discussion.
[6] *Evening Standard*, 29 January 2001.
[7] *Financial Times*, 29 February 2001.

January, John Prescott made it clear that moves to regional government were not dependent on a preceding reform of local government.[8] Beverley Hughes, the junior minister at the DETR, reiterated this approach in a debate in Westminster Hall in January 2001.[9] It was a commitment, which ministers repeated publicly on subsequent occasions. Such statements contributed to a perception that the government was preparing to act on Regional Assemblies in its second term. Thus, the *Financial Times* reported the minister's statement 'was certain to have been cleared by John Prescott' and represented 'the clearest signal yet' that the government would move on elected Assemblies. Moreover, it suggested, the calling of the committee represented growing ministerial enthusiasm for regionalism.[10]

Irrespective of whether or not the Chancellor's speech signalled his conversion to regional assemblies, the background to the new concern with regional policy appears to be two-fold. On the one hand it reflects the persistence of regional disparities within England. In November 2000, the then Trade and Industry Secretary, Stephen Byers — another of the new voices in the debate — argued:

> The economic differences between UK regions are clear and indicate that a winners' circle is emerging, with some regions keeping up and staying in touch while others slip further behind. These are the underlying causes we need to tackle through a strong, radically reformed regional policy, simply tinkering at the edges will not be enough.[11]

Underpinning this concern about persistent regional disparities is an essentially 'Keynesian' analysis of their economic consequences — that is the view that unused social and economic resources in lagging regions represent a constraint on the output growth of the national economy. In a later speech Byers sought to link the goals of 'social justice and economic efficiency' in the field of regional policy in a more or less explicitly Keynesian way:

> We do so out of a sense of social justice but also because our future economic success as a country depends on all parts and all people of the United Kingdom achieving their full potential.[12]

This concern with a 'winners' circle', however, probably also reflected a more practical political concern with the condition and mood of Labour's electoral heartlands in the run-up to the UK general election. Senior Labour figures were motivated by the need to mitigate a perception in some regions that New Labour was mainly responding to the concerns of middle England

---

[8] HC Deb, 16 January 2001, Col 184.
[9] HC Deb, 17 January 2001, col. 115WH.
[10] 'Labour signals rapid regional referendums', *Financial Times*, 11 May 2001.
[11] DTI Press Release, P/2000/761, 15 November 2000.
[12] Byers 2001.

and had little specific to offer its traditional bastions. A number of episodes contributed to this perception over the preceding period. The impact of the Bank of England's interest policy — aimed at restricting the growth of consumer demand in the South but impacting severely on those regions disproportionately dependent on manufacturing industry — had become an issue for some RDA chairs and for the media in some regions. In addition, the Prime Minister's intervention in late 1999, which appeared to cast doubt on the existence of the North/South divide, provoked a strong backlash in the northern regions — and a swift retraction.

The perception that New Labour was open to arguments in favour of regionalism was reinforced when a further influential voice was added to the debate. In a speech in his Hartlepool constituency at the end of March 2001, the former Northern Ireland secretary Peter Mandelson made a powerful call for North East regional government. Describing himself as a convert to the cause, he argued that '...we cannot achieve economic revitalisation in the North East without modernising the means of delivering our economic policies, and this means renewing the region's political institutions'. He continued:

> The first step is to introduce a democratically elected element into the existing regional chamber by establishing a regional authority for the North East that is tight in numbers and focus. The elected element would need to be based on proportional representation drawing together all the political parties and areas of the region.[13]

The speech appeared to give a powerful New Labour endorsement to regionalism, albeit in a partially elected form. Given the proximity of Peter Mandelson to the heart of the New Labour project, his intervention was seen by some as a strong signal of likely future trends.

INSTITUTIONS OF REGIONAL GOVERNANCE

The evolving debate on regional governance provided the backdrop for a number of developments in regional institutions in the period July 2000-July 2001. This section is focused on the activities of RDAs, Regional Chambers/Assemblies and Government Offices (GOs). However, events during the period also drew attention to the activities of other public bodies in the regions and the ways in which these have a bearing on the governance of the English regions.

---

[13] Quoted in Tomaney and Hetherington 2000b.

Figure 5.1. Key events relating to the English regions	
November 2000	Pre-Budget Speech announces new financial autonomy for RDAs
November 2000	Publication of Planning Policy Guidance, No 11: Regional Planning
January 2001	Gordon Brown's Manchester Speech on Regional Policy
March 2001	John Prescott and Gordon Brown announce details of new financial regime for RDAs and possible resources for Regional Chambers.
March 2001	Arts Council of England announces abolition of Regional Arts Boards
April 2001	Government Offices take on new functions from MAFF, the Home Office and the Department of Culture, Media and Sport.
April 2001	East of England Regional Assembly rejects RDA's revised Economic Strategy
May 2001	Labour's general election manifesto reaffirms Labour's commitment to create regional assemblies where there is demand
May 2001	John Prescott and Gordon Brown launch 'Ambitions for the English Regions' in Wakefield
7 June 2001	UK general election
June 2001	Major reorganisation of Whitehall Departments has implications for the regions
July 2001	Government rejects South East regional assembly plan for bypasses at Hastings

Regional Development Agencies

RDAs represented the centrepiece of Labour's policies for the English regions in its first term. In the final year of the last government Labour acted to strengthen their capacity to address regional economic problems. These moves reflected, in part, a response to criticisms — not least from business leaders — that RDAs lacked the resources and flexibility to make an impact on regional problems. At the centre of the criticism was the accusation that RDAs had too many Whitehall paymasters enforcing their priorities over regional strategies.[14] At the same time though, as noted above, moves to bolster the activities of RDAs reflected a genuine belief on the part of the Chancellor that they could play a key role in achieving his ambition of full employment. The first indication of the expanded role of RDAs came in the Spending Review 2000, which announced increased resources for RDAs (see Figure 5.2).

[14] See PIU 2000; Tomaney 2000.

Figure 5.2. Spending allocations for RDAs in 2000 spending review

(All figures £ million)	2000/01	2001/02	2002/03	2003/04
Total programme before SR2000	1,182	1,271	-	-
Total programme after SR2000	1,242	1,445	1,550	1,700
New single budget, of which:				
DETR existing	1,114	1,183		
DETR additional	60	150		
DfEE existing	49	49		
DfEE additional	0	8.5		
DTI existing	19	39		
DTI additional	0	15		
Source: *DETR News Release 489*: 21 July 2000.				

In addition to increased resources, the Spending Review also contained proposals to extend the financial flexibility afforded to RDAs. This was to be achieved by creating 'a single cross departmental funding framework' in order to overcome the problems of 'departmentalitis' that were identified by the Performance and Innovation Unit (PIU).[15] In return, it was announced, that RDAs would be given 'challenging outcome targets'.[16] The Chancellor expanded on the new approach in his pre-budget report in November 2000. This claimed that RDAs 'provide a key element in the delivery of the Government's strategy for improving UK productivity'. The report also provided details of how the single programme (also known as 'the single pot') would work. It announced that RDAs would be able to transfer up to 20 per cent out of any programme to another, so long as it is consistent with delivery objectives. It also announced the inception of a new strategic programme, which would allow RDAs to promote innovative schemes that meet their economic and other strategic aims, as a test-bed for the Single Budget and new project appraisal processes to be introduced in 2002.[17]

The DTI's White Paper on *Enterprise, Skills and Innovation,* published in March 2001, further endorsed the evolving role of RDAs.[18] It ascribed a prominent role to regional policy in meeting the Government's wider industrial policy. The White Paper claimed to adopt a new approach to regional policy concerned with 'building the capability of regions and communities':

[15] PIU 2000.
[16] HM Treasury 2000a.
[17] HM Treasury 2000b.
[18] DTI 2001.

Government must equip all regions and communities with the means to build on their own distinctive cultures, know-how and competitive advantages. This must be a bottom-up approach: the role of central Government must be to ensure that all regions and communities have the resources and capability to be winners. Strong regional policies have shown their worth in other European economies and in the USA.[19]

The White Paper proposed the notion of industry 'clusters' as the basis of its new approach to promoting economic development. Cluster development has been taken up as a major theme of the work of RDAs subsequently. (The debate around the White Paper also signalled the future shift of responsibility for RDAs from the DETR to the DTI, discussed below.)

RDA chairmen, however, remained sceptical about the degree of the Government's commitment to letting RDAs off the leash.[20] Graham Hall, the chairman of Yorkshire Forward, writing at the end of 2000, offered a series of challenges to the Government:

Firstly, the concept of the 'single pot' must be made a reality. This concept is so counter-cultural to the way Parliament votes money, the accountability mechanisms and the 'command and control' nature of large parts of Whitehall that it is not as simple as it first seems. This must consist of a clear corporate planning process, whereby the Government 'buys' a single set of outcomes — one Public Service Agreement — from RDAs, and sensible monitoring of review arrangements. It must not consist of separate corporate plans, prescriptive guidance, an excessive degree of details in planning and reporting, mid year initiatives involving RDA bidding and outputs so specific as to make any flexibility mythical. This is our biggest current challenge for Ministers.

The financial accountability arrangements should be changed to reflect the devolution of responsibility to RDAs. RDA chief executives should take sole responsibility as accounting officers and departmental permanent secretaries should lose their dual responsibility. This will help to relax the present 'control' culture of the civil service. A more fundamental review of the civil service may also be needed in the medium term.[21]

The tensions reached a high point in January 2001 when RDA chairs met senior officials at the DETR to discuss the shape of the 'single pot'. RDA chairs accused Whitehall officials of dragging their feet. One said:

The concept of the 'single pot' is so counter-cultural (to the civil service) and the accountability mechanisms, the command and control nature of Whitehall, that it makes it a quite difficult thing to get through...they find it incredibly difficult to deal with things across more than one department. Part of the argument for why you have to have RDAs is because you cannot control things from a distance and

---

[19] DTI 2001, para 3.3.
[20] Tomaney and Hetherington 2000.
[21] Hall 2000, p27.

have to be on the ground where things really happen. There is a real issue here about the modernisation of Whitehall and I have to say the jury is out at present.[22]

Notwithstanding these tensions, at a meeting with RDA chairs in Middlesbrough in March 2001, John Prescott and Gordon Brown jointly announced further details of the new scheme. (Simultaneously they announced proposals to enhance the scrutiny functions of Regional Chambers.) The Single Budget arrangements were to be in place by April 2002. In the immediate aftermath of the UK general election, with RDAs now a responsibility of the DTI, the new Trade Secretary Patricia Hewitt announced the system of general outcome targets that would apply from April 2002. These covered the areas of regional business performance, employment creation, skill formation and the recycling of brown-field land. Although the details of the agreements between the Government and the individual RDAs had yet to be finalised, RDA chairs, by July 2001, were more confident that Whitehall officials would avoid too much day-to-day interference in their work, although whether this reflected the wider views of business was unclear.[23]

Regional Chambers and Assemblies

Regional Chambers (or 'Assemblies' as most style themselves) are the other new actors in the English regions that are the product of Labour's polices since 1997.[24] The central task of Regional Chambers remains that of providing a level of scrutiny of RDAs. The role of Chambers, however, expanded in many regions during the period July 2000-July 2001 and announcements by ministers presaged an even greater role in the future.

The first indication of the Government's ambitions for Regional Chambers was contained in the Government's Planning Policy Guidance Note on Regional Planning, published in October 2000. In this note, the Government proposed that Regional Chambers should assume responsibility for the preparation for Regional Planning Guidance from regional planning conferences of local authorities. It argued:

> Given the representation of a range of regional stakeholders on each Regional Chamber, and the latter's role in relation to the RDA under the RDAs Act, it makes sense for the Chamber to take on the regional planning function. Indeed a Chamber supported by a full time regional planning, monitoring and review team would be in an ideal position to provide the necessary leadership to produce and implement an integrated spatial strategy for the region. However, the arrangements to be adopted in any particular region must be for the region to decide.[25]

[22] Quoted in Tomaney and Hetherington 2001a.
[23] Tomaney, Hetherington and Humphrey 2001.
[24] See Tomaney 2000.
[25] DETR 2000, para 2.4.

In most regions Chambers moved to assume the role of Regional Planning Conferences. In other regions, such as the West Midlands, powerful local authorities initially kept control of the regional planning process, although subsequent developments are loosening their grasp.

A further major development occurred at the meeting between John Prescott, Gordon Brown and the RDA chairs in Middlesbrough in March. At the meeting John Prescott proposed offering central government resources to assist Regional Chambers in their job of scrutinising RDAs and ensuring that their strategies and activities mesh with the wider framework of strategies for the region. A DETR discussion paper, published at the same time, offered suggestions of how the resources might be used:

> . . . by way of illustration, the way forward could involve the chambers establishing a stronger analytical or research capacity to monitor and evaluate the RDAs' plans in relation to the region's performance and to the wider strategic context within the region. In doing so they will, for example, need to lock into the work of the Regional Observatories [which monitor local social and economic conditions] and consider the links with the work on monitoring implementation of Regional Planning Guidance. It could also involve the chambers holding hearings at which the RDAs could formally explain and answer questions on their performance against their strategies and targets. In turn, the chambers will need to feed back their conclusions to the RDAs and to communicate developments to the wider regional community.[26]

Following a consultation, the Government announced a £15 million fund for Regional Chambers in July 2001, amounting to £5 million per annum for the next three years, with each Chamber receiving £500,000 per annum and £1 million available for join initiatives. The consequence of the changes was to raise the profile of Regional Chambers as regional actors. One immediate effect, for instance, was to re-open the debate — in those regions that had not already done so — about Chambers taking over the responsibilities of Regional Planning Conferences, as the Government's own Planning Policy Guidance had suggested.

Independent of Government announcements Chambers were already beginning to assert themselves as political actors in their respective regions, carrying out three distinctive roles:

• Holding RDAs to account
• Representing regions in conflicts with central government
• Policy integration

The most public effort by a Chamber to call its RDA to account occurred in the East of England. According to the *Local Government Chronicle*, 'The East of England is not noted for its political turbulence.'[27] The paper

---

[26] Quoted in Tomaney and Hetherington 2001b.
[27] *Local Government Chronicle* 'Opinion', 12 April 2001.

Name:	East of England	East Midlands	Yorkshire and Humberside	North West	North East	West Midlands	South West	South East
	Regional Assembly	Regional Assembly	Regional Chamber	Regional Assembly	Regional Assembly	Regional Chamber	Regional Assembly	Regional Assembly
Composition:								
Number of Members	42	105	35	80	63	100	117	111
Proportion appointed by local authorities	66%	63%	63%	70%	66%	68%	75%	70%
Number of stakeholders represented	14	35	13	24	19	32	38	34

Figure 5.3. Regional Chambers in England: Basic data
Source: Sandford and McQuail (2000)

suggested therefore that, 'It comes as something of a surprise that the first insurrection against the government's fudged regional policy should emanate from the east'. The 'insurrection' came about when, on 5 April, Labour and Conservative members on the East of England Regional Assembly (EERA) refused to endorse a revision of the East of England Development Agency's (EEDA) regional economic strategy (RES). EEDA is the only RDA to undertake a major revision of its RES, but chose to do so in the light of new research and the evolving institutional architecture in the region. Members of the Assembly were reportedly concerned about the environmental impact of its 3.2 per cent growth target, its alleged failure to take account of sub-regional differences, the arrangements for partnership working and a concern that questions of social inclusion had not been properly dealt with. EEDA had adopted its first version in October 1999, but agreed to revise it after EERA had voiced what its chair, John Kent, described as 'severe reservations'. Concerns raised by sub-regional partnerships prompted the Assembly to reject the strategy. Mr Kent accused EEDA of 'ducking the difficult decisions' needed to stimulate development. Rejection of the revised RES came about because EERA had previously given only its qualified endorsement to the first version of the Strategy.

EEDA reacted angrily. Its chief executive, Bill Samuel, accused EERA of being 'reluctant to commit to firm and positive action to move the region's economy forward'.[28] Although EERA eventually endorsed a revision of the RES, the events on the East of England represented a first public flexing of (admittedly) limited muscle by a Regional Chamber. Of course, as the *Local Government Chronicle* noted, the Assembly had no right of veto over the RES; EEDA is answerable to the Secretary of State. But many of the issues that surround the government's approach to the accountable governance of the English regions are highlighted in the 'eastern insurrection' and it may very well be, as the *Local Government Chronicle* put it, 'a very small-scale dress rehearsal for future battles'.

An example of a Regional Chamber being drawn into conflict with central government comes from the South East. The South East Regional Assembly (SERA), along with the South East England Development Agency (SEEDA), clashed with the Government over the latter's decision to block plans for two proposed bypasses at Hastings on the Sussex/Kent border in July 2001. The rejection was announced in a letter to Cllr David Shakespeare, leader of the Regional Assembly, in which the Secretary of State, Stephen Byers, maintained that the economic benefits of the proposed scheme did not outweigh the environmental costs. The bypasses would have damaged two Sites of Special Scientific Interest and an Area of Outstanding Natural Beauty in the South Downs.

---

[28] Quoted in Tomaney and Hetherington 2001b.

The bypasses had been a recommendation of a Government-sponsored multi-modal transport study, aimed at assisting the regeneration of Hastings, a run-down seaside town. The bypass proposal had been incorporated into broader planning priorities for the area and adopted by the Assembly (which is responsible for Regional Planning Guidance), the RDA and local authorities. Environmental campaigners welcomed the announcement. However, the Regional Assembly 'expressed fears for the successful regeneration of Hastings and the South Coast' and questioned 'the Government's commitment to the delivery of urban renaissance in the region's coastal towns'.[29] A paradoxical effect of the decision may have been to stimulate regionalism among the business sector in the South East, with local business leaders arguing that the scheme would have gone ahead if the decision had been delegated to an elected Regional Assembly.[30]

Finally, some Regional Chambers sought to establish a role for themselves as a body that can integrate public policy within the region. A good example of this is the East Midlands Regional Assembly (EMRA). EMRA launched its Integrated Regional Strategy (IRS) in June 2001. This is intended to provide a framework for the proliferation of regional strategies — in the fields of the economy, culture, environment, energy, spatial development, social inclusion, transport and housing — while placing a concern with sustainability at their heart. The principle underlying the IRS means that when the Assembly or RDA considers an issue they do not do it in isolation to other areas of concern.[31]

Government Offices

GOs remain important, if low profile, actors in the region. The period July 2000-2001 saw their roles significantly strengthened. Following the recommendations of the Performance and Innovation Unit (PIU), the Government sought to increase the range of Whitehall departments represented in GOs. The first moves came in July 2000, when the then Agriculture Secretary, Nick Brown, announced that senior staff from the Ministry of Agriculture Fisheries and Food (MAFF) would be moved into GOs in order to improve MAFF's regional policy making capacity. At the same time the Department of Culture, Media and Sport (DCMS) and the Home Office made additional appointments in the form of Regional Cultural Directors and Crime Reductions Teams, headed by Regional Crime Reduction Directors. The administrative integration of GOs will be facilitated by the introduction of a 'single pot' to meet its running costs, with some local discretion on how this is spent. The combined running costs of GOs are in the order of £100 million per annum, in support of programmes that are worth £5-6 billion. However, GOs

---

[29] Quoted in Tomaney, Hetherington and Humphrey 2001.
[30] *Financial Times*, 16 July 2001.
[31] Tomaney, Hetherington and Humphrey 2001.

will not have the kind of flexibility to move money between programmes that has been accorded to RDAs.

By September 2001, GOs incorporated a presence from the following departments:

• Department of Transport, Local Government and the Regions
• Department of Trade Industry
• Department for Education and Skills
• Department for Environment, Food and Rural Affairs
• Department for Culture, Media and Sport
• Home Office

The restructuring of GOs was hindered by the Foot-and-Mouth Disease crisis. GO officials played a central role in the fight against Foot-and-Mouth in those regions that were most badly affected — notably the North East, North West (Cumbria) and the South West (Devon). Although MAFF regional directors moved into GOs, with the aim of ensuring the work of GOs incorporates a rural perspective, the scale and endurance of the rural problems resulting from Foot-and-Mouth inevitably slowed down this development. However, GOs are likely to acquire further powers in the future. The evolving role of GOs will include providing a regional base for National Connections (the government's new 'joined-up' youth policy), Sure Start, the Children's Fund and the Neighbourhood Renewal Unit. GOs may also have a role in monitoring Local Strategic Partnerships and local Public Service Agreements.[32]

A further significant development occurred in April 2001, with the launch of the Regional Co-ordination Unit (RCU) within Whitehall. The creation of the RCU was an outcome of a report of the PIU in the Cabinet Office.[33] The aim of the RCU is to oversee the work of GOs and influence central government departments' dealings with the regions. The RCU is relatively small, comprising currently about 50 staff drawn from a range of departments across Whitehall. It incorporates the previous elements of the Whitehall machinery concerned with the financing and personnel aspects of GOs. The number of policy specialists is relatively modest, comprising about half of the RCU's total complement. In the new regime all departments are formally required to consult the RCU when introducing any new area based initiative (ABI).[34] Although the Director General of the RCU is the 'line manager' of GO Directors, the RCU preferred to see itself as standing at the heart of what he terms 'the Government Office Network', with RCU relying heavily on Regional Directors for power and influence within the Whitehall machine.

[32] Tomaney and Hetherington 2001b.
[33] PIU 2000; see also Tomaney 2000.
[34] See Tomaney and Hetherington 2001b, for a further discussion.

Regionalisation

Taken together, the changes to the RDAs, Regional Chambers and GOs represent a significant strengthening of the apparatus of governance in the English regions. However, these bodies are only the most prominent in what is currently a fractured governance of the English regions. A study for the North East Regional Assembly showed that over 20 organisations were involved in the preparation of at least 12 regional strategies, which affected many aspects of the region's life. Although the RDA, Regional Assembly and, especially the Government Office were heavily involved in the preparation of regional strategies, many other Government departments, non-departmental government bodies and other agencies were also involved. The dominant trend among these bodies is toward the creation, or strengthening, of regional structures in order to better assist them to contribute to regional strategy making. This quiet regionalisation of government structures, and simultaneous proliferation of regional strategy making is a relatively unnoticed feature of the governance of the English regions. The senior decision-makers within these organisations assume the trend will grow rather than diminish. In particular, the study demonstrated that the move to regional strategy making was seen positively, but frustrations exist about the failure to 'join up' individual strategies and the lack of capacity to implement them properly. In addition there was a broad acceptance of the need for greater accountability of the existing structure of regional governance. In short, the study revealed both the potential and current limits of existing regionalism.[35]

However, the regionalisation trend is by no means a universal one. A counter-example was the decision of the Arts Council of England (ACE) to abolish local authority dominated Regional Arts Boards (RABs). Although this event received minimal attention in the national media, it proved controversial in many of the regions. In an announcement in mid March, ACE announced plans to abolish the 10 RABs in England, by merging them with ACE. RABs currently make regional arts policy and dispense arts funding. The proposal was to create a single, new development organisation for the arts in all of England, by uniting the eleven organisations, constituting the 'arts funding system' into a single, new Arts Council of England. In its initial announcement the Arts Council suggested that its proposal commanded wide support in the regions. It rapidly emerged that this was far from the case. Among the first to condemn the proposal were the London Mayor, Ken Livingstone and the chair of the London Assembly, Trevor Phillips. MPs, the RABs themselves, and other actors in the regions (notably Regional Assemblies) also opposed the changes. In the face of this opposition ACE moderated its proposals, but ultimately ensured the abolition of the RABs.[36]

---

[35] See Tomaney and Humphrey 2001.
[36] See Tomaney and Hetherington 2001b, c for a more detailed account.

CIVIL REGIONALISM

With the exception of the North East of England, the English regions, until recently, have not been characterised by the presence of broadly based and vigorous regional campaigns. In 2000-2001, however, that picture began to change with the emergence of regional campaigns and conventions across England (see Figure 5.4). The rate of development differs substantially between regions. The North East stands out as the region with the most active debate, but developments can be seen across the northern regions and also in the West Midlands and South West. In each case the forces promoting (and resisting) regionalism are different. The divide between 'official' regionalism (as represented by Chambers, etc) and 'civic' regionalism (as represented by campaigns and conventions) is being blurred in some regions. The joint working of the North East Constitutional Convention (NECC) and the North East Regional Assembly in the production of an agreed plan for regional government exemplifies this convergence. The NECC had been formed originally, in part at least, to broaden the debate about regional government beyond the usual political channels into wider civic arenas. In the West Midlands, on the other hand, the convention chair Cllr Phil Davis (leader of Telford and Wrekin council) was elected chair of the West Midlands Regional Chamber in mid-2001. The broad pattern of development is summarised in Figure 5.4.

A significant new actor on the political scene was the Campaign for the English Regions (CFER), which sought to act as the national voice of the various regional bodies. The CFER became an important actor in media debates about the English regional government, both nationally — where the media covered the issue — and regionally where the issue began to gain in profile in some parts of England, such as the Midlands and Yorkshire. Another important aspect of the CFER's work was in parliament, providing support for those MPs who kept the regional flag flying.

PUBLIC ATTITUDES

Unlike Scotland, Wales and London, there are no regular measures of regional opinion across the English regions. Where polls are conducted about attitudes to constitutional change they tend to be concerned with the attitudes of the English in general, rather than regional differences. Where regional polls are conducted, they tend to be inconsistent in the questions they ask and, on occasion, the boundaries they use. A poll for the BBC, in September 2000, however, threw up some interesting results concerning questions of regional identity and attitudes to regional government. It was published to accompany a series of regionally based programmes on English

Figure 5.4. Civic regionalism 2001

Region	State of Civic Regionalism
North East	Campaign for a North-east Assembly formed in 1992. North East Constitutional Convention formed in 1999. NECC now working with Regional Assembly producing case for regional government. Locally conducted polls typically indicate increasing support. Currently little active opposition. Major issue for regional media.
North West	North West Constitutional Convention established by local authorities in 2000 and endorsed by some stakeholders. No civic campaign as yet, but moves are underway to establish one. Low media profile.
Yorkshire	Active regional campaign (Campaign for Yorkshire and the Humber, see: www.cfy.org.uk/) established in 1999. Convention begun in 2000, to undertake detailed work on regional government. Low public awareness, but increasing media attention.
South West	Campaign for Regional Assembly just starting. Convention launched in May 2001. Chaired by Bishop of Exeter and supported by key stakeholders, notably Liberal Democrats. Low public awareness and media interest. Boundary problems (specifically the Cornish question, where active movement exists). Strongly opposed by active UK Independence Party (UKIP).
West Midlands	Campaign for a West Midlands Assembly established in 1999. Constitutional Convention launched in July 2001, funded by Cadbury Barrow Trust. Key stakeholders becoming involved. Launch of Convention in July 2001. Emerging media interest. Active public opposition from Conservative MPs and UKIP. The weight of Birmingham means that the debate about elected mayors overshadows the regional issue.
East Midlands	Stakeholders showing interest in regionalism. Moves afoot mainly by Liberal Democrats to establish a campaign for regional government. Minimal media interest.
Eastern	Some stakeholders showing interest. Minimal public interest. Media coverage ranges from the disinterested to the actively hostile.
South East	Some stakeholders showing interest. No civic interest. Negligible media interest.

identity.[37] The respondents were asked whether they regarded themselves as English, British or European. The survey revealed that almost half of the sample considered themselves to be English, just ahead of the proportion who considered themselves British. But there were notable regional variations. Those in the East, South East and South were most likely to consider

[37] See Tomaney and Hetherington 2000.

themselves English. Those in the South West, West, North East and North were the most likely to consider themselves British. In general, regional identity was thought to be far less important than being English, British or European. However, the survey again suggested there were large regional variations. There was greater regional identity in the North East than anywhere else. Indeed, of those who had considered themselves more English or European than British, regional identity was the primary source of identity. Regional identity was also stronger the further the distance from London. Respondents were also asked for their view on an elected Regional Assembly. Overall, less than half outside London and the South East (44 per cent) wanted an elected Regional Assembly. In the northern regions the level of support was higher. The East, South and East Midlands were the least enthusiastic.[38]

The only region where polls have tended to be conducted — albeit irregularly — is the North East of England. In January 2001 the Campaign for a North-east Assembly (CNA) published the results of a survey of opinion in the Prime Ministers' constituency of Sedgefield. The questions posed broadly mirrored those asked by Mori for *The Economist* in 1999.[39] The results of the survey (conducted in association with the University of Northumbria) are summarised in Figure 5.5.

The CNA repeated the exercise in a number of other parliamentary constituencies producing somewhat similar results and further confirming the North East as an outlier as far as civic regionalism is concerned.[40]

PARLIAMENT

English regional issues tended to figure sporadically in parliamentary questions and debates. One issue that excited the attention of backbenchers was the formation of the House of Commons Standing Committee on Regional Affairs, over a year after the Government first announced its intention to do so. The Committee met for first time on Thursday 10 May — Parliament's last full day before the UK general election.

The Committee's first debate concerned 'Regional Economic Performance and Imbalances'. The Committee received a report, from the then junior DETR minister Beverley Hughes, outlining the government's approach to these matters, while MPs used the meeting to raise many of the issues that have surrounded the debate on the English regions. In particular, Northern MPs used the committee to air their grievances surrounding the operation of the Barnett Formula and to raise the issue of devolution. Only one Conservative MP, Anthony Steen, attended the debate and he began by

[38] See Tomaney and Hetherington, 2000, for a more detailed treatment.
[39] See Tomaney 2000.
[40] See Tomaney 2001b, for further discussion.

announcing his intention to leave early. The meeting was noteworthy for Beverley Hughes's restatement of the government's commitment to publish a White Paper on regional government and her reiteration of the Government's commitment not to make local government reorganisation a pre-requisite for devolution in the English regions.[41]

Figure 5.5. Attitudes to regional government in Sedgefield

	Agree	Disagree	Don't know	Total
Too many decisions about the North East region are made by central government	246 (68%)	47 (13%)	69 (19%)	362
People in the North East should have more democratic control over what happens in their region	276 (76%)	36 (11%)	48 (13%)	362
A directly elected assembly for the North East should decide on issues like generating jobs and developing major roads and public transport	251 (69%)	58 (16%)	48 (13%)	362
The people of the North East should be given the opportunity in the next two years to choose whether or not they want an elected assembly	263 (73%)	48 (13%)	51 (14(%)	362
Source: Campaign for a North-East Assembly, *Listening to Sedgefield*, Newcastle upon Tyne.[42]				

Backbenchers continued to find opportunities to raise the regional question. North East (Labour) MPs tended to lead the way, but MPs from the North West and South West (especially Liberal Democrats in the latter case) were also active. Ministerial questions were the chief mechanism, but full debates were rare. But Austin Mitchell MP sponsored a debate on 'devolution' in Westminster Hall in January 2001 which he described as 'subterfuge' for the real issue of the debate', which he described as 'regional government'.[43] In the upper house the Bishop of Durham — the chair of the North East Constitutional Convention — introduced a debate on 'the case for devolution to the English regions'.[44] The debate in the House of Commons in June

[41] HC Deb, 10 May 2001; see also Tomaney and Hetherington 2001b.
[42] See Tomaney and Hetherington 2001a.
[43] See HC Deb, 17 January 2001, Col 95WH; see also Tomaney and Hetherington 2001a.
[44] HL Deb, 21 March 2001, col: 1427; see also Tomaney and Hetherington 2001b.

2001 on the Queen's Speech — which failed to mention the English regions — was used by a number of backbenchers, their numbers bolstered by ex-ministers, to demand early action on English regional government (see below).

WHITEHALL

Throughout Labour's first term the main locus of regional policy was the Department of the Environment, Transport and the Regions (DETR), presided over by the Deputy Prime Minister John Prescott. DETR sponsored RDAs, Regional Chambers, planning policy and sponsored most of the other non-departmental public bodies that had a strong regional presence. The regional brief, however, formed only one component of this vast department. The thinking behind the creation of DETR in 1997 was that it brought together policy areas that embodied considerable spillovers. A persistent criticism of DETR, throughout its existence, was that it proved too big, with Prescott himself having a brief that was too wide to be effective. In the period before the UK general election of 2001, the future of DETR was subject to much speculation, with predictions that, in line with their evolving role in relation to the Government's industry policy, RDAs would become a responsibility of DTI. Further speculation suggested that John Prescott would move to a new role in the Cabinet Office, keeping the regional portfolio and a range of other responsibilities.

Shortly after the UK general election the Prime Minister announced major changes to the machinery of government, which had implications for the governance of the English regions.[45] Among the relevant changes were:

- **An Office of the Deputy Prime Minister** was established in the Cabinet Office. The DPM, John Prescott, will chair a number of key Cabinet Committees. These include a new Committee of the Nations and Regions, which, among other things, will develop policy on the English regions. The DPM will oversee the delivery of the manifesto pledges, as well as dealing with important cross-departmental issues, including social exclusion. The Regional Co-ordination Unit, the Government Offices in the Regions, along with the Social Exclusion Unit, now report to the DPM in the Cabinet Office. The DPM will also retain final responsibility for the production of the White Paper on regional government.
- **The new Department for the Environment, Food and Rural Affairs (DEFRA)** was created to promote green issues and the countryside. In addition to taking over responsibility for agriculture, the food industry and fisheries from MAFF, it took on the environment, rural development, countryside, wildlife and sustainable development responsibilities of the former Department of the Environment, Transport and the Regions

---

[45] Tomaney, Hetherington and Humphrey 2001, for more discussion.

(DETR). It sponsors the Environment Agency, the Countryside Agency and English Nature. It will also take on responsibility for animal welfare and hunting, previously a responsibility of the Home Office.

- **The new Department for Transport, Local Government and the Regions (DTLR)** is, according to the Prime Minister, 'designed to give sharper focus' to the old DETR's responsibilities for transport, as well as local government, housing, planning, regeneration, urban and regional policy. It assumed responsibility for the fire service and electoral law from the Home Office.
- **The Department of Trade and Industry (DTI)** assumed responsibility for the Regional Development Agencies, where they will sit alongside the department's regional economic responsibilities. The DTI also assumed sponsorship of the construction industry, which had hitherto rested with the DETR.

One important outcome of these changes concerned the production of the Government's White Paper, with responsibility being divided between the new Office of the Deputy Prime Minister and the new DTLR and the Regions, headed by a new Secretary of State, Stephen Byers, and his Regions minister, Nick Raynsford. Although both ministers were quick to promise action on regional government, they also acknowledged that they would need to balance this priority against others, such as local government reform and transport improvements.[46]

LONDON

As noted previously, a form of regional government exists in the case of London. However, the arrangements for London under the Greater London Authority (GLA) Act 1999 are markedly different from those for Scotland and Wales. In the first place, the GLA took over few central government functions. Most of the functions it acquired had previously been the responsibility of the Greater London Council before its abolition in 1986. A further distinctive feature of the GLA model is that executive authority is lodged with a directly elected mayor, whose activities are scrutinised by a 25-strong elected assembly. Although the direct functions that fall under the Mayor's authority are limited, his or her responsibilities are wide ranging. The GLA has a general power of competence, but in many areas (most notably transport) the Mayor's room for manoeuvre is constrained by the powers retained by the Secretary of State.[47]

The Mayor's direct tasks lie in the areas of emergency services, transport, economic development and policing. These powers are exercised through

---

[46] Tomaney, Hetherington and Humphrey 2001.
[47] See Tomaney 2000, 2001a.

four 'functional bodies': the London Fire and Emergency Planning Authority, Transport for London (TfL), the London Development Agency and the
Metropolitan Police Authority. The Mayor takes responsibility for the individual budgets of these bodies (but cannot switch resources between them)
and appoints the board of these bodies, which execute his strategies.
However, the Mayor has a responsibility to produce a range of statutory
plans or strategies, covering various areas of London life, which he began
drafting in the period July 2000-2001. By July 2001, two full strategies had
been issued, full drafts of three more had been prepared, and preparatory
work was under way on four more. These strategies generally require action
by a range of organisations not controlled by the Mayor and it remains to be
seen whether this 'network' form of governance can deliver improved policy
outcomes for the people of London.

  The election of Ken Livingstone as Mayor of London, following his expul-
sion from the Labour Party, complicates any analysis of the London model.
The bitterness of the election has helped to colour the attitude of the Blair
government to the Livingstone mayoralty (and vice versa) and meant that the
year to July 2001 was characterised by conflict and recrimination.

  At the centre of the dispute was a disagreement about the future of the
London Underground. The conflict has its roots in provisions contained in
the GLA Act 1999, which specified that full control over the London Underground would only be passed to TfL, once a 'public-private partnership'
(PPP) for its management was in place.[48] The Mayor and his newly appointed
transport commissioner, Bob Kiley, challenged the terms of the PPP negotiated between the government and private contractors, questioning its value
for money, its impact on safety issues and its legal basis. This meant that a
political, media and finally judicial conflict over the terms of the transfer
dominated the period to July 2001. The judicial process found in the UK
Government's favour, but the political consequences were far from clear.[49]
Otherwise the Mayor's ability to act in the transport field was limited to
making proposals for congestion charging and dedicated bus routes. The
Mayor made proposals for new Underground routes, but it was unclear how
these would be funded. The proposals for congestion charging and bus routes
proved controversial, but had the merit of stimulating a genuine debate about
the future of the private car in London.

  The Mayor's Spatial Development Strategy was also a source of contro-
versy, with its commitment to the promotion of 'skyscraper clusters'. The
Spatial Development Strategy also provided the first clear example of the
GLA's need to collaborate with the regions which surround London.

---

  [48] See section 141 of the GLA Act 1999 for the Mayor's general duty, Part IV, Chapter VII of the
GLA Act for provisions relating to the PPP; and Tomaney 2000.
  [49] Regina v London Underground Ltd and Another, Ex parte Transport for London *The Times* Law
Report, 2 August 2001.

Proposals for the development of the Thames Gateway (the area to the east of central London) mean that his strategies were discussed (and broadly approved) by the South East and East of England regional assemblies.

The Mayor also intervened in areas were he has no direct powers, but in which he can exercise his general power of competence. For instance he introduced the UK's first-ever 'Partnership Register' for same-sex relationships. In health policy (not presently an area where he can act), the Mayor has established a policy commission and now produces his own 'Health Bulletin'.

An additional feature of the Mayor's activities in the period July 2000-2001 was his willingness to make the case for additional resources for London. At the end of June 2001, Ken Livingstone set the metropolitan cat among the provincial pigeons by asking the UK Government to give Londoners some of 'their' money back. Ken Livingstone was fond of arguing that 85 per cent of his budget came directly from central government (with the balance coming from a precept on the boroughs). The resources available to the Mayor therefore depend on the financial settlement London, in general, secures from central government. The Mayor argued that as the engine of the UK economy, the capital must be allowed to keep more of the £20 billion it generates for the UK annually. He estimated that between £4 and £6 billion would help improve transport, provide more affordable housing, and fund more police officers. The Mayor's case rested on a study undertaken by Tony Travers of the London School of Economics which noted calculations from the Centre for Economics and Business Research that for every £1 spent by the Government in London the capital's taxpayers pay between £1.25 and £1.50.[50]

Inevitably, Livingstone's claims provoked an outcry in some quarters of the English regions and in Scotland and Wales. This included criticism from the South East next door. The chairman of the South East Development Agency, Alan Willett, summarised his position thus:

> London claims it is paying for the rest of the country, which just goes to show how a single statistic can distort reality. London does pay the largest amount of tax to the Exchequer, but it is also one of the largest recipients. It is the net figure that counts and the net contribution from our region is £17 billion a year, by far the largest of any region and far more than London.[51]

Part of the importance of the new structure in London lies in the assumption that the GLA model may prefigure the shape of regional government in England. The fact that the new minister at DTLR responsible for the English Regions, Nick Raynsford, was previously minister for London and therefore, largely responsible for the GLA Act reinforces that view. However, it is by

[50] See *Evening Standard*, 27 June 2001.
[51] At the annual meeting of the South East Regional Assembly, 11 July 2001; see www.southeast-a.gov.uk/reference_library/assembly_proceedings/2001/docs/110701/allan_willett_speech.doc

no means certain that such a model would have much support in those regions where a debate about regional government already exists. The powers assigned to the GLA reflect, in part, London's status as Europe's largest city-region. How relevant, for instance, is it for regions containing large rural areas? Also, given the arms-length nature of the functional bodies and the Mayor's inability to switch funds between budget heads, how does the GLA model contribute to the end of 'joined-up' government, which after all is said to be a key problem in the English regions?[52] The executive/scrutiny split has also been a source of frustration for members of the Greater London Assembly who are frank about their difficulties in influencing policy development, and itself raises major questions.

OUTLOOK

The UK general election of 2001 saw Labour's manifesto reaffirm its commitment to legislating for regional Assemblies 'where there is demand'. The manifesto was pored over by commentators and campaigners alike in the search for runes to read. In the event it sent yet more mixed signals. The manifesto revived the stipulation that 'predominantly unitary local government' was a condition for legislative action.[53] This appeared to be at odds with statements of DETR ministers over the previous period. This was taken by some as a signal of the cooling of Labour's ardour. On the other hand, hardly any attention was given to fact that the stipulation that Regional Assemblies should involve no additional public expenditure was dropped.

An additional innovation in the election campaign was the launch of a document entitled *Ambitions for the English Regions*, which set out Labour's past and future policies. While containing no surprises, it represented a radical shift in approach compared to 1997 when the English regions did not figure as a concept in Labour's election campaigning. The document was launched at a meeting in Wakefield on 30 May, which was jointly addressed by John Prescott and Gordon Brown. The meeting appeared to put the seal on a growing accord between the two about the importance of the regional issue, albeit one narrowly focused on economic development. John Prescott used the occasion to restate his commitment to English Regional Assemblies, which would be concerned with 'strategic' issues, such as economic development, planning and transport.[54] The Wakefield launch was followed by the launch of 'regional manifestos' in some of the English regions. The most detailed of these was published in the North East (*'Ambitions for the North East'*), although it was largely a reheated version of other Party documents.

---

[52] See Tomaney 2000; PIU 2000.
[53] *Ambitions for Britain*, pp. 34-5.
[54] Prescott 2001.

Taken together, these developments appeared to provide further evidence of Labour's new, but tentative, engagement with the regional issue.

The English question in the period after the UK general election looked set to be dominated by the politics of producing the White Paper on regional government. On the one hand, the UK Government's commitment to producing the White Paper signalled a new engagement with the English regions. On the other hand, some actors saw the absence of a mention for the English regions in the Queen's Speech as evidence of an enduring ambivalence on the part of the Government, notwithstanding the statements of Gordon Brown and others. The Queen's Speech debate in the House of Commons was notable for the interventions of former ministers — typically liberated by the post-Election reshuffle — calling for swift Government action on the issue. Ministers were at pains to stress their commitment to progressing English regional government. In a newspaper interview Stephen Byers suggested legislation could be brought forward in the 2002 Queen's Speech:

> What I want to do is have a White Paper, then for colleagues to agree there should be a slot in the Queen's Speech next year. I will be pushing for that. I do think it's right that if local people want to have a regional assembly we have got to be prepared to act on that. We are working on the White Paper, we will make good progress, and certainly the plan is to do it within the next six months.[55]

Ministers are likely to act when they feel pressured to do so. A key question concerns where the political pressure points lie. These might be found in the interventions in the Queen's Speech debate by ex-ministers. Freed of the ordinance of silence, and not easily dismissed as members of the 'awkward squad', these interventions by ex-ministers suggested a rockier backbench ride on the issue for the Government in its second term. The architect of New Labour, Peter Mandelson, could not have been plainer in a speech given to the Centre for Urban and Regional Development Studies at Newcastle University on the day after the Queen's Speech:

> I believe that if a second term Labour Government fails to act on regional devolution it will leave the constitutional settlement enacted by New Labour dangerously unbalanced. Indeed, it might lead some to question the legitimacy of those constitutional changes. More importantly, it will fail to address how we improve the capacity of the state to act.[56]

A further factor, already in play by the summer of 2001, was rising manufacturing job losses in Labour's northern heartlands, some in the constituencies of prominent ministers. While hardly news in regions like the North East, they promised to return the politics of the North/South divide to public attention and provide grist to the mill of devolution campaigners.

[55] *The Journal* [Newcastle] 13 July 2001.
[56] Quoted in Tomaney and Hetherington 2001c.

BIBLIOGRAPHY

Official Documents

DETR (2000). *Planning Policy Guidance Note 11: Regional Planning*. Available at: www.planning.detr.gov.uk/ppg11/index.htm

DTI (2001) *Opportunity For All In a World of Change: A White Paper on Enterprise, Skills and Innovation*. London: Department of Trade and Industry/Department for Education and Employment. (http://www.dti.gov.uk/opportunityforall).

HM Treasury (2000a) *Spending Review 2000: Prudent for a Purpose. Building Opportunity and Security for All*. (http://www.hm-treasury.gov.uk/sr2000/report/index.html)

HM Treasury (2000b) *Building Long-term Prosperity for All. Pre-Budget Report*. (Cm 4917). (http://www.hm-treasury.gov.uk/pbr2000/report/Contents.htm.)

PIU (2000) *Reaching Out. The role of central government and the regional and local level*. London: The Stationary Office.

Secondary Sources

Balls E (2000) 'Britain's new regional policy', in Balls, E and Healey, J (Ed.) *Towards a New Regional Policy: Delivering Growth and Full Employment*. London: The Smith Institute.

Balls, E. and Healey, J. (2000). *Towards a New Regional Policy: Delivering Growth and Full Employment*. London: The Smith Institute.

Brown, G. (2001). 'Enterprise and the regions', speech by Gordon Brown MP, Chancellor of the Exchequer, at UMIST on Monday 29 January 2001, HM Treasury News Release 02/01, 29 January 2001. www.hm-treasury.gov.uk/press/2001/p02_01.html

Byers, S. (2001). 'Turning Change into Opportunity: the Next Steps for Industrial Policy', Speech to the Social Market Foundation, 4 May. Www.dti.gov.uk/ministers/speeches/byers040501.html

Hall, G (2000) 'Rising to the challenge', in Balls, E and Healey, J (Ed.) *Towards a New Regional Policy: Delivering Growth and Full Employment*. London: The Smith Institute.

Mandelson, P. (2001). 'Keynote address', 'The State of the English Regions Seminar', University of Newcastle, 21 June 2001.

Prescott, J. (2001). 'Ambitions for our Regions', Wakefield, 30 May 2001. London: Labour Party.

Sandford. M. and McQuail, P. (2000). 'Unexplored Territory: Elected Regional Assemblies in England', London: Constitution Unit.

Tomaney, J. (2000). 'Regional Governance in England', in R Hazell (ed.) *The State and the Nations: The First Year of Devolution in the United Kingdom*. Exeter: Imprint Academic.

Tomaney, J (2001a). 'The new governance of London: a case of 'post-democratic' politics?', *City*, 5, 2: 225–248.

Tomaney, J. (2001b). 'Identity and politics - the regional government debate in the North East', *Northern Economic Review*, 31: 56-69.

Tomaney, J. and Hetherington, P. (2000). *Monitoring the English Regions. Report No. 1* [November 2000]. Centre for Urban and Regional Development Studies, University of Newcastle upon Tyne.
www.ucl.ac.uk/constitution-unit/leverh/index.htm

Tomaney, J, and Hetherington, P. (2001a). *Monitoring the English Regions: Report No 2* [February 2001].
www.ucl.ac.uk/constitution-unit/leverh/index.htm

Tomaney, J. and Hetherington, P. (2001b). *Monitoring the English Regions: Report No 3* [May 2001]. www.ucl.ac.uk/constitution-unit/leverh/index.htm

Tomaney, J. and Humphrey, L. (2001). *Powers and Functions of a Regional Assembly. A Study for the North East Regional Assembly.* Centre for Urban and Regional Development Studies, University of Newcastle upon Tyne.
www.northeastassembly.org.uk/publications/subpage/reggov.pdf

Tomaney, J., Hetherington, P. and Humphrey, L. (2001). *Monitoring the English Regions: Report No 4* [August 2001].
www.ucl.ac.uk/constitution-unit/leverh/index.htm

Part II

The State

6

Finance — The Barnett Formula: Nobody's Child?

David Bell and Alex Christie

INTRODUCTION

The issue of how devolution is funded in the UK was never far from the head-lines during 2000 and 2001. The funding mechanism was roundly attacked by all shades of political opinion, both in the centre and the periphery, but the UK Government steadfastly refused to countenance change, even though there have been a stream of complaints within the Labour Party, particularly among MPs from the north of England. An uneasy truce has descended, but unless this issue can be satisfactorily resolved, the tensions caused by the perceived unfairness of the system of allocating of resources between the constituent parts of the UK will undermine the legitimacy of devolution.

The funding arrangement in question is, of course, the Barnett Formula, the mechanism by which financial resources have been allocated by HM Treasury to Scotland, Wales and Northern Ireland for the last two decades. The formula was named after the Chief Secretary to the Treasury, Joel Barnett, in the Callaghan overnment, but has direct antecedents that can be traced back to the 'Goschen' formula of 1888, when the Chancellor of the day, George Goschen, used a similar mechanism to allocate revenues to local government.

But notwithstanding this long history, the Barnett Formula is now almost without friends. Even Joel Barnett, its originator, has disowned it. This chapter investigates some of the reasons why politicians have grown increasingly disenchanted with the formula during last year. It concentrates on three main issues:

1. The first concerns the complaint that the formula does not allocate a fair *level* of spending among the component parts of the UK;

2. The second concerns the growing unease that the formula is putting the nascent system of devolved government in the UK under strain;

3. The final argument is concerned with the difficulties of incorporating the Barnett Formula with the rest of the UK's fiscal structure.

But before addressing the reasons why there has been a growing clamour for change to the Barnett Formula in the last twelve months, we must first explain a little of its background and how it has suited successive UK Governments and, in particular, the Treasury, that it should survive.

THE BARNETT FORMULA

The Barnett Formula determines the *changes* in resources available to the Scottish Parliament, the National Assembly for Wales and the Northern Ireland Assembly based on a fixed share of any *changes* agreed between the Treasury and departments that operate in England (or in some cases England and Wales) in the value of 'comparable programmes'. Northern Ireland's allocation is based on expenditures in Great Britain. The share, which is updated regularly, is based on the size of the population in the relevant devolved authority as a percentage of that in England (or England and Wales, or Great Britain).

The 'comparability percentage' of each spending programme under the control of Westminster is assessed each year. The percentages are dependent on the extent to which the spending programme covers reserved or non-reserved matters. For example, comparability percentages for social security are 0 per cent in Scotland and Wales, but 100 in Northern Ireland. This is because social security is a reserved issue as far as the Scottish Parliament and the National Assembly for Wales are concerned. This is not the case in Northern Ireland, where the Assembly controls social security spending, at least in theory. Though this is an important difference in principle, in practice social security benefits in Northern Ireland are paid at the same rates as in Great Britain and the Treasury retains the right to amend the assigned budget should the Assembly choose to vary the rates paid relative to Great Britain.

For most spending programmes relating to education, the comparability percentage is 100 per cent for each of the devolved administrations. For example, the budget of the Higher Education Funding Council for England (HEFCE) is 100 per cent comparable. It was allocated a budget of £4.33 billion in 2000/01. If this increased by, say, £100 million in financial year 2001/02, then the increase in the assigned budgets would be as shown in Figure 6.1.

Thus, a commitment to increase spending on higher education by £100 million in England translates into a total financial commitment of around £120 million for the UK as a whole. It is important to note that the Barnett formula, though dependent on the changes in spending programmes in England (or GB in the case of Northern Ireland) does not place any obligation on the devolved administrations to spend the increases in the same way

Figure 6.1. Barnett-determined increases in assigned budgets resulting from £100 million increase in funding to HEFCE

Devolved Administration	Comparability percentage	Population/ Population of England	Barnett-determined increase in Budget (£million)
Scotland	100	0.1034	£10.34
Wales	100	0.0593	£ 5.93
Northern Ireland	100	0.0341	£ 3.41[1]

Source: HM Treasury 2000b

as in England (or GB). This is not a new feature brought about by devolution — the Secretaries of State for Northern Ireland, Scotland and Wales have always been free to reflect the spending priorities of their territories. The relationship between HM Treasury and the devolved administrations was codified in *Funding the Scottish Parliament, National Assembly for Wales and Northern Ireland Assembly — A Statement of Funding Policy.*[2]

The fact that the Barnett mechanism has survived the significant constitutional changes associated with devolution is a testament to the strength of the Treasury and its determination to control the key macroeconomic variables in the UK economy. Principal amongst these are the fiscal stance — the balance of government spending and taxation — and the extent of public borrowing. The Treasury's determination to control government debt led to the denial of significant borrowing powers to any of the devolved authorities. Instead, capital spending is either funded from the current budget or from Public Private Partnerships (PPPs). And Treasury determination to control taxation and public spending is evident from the extent to which the arrangements for devolution reflect its determination to micro-manage the UK fiscal stance. Take, for example, the principles relating to local council spending in Scotland:

> Should self-financed expenditure start to rise steeply, the Scottish Parliament would clearly come under pressure from council tax payers in Scotland to exercise its powers. If growth relative to England were excessive and were such as to threaten targets set for public expenditure as part of the management of the UK economy, and the Scottish Parliament nevertheless chose not to exercise its

[1] The budget assigned to Northern Ireland is reduced by a further 2.5 per cent to reflect the differential treatment of VAT in Northern Ireland. VAT payments made by Northern Ireland departments are refunded by Customs and Excise. In the rest of the UK, this is not the case and therefore departments require provision to meet their VAT commitments.

[2] HM Treasury 2000.

powers, it would be open to the UK Government to take the excess into account in considering the level of their support for expenditure in Scotland.[3]

There is clearly an implicit threat that if the Scottish Parliament fails to curb 'excessive' council spending, then the Treasury will penalise the Parliament by reducing the size of the assigned budget.

Tight control by central government has the benefit of producing 'fiscal clarity'. Federal states or states where devolved government has significant fiscal authority require legal mechanisms to resolve disputes between central and devolved governments. For example, in both Germany and Spain, the constitutional courts are charged with this duty. Disputes are frequently complex and lengthy, and thus inimical to detailed fiscal management. The German Constitutional Court has this year demanded a clarification of the principles on which transfers between the wealthier and poorer Länder take place, after some of the richer states complained about the size of the contribution they were being expected to make to poorer states.[4] The constitutional court in Spain has had to deal with long-running disputes over whether central government or the regional and municipal authorities control the salaries of government employees.

There are no parallel legal arrangements in the UK. If any of the devolved administrations are unhappy with its settlement from the Barnett Formula, the *Statement of Funding Policy* suggests that the issue should be taken up with Treasury ministers.[5] It might be possible for the relevant Secretary of State to appeal to the Joint Ministerial Committee, which is dominated by UK departments. The devolved authorities are in a very weak position in comparison to their counterparts in Germany or Spain. This may be good for fiscal clarity at the macro level, but makes life difficult for devolved administrations that are keen to differentiate their policies from those of the centre.

This issue has been addressed by Iain McLean.[6] He argues that the perceived unfairness of the Barnett Formula, the asymmetrical nature of devolution and the lack of any significant taxation powers in the devolved administrations suggest that the UK requires a 'fiscal constitution'. His preferred model is Australia, where the third party, which weighs the respective claims of the State governments, is the Commonwealth Grants Commission. It stands at arms length from the Commonwealth (federal government) and allocates revenues between the States using the principal of fiscal equalisation, which broadly implies that each State should be given resources to supply services of the same standard, if they make the same effort to raise taxes and operate at the same level of efficiency.

---

[3] Scottish Office 1997.
[4] OECD 2001.
[5] HM Treasury 2000, paras. 11.1-2.
[6] McLean 2000.

The Barnett Formula is part of a political process that allows the centre to retain tight control over the resources available to the devolved administrations and thus the extent to which they can differentiate their policies. The devolved authorities each have a cake that they can divide however they choose, but they cannot take a policy decision to change the size of the cake.

Other formulae could be used to distribute resources to the devolved authorities, yet still allow the centre to retain the same high degree of political and fiscal control. Chief among the alternatives is the so-called 'needs assessment'. This mechanism operates by allocating funds to different areas based on an assessment of the different levels of resource required to provide a common standard of service across the whole country. Our research for the Leverhulme Trust suggested that such mechanisms are commonplace throughout industrialised countries. Indeed, needs assessments are used to distribute funds to local authorities in England, Scotland and Wales and within the NHS in both Scotland and England. [7]

Our research also suggested that the Barnett Formula is unique in the developed world. There is no country other than the UK that allocates resources at a sub-national level using a formula based on changes, rather than levels of spending in relation to assessed need. We now go on to consider the three difficulties with the formula that have been highlighted in the last twelve months and that were mentioned in the introduction.

LEVELS OF FUNDING

On 19 July 2001, Joyce Quin, MP for Gateshead asked the Chief Secretary to the Treasury if he had any plans to review the Barnett Formula.[8] Her question was motivated by a widespread view in the north-east of England that this region is disadvantaged by the Barnett Formula and that a needs-based assessment would be more appropriate. The Scottish Parliament's policies such as the abolition of tuition fees, higher salaries and better conditions for teachers and better conditions of service, and the provision of free personal care for the elderly have only increased the grievance felt in the north of England. The data in Figures 6.2 and 6.3 show that there are significant differences between and among the devolved jurisdictions and the English regions.

On a per capita basis, spending in key policy areas such as health and education in Scotland and Northern Ireland remains substantially above that in England and well above the UK average. Figure 6.3 shows that the north-east and north-west of England spent significantly less per capita in 1999-2000 across most key programmes than did London and the devolved authorities.

[7] See DETR 2000 and Scottish Executive 1999.
[8] HC Deb, 9 July 2001, col. 425.

Figure 6.2. Per capita identifiable total managed expenditure by country and function 1999-2000 (in £ million)

	England	Scotland	Wales	Northern Ireland	United Kingdom
Education	659	863	682	935	685
Health and personal social services	1,041	1,271	1,180	1,193	1,072
Roads and transport	133	180	154	123	138
Housing	42	90	74	166	51
Other environmental services	134	188	242	153	144
Law, order and protective services	305	302	302	649	315
Trade, industry, energy and employment	103	171	130	293	115
Agriculture, fisheries, food and forestry	55	200	116	212	75
Culture, media and sport	88	88	140	53	89
Social security	1,682	1,865	1,983	2,069	1,724
Miscellaneous expenditure (1)	42	53	50	94	45
Total	4,283	5,271	5,052	5,939	4,453

Source: HM Treasury 2001

The argument from the north of England is that these differences cannot be justified on the basis of need. However the assertion that Scotland and Northern Ireland receive over-generous budget allocations is difficult to demonstrate if one considers the whole spectrum of government policies as a proper needs assessment should do. There has not been any UK-wide needs assessment for over 20 years. However, we can conduct a very simple needs-assessment exercise, which will indicate that the grievances of northern politicians may be genuine. To do this we have constructed a crude

Figure 6.3. Per capita identifiable total managed expenditure by region and function 1999-2000 (in £ million)

(Source: HM Treasury 2001)	North East	North West	Yorks & Humberside	East Midlands	West Midlands	South West	Eastern	London	South East	Total England*
Education	649	654	620	603	655	592	616	706	544	625
Health and personal social services	986	970	964	886	919	917	950	1190	816	957
Roads and transport	134	135	122	138	131	119	138	185	157	143
Housing	55	63	53	30	30	4	32	144	32	53
Other environmental services	153	120	116	122	130	124	123	143	134	129
Law, order and protective services	295	297	268	261	253	247	215	433	235	282
Trade, industry, energy and employment	107	96	91	84	90	93	90	98	80	91
Agriculture, fisheries, food and forestry	57	57	58	56	55	57	52	55	59	56
Culture Media and Sport	87	90	61	58	64	61	58	136	63	77
Social security	1973	1854	1655	1540	1622	1574	1454	1608	1410	1609
Central administration and miscellaneous	42	49	34	36	36	34	36	47	37	39
Total	4539	4385	4042	3814	3986	3823	3764	4746	3566	4085

* The differences in per capita spending in England as between Figures 6.2 and 6.3 are due to differences in the ability to determine **identifiable** public expenditure as between the regional level within England and between the countries of the United Kingdom. These differences have been taken account of in subsequent calculations.

indicator of relative need.[9] Rates and regulations for social security are common throughout the UK. High levels of social security payments tend to be linked with high levels of unemployment, inactivity and dependency. They are also indicative of low levels of income. Per head social security payments are thus simple, but plausible, indicators of relative need.

One way of judging the generosity of public provision in a particular region would then be to take the ratio of total identifiable expenditure to social security spending in that region. Large values of this ratio crudely indicate that overall public spending is high, given the apparent level of need and vice versa. Values for 1999-2000 are shown in Figure 6.4. It is immediately apparent that the regions in the north of England come out worst from this calculation. But interestingly, the highest level of provision is not in any of the devolved jurisdictions, but instead in London. One explanation in London's defence is that it is considerably more expensive to provide a common standard of service in London than elsewhere due to higher wages, property prices and cost of living. Similarly, costs are higher in Scotland and Wales because of the low population density. High costs in London and rurality in Scotland and Wales are not reflected in a measure of need based solely on social security payments, but it is difficult to believe that this is sufficient justification for the substantial differences in our chosen measure between these areas and those in the north of England.

Figure 6.4. Identifiable public expenditure relative to 'need' 1999-2000

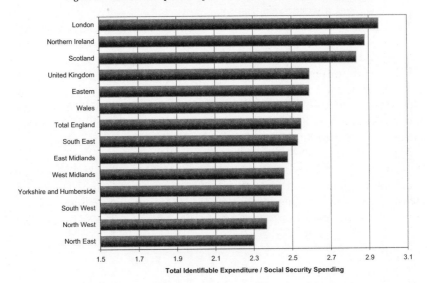

---

[9] We are grateful to Peter Jones of *The Economist* for this suggestion.

CHANGES IN FUNDING

On 9 May 2001, Mr David Trimble asked the Secretary of State for Northern Ireland if he had had discussions with the Chancellor with regard to the Barnett Formula.[10] His question was motivated by a realisation that the changes in spending proposed under the Comprehensive Spending Review (CSR) and determined by the Barnett Formula for the period 2000-2003 implied a smaller proportionate rise in spending in Northern Ireland than in Scotland, Wales or England. [11]

The reason why the increase in Northern Ireland is smaller than in other parts of the UK has to do with the so-called 'Barnett squeeze'. One of us has explained how the mathematics of the Barnett Formula implies that the process of applying population-based changes to different levels of expenditure will eventually equalise per capita public expenditure throughout the UK.[12] The Formula ensures that those areas that enjoy higher levels of per capita spending receive slightly lower proportionate rises in spending than those with lower levels of per capita spending. Hence Northern Ireland, which from Figure 6.2 has the highest per capita spending among the constituent parts of the UK, can expect the lowest increases and hence Mr Trimble's question. HM Treasury has agreed that the formula will bring about equality in per capita expenditure across the UK. In response to questioning by Ms Quin on 19 July 2001, Andrew Smith, Chief Secretary to the Treasury described it as a 'convergence formula'. The rate of convergence increases with the rate of growth in public spending in those areas to which the formula applies and with the rate of inflation.

But if the Barnett Formula is indeed a convergence formula, how sustainable are the commitments to additional spending that have been made by the devolved authorities and which these authorities very much see as measures that deliver the differentiation from Westminster that legitimises devolution? These include higher teachers' salaries in Scotland following from the McCrone Committee's Report,[13] free prescriptions for under-25s in Wales and the commitment to free personal care for the elderly that has been made by the Scottish Executive.[14]

The simple answer is that these are not sustainable in the long run. The Barnett Formula will eventually equalise per capita spending (irrespective of need) in England, Scotland, Wales and Northern Ireland. Hence any measures that imply higher levels of spending on one section of the community by the devolved authorities will have to be counterbalanced by measures

---

[10] Hansard 9 May 2001.
[11] HM Treasury 2000a.
[12] Bell 2001.
[13] Scottish Executive 2000.
[14] Scottish Executive 2001.

that imply less spending on other sections of the community. So, for example, free personal care for the elderly in Scotland might be bought at the cost of poorer nursery provision in Scotland compared to England.

Even if per capita spending is not equalised, but instead adjusted for need, the same argument that additional spending commitments would not be sustainable would still apply. This is because needs adjustments measure the spending required to deliver a *common* level of service across areas. It is implicitly based on an assumption that broadly common services will be delivered. For example, a needs adjustment would not be sustainable if there were substantively different approaches to health service funding between devolved authorities.

There is an underlying question as to whether a form of devolution that confers significant policymaking powers to sub-national governments is consistent with needs-based allocation systems that are controlled by central government. If central government is at liberty to design and amend the 'common level of service' which it is prepared to fund in the regions and which forms the basis of the needs assessment, how can sub-national governments implement policies that are significantly different from those applied at the centre? Even though such policies might have wide public support in the regions, the devolved authorities will not be able to implement the policy change unless:

1. they make significant efficiency gains in other parts of public services or;

2. they cut back on the provision of other services or;

3. they are able to find new sources of revenue to fund the desired changes.

The first option is difficult if (as is the case in the UK) there are national pay scales for a significant proportion of public service workers, and legislation constrains the way in which many public services are provided. The second is likely to inflict significant costs on other groups in society. The political costs of removing services always tend to be higher than the costs of not providing them in the first instance. The final option requires a greater degree of fiscal autonomy than the UK Treasury is currently prepared to contemplate.

The effect of the squeeze can be seen in Figure 6.5, which shows how the UK Government planned to increase spending in areas where it is reasonably predictable and which therefore are included in Departmental Expenditure Limits (DELs). For the devolved administrations, DELs incorporate the vast majority of spending programmes that are covered by the Barnett Formula.[15]

---

[15] The most important item of spending not included in DELs, because it is difficult to predict in the medium term and which is also not included in the Barnett Formula, is social security spending. Hence the Barnett squeeze does not apply to this significant component of spending, but since it is not

The CSR in 2000 set out plans for DELs for the next four years. These included substantial increases for major Whitehall departments, particularly health and education. The Barnett Formula was applied to these increases and as expected, the projected increases are smaller in areas that already enjoy high levels of per capita spending. Figure 6.5 shows the effects by comparing the planned DEL with an 'England-adjusted' DEL which applies the (higher) growth rates from the increase in DELs for those departments that operate mainly in England alone of for the UK as a whole. The difference between actual DEL and the 'Adjusted' DEL measures the 'loss' that the devolved administrations have suffered through having their DELs determined by the Barnett Formula, rather than having spending grow at the same rate as the budget for the English and UK-wide departments.

Figure 6.5. The Barnett squeeze under planned departmental expenditure limits (DELs) All figures in £ million

Scotland			
Year	DEL	Adjusted	Difference
1999-00	13,900		
2000-01	15,047	15,392	345
2001-02	16,231	16,750	519
2002-03	17,369	18,128	759
2003-04	18,428	19,454	1,026
Wales			
1999-00	7,100		
2000-01	7,758	7,862	104
2001-02	8,447	8,556	109
2002-03	9,140	9,260	120
2003-04	9,788	9,937	149
Northern Ireland			
1999-00	4,900		
2000-01	5,306	5,426	120
2001-02	5,667	5,905	238
2002-03	5,973	6,390	417
2003-04	6,294	6,858	564
Source: HM Treasury, 2001a, and authors' own calculations			

controlled by the devolved administrations, it cannot be used to make good 'losses' resulting from the Barnett squeeze. In Northern Ireland social security spending is not a reserved issue and the Northern Ireland Assembly could theoretically divert social security funds, but the Treasury only supplies funds on a claimant-count basis and to divert funds would require the Assembly to fail to meet its social security obligations.

A brief perusal of this table reveals Mr Trimble's concern about where the Barnett Formula is leading. If Northern Ireland received the same rate of growth in spending as the UK as a whole, its DEL would be 8.2 per cent higher by 2003-2004, and in Scotland, the DEL will be some £889 million less than it would have been in 2003-04 had not the Barnett squeeze taken effect. Scotland and Northern Ireland were the 'losers' from this spending review in the sense that, although they have started from a more favourable position, growth rates in the resources available to key public services will be more rapid in the regions of England during the period of this spending review. The devolved administrations in Edinburgh and Belfast are aware of this and they realise that the Barnett Formula is the culprit. Thus, the northern regions of England have spent the last year complaining that the Barnett Formula does not deliver sufficient resources compared with Scotland and Northern Ireland. Meanwhile the Scots and Northern Irish complain that the formula is not maintaining the spending advantage that they have historically enjoyed.

In reality, none of the politicians can justify their arguments for higher or lower levels of expenditure because, as we mentioned above, the Barnett Formula is a convergence formula. Convergence relies on continued growth in public spending, with the rate of convergence being greater the greater the growth rate of public spending. Unlike almost all mechanisms used to allocate resources at a sub-national level in other advanced nations, it does not reflect relative need. And since no attempt has been made to measure relative need for over twenty years, the arguments that we have seen in the last twelve months for changes to Barnett-determined allocations are built on partial and incomplete evidence.

Returning to the issue of convergence, it is clear that as far as Ms Quin is concerned, it is not happening fast enough and as far as Mr Trimble is concerned, it is happening too quickly. The Barnett Formula is caught in a pincer movement between those who want to protect their existing spending advantages and those who wish to undermine the status quo. The Barnett Formula cannot provide a valid reference point for this debate, because it is only concerned with changes and not with the relative priorities that can be attached to competing claims for resources from different parts of the UK. Until there is some intellectual basis for the discussion of relative priorities, the Barnett debate will be conducted simply on the basis of 'winners' and 'losers'.

So far, we have avoided mention of Wales. From Figure 6.3, it is clear that the Welsh DEL will only be modestly affected by the Barnett squeeze and from Figure 6.4, it appears that Wales is reasonably well resourced, given our crude indicator of need. Does this imply that Wales, unlike all other parts of the UK, is reasonably content with the Barnett formula? The answer to this question is a resounding 'no', but to see why we must consider the difficulties of integrating the Barnett Formula with parts of the UK fiscal structure and, in particular, those parts that are designed to take account of need.

THE BARNETT FORMULA AND OTHER FUNDING MECHANISMS

The European Union (EU) allocates structural funds based on measures of need that are common throughout Europe. Under its criteria, 65 per cent of the Welsh population are in areas designated as having Objective 1 status, and thus are eligible for the highest level of assistance from the structural funds. Now one might naively assume that payments under Objective 1 programmes would result in a simple transfer of funds from Europe to Wales — and that such transfers would have nothing to do with the Barnett Formula. This assumption is entirely wrong. The interaction between EU funding and the Barnett Formula has caused serious political difficulties — principally in Wales, but also in Scotland during the last year — which have only been solved by a classic British 'fudge'.

The difficulty arises because the Treasury treats such EU funding as UK expenditure, on the argument that the UK is a net contributor to the EU and thus EU grants are ultimately funded by the UK taxpayer. A large prospective increase in EU funding to England will therefore be reflected in the DELs of the relevant English departments. As well as setting limits on departmental spending, these DELs determine the assigned budget of the devolved authorities in conjunction with the Barnett Formula. Scotland, Wales and Northern Ireland will therefore benefit from increased funding even though the intention of the EU was to meet the particular needs of England. The culprit for this unintended consequence is once again the Barnett Formula.

But what if the reverse occurs? This is exactly the situation that caused crisis in the Welsh Assembly and led to the resignation of Alun Michael. In the 2000-2006 set of Structural Fund awards, the EU decided that the *relative need* in Wales merited a much higher level of support than in England. But the Barnett-determined Welsh budget did not reflect this EU priority and raised the spectre of the National Assembly having to cut back on it major spending programmes in order to meet its commitments to deliver projects agreed with the EU. Compounding this difficulty is the EU requirement that such projects attract matched funding from local sources. It is often difficult to raise such funding from private sources, but this only returns the funding burden to the public sector and ultimately the Barnett-determined Assembly budget.

This situation was so plainly crazy that in last year's CSR the Treasury changed the baseline for the Barnett formula in Wales, increasing it by

almost £300 million between 2000-2001 and 2003-2004. Aside from allevi-
ating the immediate problems of the Welsh administration, this development
raises two important issues for the future of devolution.

The first is that the CSR is the obvious vehicle for making alterations to the
Barnett baseline. The CSR has now become the Treasury's accepted vehicle
for making significant changes to the direction of government spending.
Politicians who seek to change the Barnett Formula should be aware of this
reality, particularly as the Treasury will shortly commence work on the next
CSR, which will come into effect in 2004-2005. One of us has argued previously that the optimum strategy for UK Government might be to ignore calls
for revisions to the Formula until the Barnett squeeze brings relative spending levels close to what might be expected from a needs assessment. This
should reduce the political costs of moving to a needs-based funding mechanism.[16] One difficulty with this strategy is that funding levels in Wales are
probably close to this level already, whereas it will take some time for this to
occur in Scotland and Northern Ireland. If this is likely to cause further political difficulty in Wales, it is open to the UK Government to make further
adjustments to the Welsh baseline in the next CSR.

The second issue is whether the difficulties with Europe would have been
so easily solved if the administration in Westminster had not been broadly
sympathetic to that in Cardiff. Would the Treasury have adjusted the CSR if
the relationship with Cardiff had been adversarial? So long as the devolved
administrations have no legal right to challenge Treasury decisions, they will
always be subject to UK macroeconomic priorities. Unlike many other
advanced countries, there is no arbitration mechanism, such as a constitutional court to resolve such differences.

The case of EU funding in Wales is not an isolated one. Take, for example,
the responsibility for bearing the unexpected costs associated with the
Foot-and-Mouth Disease outbreak. The UK Government decided that
Foot-and-Mouth was a UK matter and therefore compensation payments to
farmers would be met from the UK reserve. In contrast, the overrun of costs
on the Scottish Parliament will be met from a contingency fund that the Scottish Executive is building up. But what if Foot-and-Mouth had only occurred
in Wales and Scotland and the parties in power differed between Edinburgh
and Cardiff on the one hand and Westminster on the other? Without borrowing powers and with relatively small reserves, Foot-and-Mouth would have
seriously damaged the budgets of the Welsh Assembly and Scottish Parliament had the UK Government not decided that compensation payments
should be met from UK sources.

And it is not only the relationship with the Treasury that affects the progress of independent policymaking in the devolved authorities. Take, for
example, the policy of free personal care for the elderly, which has recently

[16] Bell 2001.

been investigated by the Scottish Executive. One of the key issues that will determine the overall cost of this policy to the Executive is how the Department of Work and Pensions (DWP) interprets the rules regarding payment of Attendance Allowance — a payment that is currently made as a contribution towards personal care for the elderly and infirm. Strictly applied, current DWP rules imply that Attendance Allowance will be withdrawn from the elderly in Scotland if the Executive introduces free personal care, while continuing to be available in the rest of the UK. This might seem unjust and could cause the Executive to abandon plans for free personal care, but again the devolved authority has no recourse other than political argument.

The legislation that set up the devolved institutions has left them in a weak position to resist the imposition of funding settlements decided solely by Westminster. The current situation, which relies on ad hoc adjustments and agreements, would be difficult to sustain if the devolved governments were of a different political hue from that in the centre.

One escape route would be to offer greater fiscal freedom to the devolved authorities. During the last 12 months, the Liberal Democrats, as well as the SNP have supported this approach. It also, notoriously, gained the support of 12 economists from Scottish universities in a letter written to *The Scotsman* just before the election.[17] They advocated a move towards fiscal autonomy — allowing Scotland to tax and spend on its own account.

There are a wide range of international examples where local or state governments exert varying degrees of local control over personal, sales, property and value added tax. The arguments in favour of local control over taxation and spending are broadly that:

1. Devolved governments know more about the preferences of their citizens than central government,

2. Policy differences between devolved authorities can provide valuable experiments in policy design,

3. Centrally determined rules are likely to be less flexible to meet local conditions, either due to political constraints that force equal treatment of different localities or because central government prefers simple allocation mechanisms,

4. Decentralisation protects taxpayers from excessive taxation by central government because devolved areas will compete to offer individuals and businesses lower rates of taxation.

The main arguments against devolving taxes are that:

1. There will be unwelcome 'spillover' effects from one authority to the next if they pursue different tax and spend strategies (an example

---

[17] *The Scotsman*, 18 May 2001.

might be the influx of the elderly into Scotland if its policies on long-term care are more generous than those in England),

2. There may be economies of scale in the provision of some public goods, which makes their production in a devolved setting ineffi-cient. This may be true for defence, but it is not at all obvious why it should be true for health.

3. There is an insurance argument that pooling of resources to help areas experiencing difficult economic conditions is more easily brought about if there is a central authority able to control transfers to the poorer areas.

Whatever the merits of the former arguments, they have failed to persuade any UK Government that they offset the case against extending fiscal powers to the devolved authorities. National governments have not seen the paradox in their own behaviour as they consistently resist the transfer of taxation powers to the EU.

Other forces resisting change include the Labour Party in Scotland — both because it fears a significant worsening of Scotland's funding position and that such a move would play into the hands of the nationalists. The Treasury is fairly predictable in its resistance to any diminution of its macroeconomic control over the economy. It is unlikely that the devolved authorities will be permitted any move toward even a small extension of their fiscal powers in the short to medium term.

CONCLUSION

During the last twelve months, the main issue relating to finance and resources in the devolved administrations has been the Barnett Formula. It has been assailed by politicians from the regions of England who think its *level* of support is too generous to the devolved authorities. From the other side it has been criticised by politicians from the devolved Parliament and Assemblies who feel that Barnett-determined *changes* in funding to their institutions are insufficient to enable them to show that devolution is making a real difference. It is also is a very curious bedfellow to other forms of support to the devolved authorities, particularly those that are based on some form of 'needs assessment'.

The Barnett Formula will continue to 'squeeze' the devolved authorities until the present spending review ends in 2003-2004. The present adminis-tration may decide to postpone a thorough review of the Barnett Formula until the following CSR, by which time the 'squeeze' may have brought Scotland and Northern Ireland much closer to the levels of funding that a needs assessment might imply. Some interim arrangements for Wales may again be necessary.

The mechanisms that are used to resolve differences over funding between the centre and the devolved authorities overwhelmingly favour the centre. If the issue of rebalancing these is not addressed, then the ability of the devolved bodies to deliver significantly differentiated polices will be seriously compromised. And ultimately this will only serve to devalue the process of devolution in the public perception.

BIBLIOGRAPHY

Official Documents

Department of the Environment Transport and the Regions (2000*). Local Government Finance, SSA Background*. Available at www.local.dtlr.gov.uk/finance/ssa/ssas.htm

HM Treasury (1979). *Needs assessment study : the report of an Interdepartmental Study co-ordinated by HM Treasury on the relative public expenditure needs in England, Scotland, Wales and Northern Ireland.*

HM Treasury(2000a). Spending Review 2000. Available at

HM Treasury (2000b). *Funding the Scottish Parliament, the National Assembly for Wales and the Northern Ireland Assembly, Statement of Funding Policy* (2nd Edition), July. Available at www.hm-treasury.gov.uk/pdf/2000/sfp4.pdf

HM Treasury (2001). *Public Expenditure Statistical Analysis 2001-2002.*

Scottish Executive (1999). *Fair Shares for All: Report of the National Review of Resource Allocation for the NHS in Scotland.* Available at www.scotland.gov.uk /library2/doc01/fsag-00.htm

Scottish Parliament (2001). Community Care and Health (Scotland) Bill, Policy Memorandum. Available at Scottish Office (1997). *Scotland's Parliament* (the devolution White Paper). Available at www.scotland.gov.uk/government /devolution/scpa-10.asp

Scottish Office (1997). *The Scotland Bill — A Guide.*

Secondary Sources

Bell, D. N .F. (2001). The Barnett Formula, unpublished mimeo. Department of Economics, University of Stirling.

McCrone, G. (1999). 'Scotland's Public Finances from Goschen to Barnett'. *Fraser of Allander Institute Quarterly Economic Commentary.* Vol. 24 No. 2.

McLean, I. (2000). 'A Fiscal Constitution for the UK' in Chen, S. and Wright, T. (eds) *The English Question.* The Fabian Society, pp 80-95.

Organization for Economic Co-operation and Development (2001). *Economic Survey of Germany 2001.* Available at www.oecd.org/publications/Library/ webook/01-2001-17-1/5.htm

Twigger, R. (1998). *The Barnett Formula* House of Commons Library Research Paper 98/8.

7

Intergovernmental Relations a Year On
Whitehall still Rules UK?

Alan Trench

In 1999-2000, intergovernmental relations (IGR) were largely driven by paper. The framework of intergovernmental agreements needed to manage devolution was only conceived when Parliamentary consideration of the devolution legislation was fairly advanced, and putting them in place took up much of the first year of devolution. As Robert Hazell described last year, this was a complex task.[1] Devolution has now become the framework within which policy is made, rather than a policy in itself, and in that setting it becomes easier to see how IGR actually works under devolution.

Robert Hazell also noted last year the informality and low-key nature of the arrangements established for IGR. The system reflected the preference of the British civil service for recording everything in writing but also maintaining flexibility and the scope to adjust policy in a pragmatic way. That tendency has become very clear in 2000-2001, as IGR has become even more informal and low-key. Over the last year it has been characterised as involving very little by way of high politics and relatively limited involvement by politicians, a high overall level of consensus between governments, and a public profile so low that at times it has vanished altogether. Yet even if one does not notice it, IGR is there and of immense importance; if this particular dog remains silent at night, its failure to bark is itself significant and indicates a good deal about the way potentially-contentious issues are dealt with.

This chapter will seek to describe and assess the developments in the formal machinery and the informal machinery over the last year. This chapter will review the formal system as discussed by Robert Hazell in last year's chapter, look at its working in practice, and then assess the significance of three key areas — Westminster legislation, finance, and European Union (EU) and international policy — in IGR. It concludes by assessing the implications of the way IGR is presently working. There are obvious overlaps with other chapters of this book (notably Chapters 6, 8 and 9) and to an extent this chapter is drawing together themes discussed in more detail in those chapters, but all the authors have sought to keep such overlaps to a minimum.

Much of the material for this chapter derives from research being carried out at the Constitution Unit for a project on IGR funded by the Leverhulme

---

[1] Hazell 2000. For an account of the institutional framework of IGR, see Burrows 2000, chap. 5.

Trust as part of the Unit's 'Nations and Regions' programme. This project is a five-year study to assess the UK's developing system of IGR in comparative context. As well as documentary analysis, it has involved lengthy interviews with officials in Whitehall departments (central departments such as the Cabinet Office, the territorial offices and front-line departments) and the devolved administrations. The interviews are semi-structured and unattributable to the individuals involved. They have done a good deal to illustrate to me how the UK's system of intergovernmental relations is now working, and I am grateful to all the interviewees for their help and their candour. The usual disclaimer, or course, applies.

Figure 7.1. Key events in intergovernmental relations, 2000-01

1 September 2000	Meeting of (full) Joint Ministerial Committee (JMC)
11 October 2000	Death of Donald Dewar, First Minister of the Scottish Parliament
24 January 2001	Resignation of Peter Mandelson as Secretary of State for Northern Ireland; appointment of Dr John Reid to replace him, and of Helen Liddell as Secretary of State for Scotland
19 February 2001	First suspected case of Foot-and-Mouth Disease identified
1 March 2001	Meeting of JMC (EU)
28 May 2001	Adoption of 'Flanders Declaration'
7 June 2001	UK General Election

THE FORMAL APPARATUS FOR INTERGOVERNMENTAL RELATIONS

The Joint Ministerial Committee

The JMC has had very limited use over the past twelve months. It was established as the main forum for bringing together the four governments and with wide-ranging formal terms of reference (see Figure 7.2) and a further remit to try to resolve bilateral differences between the UK Government and one of the devolved administrations, with a requirement to meet at least once a year.

As well as the main JMC of the Prime Minister (accompanied by the Deputy PM and the territorial Secretaries of State) and the First Ministers of the devolved administrations and their deputies, there are various 'functional' JMCs. Those originally established had remits for Health, the Knowledge Economy, Poverty and the EU, and the Memorandum of Understanding (MOU) noted the possibility of others being established for Agriculture ministers and Environment ministers.[2]

[2] Lord Chancellor 2000, Annex A1, para A1.4.

**Figure 7.2. Terms of reference of the Joint Ministerial Committee
Source: Lord Chancellor 2000, Annex A1, paragraph A1.2.**

a.   to consider non-devolved matters which impinge on devolved
     responsibility, and devolved matters which impinge on non-devolved
     responsibilities;

b.   where the UK Government and the devolved administrations so agree, to
     consider devolved matters it is beneficial to discuss their respective
     treatment in the different parts of the United Kingdom;

c.   to keep the arrangements for liaison between the UK Government and the
     devolved administrations under review; and

d.   to consider disputes between the administrations.

In fact there have been few meetings of the JMC (in any form) over the last
year. The main JMC had its first (and so far only) meeting in November
1999. After a flurry of meetings in spring 2000, the JMC for Health met in
June 2000 and October 2000, and the JMCs on Poverty and the Knowledge
Economy have not met since May 2000. The JMC on EU affairs met on 1
March 2001,[3] but its meeting produced no communique and according to
officials involved was mainly used by the Foreign Secretary, Robin Cook, as
a briefing meeting for the Stockholm EU summit.

The decline in meetings of the JMC reflects a number of factors. Part of the
reason is the smoothness of relations between the four administrations —
itself partly because of the wide range of agreement between them, and also
partly because the issues that do emerge are being satisfactorily dealt with at
lower levels (between officials, or bilaterally between ministers) and so do
not need airing in such a forum. Another part of the explanation is political.
The functional JMCs were very much the creation of certain senior politicians (the names of Gordon Brown, the Chancellor, and the Prime Minister
were particularly mentioned) and reflected their concerns. A combination of
pressures of time as the UK general election loomed and the fact that the
functional JMCs had done what they were initially needed to do meant that
the political impetus died.

Perhaps the most important reason, though, is terminological. Officials
have emphasised that the main difference between a JMC and a quadrilateral
meeting of ministers is the name used, and whether the UK end of the Secretariat is provided by Cabinet Office or the UK department concerned. (One
might add that for a JMC a press release is normally issued afterward.)
Several functional groups of ministers have met regularly without calling
their meetings a JMC. This has applied to the frequent (usually monthly)
meetings of agriculture ministers, to ones of health ministers, and others as

---

[3] See *The Scotsman,* 2 March 2001; FCO News release, 28 February 2001.

well (discussed in more detail below). In reality ministers continue to meet, but informally and outside the JMC framework.

The September meeting of the full JMC issued a lengthy communique.[4] It agreed three 'action points':

- 'Formal stock-takes' of the MOU and concordats
- continued co-ordination over the legislative programmes at Westminster and the devolved assemblies, so as 'to ensure that legitimate interest in each other's programmes is fully built into the process of preparing legislation, not treated as an optional extra'
- continued informal dialogue, to strengthen relations between administrations.

In fact, the MOU had been reviewed only shortly before the September meeting. A revised version, Cm 4806, was issued in July 2000 to replace the version issued in October 1999 (Cm 4444), incorporating the Northern Ireland Executive Committee as well as Scottish ministers and the National Assembly's Cabinet. And when it is complete it is unlikely that the 'stock-take' of the MOU or concordats will result in any significant changes.

The British–Irish Council and the North–South Ministerial Council

A year ago these were important institutions.[5] They brought a different perspective to IGR, as they concerned not so much relations between different governments within a state as relations between governments within two different states, the UK and the Republic of Ireland. By September 2001, however, they had vanished off the radar.

The North-South Ministerial Council (NSMC) continues to meet regularly in its more technical 'sectoral' formats, but has not met in plenary since 26 September 2000. And some sections are more active than others — the Foyle, Carlingford and Irish Lights Commission has met almost quarterly, but Language last met in December 2000 and neither the Education nor the Food Safety and Health Sectoral Councils have met since July 2000 (unsurprisingly, given that David Trimble had barred the Sinn Féin ministers from NSMC meetings, and these are included in the portfolios of Martin Mcguinness and Bairbre de Brún; see Chapter 4).

The stalling of the British–Irish Council is also largely due to the stalemate in the peace process. It has not met in plenary since December 1999, with meetings arranged in 2001 cancelled due to the state of the peace process (and one in October 2000 because it coincided with the funeral of Donald Dewar). There have been a number of lower-profile ministerial meetings, of Environment ministers in October 2000 and of Transport ministers in

---

[4] Available on the internet at www.cabinet-office.gov.uk/constitution/devolution/jmc/jmc.htm
[5] See Hazell 2000.

December 2000, and work continues at the official level, but until the peace process is in less fragile a state it is unlikely that this will resume.

Concordats

The concordats entered into before July 2000 included, as a standard provision, the requirement that their operation be reviewed after 12 months. The 'action point' from the September 2000 JMC appears simply to have been a reiteration of this. That review of the concordats has been ongoing, but has seldom resulted in anything more than typographical changes and the updating of references. One exception was the concordat between the former Department for Environment, Transport and the Regions (DETR) and the National Assembly for Wales, which was changed to provide for the synchronisation of consultation exercises such as that on local government finance. Officials have spent only limited time on the review, fearing that it could turn into a lengthy and largely futile exercise, and given the limited need they have seen for it.[6]

At the same time, the network of concordats has been expanded. Figure 7.3 shows the new concordats issued over the last 12 months.

Figure 7.3. Concordats concluded between July 2000 and July 2001	
Concordat between:	*Date*
National Assembly for Wales and Health & Safety Executive	June 2000
Northern Ireland Office and Northern Ireland Executive Committee	August 2000
National Assembly for Wales and Ministry of Agriculture, Fisheries and Food	October 2000
National Assembly for Wales and Wales Office (Office of Secretary of State for Wales)	January 2001
National Assembly for Wales and Home Office	April 2001

The gaps in the network of concordats are therefore being filled. It is unlikely of course ever to be completed (whatever that might mean), and recent comparative research on intergovernmental relations has found that such instruments are often concluded to deal with a specific issue, especially one which is left unclear by the main constitutional settlement.[7] It is worth noting that the newer concordats serve somewhat different functions to earlier ones. For example, as well as the usual provisions about sharing of information and consultation, the concordat between the National Assembly and the Ministry of Agriculture, Fisheries and Food (MAFF) is largely concerned with EU

[6] Interviews with Whitehall and National Assembly officials, July-August 2001.

[7] Poirier 2001a, b. For a discussion of the legal significance of concordats, see also Rawlings 2000.

matters, and sets out in some detail how these should be dealt with (including the implementation of EU obligations into domestic law), amplifying to a considerable degree on what the main Concordat on Co-ordination of EU Policy Issues[8] says about such matters. The concordats between the devolved administrations and the territorial offices are attempts to clarify the functions of the territorial Offices (which themselves have been the subject of some discussion; see Chapter 8 for more details). In the Northern Irish case, the concordat is also an attempt to ensure that ordinary business can continue to be dealt with smoothly despite the erratic progress of the peace process and the role that the Northern Ireland Office plays in orchestrating the peace process.[9]

THE SYSTEM AT WORK

The fact that only limited use of the formal frameworks for making devolution work has been made over the last year is enough to suggest that other ways of dealing with IGR have emerged. The interviews carried out for this project suggest strongly that this is the case. These formal frameworks were in any case limited compared with those in other states.[10] This is not to say that the original principles of the settlement have been abandoned; the MOU states:

> The UK Government and the devolved administrations believe that most contact between them should be carried out on a bilateral or multi-lateral basis, between departments which deal on a day-to-day basis with the issues at stake. Nonetheless, some central co-ordination of the overall relationship is needed. ... The UK Government and the devolved administrations commit themselves, wherever possible, to conduct business through normal administrative channels, either at official or ministerial level.[11]

Before considering how the system works in certain policy areas, it is worth looking at the players in the system itself.

Ministers

As noted above, ministerial co-operation is key to IGR in the UK. Much routine business continues to be dealt with by correspondence (sometimes simply between officials, sometimes between ministers, particularly for sensitive matters). The formal system of regular meetings in the framework of the JMC has been set aside — largely because an informal system has emerged instead. This operates more at the functional level than as a parallel to the main JMC, and how much it works depends on the subject areas

[8] Part II, Annex B to Lord Chancellor 2000.
[9] Interview with Northern Ireland Office official, July 2001.
[10] See Cornes 1999.
[11] Lord Chancellor 2000, paras 22 and 24. The wording was the same in the 1999 version.

involved. For example, the four agriculture ministers meet monthly, while the health or sports and culture ministers meet much less often. Officials from both the UK Government and the devolved administrations consider that such meetings have generally worked well, and that ministers have found much common ground when meetings take place. The use of meetings as a co-ordination mechanism is ingrained in British public administration, and such inter-ministerial meetings are now also part of the fabric of government. In fact, they are so numerous that is not practicable to keep records of them, at least centrally.[12]

The fact that ministerial meetings take place outside the framework of the JMC is regarded by officials simply as a matter of how the meeting is 'badged'. However, the framework within which the meeting is held has a greater significance than this. It affects the secretariat for the meeting — secretariats for JMC meetings are provided by a joint secretariat of central officials (from the former Constitution Secretariat, now known as the Nations and Regions Division, in the UK Cabinet Office, the Constitution Units of the Scottish Executive and National Assembly, and the Executive Secretariat in the Office of the First Minister and Deputy First Minister in Northern Ireland), while secretariats for 'ordinary' ministers' meetings are provided from within the departments or ministerial private offices involved. That has staffing implications and may affect the way that information is shared and the organisation of such meetings co-ordinated. It also affects publicity, and the extent to which the public becomes aware of such meetings; while JMC meetings are the subject of press releases and usually attract some news coverage, no such publicity is given to ordinary quadrilateral meetings. They, and what is decided at them, can be immensely influential — but will only become known to the public if those present decide it should.

Ministers are, by definition, political creatures. The question therefore arises of what effect party politics has on IGR. Officials note that party politics seldom, if ever, play a major role; one said that it was impossible to tell which parties ministers at a particular functional meeting came from as it had no apparent effect on their behaviour or the positions they adopted. This is the more telling as one of the ministers from a devolved administration at the meeting in question was a Liberal Democrat (and Northern Ireland ministers are always outside the Labour fold as well). During the Foot-and-Mouth crisis, it was notable how muted the devolved administrations were in their criticism of the positions determined by the UK Government — often more restrained than different UK departments and ministers were themselves.[13]

What is unclear, however, is how well such mechanisms for co-operation would continue to work if there were less political common ground between

---

[12] Interview with Cabinet Office official, July 2001.

[13] See Masterman 2001, and the section on 'IGR in crisis: Foot-and-Mouth Disease' below.

the ministers. The hard issues remain: whose decision applies where the UK Government and a devolved administration disagree? What happens if the two governments pursue conflicting policies within the areas in which each of them is competent? What happens if the UK Government were to seek to use its powers to overrule a devolved administration regarding a devolved matter? Political consensus not only means that these issues have not occurred, but that the institutional mechanisms put in place to deal with them have in fact been weakened by disuse over the last year.

Officials

Much of IGR in fact happens between officials. Each of the four administrations has a specialist unit dealing with intergovernmental relations. These are all small — four or five officials in the Cabinet Office, two or three in Wales and Scotland. The Cabinet Office's staff formerly were known as the Constitution Secretariat, and that secretariat also embraced responsibility for other elements of the Government's constitutional reform programme (notably human rights and reform of Parliament, particularly the House of Lords). As detailed in Chapter 8, the changes to the machinery of government announced immediately after the UK general election have resulted in the break-up of this and its re-creation as the 'Nations and Regions Division' of the General Policy Group. The Constitution Units in the Scottish Executive and National Assembly for Wales were unaffected by such changes, though — like the Nations and Regions Division — their focus is also split. Certainly in Wales, they are concerned as much if not more with matters relating to the National Assembly's Cabinet as with IGR issues.[14] It would not be practicable for all IGR issues to be routed through the central teams, which become involved only in specific circumstances — where issues are particularly complex or politically sensitive, or occasionally where desk officials find themselves out of their depth.[15] That was never intended under the MOU (see above, p. 158).

The UK's system works in part because it is highly decentralised, a characteristic of the UK's central administrative apparatus more generally.[16] At the level of interaction between front-line or desk civil servants working for different administrations, contact often happens daily, by phone or e-mail. Policies and their implementation are discussed regularly and routinely. The way interviewees suggested this was a normal part of life leads one to characterise it as a 'co-ordination reflex'. This is of course quite in keeping with the spirit of the concordats, particularly their concerns with avoiding surprises, ensuring advance warning of policy initiatives and promoting consultation

[14] Interview with National Assembly official, July 2000.
[15] Interviews with Cabinet Office and devolved administration officials, July-August 2001.
[16] See Daintith and Page 1999, especially chaps. 2, 10 and 12.

about initiatives which might affect another order of government, and can be regarded as that intention becoming reality. It is also helped by the fact that officials remain part of a single Home Civil Service, so are dealing with people who are colleagues rather than counterparts from a different service, and who in many cases were immediate colleagues only three years ago.

One consequence of this process is that issues have been aired thoroughly by the time they reach more senior levels of officials, or are passed to the central units specialising in IGR. This winnowing process means that the more senior levels are dealing with genuine issues that call for their expertise, while meaning a wide range of officials are exposed to IGR issues at various stages of their careers. This happens both on an ad hoc basis and as part of the regular round of meetings that support government. One significant factor in this is the weekly meeting of permanent secretaries and other very senior officials at the Civil Service Management Board, which of course includes Muir Russell and Jon Shortridge, Permanent Secretaries to the Scottish Executive and National Assembly respectively; that appears to deal with most of the high-level issues of IGR affecting officials. However, the committee of senior officials (at Permanent or Deputy Secretary level) shadowing the JMC has fallen into disuse, having met only once, in November 1999.[17]

One somewhat surprising aspect of the system at official level is the extent to which it consists of bilateral contacts between the devolved administrations and the centre. Each set of officials in a devolved administration has regular and close contact with their opposite numbers in the UK Government, in person and by phone or e-mail. Each side said they were fully briefed about the activities of the other (although some devolved administration officials suggested that there were sometimes problems with being informed about what is happening in Whitehall). What happens rather less, however, is contact either among all four administrations or trilaterally between devolved administration officials only (excluding the UK Government). In some areas, trilateral contact happens only rather casually, and in relation to occasional four-government meetings — 'when we are at the same meetings with the UK Government we try to meet for dinner beforehand'.[18] This was said to be because informal contact and co-operation worked very well and more formal or regular contact was unnecessary. In other areas, co-operation had not reached that level, but e-mail circulation groups of the devolved administrations have recently been set up; in these areas, the officials were conscious that such co-operation might be useful, but pressures of time and other priorities had meant it had been postponed.[19]

---

[17] Interview with Cabinet Office official, July 2001.
[18] Interviews with devolved administration officials, June-August 2001.
[19] Interviews with devolved administration officials, July 2001.

A further reason for the lack of contact between the devolved administrations is the differences between the three sets of devolution arrangements. This was cited by a number of interviewees, from both UK Government and the devolved administrations. It means that there is only a limited amount of common ground between the devolved administrations; both Scotland and Wales find the problems of Northern Ireland, chiefly arising from the peace process, of intellectual interest but little practical concern. Welsh interviewees pointed out that Wales, being largely rural and with generally evenly spread population, had quite different concerns from Scotland with a wealthier, more urbanised, more industrial population — one felt Wales had more in common with the Republic of Ireland as a result.[20] Certainly the different structures for devolution to Scotland and Wales mean that the preoccupations of each are unique; Scotland does not share the Welsh concern with Westminster primary legislation, and Wales does not share Scottish concerns with what exactly is devolved and what is reserved. Finance further complicates the matter, although finance officials appear to have the most professional common ground, even if they have the least common ground in terms of the policy they wish to see pursued by the UK Government (see section on Finance below, and Chapter 6).

The Territorial Offices

The role of the territorial Offices is discussed in detail in Chapter 8 and will not be duplicated here. So far as IGR is concerned the role of the territorial Offices remains unclear, given the extent of bilateral links between the devolved administrations and UK departments. As noted above, the intention never was that the territorial Offices should monopolise contact between the UK Government and the devolved administrations, and they do not, only becoming involved when needed to, although there is also regular liaison in the form of a weekly meeting between the Secretary of State and the First Minister, at least in Wales.[21] At least one territorial Office conceives of itself as being expert in no particular policy area, but rather in the devolution settlement for that territory as a whole[22]. Interviewees from both the UK Government and the devolved administrations considered that, when the territorial Offices had become involved in a matter, they had played a useful part, mediating in and defusing differences between administrations before the issue became a dispute. The 'honest broker' role is properly played; there has been at least one occasion when a territorial Secretary of State has presented views to Cabinet committee which they did not share, acting as the devolved administration's spokesman even when they disagreed with it,[23]

---

[20] Interviews with National Assembly for Wales officials, August 2001.

[21] Interviews with National Assembly and Wales Office officials, August 2001.

[22] Interview with territorial Office official, August 2001.

[23] Interview with devolved administration official, July 2001.

and officials regard the Secretaries of State and their staff as having acted openly and honestly in playing their role. Like the devolved administrations, while the territorial Offices keep in touch with each other informally, they have no formal mechanisms for doing so — especially as the Heads of the Scotland and Wales Offices are not members of the Civil Service Management Board, although the Permanent Secretary of the Northern Ireland Office is. There is also sufficient difference between the concerns each Office deals with to mean that more formal or regular contact would give little benefit.[24]

While this is a testament to the commitment of those involved in ensuring devolution works, and their goodwill toward the devolved administrations, it does not deal with the difficult questions about the future of the Offices, or the tensions inherent in the Janus-faced approach of the Offices, representing both the UK Government in their territories and the devolved administration to the UK Government.[25]

LEGISLATION AT WESTMINSTER

The territorial issues of Westminster legislation are discussed in Chapter 9. What is of interest in the present context is Westminster's role as forum for IGR, or focus of it.

Part of the reason why Westminster has become important is the volume of Sewel resolutions for matters affecting Scotland. Officials consider that the number of these is much greater than had been expected before devolution took place, and that they expected this to be a rarely-used device to deal with a particularly difficult issues where demarcation of devolved and reserved matters was in doubt. Instead, they have been used in a variety of circumstances, some arising from overlapping competences of the two levels of government and some from the workload of the Scottish Parliament. At least one official sees this as offering the advantage of enabling areas of uncertainty about powers to be resolved straightforwardly and amicably, without need for an amendment of the Scotland Act 1998 on each occasion.[26] This is discussed in more detail in Chapter 9. One example particularly worth noting is the (Westminster) International Criminal Court Act 2001, to make provision for implementation of the Statute of the International Criminal Court. While this gives effect to the UK's international obligations and so deals with reserved matters, it also affects both extradition law and criminal procedure, so also affects matters devolved to Scotland. The Westminster Act therefore only makes substantive provision for England and Wales and Northern Ireland, and a separate Act of the Scottish Parliament (the International

---

[24] Interviews with territorial Office officials, August 2001.

[25] For further discussion, see Hazell 2001.

[26] Interview with UK Department official, June 2001.

Criminal Court (Scotland) Act 2001) makes provision for application of the statute in Scotland. Nonetheless, there was also a Sewel resolution for the Westminster legislation as it was found impossible not to deal with devolved matters in drafting the Westminster Act.[27]

Wales raises a different set of issues. Executive devolution means that the National Assembly has to obtain powers from Westminster whenever the development of a distinctively Welsh policy involves a change in primary legislation. The last year has seen the enactment of the first Wales-only Act since devolution, the Children's Commissioner for Wales Act 2001, as well as provisions for Wales in the Learning and Skills Act 2000 and the Care Standards Act 2000 that are both substantial and substantially different from those for England. The Local Government Act 2000 and the Transport Act 2000 also had significant effects for areas that are devolved in Wales. Westminster legislation varies significantly in the way it deals with how the National Assembly will exercise the functions involved. In some cases, it allocates functions to 'the appropriate minister', defined as the Secretary of State for England and the National Assembly for Wales. In others, specific provisions set out precisely what the National Assembly may do, in a structure that reflects a significantly different policy for Wales (the Learning and Skills Act 2000 is a good example, with provisions in Parts II and IV that parallel but differ a good deal from those for England in Parts I and III).[28] Cases where the legislative provisions have given more limited powers to the National Assembly than to the Secretary of State, such as the limited powers for the Assembly to make commencement orders for the application of the Local Government Act 2000 in Wales, or to be able to repeal old provisions (so-called 'Henry VIII' powers) under that Act, have been very controversial.

A further issue is Wales's access to Westminster to be able to introduce Wales-only legislation. Parliamentary time is a scarce, and precious, commodity. Where Welsh measures can be incorporated into an existing bill, they are not likely to consume a great deal of Parliamentary time — but this depends on the provisions falling within the scope of the existing bill and the UK department promoting it agreeing to a measure (possibly expressing a rather different policy to the department's own one for England) being included. A Wales-only measure, like the Children's Commissioner for Wales, can only be included on the Parliamentary timetable if the responsible Cabinet Committee, LP, agrees; it requires the sponsorship of the Secretary of State for Wales, and at least non-opposition of various other UK ministers. At each stage, therefore, the process of securing time at Westminster for

---

[27] The Westminster Act received Royal Assent on 11 May 2001 and the Scottish Act on 21 September 2001.

[28] For further discussion, see Patchett and Osmond 2001.

legislation requires extensive inter-governmental bargaining, and a significant degree of goodwill toward Wales.

Against this setting, it is no surprise that legislation is identified by officials concerned with Welsh devolution as a major area of intergovernmental activity in its own right. It occupies a large amount of the time of officials in the Cabinet Secretariat at the National Assembly and the Wales Office as well as in the functional areas affected. The nature of the powers given to the Assembly are the subject of considerable debate between the UK departmental officials promoting a bill and their counterparts from the National Assembly and Wales Office, which ultimately are referred to ministerial level for endorsement or resolution. The approaches taken to such matters vary a good deal between Whitehall departments, with some being regarded as much 'better' or less sceptical about the devolved administrations than others.[29] Although the principles stated in the Devolution Guidance Note on primary legislation affecting Wales[30] are now published, the Note is not exhaustive (for example, the National Assembly would normally expect to have responsibility for commencement of legislation it administers in Wales, and for any specifically Welsh public bodies, but these issues are not dealt with in the Note[31]). Welsh officials do not usually formally become members of bill teams, even where legislation contains separate provisions for Wales — although they co-operate fully with the UK department's bill team in such cases, including attending Parliamentary debates to brief the UK ministers leading the bill.[32]

There remain serious problems with Welsh Westminster legislation. Because provisions affecting Wales vary so much from Act to Act, practical administration is made much harder. Moreover, the extent of variation means that the devolution settlement for Wales set out in the Government of Wales Act 1998 and the transfer of functions orders[33] is, in effect, being re-written in small increments by each new Westminster Act affecting devolved matters. In other words, Wales's need for recourse to Westminster for primary legislation and the form that legislation takes has exactly the opposite effect to Scotland's unexpected use of Westminster legislation through the Sewel resolution mechanism. This process of negotiation is one in which Wales starts at an inherent disadvantage, as it relies on others' goodwill and has few institutional means to secure what it needs if those others fail to deliver. The precedents set so far have by and large been good for Wales,

---

[29] Interviews with National Assembly and Whitehall officials, July-August 2001.

[30] Devolution Guidance Note 9, 'Post Devolution Primary Legislation affecting Wales' available on the Cabinet Office website at
www.cabinet-office.gov.uk/constitution/devolution/guidance/dgn.index.htm

[31] Interview with National Assembly official, August 2001.

[32] Interviews with National Assembly and UK Government officials, August 2001.

[33] The National Assembly for Wales (Transfer of Functions) Order 1999, SI 1999 no. 672, The National Assembly for Wales (Transfer of Functions) (No. 2) Order 1999, SI 1999 no. 2787 and the National Assembly for Wales (Transfer of Functions) Order 2000, SI 2000 no. 253.

giving it time and legislation appropriate for Welsh needs, and good for devolution too by enabling the systems put in place to work. Nonetheless, the question remains of how robust they would be if the present high levels of goodwill were to decline.

FINANCE

Finance remains potentially the most unsettled aspect of devolution. The key issues are how the Barnett Formula works, how that affects the room for manoeuvre of the devolved administrations, and whether and in what ways it might change. These issues are of course discussed in Chapter 6 and will not be duplicated here. Its importance for IGR lies in the extent to which finance affects other aspects of relations between the four administrations, and the extent to which their relations involve dealing with finance issues.

One advantage of the Barnett Formula noted by interviewees is its certainty; if an item attracts a 'Barnett consequential', the Treasury pays the amount involved as part of the block grant to the devolved administration.[34] Yet this conceals the question of what attracts a Barnett consequential. This largely depends on whether an item of spending is classed as being England-only (in which case it attracts the consequential) or UK-wide (in which case it does not). Thus the re-categorisation of the central government subsidy for London Underground as an England-only service rather than a UK-wide one, as it was originally classed prior to the 2000 Comprehensive Spending Review (CSR), meant that significant extra payments were made to Scotland, though not the devolved administrations. (Contrast this with the position of the Channel Tunnel Rail Link, which is treated as having UK-wide benefit and therefore attracts no such payment, although the project's benefit will in reality mainly be limited to London and south-east England.)[35] The way spending programmes and sub-programmes are classed is an area where there is scope for negotiation between the devolved administrations and the Treasury, if only during the CSR process, in contrast to most other aspects of Barnett.

There are two other areas where Barnett leaves room for adjustment if not negotiation. One is in-year adjustments, mainly being calls on the UK reserve arising from unexpected contingencies. The other is payments outside the scope of Barnett altogether. Both have been significant factors over the last year — crises such as Foot-and-Mouth Disease (and its effect on tourism across the whole UK), late winter and spring flooding and the Corus closures (for Wales) all brought calls for significant additional funding (for

[34] See HM Treasury 2000, para 2.2. programmes which are comparable and therefore attract the consequential payment are set out in Annex C, the Schedule of Comparable Sub-programmes.

[35] See HM Treasury 2000, Annex C, p43; the grant for the London Underground is classed as the Metropolitan Railways Passenger Services grant.

England as well as the devolved administrations) outside the scope of Barnett. As the Statement of Funding Policy states:

> There is no automatic application of the Barnett formula to Reserve claims made by departments of the UK Government. Reserve claims may be higher or lower than a population share depending on the circumstances of the claim or other pressures facing the United Kingdom Government.[36]

Thus access to the UK reserve depends on making a case acceptable to the Treasury about the need of the devolved administration and its territory. The Treasury's determination is final, subject to the Secretary of State for the territory raising the matter with the Chief Secretary to the Treasury and then pursuing the matter to the JMC or the UK Cabinet. No occasion has yet arisen when a matter has been taken to the JMC, but the in-year adjustments have been a cause of hard negotiation with the Treasury over the past year — the tourism effects of Foot-and-Mouth being a notable example.[37]

Payments outside the scope of Barnett have been significant in defusing at least one potential major area of dispute between the National Assembly for Wales and the Treasury. This is in the area of matching funding for Objective 1 projects, which of course triggered the fall of Alun Michael in early 2000.[38] Such funding has the effect of making it unattractive for the Assembly Cabinet to object too strongly to the overall terms of the Barnett Formula, even if these do disadvantage Wales, as the settlement viewed more broadly has been made more generous to Wales.

These areas both highlight flaws in the structure of devolution. Both hand a great deal of discretion to the Treasury, and any disagreement between the devolved administration and the Treasury can only be pursued if they consider it is sufficiently important (given the trade-offs that may be lost if the matter is pursued), and if the Secretary of State supports the devolved administration. Pursuit of the matter to the JMC means increasing the stakes still further. It also means raising the issue not just before a larger audience but in what is scarcely a neutral forum, since the JMC includes both numerous UK ministers and the other devolved administrations (which may have an interest in seeing another devolved administration lose out if they may benefit). Taking the matter further, to the UK Cabinet, is even less favourable; the devolved administration would not even be able to attend itself to be heard, and as the UK Government both makes the decision and provides the funds it would effectively be judge in its own cause.

This raises issues about the suitability generally of the JMC for resolving what in essence are bilateral disputes, but in the case of finance the issues, while avoided up to now, remain likely to become acute.

---

[36] HM Treasury 2000, para 9.2. i, p21.
[37] Interviews with devolved administration finance officials, July-August 2001.
[38] See Osmond 2000, especially p39 and pp. 45-7.

EU AND INTERNATIONAL MATTERS

One aspect of devolution becoming more established is that external matters have become more prominent over the last year. This has included visits overseas by Scottish, Welsh and Northern Irish politicians (notably by Henry McLeish to the US for 'Tartan Day' and by Rhodri Morgan to Patagonia) as well as visits to Scotland and Wales by politicians from overseas (such as the visit by President Mbeki of South Africa to Edinburgh). More generally, it has embraced the devolved administrations taking a greater role on the European and world stages, which is important for IGR both in itself and because of its effects on relations within the UK. Co-ordination of visits (both to the devolved territories and by their representatives) is an area where the Foreign and Commonwealth Office (FCO) sees itself as being able to contribute expertise.

The EU is perhaps the most important overseas forum for the devolved administrations.[39] Explanation of the UK's line for the Stockholm EU summit was, as noted above, the reason for holding a meeting of the JMC (EU) on 1 March 2001. The use of this forum has an added attraction for the devolved administrations as, unlike other JMCs, this one comprises the members of the main Cabinet committee on EU matters (EDOP) as well as the First and Deputy First Ministers of the devolved administrations; it therefore presents an opportunity to influence all the key decision-makers for EU policy, and to participate directly in UK Government discussions. For the devolved administrations the effectiveness of this does not seem to be affected by the lack of any formal outcome to the meeting (which produced no communique, only a 'statement' recording that it had happened). The problem with slow implementation of Community obligations noted last year, particularly in Wales, remains.[40] The National Assembly is trying to find ways of speeding up its legislative processes to improve its record, with some success. The backlog appears, however, not to be causing extra tension with the UK Government, nor has it yet resulted in actual or threatened infraction proceedings under Article 226 of the EC Treaty for breach of Community law.[41]

Both Scotland and Wales have active representations in Brussels — in Scotland's case, at Scotland House and in Wales's at the Welsh European Centre. These include representatives of other national interests as well as of the devolved administration, and exist to represent the distinct interests of Scotland and Wales, not those of the UK. (In addition, one or two Scottish Executive officials are seconded to the UK's Permanent Representation to

---

[39] For a discussion, see Hogwood et al 2000 and Bulmer et al 2001.
[40] Hazell 2000, pp. 174-5.
[41] Interviews with UK Government and National Assembly officials, July-August 2001.

the EU, or UKREP — but they represent UK interests there, not Scottish ones). Their status is therefore somewhere between that of the unofficial local authority and English regional representations (and those from other member states), which are common in Brussels, and the diplomatic missions of member states themselves. Curiously, though, the officials from the devolved administrations enjoy diplomatic status in Brussels through UKREP[42] — even though their colleagues in the same building will not have that status. Their status is rather ambiguous as part-lobbyist and part-formal representative.

This is not the only anomaly in the relations between the devolved administrations and the EU. Ministers from the devolved administrations have attended a significant number of meetings of the Council of Ministers (in Scotland's case, 22 since 1999[43]). This obviously does not include every Council meeting; there are of course many Councils which do not touch on devolved matters (for example, Internal Market Councils). Scottish attendance is fairly regular at Agriculture and Fisheries Council meetings, less frequent but still regular for Environment Councils, and sporadic at Justice & Home Affairs, Health and Education Councils, with the decision to attend taken on the extent to which the agenda affects matters of concern to Scotland and bearing in mind the costs of attending (working time spent as well as travel costs). Such ministers are of course there to represent the UK and therefore have to adhere to the agreed UK line (as well as respecting the confidentiality of discussions leading to the meeting)[44]. So far devolved ministers have on occasion been the lead or sole minister from the UK at Council meetings; for example, Susan Deacon at the Health Council meeting on 14 June 2001. Although such Scottish ministers are clearly wearing a UK hat, they are not of course accountable to Parliament for what happens at that meeting. The UK minister remains accountable — but as she or he has no responsibility for or control over the actions of the Scottish minister (in the way she or he would for a departmental junior minister), the reality of that accountability has to be questionable. On the other hand, the Scottish Parliament treats these meetings as different to other ones, and MSPs have sought information about or sought to hold the Scottish minister in question accountable for what happened — although as foreign affairs and the EU are reserved matters under Schedule 5 to the Scotland Act 1998, there is in fact no such accountability. To create a situation where one minister attends a meeting, for which they are responsible to a Parliament of which they are not a member but not to the one of which they are a member, is strange indeed.

---

[42] Interview with devolved administration officials, August 2001.

[43] Interview with Scottish Administration officials, August 2001.

[44] Lord Chancellor 2000, paras B1.4, B4.4, B4.12-15; interview with Scottish Executive officials, August 2001.

The other controversial external issue of the year has been the Flanders Declaration. This 'political declaration of the constitutional regions Bavaria, Catalonia, North-Rhine Westphalia, Salzburg, Scotland, Flanders and Wallonia' was made on 28 May 2001 in Brussels, and is an attempt to influence the agenda for the EU's 2004 Intergovernmental Conference (IGC) so as to improve the position within the EU of the 'constitutional regions'[45]. Scottish signature of the declaration was approved in June by the Scottish Parliament, but not without some criticism,[46] while the UK Government has remained conspicuously silent in public. The declaration was in fact the subject of discussion between the Scottish Executive and the FCO while still a draft, but the Scottish Executive did not seek FCO approval for signature and the FCO's views concerned consistency with UK Government policy rather than approval or disapproval as such.[47] Whether the declaration will succeed in securing a voice for the 'constitutional regions' at the 2004 IGC remains unclear; but pressure for the interests of such regions to be more closely involved in EU decision-making is a concern already raised by the German government and is unlikely to go away.

IGR IN CRISIS: FOOT-AND-MOUTH DISEASE

This is not the place to give a detailed account of the crisis over Foot-and-Mouth Disease between the late winter and summer of 2001.[48] What is interesting is the extent to which this was an intergovernmental crisis, and highlighted the extent to which the four administrations co-operate much of the time. This aspect of the crisis was not readily apparent in England (it was hardly covered by the London-based media), although it was in Wales and Scotland.

The interests involved also varied greatly. For Wales, being more reliant on agriculture and rural tourism than most other parts of the UK, the crisis was more serious than in more urbanised areas, while for Scottish ministers, with only a small part of Dumfries and Galloway directly affected by the disease but a large tourism industry across the whole country affected by the restrictions on access to the countryside, eradicating the disease by culling rather than controlling it with vaccination is likely to have seemed rather less

---

[45] The text of the declaration and details of the preparatory work is available on the internet from: www.eu2001.be/Main/Frameset.asp?reference=23-01.03-01.05-01&lang=en
Wales was also involved in preparatory work on the declaration but so far has not signed it.

[46] See the debate on 'Scotland's Place in the World', 21 June 2001; Minutes of Proceedings, vol. 3, no. 11, session 1.

[47] Interview with FCO official, July 2001.

[48] Such an account has not yet been written, but for a brief introduction see the special report 'Lessons of a crisis that will reach far across the land' *Financial Times,* 5-6 May 2001 and also Rawnsley 2001, chap. 23. For accounts of how the crisis looked from Wales and Scotland see Mitchell 2001 and Osmond 2001. See also Masterman 2001, pp. 14-16.

attractive than it did in Whitehall.[49] It is therefore remarkable that Scottish and Welsh ministers stuck so closely to the line adopted by the UK Government — more so, at times than UK ministers.[50] At the same time, the legal position was far from clear. The main piece of legislation governing such a situation is the Animal Health Act 1981, although this does not take account of restrictions imposed by the European Community institutions which fall to be implemented under the European Communities Act 1972. In broad terms, this meant that MAFF exercised some functions for England or in some cases England and Wales, which were devolved to one or more of the devolved institutions (though to add to the confusion different ones were devolved in each territory). MAFF also retained a number of Great Britain or UK-wide functions. Thus the export ban required MAFF to act, while movement restrictions or footpath closures were for the devolved administrations to deal with. Effective management of the crisis would therefore have to involve the four administrations co-operating both in creating the legal and administrative framework and in implementing on the ground the actions decided on.

Officials regard the intergovernmental aspects of the crisis as having been well handled. In Wales, an operations room brought together staff from the National Assembly and MAFF as well as the State Veterinary Service, the Army, the Police and on occasion others such as the Environment Agency. Centrally (at least after 23 March 2001), the crisis was handled using the 'COBRA' system from the Cabinet Office. The National Assembly had been directly involved in COBRA during the September 2000 fuel crisis. It was not involved in it during the Foot-and-Mouth crisis — although the Wales Office was, and provided liaison to the National Assembly (a rare example of the territorial office doing this for an operational rather than policy matter). By contrast, the Scottish Executive was included in COBRA directly.[51]

It is remarkable that co-operation went so well in such a charged situation. However, it may be the charged atmosphere that helped ensure that co-operation went well — coupled with the sort of 'co-ordination reflex' mentioned above. The conditions meant that civil servants dealt with the crisis first (no simple job for the lawyers, at least) and considered other issues later. The fact that politicians in the devolved administrations may have had different concerns to those of UK-level politicians did not, in practice, affect to any

---

[49] Scottish Executive officials deny this was the case, however; interview, August 2001.

[50] Compare the attitude of Nick Brown, then Minister for Agriculture Fisheries and Food, reported in 'Brown bridles at "military takeover" of Maff' *Sunday Telegraph,* 25 March 2001 with that of the (Liberal Democrat) Scottish Rural Affairs Minister Ross Finnie reported in 'Scotland says it will not change policy', *Financial Times,* 18 April 2001. See also 'Finnie suggests slaughter will never be used again' *The Scotsman,* 11 May 2001 for a later, limited criticism of the UK policy.

[51] Interviews with UK Government, National Assembly and Scottish Executive officials, July-August 2001.

significant degree the way the crisis was handled. This suggests that the principles of devolved decision-making have yet to penetrate very deeply.

CONCLUSIONS

No-one could seriously question that IGR has had a smooth time in 2000-1. No disputes have been referred to the JMC for resolution, let alone determined by litigation, nor is there any great indication that this will change in the immediate future. All involved describe relations between the administrations as good. Something of the caution showed early on has dissipated — witness the difference between the Devolution Guidance Notes on primary legislation for Scotland, published early in 2000 and for Wales (in February 2001).

Tensions remain, however. Some occasionally break to the surface, for example in complaints from devolved administrations that they are not kept fully informed by Whitehall about developments there, although they keep Whitehall abreast of what they are doing. Some lie in issues that have not yet been tackled properly, finance being the notable example. Some lie in the structure of relationships that form the basis for IGR — finance again, being so substantially in the hands of the Treasury, being one example, and the way Wales has to negotiate over Westminster primary legislation being another. In many respects, these are issues which do not yet call for resolution, so they have not been resolved; a case of not crossing bridges before one comes to them. Where difficult issues have been tackled, there is clearly a conscious attempt to try to ensure that good precedents rather than bad ones apply, and to establish the principle that devolved matters are indeed devolved and should be left to the devolved administrations and assemblies to sort out.

This still leaves some major problems. One is public awareness of IGR. The interest shown in the process by members of the devolved assemblies is limited, as is coverage of the subject in the press and broadcast media (the London-based media scarcely cover it at all). Some areas, notably finance, attract more attention than others, but it is hardly a hot topic. As much of IGR happens in the background, unobtrusively, this is no surprise. But the declining use of the formal institutions (notably the JMC) means that coverage is even less than it might be. Eventually this lack of interest will change, and with it will come allegations that everything was fixed by behind-the-scenes meetings without regard to the principles of devolution as publicly understood.[52] Such an allegation will cause disillusion even if it is groundless, but the lack of openness will give it credibility whatever the truth may be.

---

[52] See Poirier 2001a and 2001b for criticisms of intergovernmental agreements as a means of de facto amendment of a constitutional settlement.

The second problem is related. The very smoothness of relations between administrations has fuelled the expectation that such smoothness will continue, although it is inevitable that disputes will develop at some point, and these may be major and fundamental. The declining use of the formal mechanisms for IGR (notably the JMC framework) and the increasing use of informal channels means that the system's capacity to deal with more troubled conditions is diminished. Would it be robust enough to cope with a major difference between London and one of the devolved administrations without that affecting other areas of co-operation or the other administrations? How the system would cope with major political differences (whether arising from a Conservative government in London or, more realistically in the near future, nationalist ones in Cardiff or Edinburgh)? Officials following conflicting lines, and under instructions not to resolve differences but to bring them into the political arena, would find themselves in a position that would certainly challenge them. The high level of trust that presently characterises the system may not always exist. There may be lessons to be drawn here from Northern Ireland, where the problems caused by a deeply divided coalition government and a troubled peace process have led to a more formal approach from the UK Government toward the devolved administration.

These are early days for IGR. So far things have undeniably worked well. For them to continue to do so may require Whitehall to loosen the strings of the devolved administrations yet further.

BIBLIOGRAPHY

Official Documents

HM Treasury (2000). *Funding the Scottish Parliament, National Assembly for Wales and Northern Ireland Assembly: a statement of funding policy.* London: HM Treasury.

Lord Chancellor (2000). *Memorandum of Understanding and supplementary agreements between the United Kingdom Government, Scottish Ministers, the Cabinet of the National Assembly for Wales and the Northern Ireland Executive Committee*, Cm 4806. London: The Stationery Office.

Secondary Sources

Cornes, R. (1999). 'Intergovernmental Relations in a Devolved United Kingdom: Making Devolution Work' in R. Hazell (ed.) *Constitutional Futures: a history of the next ten years*. Oxford: Oxford University Press.

Bulmer, S., Burch, M., Carter, C., Hogwood, P. and Scott, A., (2001) *European Policy-making under Devolution: Britain's New Multi-level Governance.* Manchester: European Policy Research Unit, Department of Government.

Burrows, N. (2000). *Devolution.* London: Sweet & Maxwell.

Daintith, T. and Page, A. (1999). *The Executive in the Constitution: structure, autonomy and internal control.* Oxford: Oxford University Press.

Hazell, R. (2000). 'Intergovernmental Relations: Whitehall Rules OK?' in R. Hazell (ed.) *The State and the Nations The first year of devolution in the United Kingdom.* Exeter: Imprint Academic.

Hazell, R. (2001). *Three into One Won't go: the future of territorial Secretaries of State.* London: Constitution Unit.

Hogwood, P., Carter, C., Bulmer, S., Burch, M. and Scott, A., 'Devolution and EU policy making: the territorial challenge' *Public Policy and Administration* vol. 15 no. 2, pp. 81-95.

Laffin, M., Thomas A., and Webb, A. (2000). 'Intergovernmental relations after devolution: the National Assembly for Wales' *Political Quarterly* vol. 71 no. 2, pp. 223-233.

Masterman, R. (2001). *Devolution and the Centre: Monitoring Report* [Feb–May 2001]. London: The Constitution Unit.

Mitchell, J. (ed.) (2001). *Scotland: Monitoring Report* [Feb–May 2001]. London: The Constitution Unit.

Osmond, J. (2000). 'A Constitutional Convention by Other Means: the First Year of the National Assembly for Wales' in R. Hazell (ed.) *The State and the Nations The first year of devolution in the United Kingdom.* Exeter: Imprint Academic.

Osmond, J. (ed.). *Farming Crisis Consolidates Assembly's Role: Monitoring the National Assembly March to May 2001.* Cardiff: Institute of Welsh Affairs.

Patchett, K and Osmond, J. (2001). *Enhancing Welsh Input into Westminster Legislation: the IWA's contribution to the National Assembly's operational review.* Cardiff: Institute of Welsh Affairs.

Poirier J. (2001a). 'The Functions of Intergovernmental Agreements: Post-devolution Concordats in a Comparative Perspective' *Public Law* Spring 2001, pp 134-157.

Poirier J. (2001b). *The Functions of Intergovernmental Agreements: Post-devolution Concordats in a Comparative Perspective.* London: Constitution Unit.

Rawlings, R. (2000). 'Concordats of the Constitution' *Law Quarterly Review* vol 116, pp. 257-286.

Rawnsley, A. (2001). *Servants of the People: the inside story of new Labour* revised edition. London: Penguin Books.

8

Devolution and the Centre[1]

Roger Masterman and James Mitchell

INTRODUCTION

Much of the debate on devolution before the enactment of the various pieces of devolution legislation was parochial. It had been parochial in concentrating on the opportunities, problems and implications of devolution within Scotland, Wales and Northern Ireland; little attention had been paid to devolution's impact on the UK as a whole or on the 'centre' — Whitehall and Westminster. One of the paradoxes of devolution was that it had been framed in Scotland and Wales in nationalist terms, yet it was sold as a means of maintaining the Union. So long as devolution remained an opposition desire, the significance of its UK and particularly Whitehall implications could be ignored. Historically, much had been made by parliamentarians of the implications for Westminster, or at least the House of Commons, of devolution — the West Lothian question — though there is little evidence that the English public found this important. Few seemed to know and fewer still cared that devolution would have an impact on Whitehall. Only a few academics, commentators and those working in Whitehall appreciated that this was an important matter.[2]

It was against this background of lack of preparation that the Government legislated for devolution. The idea of a Joint Ministerial Committee (JMC) to bring the four governments together emerged late at night in a Government amendment in the House of Lords.[3] Concordats between UK departments and the devolved administrations entered the vocabulary of British politics and became almost a panacea for the resolution of all kinds of disputes. The concordat became the shibboleth of devolutionists in much the same way that subsidiarity has for supporters of further European integration.

Significantly, the emphasis was on formal institutions. Frequent references were made to the need for co-operation and, at least implicitly, a new,

[1] The research for this chapter forms part of the work undertaken on the 'Devolution and the Centre' project funded by the ESRC Devolution and Constitutional Change Programme (reference no. L29252026). The authors are grateful to John Rhodes for his work in carrying out the interviews for this project.
[2] For a prediction of the effects of devolution on Westminster and Whitehall see The Constitution Unit, 1996, pp. 99-119, or Hazell and Morris 1999.
[3] HL Deb, 28 July, col.1487.

more pluralist political culture at the centre that would allow devolution to succeed, but these tended to be exhortations rather than detailed recommendations. There has been some evidence that a change in attitude has begun (or at least signals of that) but it remains too early to predict confidently that devolution signifies a shift in Whitehall culture.

And while the devolved UK is repeatedly cited by UK ministers as evidence of a revitalised union,[4] Whitehall remains inconspicuous. Despite its radical implications for the constitution — or at least for Whitehall — devolution has evolved since its enactment in a pragmatic, evolutionary, even typically British manner. To date, devolution has not so much resulted in a revolution in Whitehall so much as Whitehall has adapted to accommodate devolution. That may be testimony to the enduring strength and adaptability of the constitution or its innate conservatism.

In their contribution to *Constitutional Futures: A History of the Next Ten Years* in 1999 Robert Hazell and Bob Morris suggested that devolution would result in a number of changes to the machinery at the centre of the UK Government, Whitehall:

- the end of the territorial Secretaries of State;
- the end of the unified home civil service;
- the use of concordats and the development of legal and political structures of intergovernmental relations;
- the use of the JMC on devolution as the main forum for the debate of devolution issues;
- the establishment of devolution units within individual departments;
- representation of the devolved administrations in London; and
- representation for the devolved administrations to the European Union (EU).[5]

Of these predictions, only the less radical have so far come to fruition. Concordats have been agreed between Whitehall departments and the devolved administrations. The JMC on Devolution has acted as a forum for the discussion of various cross-border issues (although during the past year meetings have been infrequent). Whitehall departments have responded to devolution through the creation of devolution and nations and regions teams and the devolved administrations are beginning to make their presence felt on a European scale. However, the Scotland, Wales and Northern Ireland Offices remain (albeit with roles that have changed since devolution) and the civil service remains unified within Great Britain.

---

[4] See for example: WO Press Release, 'Speech by the Secretary of State for Wales, Paul Murphy, to the Regional Government and Devolution Conference in Valencia,' 31 October 2000; 'Cook says devolution will help ensure UK unity,' *The Herald*, 20 April 2001; 'Liddell aims to build on Holyrood-Westminster links', *The Herald*, 8 May 2001.

[5] Hazell and Morris 1999, pp 136-155.

Figure 8.1. Key events in Whitehall: 2000-1

31 October 2000	Secretary of State for Wales Paul Murphy MP, addresses Regional Government and Devolution Conference in Valencia.
23 January 2001	Resignation of Peter Mandelson MP from post of Secretary of State for Northern Ireland.
24 January 2001	Appointment of Dr John Reid MP as Secretary of State for Northern Ireland and appointment of Helen Liddell MP as Secretary of State for Scotland.
11 February 2001	Resignation of Frank Roy MP as PPS to Helen Liddell, to be replaced by Jim Murphy MP.
27 February 2001	DGN 9 (Post-Devolution Primary Legislation Affecting Wales) published.
27 February 2001	DGN 5 (The Role of the Secretary of State for Northern Ireland Post-Devolution) published.
4 March 2001	William Hague MP announces that an incoming Conservative government would retain the post of Secretary of State for Scotland.
9 March 2001	Prime Minister Blair tells press of mistakes made by 'not letting go' of affairs in Wales, post-devolution.
23 March 2001	Revised edition of DGN 6 (Circulation of Inter-Ministerial and Inter-Departmental Correspondence) published.
19 April 2001	Robin Cook MP, Foreign Secretary, announces that devolution will 'stand the test of time as one of this Government's most radical achievements.'
11 May 2001	Children's Commissioner for Wales Act receives Royal Assent.
7 June 2001	Labour win the UK general election, confirming second term in office with another landslide victory.
8 June 2001	Reshuffle of Cabinet, with new responsibilities for the Deputy Prime Minister and departments responsible for the English regions.
11 July 2001	Cabinet Office press release outlines the structure and responsibilities of the new Office of the Deputy Prime Minister.

These expectations were based on an appreciation of administrative processes — Hazell and Morris had avoided emphasising the party-political implications. All things being equal, these expectations were logical. We may surmise that one reason for the limited, indeed relatively conservative, nature of the changes that have been brought about has been the party political considerations that tend to be of particular importance in an election year.

However, had this been entirely correct, we might have expected the Blair government, re-elected with a huge majority, to use the opportunity of a post-election situation to press ahead with the more radical, and potentially politically sensitive, ideas. Instead, there has been little evidence of this. This appears to reflect a mixture of constitutional conservatism on the part of the government and party political considerations that pre-election had resulted in the government making commitments that have bound it even after it secured its second term.

As well as drawing on official documents and the published secondary literature, this chapter is based on interviews with over 40 UK government officials carried out in the spring and summer of 2001 for the 'Devolution and Whitehall' project being undertaken by the authors and Professor Robert Hazell at the Constitution Unit, which forms part of the ESRC's Devolution and Constitutional Change programme. It will examine how the centre has responded to devolution, dealing specifically with the courts, the impact of devolution on Whitehall departments and the territorial offices, and the changes to the central machinery of government made in June 2001 that will shape the way central government deals with devolution in the future.

DEVOLUTION AND THE COURTS

When preparations were being made for devolution, many observers expected that it would result in a great deal of work for lawyers. Even if the four governments avoided their differences becoming legal disputes, there was plenty of scope for challenges by third parties to the actions of the devolved institutions, questioning the extent of the bodies' statutory powers. To deal with such challenges each of the devolution Acts contains a schedule setting out a detailed procedure for dealing with 'devolution issues', which are largely issues of whether an Act or piece of secondary legislation is within the competence of that particular devolved institution.[6] Such issues are to be referred to the Judicial Committee of the Privy Council, and the law officers of the UK government and devolved administrations may be heard in the legal proceedings on them. The legal effect of giving such powers to the Judicial Committee (rather than to the House of Lords' Appellate Committee) has itself been the subject of some discussion, as it creates a 'dual apex' in the UK's judicial system.[7] It also means that a UK court sitting in London has become, in practice, the final court of appeal for certain Scottish criminal matters.

What has been striking, however, is the little use that has in fact been made in the first two years of devolution of the 'devolution issues' procedure. For

[6] Scotland Act 1998, Schedule 6; Government of Wales Act 1998, Schedule 8; Northern Ireland Act 1998, Schedule 10. For a discussion, see Burrows 2000, chap. 6.

[7] See Le Sueur and Cornes 2001, especially chaps. 2 and 5.

government lawyers advising on the powers of the devolved administrations and assemblies there may be a good deal of devolution-related work, but few other lawyers have been greatly affected. While the procedure has been used in a number of cases (three in 2000, and four to 31 July 2001), with one exception these have all concerned criminal prosecutions brought in Scotland. The challenges have been brought on the ground that the prosecution is contrary to the defendant's human rights protected under the Human Rights Act 1998 and section 57 (2) of the Scotland Act 1998.[8] The last year has however seen the first exception to that, in the case of *Anderson, Reid & Doherty v. Scottish Ministers and Advocate-General for Scotland.* This case challenges the lawfulness of the first Act passed by the Scottish Parliament, the Mental Health (Public Safety and Appeals) (Scotland) Act 1999, which provides for the continued incarceration of prisoners suffering from untreatable personality disorders (notably psychopathic disorders) as well as mental illness. This case, like previous challenges, is based on human rights grounds (Article 5 of the European Convention on Human Rights), and the Court of Session had little difficulty in dismissing the application when it was heard in May-June 2000.[9] The case came before the Judicial Committee in July 2001 but no judgment had been issued before the court rose for the summer.

Such legal challenges to the legislation and other decisions taken by the devolved institutions are likely to become more common over time. While Scotland will probably remain the principal object of such challenges, Wales and Northern Ireland are unlikely to be wholly immune. Whether the 'judicial architecture' of the UK will be adequate to cope with them is doubtful and has already, for example, been questioned by the UK's Senior Law Lord, Lord Bingham of Cornhill.[10] Already, however, the role of the Judicial Committee of the Privy Council is exciting some discussion in Scotland.[11] The supremacy of the Scottish High Court of Justiciary as the final court of appeal for Scottish criminal matters was carefully preserved under the Union with England of 1707. It has therefore come as quite a surprise to find that jurisdiction has in fact passed to a UK court, and doubly so that this is a consequence of devolution. This is aggravated by the detailed aspects of Scottish criminal law and procedure that have been the subject of appeals to the Judicial Committee, and by the apparent ignorance of Scottish law and procedure exhibited in those judgments. This legal intervention has proved a

---

[8] This prohibits a member of the Scottish Executive, including the Lord Advocate, from doing an act that is incompatible with Convention rights. See also sections 29 and 54 of the Scotland Act 1998, the former stating that all provisions of Acts of the Scottish Parliament are beyond the Parliament's legislative competence to the extent they are incompatible with Convention rights, and the latter providing that secondary legislation made by Scottish ministers is not competent to the extent it is incompatible with Convention rights.

[9] [2001] SC 1, 16 June 2001. The Court consisted of the Lord President, Lady Cosgrove and Lord Philip.

[10] See 'The Supreme Sacrifice', *The Times*, 17 July 2001.

[11] See Le Sueur 2001 and Le Sueur and Cornes 2001.

particular source of concern to those who expected that the requirement to act only in accordance with human rights obligations would prove a rather remote restriction rather than an immediate and tangible constraint.

THE IMPACT OF DEVOLUTION ON WHITEHALL

With a cross-departmental emphasis on good practice and establishing sensible working arrangements with the devolved administrations the Whitehall response to devolution throughout 2000-2001 can clearly be termed pragmatic. The terminology of concordats and Devolution Guidance Notes (DGNs) has permeated every level of central government, ensuring that, for the most part, change has been in a practical rather than organisational sense.[12] Whitehall departments have responded to devolution by raising awareness and ensuring that the language of devolution was instilled in decision-making processes.[13] However, in keeping with the fragmented structure of UK central government, each department determined for itself what approach it should adopt.[14]

The establishment of 'devolution units' provides a practical example. The function of these generally small teams has been to provide information and increase familiarity with the complex and asymmetric distribution of powers following devolution within the department. Examples include the International and Constitution Branch in the Department of Health and the Regional Co-ordination and Devolution Directorate in the Department of Transport, Local Government and the Regions (DTLR). Such teams have, however, been largely reserved to the main departments providing front-line services, and accordingly the Ministry of Defence and the Department for Culture, Media and Sport do not have in-house devolution expertise. One exception was the devolution team in the Foreign and Commonwealth Office (although it has been wound down during the year). A particularly good example remains the DTLR's Regional Co-ordination and Devolution Directorate, originally established during the passage through Westminster of the three devolution Acts of 1998. Whitehall officials consider that such groups remain necessary, two years after the devolved administrations were established, due to continued questions over the division of powers between administrations caused by changes in policy, new legislation, and most recently the changes to departmental remits following the 2001 UK general election (discussed in more detail below).[15]

---

[12] The increase in use of the terminology of devolution has been seen in House of Commons debates. A basic search for 'concordat' in 1994 comes up with no hits, five for 1995, 20 for 1996, 63 for 1997, 329 for 1998, 400 for 1999, down to 248 for 2000 and 483 by end of June 2001.

[13] Interviews with Whitehall officials, March–July 2001.

[14] See Daintith and Page 1999, chaps. 2 and 10.

[15] Interview with Whitehall official, July 2001.

A number of departments had the benefit of retaining the majority of their pre-devolution functions. The Department for Education and Employment (DfEE) did not cede any functions to the devolved administrations (the Welsh and Scottish Offices already dealt with education matters in those countries) and so relationships, originally established with officials in the three territorial departments, could carry on much as they were with the three devolved administrations. And yet although the role of the department and its Secretary of State remained virtually unchanged, DfEE was initially slow to respond to the demands of liaising with the separate administrations.[16] Within the department the view that the effects of devolution would be minimal made it hard to generate interest in looking at the impact of devolution. Interest was quickly stimulated, however, by the announcement of the Scottish Executive's policy divergence from Whitehall over university tuition fees. While this triggered a change in approach this lay in practice rather than organisation, and it fell to the department's strategy division to raise awareness of the new settlement and its intricacies throughout the department.[17]

Other departments were perhaps not as fortunate and found that their responsibilities had narrowed on some levels while remaining static on others; where potential problems arose, it was in the interaction between levels. For example, while parts of DTLR transport policy remain a UK-wide responsibility (vehicle standards and emissions), others stretch only as far as Great Britain (licensing, roadworthiness and insurance), while others have been narrowed yet further to apply to England alone (roads policy). Mapping the scope of a UK department's responsibilities in this way is complex for the observer and no doubt confusing for many civil servants. Officials report that in dealing with the interaction between these policies in a pragmatic way, and in close co-operation with the devolved administrations, disputes over competences have been identified and resolved before becoming problematic. And while some departments may have been slower than others to catch on, the consensus is that interaction between departments, the territorial offices and the devolved administrations now comes as second nature when necessary.

The emphasis on partnership, emphasised through ministerial rhetoric and put into practice at the official level, has ensured that potential problems over policy divergence between administrations, the future of the unified civil service and claims of Whitehall control-freakery have, thus far, been largely diverted (see also Chapter 7).

THE WORK OF THE TERRITORIAL OFFICES

The three territorial offices — the Scotland Office (SO), Wales Office (WO) and Northern Ireland Office (NIO) — retain a key role even after devolution.

---

[16] Interview with Whitehall official, April 2001.
[17] Interviews with Whitehall officials, April–May 2001.

They link the devolved administrations with the UK government, and their Secretary of State acts as advocate for that territory within the UK Government. The NIO retains other functions as well, notably regarding security and policing, and the Northern Ireland Secretary also has the power to suspend devolution under the Northern Ireland Act 2000. What the territorial offices continue to do in post-devolution Whitehall is worth investigating in detail.

The Scotland Office

The Scotland Office departmental report 2001 detailed the role of the office:

- to promote the devolution settlement for Scotland;
- to continue to represent Scottish interests within the UK government on matters reserved to the UK Parliament;
- to exercise certain residual functions in reserved areas, notably under the Scotland Act 1998, but also in relation to elections and private legislation;
- to pay grant to the Scottish Consolidated Fund;
- to provide legal advice and services to the UK government as regards Scots law.[18]

Its functions are therefore representative (both of Scotland to the UK Government, and vice versa), administrative (paying grant, advising on Scots law) and executive (to only a limited degree, for reserved matters). The SO is currently split into four divisions: the Parliamentary and Constitution Division, the Economy and Industry Division, the Social and Home Affairs Division, and the Finance and Administration Unit. The latter three are based in Edinburgh and Glasgow, with only the Parliamentary and Constitution Division residing south of the border, at Dover House in Whitehall.

A good deal of the work of the SO has centred around acting as an interface between Whitehall departments and the Scottish Executive. Areas of potential conflict or tension have been referred to the SO and its Secretary of State, allowing the stability of the settlement to be monitored and minimising accusations of 'control freakery' being levelled at Whitehall departments.[19] The SO has also performed a monitoring role — scrutinising legislative proposals from both Westminster and Holyrood in an attempt to identify clashes of competence. The SO and Office of the Advocate General have worked in tandem on this exercise, with over 40 of the SO's 100 or so staff having legal expertise.[20] In parallel with this the 2001 departmental report listed eleven Orders in Council passed under the Scotland Act 1998 between April 2000 and March 2001 for the purposes of 'fine-tuning' the devolution settlement.[21] As of September 2001 another seven Orders in Council have

---

[18] SO 2001, Cm 5120, p6.
[19] Interview with Whitehall official, July 2001.
[20] Interview with Whitehall official, July 2001.
[21] SO 2001, CM 5120, at Annex 10 (Scotland Act Orders Made 2000-2001).

been added to this list, with a further Transfer of Functions Order to be made by the Privy Council in October 2001. The process of monitoring the legislative competence of the Scottish Parliament and making amendments to the devolution arrangements through Orders in Council has constituted a large part of the work of the SO since devolution.[22]

The SO retains a role in developing UK policy in relation to reserved matters. Incidences of the involvement of the SO include the Scottish economy,[23] the promotion of overseas trade interests, and government decisions affecting the oil and gas industry in Scotland.[24] The departmental report 2001 addresses these matters in the language of co-operation and partnership favoured by many of the Whitehall documents on devolution:

> Good working relations have been established with the Scottish Executive and relevant Whitehall Departments with responsibility for reserved matters, which has been important to enable Scottish Ministers effectively to present UK policies in Scotland.

In his role as Secretary of State for Scotland John Reid was being increasingly seen as 'a government trouble shooter',[25] and much has been made of his 'expansionist' view of the post, leading to friction with the then Scottish First Minister, Donald Dewar.[26] (It is notable how the staffing of the SO grew while he was Secretary of State.) But his work in and for the SO has also been portrayed in a favourable light, for example by Donald Macintyre of *The Independent*: 'Reid's strategic achievement in Scotland has been to give the Scotland Office, denuded of actual power, the authority it has.'[27]

Figure 8.2. Ministers in the Scotland Office, at July 2001

Helen Liddell	Secretary of State for Scotland	Appointed January 2001
George Foulkes	Minister of State for Scotland	Appointed January 2001
Jim Murphy	PPS	Appointed February 2001
Sandra Osborne	PPS	Appointed January 2001
Lynda Clark QC	Advocate General	Appointed May 1999

[22] Interview with Whitehall official, July 2001.

[23] Including the designation of assisted areas and regulation of the energy and financial services sectors in Scotland (for further details see SO 2001, p2).

[24] *Ibid*, pp. 2-3.

[25] 'Reid takes over Ulster role', *The Times*, 25 January 2001.

[26] Hazell 2001, p15.

[27] 'The Blairite bruiser', *The Independent*, 27 January 2001.

Helen Liddell was elevated to the post of Secretary of State for Scotland on 24 January 2001, following Reid's departure to the NIO. Liddell was previously minister for Energy at the Department of Trade and Industry (DTI), and between 1995 and 1997 was the junior opposition spokeswoman on Scotland. Reid had established a role for himself when Donald Dewar had been First Minister. This, allied with the fact that Henry McLeish is a much weaker First Minister, eased the task for Liddell on her appointment as Secretary of State for Scotland (see also Chapter 3).

The Wales Office

The role of the WO post-devolution is to ' . . . support the Secretary of State in his role of representing Wales in the UK government, representing the UK government in Wales, and ensuring the smooth working of the devolution settlement for Wales.'[28] In line with this role the WO's departmental report 2001 lays down the office's objectives as follows:

- to maintain effective working relationships with the Assembly and to ensure that the devolution settlement continues to operate equitably in the best interests of Wales;
- to ensure that the interests of Wales are fully taken into account in primary legislation which affects the Assembly's responsibilities;
- to promote Welsh interests in functions retained by the UK Government;
- to promote effective communication and co-ordination of policy in areas which straddle the boundary between transferred and retained functions;
- to keep under review the operation of the funding policy for the devolved administrations.[29]

Again, the roles are representative, administrative and executive. The representative function is rather different, however, given the nature of the Welsh settlement. As Welsh primary legislation has to be made at Westminster, the task of liaising between the UK department on one hand and the National Assembly on the other, and understanding the Welsh settlement from a UK government point of view, falls to the WO. The principles governing the process are laid down in DGN 9, issued in February 2001 after protracted discussions between the WO, Cabinet Office and National Assembly. (See Chapter 7 for further discussion of the legislative process affecting Wales, and Chapter 9 for discussion of how Westminster legislation has dealt with Welsh issues.)

One obligation is for the Secretary of State for Wales, Paul Murphy MP, to attend a debate at the National Assembly on the Queen's Speech and the UK government's legislative programme and on 18 December 2000 he duly attended at the National Assembly. And 2000-1 saw a major legislative

---

[28]   WO 2001, Cm 5121, p6.
[29]   *Ibid.*

achievement, which had involved much work for the WO. Following the publication of the report of the Waterhouse Inquiry into abuse of children in care in north Wales, close co-operation between the WO, the UK Department of Health and the National Assembly had already allowed the creation of a Children's Commissioner for Wales in Part V of the Care Standards Act 2000. The powers of the Commissioner were greatly extended in the Children's Commissioner for Wales Bill, the first Wales-only legislation to be proposed at Westminster following devolution, which gained Royal Assent on 11 May 2001 after an uncontroversial passage through both Houses of Parliament.

The 2000-2001 Parliamentary session saw other legislation similarly involving consultation with the WO — such as the Local Government Act 2000, the Transport Act 2000 or the Learning and Skills Act 2000. In addition the WO has been active in developing Welsh interests in reserved matters; in 2000-1 this particularly involved Home Office and Treasury responsibilities.[30]

Figure 8.3. Ministers in the Wales Office, at July 2001

Paul Murphy	Secretary of State for Wales	Appointed July 1999
Don Touhig	Parliamentary Under-Secretary	Appointed June 2001

The Northern Ireland Office

Following the resignation of Peter Mandelson from the post of Secretary of State for Northern Ireland in January 2001, John Reid was appointed to succeed him. Under the Blair administration Reid had served as a junior minister at the Ministry of Defence, and as Minister for Transport. From 1999 he was Secretary of State for Scotland. Given the sensitivities of Northern Ireland it is also significant that Reid is a Catholic.

Figure 8.4. Ministers in the Northern Ireland Office, at July 2001

John Reid	Secretary of State for Northern Ireland	Appointed Jan. 2001
Jane Kennedy	Minister of State	Appointed June 2001
Des Browne	Parliamentary Under-Secretary	Appointed June 2001

Despite the inevitable 'stop-start' nature of devolution to Northern Ireland thus far, as a result of both the suspension of the devolved institutions

---

[30] WO departmental report 2001, pp. 7-8. Particular interest has been paid by the WO to crime and policing in Wales. In addition the WO has established regular contact with the Treasury's Devolved Countries and Regions Team.

between February and May 2000 and the replacement of Peter Mandelson by John Reid as Secretary of State in January 2001, the NIO has maintained a commitment towards making devolution work. This commitment is perhaps best illustrated by the self-denying ordinance against initiating new policy from the centre imposed by NIO ministers during the 2000 suspension. Of course, the extra dimension imposed by the Belfast Agreement adds to the responsibilities of the NIO; the NIO has to ensure that the political conditions enable the peace process to continue, with the eventual goal being a second stage of devolution to Northern Ireland.[31]

The retention of responsibility for law and order and security functions ensures that the role of the Secretary of State for Northern Ireland bears a heavier policy burden than the equivalent post in the Scotland and Wales Offices and that the NIO retains an active role in the administration of the province. For as long as policing, criminal justice and prisons lie within the remit of the NIO there is little chance that the department will be significantly reduced in size or even significantly reformed in the near future. This wider jurisdiction is reflected in the aim of the NIO, as set down in the departmental report 2001:

> To secure a lasting peace in Northern Ireland, based on the Good Friday Agreement, in which the rights and identities of all traditions in Northern Ireland are fully respected and safeguarded and in which a safe, stable, just, open and tolerant society can thrive and prosper.[32]

In contrast to the other territorial departments, ensuring the smooth operation of the devolution settlement is one of many responsibilities for the NIO. In March 2001 relationships between the NIO, Whitehall departments and the Northern Ireland administration were described as 'positive and constructive.'[33] And in these fields significant steps have been made; following the recommendations of the Patten Report, the Police (Northern Ireland) Act received Royal Assent on 23 November 2000, the Office of the Police Ombudsman was opened in November 2000 and, perhaps most symbolically, the Maze Prison was closed in September 2000, following the continued release of prisoners under the Northern Ireland (Sentences) Act 1998. It was these responsibilities that were to largely exclude the NIO from the debate over the future role of the territorial Secretaries of State throughout 2000-2001.

The Continuing Roles of the Territorial Secretaries of State

Much of the debate surrounding the machinery of government prior to the 2001 UK general election concerned the future of the territorial Secretaries

---

[31] DGN 5 (The Role of the Secretary of State for Northern Ireland) recognises the commitment towards further devolution to Northern Ireland.

[32] Northern Ireland Office 2001, Cm 5122, p8.

[33] *Ibid*, p9.

of State. Indeed within Whitehall (and outside it) views on the future of the offices were polarised, especially with regard to the role of the Secretary of State for Scotland; most civil servants agreed that the office 'brought value' to the devolution settlement, and provided an avenue into Whitehall business for the Scottish administration, but a vocal minority insisted that post-devolution a separate department of state for Scotland simply could not be justified.[34]

Since the transfer of powers from the old Scottish Office to the Executive in Edinburgh it has been alleged that it is becoming increasingly unclear what the actual role of the Scottish Secretary is.[35] The official position is that the Secretary of State remains to ensure the smooth implementation of the devolution arrangements and to oversee relations between Whitehall and Holyrood, and yet since devolution the office has undergone a more profound change. One of us has suggested that during the tenure of John Reid the office became the post of 'Minister for Spin' due to having more time on his hands than fellow cabinet members as a result of a lighter policy burden.[36] These claims were countered by Helen Liddell who asserted that in her first seven weeks in the job she had been 'run ragged.'[37] When the issue was raised at Westminster by the Conservative MP James Gray in a written question, he received a rather terse response:

> *Mr Gray*: To ask the Secretary of State for Scotland what discussions she has had with the Prime Minister concerning the future of her department.
> *Mrs. Liddell*: I have regular discussions with the Prime Minister on a wide range of issues... [38]

Of the three territorial Secretaries of State, the office of Secretary of State for Scotland remains the most obvious candidate for reform. With the demands of the ongoing peace process in Ireland it would be almost impossible to alter the position of the NIO. While the Welsh Secretary has to represent the interests of the National Assembly in the legislative process at Westminster, the office of Scottish Secretary seems prima facie the most redundant. Various suggestions for change were tabled in the run-up to the general election, amid speculation that this was where Blair — notoriously reluctant to tamper with the organisation of Whitehall — would choose to cut. Robert Hazell's argument was that a 'Secretary of State for the Union' could:

> ... take a more strategic and forward looking view, and lead government thinking on the unresolved issues of devolution: finance, representation at Westminster

---

[34] Interviews with Whitehall officials, May and July 2001. See also Hazell, 2001, p14.

[35] See Parry and Jones 2000, and James Mitchell, 'Tell us again, what does the Scottish Secretary do?', *The Sunday Times* (Scotland edition), 28 January 2001.

[36] *Ibid.*

[37] 'Liddell 'run ragged' as Scottish Secretary', *The Herald*, 20 March 2001.

[38] House of Commons Written Answers, 3 April 2001, Column 169W.

and the English Question. A combined Secretary of State could also help to ensure mutual learning between the devolved administrations and the UK government from the policy experiments released by devolution.[39]

This was echoed publicly by one other think-tank.[40] The debate surfaced in the media, with reports in the run-up to the UK general election that this would happen.[41] The Tories picked up on the issue too; writing in *Scotland on Sunday*, William Hague, then Leader of the Opposition but using terms that have become familiar through their use by government ministers, outlined the Conservative Party's plans to 'strengthen the Union and improve the government of Scotland.'[42] Hague argued that to ensure a strong voice for Scotland at Westminster and in Europe it would be necessary to retain the post of Secretary of State for Scotland. Labelling any plans to remove, or merge, the offices 'a serious mistake', Hague proposed an increased UK role in Cabinet for the Secretary of State for Scotland allowing the post holder to lead UK delegations at an international level. (It was generally not noticed that Hague planned to combine the office with another Cabinet post, as part of his plans to reduce the overall size of the Cabinet; in reality the SO would have become an appendage to a larger Whitehall department.)

Despite the suggestion that the SO bears a lighter policy load than prior to devolution, the staff of the SO has increased to 107. The WO too has six more staff in April 2001 than it did the previous year, taking its total number up to 46, while the total staff of the NIO has remained static, at 190.

Figure 8.5. Staff of the territorial offices [43]

	Northern Ireland Office	Scotland Office	Wales Office
April 2000	190	86	40
April 2001	190	107	46

What do all these people in the SO do? The role of the SO post-devolution is clearly limited. While Westminster legislation has turned out to be more complex than was expected before devolution (see Chapter 9), the bulk of that work falls on the WO rather than the SO. The SO's functions are

[39] Hazell 2001, p5.

[40] See, for example, Hunt, 'Remodelling Government', IPPR, summarised in *The Times*, 16 December 2000.

[41] See 'Blair plans Ministry of Justice in big shake-up of Whitehall,' *The Independent*, 20 March 2001; 'Downing St studies ways to reshuffle ministry pack,' *Financial Times*, 12 March 2001. There have, however, also been reports that the Government's plan to create a Secretary of State for the Union had been 'shelved for the foreseeable future', see for example 'Scotland Minister "has no job to do"', *The Herald*, 19 March 2001.

[42] 'Play the Scottish Card', *Scotland on Sunday*, 4 March 2001.

[43] Sources: SO, 2000, 2001; WO 2000, 2001; figures for the NIO were taken from Civil Service Staffing Statistics, available at www.cabinet-office.gov.uk/civilservice/index/statistics.htm as no comparable figures were contained in the NIO departmental reports.

comparatively limited. One suggestion is that the size of the office was due to empire building by Reid; this is rejected by officials, but a public case why the office needs to be so large has still not been made.

GOVERNMENT AT THE CENTRE

At the heart of central government lies a small network of officials charged with making sure the whole machine works. For present purposes 'the centre' is treated as the central departments of state — not just the Cabinet Office, and the network surrounding the Prime Minister at 10 Downing Street, but also HM Treasury. However, Number 10 plays only a limited day-to-day role in devolution, and is mainly concerned with aspects of inter-governmental relations. The Treasury too has scaled down its involvement with devolution matters, having only a relatively small team dealing with devolution. The Cabinet Office is, however, a prominent player, not just at the interface with the devolved administrations but also acting as a resource for other Whitehall departments.

HM Treasury

At first glance it appears that the Treasury plays a central part in devolution. In contrast to the legal arrangements, finance remains heavily centralised. Funding is allocated to the devolved administrations according to the Barnett Formula (discussed in detail in Chapter 6), by the UK Government which continues to have sole responsibility in this area. However, the Barnett Formula is simple to administer even if it is complex in its working and effects. The Treasury does have a devolved countries and regions team, but this is small (nine officials). As Chapter 7 discusses, the role of the Treasury in dealing with the devolved administrations is relatively limited — certainly nothing like the detailed control of spending that UK departments face through departmental expenditure controllers.[44] When settlements are relatively generous to the devolved administrations (as with Wales and the funding for Objective 1 in the 2000 Comprehensive Spending Review; see Chapter 6), that happens for political reasons rather than administrative ones. Officials are of course adamant that the Barnett Formula is not open for review or even discussion. While finance remains centralised at the UK level, and for all the power of the Treasury in finance matters, at an administrative level the Treasury is not in fact an active player in devolution.

Cabinet Office: The Constitution Secretariat

Various arms of the Cabinet Office are and have been involved in the management of devolution. Two of the most notable examples are the

---

[44] See Thain and Wright 1995.

Central Secretariat, with responsibility for civil service staffing, and the European Secretariat, which carries responsibility for EU matters. The most prominent however, has been the Constitution Secretariat.

The Constitution Secretariat was established following the 1997 general election to manage the incoming Labour government's extensive constitutional reform agenda. It was placed at the focal point of the Whitehall machinery dealing with devolution. The Secretariat forged close contacts with the central co-ordination units in each of the devolved administrations, encouraged bilateral contact between departments and the devolved administrations, and rightly saw devolution as a process, not an event.[45] The Constitution Secretariat's website detailed its role as:

- to work alongside departments with lead responsibility for each element of the Government's constitutional reform programme;
- to service the collective decision-making necessary to deliver the Government's objectives;
- to undertake a co-ordinating role in bringing together interested departments and ensuring cohesion across the programme as a whole;
- to act as the secretariat to the Joint Ministerial Committee on Devolution (JMC); and
- to act as the secretariat for the British–Irish Council (BIC).[46]

Co-ordinating the government's constitutional agenda across Whitehall was undeniably necessary, but was in practice more concerned with raising awareness and managing relationships than the implementation of policy. But the additional brokering role with the devolved administrations (see Chapter 7), provided an essential means by which potential disputes could be identified and dealt with without resort to the formal machinery set up under the *Memorandum of Understanding* (MOU).[47] Although prior to devolution, officials at the centre believed that the co-ordination mechanisms set up under the MOU would be regularly invoked to deal with potentially divergent policy positions between the administrations, this has not been the case. The success of the Constitution Secretariat in this management role can be attributed to various factors:

- the simple fact that prior to devolution there were no explicit supervisors of relations between Whitehall departments and the territorial offices;[48]
- consultation between UK departments and the devolved administrations has been encouraged, and has continued between individuals with established working relationships;

---

[45] Interview with Whitehall Official, May 2001.
[46] www.cabinet-office.gov.uk/constitution/index.htm (visited June 2001).
[47] Cabinet Office 2000, Cm. 4806.
[48] Interview with Whitehall official, March 2001.

- the devolved administrations have regularly attended meetings in White-hall and received papers.[49]

Despite the practical change which devolution has effected in Whitehall, the reality of the progression has been one of evolution rather than revolution.[50] Indeed those at the centre remain relaxed about the potential discord which many have predicted will result in the event of a devolved nationalist admin-istration, believing that good working relations at official level can minimise tensions. With the emphasis during 2000-2001 on maintaining working rela-tionships and putting into practice the principles enshrined in the MOU and accompanying concordats, many officials believe that the desire of politi-cians to provide 'good service', reinforced by established working practices, will enable relations between the four administrations to continue much as they do at present.[51]

The Mechanics of Devolution: Devolution Guidance Notes

Adding to the values of co-operation and consultation inherent in the MOU the Constitution Secretariat has continued to produce DGNs throughout 2000-2001.[52] Though formally only guidance to Whitehall departments and their officials about how to deal with devolution matters, DGNs are as a matter of practice drafted in conjunction with the devolved administrations affected and so represent agreed positions about detailed matters of adminis-tration. That means they are particularly useful to outside observers as a guide to how devolution is supposed to work from day to day.[53] A full list is reproduced below.[54]

By the end of July 2001 the only DGN which remained unpublished was DGN 7 (*Court Proceedings regarding Devolution Issues under the Scotland Act 1998 and the Government of Wales Act 1998*). This is perhaps surprising bearing in mind the amount of litigation already heard by the Judicial Committee of the Privy Council under the Scotland Act 1998, and now the first challenge to Scottish legislation has been heard, the Government's seeming lack of progress on this front is perplexing.[55]

Some of the recent DGNs are worth noting. DGN 9, *Post-Devolution Primary Legislation Affecting Wales*, agreed between the UK government

[49] Interview with Whitehall official, June 2001.

[50] Interview with Whitehall official, May 2001.

[51] Interview with Whitehall Official, May 2001.

[52] For details of previous DGNs published see Hazell, 2000, pp. 161-163.

[53] To this extent DGNs can be said, like concordats, to function as 'soft law': see Rawlings 2000.

[54] All DGNs are available on the Cabinet Office website at www.cabinet-office.gov.uk/constitution/devolution/guidance/dgn.index.htm

[55] For further details of the case see the August 2001 Devolution and the Centre Monitoring Report available on the Constitution Unit website (www.ucl.ac.uk/constitution-unit/). For further details of the cases involving devolution issues heard by the Judicial Committee see Le Sueur and Cornes, 2001, pp. 22-24.

Figure 8.6. Devolution Guidance Notes published at August 2001

DGN1	Common Working Arrangements (21 January 2000)
DGN2	Handling Correspondence under Devolution (21 January 2000)
DGN3	Role of the Secretary of State for Scotland (21 January 2000)
DGN4	Role of the Secretary of State for Wales (21 January 2000)
DGN5	Role of the Secretary of State for Northern Ireland (27 February 2001)
DGN6	Circulation of Inter-Ministerial and Interdepartmental Correspondence (Revised 23 March 2001).
DGN7	Court Proceedings regarding Devolution Issues under the Scotland Act 1998 and the Government of Wales Act 1998 (to be published)
DGN8	Post Devolution Primary Legislation affecting Northern Ireland (Published April 2001)
DGN9	Post Devolution Primary Legislation affecting Wales (27 February 2001)
DGN10	Post Devolution Primary Legislation affecting Scotland (21 January 2000)
DGN11	Ministerial Accountability after Devolution (28 July 2000)
DGN12	Attendance of UK Ministers and Officials at Committees of the Devolved Legislatures (30 March 2000)
DGN13	Handling of Parliamentary Business in the House of Lords (30 March 2000)

and the Cabinet of the National Assembly, sets down guidance to be followed by Whitehall departments when dealing with legislation affecting the Assembly's responsibilities. Like other DGNs, the document encourages interaction between administrations from an early stage. Although it notes that policy control remains with the UK government, it outlines that the Cabinet of the Assembly must be consulted on Westminster bills which purport to:

- confer new functions on the Assembly;
- alter the Assembly's existing functions (including legislation on, for instance, freedom of information, which would affect the overall discharge of its duties and those public bodies for which it is responsible); or
- otherwise affect areas which are the responsibility of the Assembly, including where it will otherwise be responsible for implementation in Wales, though policy control remains with the UK Government.[56]

Early identification of possible disagreements is fundamental; by the time any proposed legislation reaches the Cabinet's Legislative Programme

[56] DGN 9, para 1.

committee (LP) to gain drafting authority and a commitment for parliamentary time, those issues need to have been addressed and, as far as possible, resolved. The approach is strikingly different to that outlined in DGN 10 on primary legislation for Scotland of a year earlier, indicating a more relaxed view about the practicalities of devolution a year on.

DGN 8, *Post-Devolution Primary Legislation* affecting Northern Ireland, was published by the Cabinet Office in April 2001, and again stresses the importance of co-operation and early consultation. Bearing in mind the sensitive political climate in Northern Ireland it is not surprising that DGN 8 is termed in much stronger language than its Welsh equivalent. While legislative proposals affecting Wales must be referred to the National Assembly, in Northern Ireland similar referrals must be made at the earlier policy stage. The DGN goes as far as to recommend that Whitehall departments should liaise with their Northern Ireland counterparts when 'considering' legislation on reserved matters (particularly on matters which may in the future be devolved).

DGNs are complemented by *Devolution in Practice: a checklist for officials*, agreed by members of the four UK administrations and issued in spring 2001. The document offers a set of principles to be referred to by officials during their dealings between administrations and unsurprisingly emphasises communications, consultation and confidentiality. It complements the values enshrined in the MOU and notes the importance of 'effective and efficient relationships between the administrations' to make the system work.[57]

Remodelling the Centre

To widespread surprise Blair embarked on a major re-organisation of the machinery of government in the wake of the UK general election. And he did not do the expected — despite all the discussion over the future of the territorial departments and their Secretaries of State, these were almost the only parts of central government to be left untouched.

The change reached far and wide. One effect is that responsibility for constitutional affairs is now divided between just two Whitehall departments: the Lord Chancellor's department and the Cabinet Office. While the transfer of human rights, freedom of information and data protection from the Home Office to the Lord Chancellor's department has left the former resembling a Ministry of the Interior, the latter seems to have taken on the role of a Ministry of Justice in all but name.

The creation of the Office of the Deputy Prime Minister following the general election heralds a potential strengthening at the centre of Whitehall. The appointment of John Prescott to the position of 'Cabinet enforcer,' a

---

[57] Available at: www.cabinet-office.gov.uk/constitution/devolution/devolution.htm

more significant figure than previous incumbents and supported by four ministers,[58] indicates an increased role for Prescott, not least with regard to devolution. Some of the responsibilities are relatively light; the Deputy Prime Minister (DPM) carries ministerial responsibility for the BIC and will deputise when necessary for the Prime Minister at meetings of the Council. As the Council has fallen into disuse during 2000 (see Chapter 7), this is unlikely to be onerous. More important is the fact that Prescott also chairs the new Cabinet Committee on the Nations and Regions (CNR)[59] which replaces the former Devolution Policy (DP) committee chaired by Lord Irvine. CNR has broad terms of reference: 'To consider policy and other issues arising from devolution to Scotland, Wales and Northern Ireland; and to develop policy on the English Regions.'

Prescott also has serious back-up in his new role. Following the general election the Constitution Secretariat has been remodelled and merged into a Devolution and Regions Division of the Cabinet Office's General Policy Group. While retaining general responsibility for managing devolution and its role as secretariat for the Joint Ministerial Committee on Devolution and BIC, the group will also be involved in the production of the White Paper on Regional Governance (and took over officials from the former DETR for this). Devolution has become a free-standing area incorporating aspects of policy on the English regions but separate from the (now largely completed) constitutional reform agenda. Like the Constitution Secretariat — the Devolution and Regions division will be involved primarily in the business of relationships rather than policy, becoming involved when cross-administration issues are at stake, when information or advice on the devolution arrangements are requested, or when the Westminster legislative programme is involved, much as the Constitution Secretariat was. Added to this the DPM's responsibility for the Regional Co-ordination Unit and the nine Government Offices in the Regions, 2001 has seen a significant increase in the number of officials reporting to the Cabinet Office.

With regard to regional government for England, no less than three departments are involved (see also Chapter 5). The Government Offices for the Regions and the Regional Co-ordination Unit will report to the DPM in the Cabinet Office. Responsibility for the Regional Development Agencies has been transferred to Patricia Hewitt at the DTI, with only 'regional policy' remaining at what is now the DTLR). Following this division of

[58] Barbara Roche MP, Christopher Leslie MP, Lord Macdonald of Tradeston and Baroness Morgan of Huyton.

[59] It is chaired by the Deputy Prime Minister and its other members are the Leader of the Commons, the Lord Chancellor, the Home Secretary, the Secretaries of State for Environment, Food and Rural Affairs; Work and Pensions; Transport, Local Government and the Regions; Health; Trade and Industry; Education and Skills; Culture, Media and Sport; Northern Ireland, Wales and Scotland; the Chief Secretary to the Treasury, the Leader of the Lords, the Chief Whip, the Minister without Portfolio, the Attorney General, the Advocate General for Scotland, and the Minister of State at the Cabinet Office (Barbara Roche). The Foreign and Defence Secretaries also receive papers.

responsibility, press reports suggested that after having completed the forth-coming White Paper on English regional government Prescott would hand over the implementation of the policy to Stephen Byers in the DTLR. Regional Government was always going to be the subject of fierce Whitehall turf wars; this division of responsibility can only increase that risk.

Daintith and Page observed in 1999 that, 'The role of the centre is no longer confined to advice and assistance; it is also increasingly one of encouraging and exhorting departments and agencies to move in desired directions.'[60] While the Constitution Secretariat concerned itself with the 'management' of devolution here we may be seeing the development of a more active centre. One of the criticisms of the Constitution Secretariat was that, although it had a clear understanding of the decisions made by the devolved administrations, it was inherently reactive, and not strong enough to exert an influence on the ways in which departments worked.[61] The remodelled centre may indeed prove to be a driving force behind policy on devolution to the nations and regions, if problems over the division of responsibility surrounding devolution to the English regions can be overcome.

CONCLUSION

Noreen Burrows has noted that in a country 'whose constitutional mantra is that there is no written constitution, the deference to the written word in the devolution process is astonishing.'[62] In addition to the primary legislation itself, there is secondary legislation, written codes and concordats. It is not so much that a formal written constitution is in the making, but that devolution has spawned a substantial written addition to 'the set of laws, rules and prac-tices that create the basic institutions of the state and its component and related parts.'[63] Within the text of concordats and DGNs alone we are seeing a codification of 'the relationship[s] between the different institutions' of the state, a codification which may redefine the operation and study of the United Kingdom constitution in years to come.[64]

Nonetheless, Whitehall has accommodated devolution without too much difficulty. In large measure this is because devolution did not involve a new layer of government but changes in the accountability of an existing struc-ture. Whitehall has long understood that the component parts of the UK are treated differently, that the UK is a union, not a unitary state. Changes that have been introduced post-devolution have built on existing arrangements.

[60] Daintith and Page 1999, p385.
[61] Interviews with Whitehall officials, March 2001, July 2001.
[62] Burrows 2000, p2.
[63] House of Lords Select Committee on the Constitution, *Reviewing the Constitution: Terms of Reference and Method of Working*, 11 July 2001, HL 11, para 50.
[64] *Ibid.*

However, it remains early days. It is too early to say whether the growth of the 'written word' suggests a 'carefully controlled process'[65] or codification embodying a union state.

BIBLIOGRAPHY

Official Documents

Cabinet Office (2000). *Memorandum of Understanding and supplementary agreements*. Cm 4806.

Northern Ireland Office/Her Majesty's Treasury (2001). *The Government's Expenditure Plans 2001-02 to 2003-04 and Main Estimates 2001-02: Northern Ireland Office 2001 Departmental Report*. Cm 5122.

Scotland Office (2000). *The Government's Expenditure Plans 2000-01 to 2001-02: Departmental Report by the Scotland Office*. Cm 4619.

Scotland Office (2001). *The Government's Expenditure Plans 2001-02 to 2003-04: Departmental Report by the Scotland Office*. Cm 5120.

Wales Office (2000). *The Government's Expenditure Plans 2000-01 to 2001-02: Departmental Report by the Wales Office*. Cm 4620.

Wales Office (2001). *The Government's Expenditure Plans 2001-02 to 2003-04: Departmental Report by the Wales Office*. Cm 5121.

Secondary Sources

Burrows, N. (2000). *Devolution*. London: Sweet and Maxwell.

Constitution Unit (1996). *Scotland's Parliament: Fundamentals for a new Scotland Act*. London: Constitution Unit.

Daintith, T. and Page, A. (1999). *The Executive in the Constitution*. Oxford: OUP.

Hazell, R. (2000). 'Intergovernmental Relations: Whitehall Rules OK?', in Hazell, R. (ed.), *The State and the Nations: The First Year of Devolution in the United Kingdom*. London: Imprint Academic.

Hazell, R. (2001). *Three into One Won't Go: The Future of the Territorial Secretaries of State*. London: Constitution Unit.

Hazell, R. and Morris, B. (1999). 'Machinery of Government: Whitehall', in Hazell, R (ed)), *Constitutional Futures*. London: Oxford University Press.

Le Sueur, A. (2001). *What is the Future for the Judicial Committee of the Privy Council?* London: Constitution Unit.

Le Sueur, A. and Cornes, R. (2001). *The Future of the United Kingdom's Highest Courts*. London: Constitution Unit.

Parry, R. and Jones, A. (2000). 'The Transition from the Scottish Office to the Scottish Executive', 15(2) *Public Policy and Administration* 53.

Rawlings, R. (2000). 'Concordats of the Constitution' *Law Quarterly Review*, vol. 116.

Thain, C. and Wright, M. (1995). The Treasury and Whitehall: the planning and control of public expenditure 1976-1993. Oxford: Oxford University Press.

---

[65] *Ibid.*

9

Devolution and Westminster

Roger Masterman and Robert Hazell[1]

INTRODUCTION

Devolution had an immediate impact on the range of issues which could be discussed or legislated on at Westminster. Consequently the procedures and conventions under which Parliament operates underwent a vast change in a short period of time. But, as Russell and Hazell observed in *The State and the Nations* in 2000, changes to the parliamentary process during the first year of devolution were piecemeal and minimalist.[2] More recently commentators on the Westminster response to devolution also support this view. Writing at the end of 2000, Cowley and Stuart commented:

> The year 2000 could have been a year in which Parliament began to deal with the consequences of devolution . . . Instead, for the most part Parliament continued to treat devolution as a problem that would go away if it were ignored for long enough . . .[3]

And in summer 2001 the Hansard Society Commission on Parliamentary Scrutiny described the situation as follows:

> Parliament has been slow to adapt its own procedures in the face of these sizeable constitutional reforms . . . and as the Procedure Committee noted in its report on the Procedural Consequences of Devolution there is a degree of confusion as to what can and cannot be discussed in London. Since devolution certain matters are now ruled inadmissible by the Speaker if they relate to devolved matters. Yet defining the specific ministerial responsibilities of the Scotland Office or Wales Office is not straightforward. There are many issues which overlap, where responsibility is not clear. The fear of some who gave evidence to the Procedure Committee was that this ambiguity would allow ministers in the Westminster Parliament to define those areas where they are willing to answer questions.[4]

The way in which Parliament has reacted to devolution has been largely reactive and responsive. Action has generally been taken only in response to

---

[1] Particular thanks are due to Meg Russell for her work on the impact of devolution on Westminster.
[2] Russell and Hazell 2000, p219.
[3] Cowley and Stuart 2001, p238.
[4] Report of the Hansard Society Commission on Parliamentary Scrutiny 2001, para 1.13.

some challenge to the established procedures of Westminster, and generally in response to small procedural matters rather than to bigger issues of substance. This inertia is most clearly illustrated by the lack of a convincing answer to the 'English Question'. In this as in other things Westminster follows the pattern set by the government, which is inevitable in a parliamentary system where the lead for parliamentary reform comes from the executive.[5] Only in the House of Lords, the chamber which is not dominated by the executive, are there signs that Westminster is beginning to take a more active interest, through the Lords' new Committee on the Constitution.

An MP who had left Parliament in 1997, on the eve of devolution, and returned to the House of Commons today would find very little changed so far as a result of devolution. Scotland and Wales are still over-represented in terms of the number of their MPs.[6] There is still the full range of Scottish, Welsh and Northern Irish committees (Grand, Select and Standing) even though there should be less Scottish, Welsh and Northern Irish business for Westminster to consider. There is still a separate question time every month for each of the territorial Secretaries of State, although they have much less to answer for. These are matters which eventually Westminster will start to rationalise, but for the moment most of the pre-devolution structures and procedures have been left in place.

The story in this chapter is mostly one of minor rather than major changes. The chapter begins with a brief chronology of the main events at Westminster (Figure 9.1), before analysing the changes in the membership of the new House of Commons following the general election in June 2001. We then look at Westminster's legislative output, analysing how Westminster legislates sometimes for the whole UK, sometimes for one of its constituent parts; and how Westminster continues to legislate for Scotland, even on matters now devolved to Scotland. We then turn to the changing work of the territorial committees: the Scottish, Welsh and Northern Ireland Select Committees, and Grand Committees, and the strange case of the short-lived English committee, the Standing Committee on Regional Affairs. That leads into a section on the English Question, and William Hague's proposal for 'English votes on English laws'. The chapter concludes with a discussion of the potentially more significant changes in response to devolution which are starting to be made in the House of Lords.

---

[5] A salutary reminder from an expert insider is Andrew Kennon 2001.

[6] Scotland has 72 MPs and Wales 40. If their representation was brought into line with the English quota they would have 57 and 33 respectively. Scottish representation is due to be reduced in the current Boundary Commission review (Scotland Act 1998, s.86), due to report between 2002 and 2006; but there are no plans to reduce Welsh representation.

Figure 9.1. Key events at Westminster, July 2000–July 2001

23 October 2000	Michael Martin MP elected to replace Betty Boothroyd as Speaker of the House of Commons.
13 Nov. 2000	William Hague gives speech at Magdalen College Oxford proposing 'English votes on English laws.'
30 Nov. 2000	Prorogation of Parliamentary Session 1999-2000.
6 Dec. 2000	Queen's Speech — opening of the 2000-2001 Parliamentary Session.
8 February 2001	Membership of the House of Lords Committee on the Constitution announced.
13 March 2001	Membership of the House of Commons Standing Committee on Regional Affairs announced.
21 March 2001	House of Lords debate on devolution to the English regions.
10 May 2001	First meeting of the Standing Committee on Regional Affairs since 1978.
11 May 2001	Children's Commissioner for Wales Act receives Royal Assent.
11 May 2001	Dissolution of Parliament.
7 June 2001	General election — Labour administration re-elected with a majority of 167.
8 June 2001	William Hague announces that he will step down as leader of the Conservative Party.
19 June 2001	Publication of the Hansard Society Commission Report on Parliamentary Scrutiny: *The Challenge for Parliament: Making Government Accountable.*
20 June 2001	Queen's Speech — Opening of the 2001-2002 parliamentary session.
20 July 2001	Parliament adjourns for the summer recess.

THE HOUSE OF COMMONS

The State of the Parties, July 2001

The UK general election of June 2001 was the first since the devolved admin-istrations assumed their functions during the summer of 1999. Following the general election of 7 June the division of Westminster seats among the parties showed little change. Having lost all their seats outside England in 1997, the Conservatives gained just one in Scotland; and in terms of their electoral representation they continued to be an overwhelmingly English party. Labour was completely dominant electorally in England, Scotland and Wales.

Figure 9.2. Territorial and party strength in the new House of Commons, July 2001

	Lab	Con	Lib Dem	Other	Total
England	323	165	40	1	529
Scotland	56	1	10	5	72
Wales	34	0	2	4	40
Northern Ireland	0	0	0	18	18
Total	413	166	52	28	659

Source: House of Commons Information Office

The End of Dual Mandates

From the devolution point of view, the main change in the new Parliament was the disappearance of all the dual-mandate MPs except for those in Northern Ireland. A total of 17 dual-mandate MPs stood down at the election, choosing to focus on their work in the devolved administrations. Only one, Alex Salmond MP, former leader of the Scottish National Party, in a surprising move announced that he was going to stand down as a Member of the Scottish Parliament to focus on a 'crucial general election campaigning role' for the SNP at Westminster.[7] Both the Scottish National Party (SNP) and Plaid Cymru (PC) had faced some criticism that post-devolution they would be fielding their B-team at Westminster. But the dilemma was one facing all parties, as they came to realise that post-devolution they needed effective leaders both at Westminster and at the devolved level. For the SNP Salmond will ensure they maintain an effective presence at Westminster. For the main political parties the search has been in reverse — Labour, the Conservatives and Liberal Democrats have all had to seek out new political talent to lead their parties at the devolved level.

Figure 9.3. Westminster MPs with experience of the devolved institutions

Formerly Member of the Scottish Parliament:		
Alex Salmond	SNP	Banff and Buchan
Formerly Member of the National Assembly for Wales:		
Alun Michael	Labour	Cardiff South and Penarth

Source: House of Commons Information Office

Salmond remains the only MP at Westminster with first-hand experience of devolution to Scotland. Alun Michael, former First Secretary of the

[7] 'Salmond opts for Westminster in change of heart', *The Guardian*, 11 January 2001, 'Salmond defies Westminster critics', *The Herald*, 16 January 2001.

National Assembly for Wales, is now a junior minister in the Department of the Environment Food and Rural Affairs (DEFRA).

Figure 9.4. Dual-Mandate MPs in the 1997-2001 Parliament who did not contest their seats in 2001

Members of the Scottish Parliament:		
Malcolm Chisholm	Labour	Edinburgh North & Leith
Roseanna Cunningham	SNP	Perth
Margaret Ewing	SNP	Moray
Sam Galbraith	Labour	Strathkelvin & Bearsden
Donald Gorrie	Liberal Democrat	Edinburgh West
John Home Robertson	Labour	East Lothian
John McAllion	Labour	Dundee East
Henry McLeish	Labour	Fife Central
Alasdair Morgan	SNP	Upper Galloway & Nithsdale
John Swinney	SNP	Tayside North
Jim Wallace	Liberal Democrat	Orkney and Shetland
Andrew Welsh	SNP	Angus
Members of the National Assembly for Wales:		
Ron Davies	Labour	Caerphilly
Ieuan Wyn Jones	Plaid Cymru	Ynys Môn
John Marek	Labour	Wrexham
Rhodri Morgan	Labour	Cardiff West
Dafydd Wigley	Plaid Cymru	Caernarfon
Member of the Northern Ireland Assembly:		
John Taylor	Ulster Unionist	Strangford

Source: House of Commons Information Office

The loss of these dual-mandate MPs has removed one of the informal links between Westminster and the Scottish Parliament and National Assembly for Wales. However the effectiveness of the links has been called into question — at least one MP has commented on the fact that dual-mandate MPs from Scotland, Wales or Northern Ireland rarely attended Westminster sittings.[8] Five members of the House of Lords also hold seats in the devolved bodies in Wales, Scotland and Northern Ireland.[9]

---

[8] Interview with Westminster MP, March 2001.

[9] Lord Selkirk of Douglas (James Douglas-Hamilton), Lord Steel of Aikwood (Sir David Steel) and Lord Watson of Invergowrie in the Scottish Parliament; Lord Elis-Thomas in the National Assembly for Wales; and Lord Alderdice in the Northern Ireland Assembly. Lords Steel, Elis-Thomas and Alderdice are all presiding officers of their respective assemblies.

Northern Ireland is a big exception. A majority of MPs from Northern Ireland are dual-mandate MPs, holding their Westminster seats in conjunction with seats in the Northern Ireland Assembly.

Figure 9.5. MPs holding seats in the Northern Ireland Assembly, July 2001

Gerry Adams	Sinn Féin	Belfast West
Roy Beggs	Ulster Unionist	East Antrim
Gregory Campbell	DUP	East Londonderry
Nigel Dodds	DUP	Belfast North
Pat Doherty	Sinn Féin	West Tyrone
Michelle Gildernew	Sinn Féin	Fermanagh and South Tyrone
Seamus Mallon	SDLP	Newry and Armagh
Martin McGuinness	Sinn Féin	Mid Ulster
Rev Ian Paisley	DUP	North Antrim
Iris Robinson	DUP	Strangford
Peter Robinson	DUP	Belfast East
David Trimble	Ulster Unionist	Upper Bann

Source: House of Commons Information Office

Twelve of the eighteen MPs from Northern Ireland following the 2001 UK general election also hold seats in the Northern Ireland Assembly. John Hume, the Social Democratic and Labour Party (SDLP) Member of Parliament for Foyle, resigned his seat in the Northern Ireland Assembly on 1 December 2000.

Nationalist Parties Form Joint Party Group

Another change in the new Parliament is that, after discussions with the Speaker, the SNP and PC announced that they had formed a joint group in order to achieve more speaking rights in the House and better representation on Select Committees.[10] The group, now comprising nine MPs, will be the fourth largest in the Commons, above the Ulster Unionists.

When membership of the parliamentary select committees was announced on July 16 2001, the decision to form a parliamentary group did not seem to pay dividends with the nationalist parties being awarded five seats between them, the same number as they had held at the beginning of the previous Parliament in 1997. In July 2001 the newly elected Scottish National Party MP Michael Weir was awarded a seat on the Scottish Affairs Committee, while Alasdair Morgan gained a seat on the Trade and Industry Select

[10] 'Welsh link up with the Scots', *The Times*, 28 June 2001.

Committee. PC MP Adam Price gained a seat on the Welsh Affairs Committee and Simon Thomas will sit on both the Environmental Audit Committee and Commons Select Committee on Catering.[11]

WESTMINSTER LEGISLATION

The period July 2000 to July 2001 spanned two Parliamentary sessions: 1999-2000, and 2000-2001. During this period 58 Acts of Parliament received Royal Assent. Just over half of these (33 Acts) applied to the whole of the UK. In the next largest category (20 Acts) Parliament was legislating just for England and Wales.

Figure 9.6. Territorial extent of legislation passed during 1999-2000 parliamentary session

United Kingdom	16
Great Britain	4
England and Wales	16
Northern Ireland	1
Total	37

Figure 9.7. Territorial extent of legislation passed during 2000-2001 parliamentary session

United Kingdom	17
Great Britain	0
England and Wales	4
Northern Ireland	0
Total	21

Legislating for Scotland

The Westminster Parliament also continues to legislate to a surprising extent for Scotland, even on matters which are now devolved. During the passage of the Scotland Act it was anticipated that Westminster would continue sometimes to legislate for Scotland; an understanding known as the 'Sewel convention' after it was first proposed by the then Scottish Office minister Lord Sewel.[12] It was generally believed that this licensed legislative trespassing would happen only occasionally. In practice it seems to be happening

---

[11] In 1997 the SNP and PC held five seats between them on the Scottish and Welsh Affairs Committees, the Trade and Industry Committee, the Environmental Audit Committee and the European Legislation Committee.

[12] See further: Devolution Guidance Note 10, *Post Devolution Primary Legislation Affecting Scotland.*

regularly. Of the 58 Acts of Parliament which received Royal Assent between July 2000 and July 2001 thirteen were endorsed by way of a Sewel Resolution made by the Scottish Parliament (they are divided by Parliamentary session in the table below).

Figure 9.8. Acts passed for which Sewel resolutions made by the Scottish Parliament

1999-2000 Parliamentary Session:
Limited Liability Partnerships Act 2000.
Care Standards Act 2000.
Sea Fishing Grants Act 2000.
Government Resources and Accounts Act 2000.
Regulation of Investigatory Powers Act 2000.
Race Relations (Amendment) Act 2000
Insolvency Act 2000.
Political Parties, Elections and Referendums Act 2000.
Criminal Justice and Court Service Act 2000.
Sexual Offences (Amendment) Act 2000.
2000-2001 Parliamentary Session:
Health and Social Care Act 2001.
International Criminal Court Act 2001.
Armed Forces Act 2001.

Two things are worth noting about this table. First is the statute which is missing. A significant omission from the above list is the Health Service Commissioners (Amendment) Act 2000: an act passed at Westminster which trespassed on matters which were devolved to Scotland, but was not the subject of any Sewel resolution or debate in the Scottish Parliament.

Second is the inclusion in the list of Acts which only trespassed marginally on devolved matters. Some of the statutes fell squarely within the powers of the Scottish Parliament (for example the Sexual Offences (Amendment) Act),[13] but others are more borderline. By erring on the side of caution the UK Government would be following the advice which it promulgated in Devolution Guidance Note (DGN) 10, which states that:

> . . . consent need only be obtained for legislative provisions which are specifically for devolved purposes, although it will be good practice to consult the Scottish Executive on changes in devolved areas of law which are incidental to or consequential on provisions made for reserved purposes.[14]

---

[13] As observed by Baroness Blatch, HL Deb, 11 April 2000, Col. 98.

[14] DGN 10, para 2(3).

An example of the latter is the Race Relations (Amendment) Act, which is squarely within the competence of Westminster, since equal opportunities and race relations are reserved matters. But the Act contains sections which touch on issues of criminal justice which are devolved to Scotland, and for that reason was endorsed by the Scottish Parliament by way of Sewel resolution on 25 May 2000.[15]

Legislating for Wales

In Wales the division of legislative responsibility is very different. Westminster continues to pass all primary legislation for Wales, and the National Assembly has powers of secondary legislation only. This makes it the more important for there to be effective procedures which enable Wales to feed in views about the primary legislative framework. Those procedures are outlined in DGN 9, *Post Devolution Primary Legislation Affecting Wales*. The DGN states that the Cabinet of the Assembly should always be consulted on bills which confer new functions on the Assembly, alter the existing functions of the Assembly, or otherwise affect areas which are the responsibility of the National Assembly for Wales (NAW) (including where implementation is a matter for the Assembly, although control of the underlying policy remains with the UK government).

Even at this early stage of devolution we can see patterns emerging in the Westminster legislation which impacts on the devolved responsibilities of the National Assembly. For the majority of Acts which relate to devolved competences there is a simple read-across provision — the National Assembly will receive equivalent powers to the relevant Secretary of State.

Less frequent, however, are Acts which although conferring powers on the NAW, do not do so to the same extent as the relevant Secretary of State. An example is the Local Government Act 2000 which gives the NAW various powers with regard to local authorities, but reserves to the Secretary of State powers over commencement orders and 'Henry VIII' provisions.

Finally there are those Acts which allow the development of a separate policy framework for Wales, the most obvious example so far being the Care Standards Act 2000 which established the Office of Children's Commissioner for Wales. The powers of the Commissioner were extended in the Children's Commissioner for Wales Act which received Royal Assent on 11 May 2001. This was the first formally Wales-only legislation introduced at Westminster at the instigation of the National Assembly. The Act legislated to give effect to the recommendations of Sir Ronald Waterhouse's inquiry into child abuse in Wales, which had not been published at the time of passing the Care Standards Act. The Act had an uncontroversial passage through Westminster and had cross party support within the National Assembly for

---

[15] Scottish Parliament Official Report, 25 May 2000, Cols. 1059-1078.

Wales. It stimulated some MPs at Westminster to question why there was no parallel legislation for England.[16]

The Queen's Speech given on 20 June 2001 indicated that the next Wales-only legislation likely to be debated at Westminster would involve plans to reform the National Health Service in Wales in line with proposals agreed by the National Assembly early in 2001.[17] In July 2001, however, it was announced that the clauses of the draft NHS (Wales) Bill had been merged into the NHS Reform bill.[18]

Legislating for Northern Ireland

The Northern Ireland Assembly has significant legislative powers broadly comparable to those of the Scottish Parliament. As with Scotland, DGN 8, *Post-Devolution Primary Legislation affecting Northern Ireland*, provides that the UK Government would 'not normally legislate with regard to devolved matters except with the agreement of the devolved legislature'.[19] Under the DGN it remains the responsibility of the devolved administration for seeking agreement after an approach by the UK government. In practice it has been left to the Executive Committee to decide whether further action needs to be taken by the Northern Ireland Assembly, and in operation has proved less formal than the Sewel procedure as evident in the Scottish Parliament.

It should be noted at this point that Westminster continues to deal with controversial legislation dealing with Northern Ireland. One example of this is the Disqualifications Act 2000. The primary purpose of the Act was to remove the disqualification for membership of the House of Commons and the Northern Ireland Assembly of persons who are members of the legislature of Ireland (the Oireachtas). Lord Falconer of Thoroton, presenting the bill on behalf of the government stated that the purpose of the bill was to:

> . . . enable members of the Irish legislature to stand for election to the House of Commons and the UK devolved legislatures, thereby giving them equal treatment with Members of Commonwealth legislatures and the same rights as other non-elected Irish citizens.[20]

Opponents of the bill, however, criticised it as a sop to Sinn Féin, who would be its main beneficiaries. During the course of the Lords debates the bill was described as 'a constitutional monstrosity'[21] and came under fire for lacking

[16] HC Deb, 16 January 2001, Col. 212. Interview with Westminster MP, January 2001.
[17] HL Deb, 20 June 2001, Col. 5. See also *Improving Health for Wales: A Plan for the NHS with its Partners* (National Assembly for Wales, 2001), available at: www.wales.gov.uk/healthplanonline /health_plan/index.htm
[18] See Osmond 2001, p14.
[19] DGN 9, para 1.
[20] HL Deb, 27 July 2000, Col. 706.
[21] HL Deb, 6 November 2000, Col. 1254.

popular and parliamentary support, and for having no foundation in the Belfast Agreement.[22]

Despite a successful wrecking amendment by Conservative peers on 20 November 2000, prompting suggestions that the bill would be dropped,[23] the government pressed ahead with the Bill and its Royal Assent was granted on 30 November 2000. Other controversial legislation included the Northern Ireland Act 2000, which grants the Secretary of State for Northern Ireland the power to suspend the devolved institutions, and legislation relating to policing reform.

THE WORK OF THE TERRITORIAL COMMITTEES

Scotland, Wales and Northern Ireland still retain their separate committee structure at Westminster, with three different kinds of committees. There are the Scottish, Welsh and Northern Ireland Select Committees, to scrutinise the work of the three territorial Secretaries of State. There are the much larger Scottish, Welsh and Northern Ireland Grand Committees, which consist of all the MPs sitting for Scotland, Wales and Northern Ireland respectively. And there is still the possibility of a Scottish, Welsh or Northern Ireland Standing Committee, to take the committee stage of legislation applying to one of the territories.

Although the UK government has made no move to rationalise the pre-devolution committee structure, MPs recognise the need to do so. A survey of MPs conducted by the Constitution Unit during 2000 produced interesting responses with regard to territorial committees at Westminster. Results indicated a high degree of agreement between MPs that there should be fewer forums at Westminster to discuss Scottish-only issues, with no MP suggesting that there should be an increase in such forums. It was also largely agreed that there should be fewer Wales-only forums (a view demonstrated more markedly by Conservative responses).[24] And there was strong support for more English-only, or English regional, forums amongst MPs.

The Territorial Select Committees

Following devolution to Scotland, Wales and Northern Ireland the remits of the territorial Select Committees have been altered to allow the scrutiny of

[22] HL Deb, 27 July 2000, Col. 709. Subsequent to the passing of the Act a number of Parliamentary questions were tabled by Lord Laird asking where and when the support of the Irish Government for the Disqualifications Bill was gained (HL Written Answers, 21 December 2000, WA 87; 19 February 2001, WA 84). Each received an equally elusive answer.

[23] 'Ireland Bill may have to be ditched,' *The Times*, 22 November 2000; 'Ministers may sacrifice bill to aid Trimble,' *The Guardian*, 22 November 2000.

[24] A survey of MPs for the Devolution and Westminster Project funded by the Leverhulme Trust and carried out by Meg Russell, summer 2000. Results will be published by the Constitution Unit in due course.

not only the workings of each territorial office, but also relations between that office and its corresponding devolved administration.[25] The work of the Wales and Northern Ireland Committees during 2000-2001 has reflected this expansion of their role with each conducting a reassessment of their role in the post-devolution Parliament. The Scottish Affairs Committee does not appear to have engaged in a similar rethink, and produced just two reports in 2000-1, compared with four from the Welsh Affairs Committee and eight from the Northern Ireland Affairs Committee (see Figures 9.9–9.11).

Figure 9.9. Welsh Affairs Committee reports published, 2000-1

21 Dec. 2000	The Work of the Committee since Devolution	HC81
15 Jan. 2001	Social Exclusion in Wales	HC 365 I-II
28 March 2001	Wales in the World: The Role of the UK Government in Promoting Wales Abroad	HC38
11 May 2001	Welsh Young Offenders held outside Wales: Interim Report and Proposals for Further Inquiry	HC511

It has been suggested that this comparative lack of action has of late been, in part, caused by the debate over the future of the Scotland Office held in the run-up to the 2001 general election.[26] But perhaps equally the case is that because of the reduced range of Scotland Office responsibilities the Scottish Affairs Committee is finding it harder to identify topics for investigation.[27] But nevertheless, in the face of similar alterations to the scope of potential inquiries, both the Northern Ireland and Welsh Affairs Committees have tackled the impact that devolution will have on their work in significantly more detail than the Scottish Affairs Committee. Despite taking evidence on the work of the Scotland Office in early 2000,[28] and submitting a memorandum to the Liaison Committee which deals with the Committee's work post-devolution,[29] the Scottish Affairs Committee has not looked into the ramifications of the new constitutional settlement since its report on Multi-Layer Democracy, published in 1998.[30]

---

[25] Standing Order No. 152.

[26] Interviews with Westminster MPs, March–April 2001. For further details of the debate over the future of the territorial offices see Chapter 8, on Devolution and the Centre.

[27] Interview with Westminster MP, December 2000. Indeed, in a memorandum to the Liaison Committee, the Scottish Affairs Committee indicated that devolution had narrowed its range of interests (Liaison Committee 2001).

[28] Scottish Affairs Committee 2000, vol. i. The Scottish Affairs Committee has, in its memorandum to the Liaison Committee, suggested that it may return to this topic in the future.

[29] Liaison Committee 2001.

[30] Scottish Affairs Committee 1998.

Figure 9.10. Northern Ireland Affairs Committee reports published, 2000-1

4 August 2000	Public Expenditure in Northern Ireland: Inward Investment.	HC 198 I-II.
4 August 2000	Northern Ireland Railways: Financial Provision for New Rolling Stock in 2000-1.	HC 512.
28 Feb. 2001	The Northern Ireland Prison Service.	HC 263.
11 April 2001	The Parades Commission.	HC 120 I-II.
11 April 2001	Relocation Following Paramilitary Intimidation.	HC 59 I-II.
11 May 2001	The Parades Commission — Supplementary Report.	HC 521.
29 June 2001	Miscellaneous Financial Matters and the Government's Response to the Committee's Third Report Session 1999-2000.	HC 458.
13 July 2001	Legal Aid in Northern Ireland.	HC 444.

Figure 9.11. Scottish Affairs Committee reports published, 2000-1

19 July 2000.	Poverty in Scotland.	HC 59 I-II.
1 May 2001.	The Drinks Industry in Scotland: Issues and Concerns.	HC 114.

In its report *The Work of the Committee Since Devolution*,[31] the Welsh Affairs Committee indicated that:

> We have taken a flexible approach to the interpretation of the new terms of reference. The primary functions of the Wales Office include promoting the interests of Wales in policy formulation by the UK Government, promoting UK Government policies in Wales, consulting the National Assembly on the Government's legislative programme and steering primary legislation through Parliament. We believe that this gives us a broad remit to examine the impact of UK Government policy in Wales, as well as more technical issues such as the mechanics of the devolution settlement and the calculation of the National Assembly's budget.[32]

That the Welsh Affairs Committee have interpreted this remit broadly is demonstrated by their subsequent inquiries into European structural funds, the impact of the Transport bill in Wales, and social exclusion in Wales, all of

[31] Welsh Affairs Committee 2000.
[32] *Ibid,* para 9.

which deal with the impact of UK government policies in Wales.[33] Indeed the Committee believes that this broader approach to matters has helped to define their role, post-devolution:

> Unlike the position in Scotland, where a large measure of responsibility for primary legislation has been devolved, much of the primary legislation passed at Westminster affects Wales directly and we believe that we can play a useful role in taking up Assembly Members' concerns about matters which fall within the responsibility of the UK Parliament.[34]

In addition to this expansion of the Committee's areas of interest, meetings have taken place, both formally and informally, with representatives of the Assembly, a trend which the Committee would favour the continuation of in the future where appropriate.[35]

In keeping with the expansion of the interests of the Welsh Affairs Committee it announced in February 2001 that it will be conducting an inquiry into the 'way in which Welsh interests, including the interests of the National Assembly, are taken into account in the drafting of primary legislation and its passage through Parliament.'[36] This topic was proposed by the Assembly's committee chairs at one of their regular meetings with the Welsh Affairs Committee. At the time of writing the Committee continues to receive memoranda related to this course of inquiry and is expected to return to it in 2002.[37] Bearing in mind the spirit of co-operation which is emerging between the Welsh Affairs Committee and the National Assembly the former may provide the latter with a louder voice at Westminster with regard to any proposed reforms emanating from Cardiff. Any proposals made by the Committee will have to be afforded a formal UK government response.

In the Annual Report of the Northern Ireland Affairs Committee[38] the Committee drew attention to its relationship with the Northern Ireland Office. Relations between the two were described as 'generally good' with the Northern Ireland Office keeping the Committee 'adequately informed of general developments'.[39] Similarly to the Welsh Affairs Committee, although in practice at a less advanced stage, relations between the Committee and the Northern Ireland Assembly were also high on the Committee's list of priorities and it was predicted that growing links between the two

---

[33] *Ibid*, para 10.

[34] *Ibid*, para 24.

[35] *Ibid*, paras 29-31.

[36] Welsh Affairs Committee, Press Notice No. 7 of Session 2000-01, 12 February 2001.

[37] Such an inquiry will be running in conjunction with two reviews of the workings of the National Assembly currently underway in Cardiff, on which see Chapter 2 'In search of stability: coalition politics in the second year of the National Assembly for Wales', and Osmond 2000.

[38] Northern Ireland Affairs Committee 2001.

[39] *Ibid*, para 23.

would yield benefits for accountability through the strengthening of 'parliamentary oversight of both Executives.'[40]

Of particular note were the Committee's observations with regard to the new procedure for legislation by way of Order in Council under the Northern Ireland Act 1998. Under s.85 of the Act a new procedure was introduced whereby proposed legislation on certain reserved matters would have the opportunity to go before the Commons and its Committees before its approval. The Northern Ireland Affairs Committee recommended that:

> . . . there should be a presumption that each such proposal will in any event be debated in the Northern Ireland Grand Committee. We also recommend that consideration be given to introducing into the Northern Ireland Grand Committee, for use when considering proposals for draft Orders in Council, a procedure similar to that used in European Standing Committees, whereby Ministers of the Crown may make statements about the proposal and answer questions thereon for a period, before the Committee embarks on the debate. Use of such a procedure might make the Committee's scrutiny even more effective.[41]

While the Northern Ireland Affairs Committee retains a larger scrutiny role than either its Welsh or Scottish counterparts, and while the Welsh Affairs Committee has re-invented itself following devolution, the Scottish Affairs Committee has been, if not inactive, then slow to respond to the post-devolution climate at Westminster. Devoting almost the entire year to its work on the drinks industry in Scotland the Committee has, as yet, failed to make attempts comparable with those of the Welsh Affairs Committee to come to terms with its redefined role following devolution.

The Work of the Grand Committees

The Scottish, Welsh and Northern Ireland Grand Committees consist of all the MPs sitting for Scotland, Wales and Northern Ireland. They are essentially territorial clubs, with few powers, and when in the 1992 Parliament the Major government tried to breathe life into them as an alternative to devolution, they were dismissed by Labour as mere talking shops. Their role as a voice for the territory has passed to the devolved assemblies. In reflecting on their role at the first meeting of the Welsh Grand Committee in the new Parliament the Secretary of State for Wales, Paul Murphy MP, confirmed that they are essentially clubs, providing territorial MPs with the opportunity to get together:

> The role of the Welsh Grand Committee needs to be examined occasionally and we need to reflect on why we meet in the House according to such a format. It is important that we meet in this way. Everyone knows that 40 Members of Parliament represent the people of Wales in the House, and our Committee gives

[40] *Ibid*, para 31.
[41] *Ibid*, para 28.

us an opportunity, which has perhaps become more significant since devolution, to talk about various matters, some of which may be devolved, but which have a resonance for us all because we are public representatives . . . Our Committee gives Members representing Welsh constituencies the opportunity to get together.

Figure 9.12. Meetings of the Welsh Grand Committee, 2000-1

Date:	Subject of Debate:
19 July 2000	Comprehensive Spending Review.
11 December 2000	Legislative Programme and Pre-Budget Statement.
13 February 2001	Building Safer Communities.
12 March 2001	Budget Statement and its Implications for Wales.
3 July 2001	Legislative Programme.

Figure 9.13. Meetings of the Northern Irish Grand Committee, 2000-1

Date:	Subject of Debate:
5 July 2000	Devolution in Northern Ireland.
29 November 2000	Juvenile Justice.
8 February 2001	Human Rights and Equality in Northern Ireland.
22 March 2001	Life Sentences (Northern Ireland). Financial Investigations (Northern Ireland).

Figure 9.14. Meetings of the Scottish Grand Committee, 2000-1

Date:	Subject of Debate:
10 July 2000	Employment Policy.
28 March 2001	Oil and Gas Industry.

Views amongst MPs as to the continuing usefulness of the Territorial Grand Committees are polarised. During the tenure of John Reid as Secretary of State for Scotland the Scottish Grand Committee was seen by some as becoming nothing more than a campaigning tool for the government and more generally by others as an irrelevance.[42] Nevertheless, others saw the Committee as a useful way to hold the government to account and attract the Scottish press to Westminster matters.[43] But in parallel with the Scottish Affairs Committee the Grand Committee has, in comparison with its Welsh

---

[42] Interviews with Westminster MPs, February 2001.
[43] Interview with Westminster MP, March 2001.

and Northern Irish counterparts, been relatively inactive, meeting only twice during 2000-1.

Opinions of Welsh MPs are again diverse. The Welsh Grand Committee has met on a more regular basis and is seen as a useful forum for backbenchers to make speeches[44] and has been favourably compared to the National Assembly for Wales in its scrutiny role.[45] Others however see it as meaningless.[46] However, there seems to be a consensus that, were the Grand Committee to have an increased role with regard to Welsh legislation, then its future would be secured.[47] Otherwise, many predict that there will be a gradual withering of the Grand Committee system.

CHANGES IN PROCEDURE

There were few procedural changes as a result of devolution during 2000-1. Most of the rulings on which matters would no longer be admissible (because they were now devolved) were dealt with during the first year of devolution.[48] However, occasional reminders were provided by the Speaker as to what was, and was not, in order. Some of these bordered on the absurd. For example, the Speaker, Michael Martin, told Parliamentary clerks only to accept written questions referring to the First Secretary of the National Assembly for Wales after a number of questions had referred to Rhodri Morgan as the First Minister, the title he has adopted.[49]

The Lords is not immune to such self-importance, but it has also addressed procedural issues of greater substance. One of these involved making more transparent the implications of Westminster legislation for the devolution settlement in Wales. It is becoming a serious problem that there is no uniform approach in Westminster drafting to conferring new powers on the National Assembly for Wales.[50] The Select Committee on Delegated Powers and Deregulation noted from its experience discussing the Transport Bill (now the Transport Act 2000) that powers delegated to the National Assembly were scattered throughout the bill and it was therefore difficult to pin-point them. Consequently it recommended that all departments, when drafting the accompanying memoranda to bills, produce a supplementary list of all clauses which (purport to) delegate powers to the National Assembly.[51]

---

[44] Interview with Westminster MP, February 2001.

[45] Interview with Westminster MP, March 2001.

[46] Interviews with Westminster MPs, March 2001.

[47] Interviews with Westminster MPs, January — March 2001.

[48] Russell and Hazell 2000, p187-194.

[49] HC Deb, 15 November 2000, Col. 939. The UK government displayed similar sensitivity when Henry McLeish as the new First Minister wanted to refer to the Scottish Executive as the Scottish government.

[50] Rawlings 2001, pp 54-80.

[51] Select Committee on Delegated Powers and Deregulation 2000*a*, paras 70-71.

However at the end of the 2000-1 Parliamentary session, evidence of this recommendation being put into practice has been conspicuous only through its absence. This is despite the fact that Devolution Guidance Notes, issued to Whitehall departments by the Cabinet Office, have also made equivalent recommendations and state that papers outlining the effects of proposed legislation on devolved competences should be available to the Cabinet Committee on the Legislative Programme (LP).[52] If a 'devolution impact statement' is available to Cabinet for each bill, it should also be made available to Parliament.

THE ROLE OF MEMBERS OF PARLIAMENT

Devolution has significantly reduced the scope for debate and scrutiny at Westminster of Scottish and Welsh matters. The strongest evidence of this is the marked decline in the number of written parliamentary questions to the Scotland Office and the Wales Office in the two years since devolution, set out in the tables below. The thousands of questions asked before devolution now go to ministers in the Scottish Parliament and National Assembly. The number of oral questions has not declined so sharply because separate question times have been preserved for the three territorial Secretaries of State (although shortened from 40 to 30 minutes), and the space is there to be filled.

Figure 9.15. Parliamentary questions to the Welsh Office and Wales Office, 1997-2001

	1997/1998 (18 months)	1998/1999 (12 months)	1999/2000 (12 months)	2000/2001 (5 months)
Oral	370	180	264	79
Written	2150	1075	576	187

Source: House of Commons Information Office

Figure 9.16. Parliamentary questions to the Scottish Office and Scotland Office, 1997-2001

	1997/1998 (18 months)	1998/1999 (12 months)	1999/2000 (12 months)	2000/2001 (5 months)
Oral	492	278	155	88
Written	2388	53	396	201

Source: House of Commons Information Office

---

[52] DGN 9, para 7; DGN 10, para 8; DGN 8, para 7.

Figure 9.17. Parliamentary questions to the Northern Ireland Office, 1997-2001

	1997/1998 (18 months)	1998/1999 (12 months)	1999/2000 (12 months)	2000/2001 (5 months)
Oral	286	200	191	87
Written	2377	1104	930	399

Source: House of Commons Information Office

Although the scope of questions that can be raised by both Scots and Welsh MPs, post-devolution, has been limited many have sought to redefine themselves to exert an influence on Westminster. One Welsh MP suggested that although many of areas of interest and expertise have been transferred to the NAW the job for MPs representing Welsh constituencies is to ensure that the voice of Wales is still heard.[53] At a meeting of the Welsh Grand Committee in July 2001 Paul Murphy emphasised the continuing role of Welsh MPs:

> Our role in the devolution settlement is to fulfil two functions in respect of devolved matters: first, to ensure that we get the resources . . . and, secondly, to provide the legislative tools to enable the Assembly to go about its business in delivering the services that it is charged to deliver. On non-devolved matters, we shall play our part in the House of Commons and as legislators.[54]

There exists a view, most prominently held among Conservative MPs, that the role of members representing Scottish constituencies has significantly diminished in practice. Although, as with Welsh MPs, many Scots have sought out new areas of work and become involved with areas of UK-wide interest.[55] With regard to voting habits, many Scots MPs continue to vote on matters affecting England and Wales only but there are some who have consciously abstained from voting on matters which do not affect Scotland.[56] But regardless of the personal tendencies of Scots members, the debate over their role, at least amongst English members, looks set to continue for some time.

THE ENGLISH QUESTION

The outstanding, and recurrent, challenge to the established Westminster order post-devolution remains the English Question.[57] Russell and Hazell, in *The State and the Nations*, discussed the English Question in terms of the four proposals that had been put forward for its remedy: the creation of an

---

[53] Interview with Westminster MP, January 2001.
[54] Meeting of the Welsh Grand Committee, 3 July 2001.
[55] Interviews with Westminster MPs, January–February 2001.
[56] Interview with Westminster MP, March 2001.
[57] For further detail see Hazell 2000.

English Parliament, regional assemblies in England, 'English Votes on English Laws' or new English structures at Westminster.[58]

As Russell and Hazell observed, popular support for an English Parliament is negligible.[59] The Campaign for an English Parliament remains the only body committed to such a step, and its influence remains marginal. It has not attracted the support of any political heavyweights, although the idea surfaces occasionally in debates at Westminster. In a short debate on Constitutional Change in the House of Lords the Conservative peer Lord Renton asked whether devolution had 'made the trend towards an English national parliament at Westminster irreversible?' Lord Irvine was dismissive of the question, saying 'I do not believe that there is any appetite in England for a national parliament for England.'[60]

Further constitutional reform may go some way towards answering the political aspect of the English Question, were elected Regional Assemblies to have jurisdiction over some of the England-only policies regularly raised in debates over the English Question, for example health policy and education.[61] Nevertheless, it is unlikely that powers equivalent to the devolved administrations will be granted to English regional bodies, and so there remains the likelihood of Scottish members being able to debate English matters at Westminster.

English Votes on English Laws

William Hague outlined the action that would be taken by an incoming Conservative government in a speech at Magdalen College, Oxford, on 13 November 2000.[62] Hague stated that one of his first acts as Prime Minister would be to prevent Scottish MPs from voting on matters dealt with in the Scottish Parliament by MSPs. All MPs at Westminster would remain able to vote on matters of UK-wide application such as taxation, defence, social security and foreign policy. Quoted in *The Times* the Labour response accused Mr Hague of attempting to create an 'English Nationalism bandwagon', while Alistair Morgan of the Scottish National Party denounced Mr Hague's speech as 'typical Tory anti-Scottishness.'[63]

---

[58] Russell and Hazell 2000, p202-214 and Hazell 2000.

[59] Russell and Hazell 2000, p203-204. But see Figure 10.3, which suggests that support for regional assemblies and an English Parliament may be about equal.

[60] HL Deb, 3 April 2001, Cols. 719-722.

[61] For a fuller analysis of the Government's proposals for elected regional government for England see Chapter 5, on the English Regions.

[62] *A Conservative View of Constitutional Change*, Speech at Magdalen College, Oxford, 13 November 2000.

[63] 'Scots MPs would lose vote under the Tories,' *The Times*, 14 November 2000. Anti-Scottish tendencies were raised at a number of points throughout the year: see for example: 'English MPs to oppose Scot as new Speaker,' *The Daily Telegraph*, 24 August 2000. The issue of Scots domination of the Cabinet was raised later in the year: in a letter to the Commission for Racial Equality (CRE) in which he explained his reasoning behind not signing its anti-racism pledge, the Conservative MP for

Hague's proposal, a step back from the English Parliament he first suggested in 1998,[64] provoked much comment. Professor Vernon Bogdanor sparked a succession of letters to the editor of the *Financial Times* through an article responding to Hague's suggestion for English votes on English laws.[65] Professor Bogdanor argued that under our constitution the government of the day is responsible to the House of Commons for all issues, whether domestic or non-domestic. By implementing Mr Hague's proposal of English votes on English legislation this principle of 'collective responsibility' would be weakened by effectively removing the majority of any Labour government which might be reliant on their members in Wales and Scotland for an overall majority in the Commons.

The Conservative Election Manifesto duly contained the commitment to English votes on English laws.[66] However, since William Hague's resignation as Conservative leader, his successor, Iain Duncan Smith, has not revealed his position on the issue.

The Government's Position on the English Question

On 27 June 2001, Edward Leigh MP lamented the Government's lack of interest in resolving the debate:

> . . . although we have argued about the West Lothian question for four years, there is still no answer. Our English constituents are still faced with the fact that Scottish MPs vote on our health, education, policing, agriculture, transport, housing policy and much else, whereas we have no say on Scottish matters. We should point that out again and again because it is a denial of natural justice . . . it is a matter of justice, and it must be dealt with. The Government cannot ignore it.[67]

The government seem to have made a point of failing to address the widespread concerns over the issues surrounding the English Question. Its stance is epitomised by Lord Irvine's famous response that the best way to answer the English Question is to stop asking. William Hague's retort was that the best way to find an answer to the Question might be to stop asking Lord Irvine.[68]

Instead of addressing the issue directly, the government response has been to either criticise the hypocritical attitude of the Conservative Opposition or emphasise the fact that the Westminster Parliament remains the Parliament of the United Kingdom. The latter most closely resembles an 'answer' to the

Yorkshire East, John Townend, added that the English considered themselves 'ignored by a government dominated by Scots ('Tory complains of Scots domination', *The Herald*, 27 April 2001).'

[64] *Change and Tradition: Thinking Creatively about the Constitution*, speech to the Centre for Policy Studies, 24 February 1998.

[65] 'West Lothian is not the question,' *Financial Times*, 21 November 2000.

[66] Conservative Party, *Time for Common Sense*, 2001, p46.

[67] HC Deb, 27 June 2001, Col. 674.

[68] Hazell 2000, p17.

question, perhaps most akin to that of Vernon Bogdanor. An example of the former is perhaps best illustrated by the following response to a question from the Conservative Member, Dominic Grieve, by the former Scotland Office minister, Brian Wilson:

> It comes ill from a Tory to seek that sort of absolutist solution to a relative problem. When legislation that was already devolved administratively was carried out in this House, I do not remember the hon. Gentleman or any of his colleagues thinking that it was a great constitutional outrage that the Tories ruthlessly used their majority to drive through Scottish legislation against the will of the people of Scotland. There is, by the will of this Parliament, a devolved responsibility to the Parliament in Scotland over certain areas, but that does not change the constitutional position of this House or Members of this House.[69]

The then Home Secretary, Jack Straw, illustrated the latter approach during the second reading in the Commons of the contentious England and Wales-only Hunting Bill by responding to suggestions that Scottish members should be prevented from participating in the discussions of the bill with a forceful reassertion of Westminster as not only the sovereign parliament, but also as the Parliament of the Union:

> I happen to believe in the sovereignty of the Parliament of the United Kingdom of England, Wales, Scotland and Northern Ireland and believe that every member elected to the Parliament has a right to legislate, subject to previous legislation, in respect of every part of the United Kingdom.[70]

New English Structures at Westminster

Westminster Hall had been mooted as a further possible forum for the discussion of territorial matters, initially by the Procedure Committee in 1999.[71] Although debates in Westminster Hall have occasionally dealt with English regional issues, most have tended to be driven by members' individual constituency interests rather than anything else.

The first England-only forum, the Standing Committee on Regional Affairs, finally met in May 2001, over a year after Margaret Beckett, Leader of the House of Commons, announced that it was to be revived.[72] The Committee met on 10 May 2001, the day before the dissolution of Parliament, devoting its first and last meeting to regional economic performance and imbalances. Membership of the Committee had been announced on 13 March 2001 (see the table below) under the joint chairmanship of Bill O'Brien (Labour) and Jonathan Sayeed (Conservative). Although the Committee has a standing membership of 13, any MP representing an

---

[69] HC Deb, 19 December 2000, Col. 190.
[70] HC Deb, 20 December 2000, Cols. 380-381.
[71] Russell and Hazell 2000, p195.
[72] HC Deb, 11 April 2000, Col. 289.

Figure 9.18. Membership of the Standing Committee on Regional Affairs, announced 13 March 2001

Bill O'Brien (Joint Chair)	Labour	Normanton
Jonathan Sayeed (Joint Chair)	Conservative	Mid Bedfordshire
Joe Ashton	Labour	Bassetlaw
Candy Atherton	Labour	Falmouth and Camborne
Karen Buck	Labour	Regent's Park and Kensington North
David Chidgley	Lib. Dem.	Eastleigh
Louise Ellman	Labour	Liverpool Riverside
Nigel Evans	Conservative	Ribble Valley
Christopher Fraser	Conservative	Mid Dorset and North Poole
Andrew George	Lib. Dem.	St Ives
Denis Murphy	Labour	Wansbeck
Ian Pearson	Labour	Dudley South
Laurie Quinn	Labour	Scarborough and Whitby
Anthony Steen	Conservative	Totnes
Derek Wyatt	Labour	Sittingbourne and Sheppey

English constituency may attend and speak at its meetings. It is a kind of English Grand Committee, and like the other Grand Committees has no effective powers.

The long delay in establishing the Committee was, according to Beverley Hughes MP, attributable to Conservative lack of interest.[73] Indeed as Russell and Hazell observed, at the time the resurrection of the Standing Committee was announced the 'Conservatives were dismissive of the proposals, considering them no substitute for separate treatment of English legislation.'[74] This was reflected at the first meeting of the Committee which was attended by only one Conservative MP, Anthony Steen, who left shortly after the start of the meeting. Nine of the standing members of the Committee attended, with a further six MPs — the North East of England being particularly well represented..

Due to the lack of cross-party support for the Standing Committee on Regional Affairs it remains doubtful whether the short-lived experiment will be revived. It will be a pity if nothing is done because there is strong support for more English regional forums at Westminster amongst all except

[73] Standing Committee on Regional Affairs, 10 May 2001 (available at: www.publications. parliament.uk/pa/cm/cmpubns.htm).
[74] Russell and Hazell 2000, p211.

Conservative MPs.[75] Conservative MPs also favour more English forums, but they favour additional forums for the discussion of English-only, rather than English regional, issues.[76] The timing of the first meeting of the Committee cannot have encouraged those who may have attended, and indicates a certain lack of enthusiasm for the Committee on the part of the government. The doubts on the part of the Conservative Party remain that, without legislative powers, the Committee will be nothing more than a talking shop and a sop to English regionalism.[77] The Committee has not, as at August 2001, been re-appointed in the new Parliament.

THE HOUSE OF LORDS

In the upper house the response to devolution is closely linked to the continuing debate about reform of the House of Lords. The major parties are all agreed that a fully reformed House of Lords should contain members elected to represent the nations and regions, giving the second chamber more of a quasi-federal role. The only disagreement is what proportion of the second chamber should be elected, with the Liberal Democrats favouring an all-elected second chamber, the Conservatives a majority, but the Labour Party only a minority of elected members. The Blair administration maintains its commitment to further reform of the House of Lords based on the recommendations drawn up by Lord Wakeham's commission in January 2000.[78] The pledge to continue with stage two of reform of the upper house was cemented with the promise of legislation, following consultation, contained in the Queen's Speech of June 2001.[79] Following the Queen's Speech the Lord Chancellor, Lord Irvine, promised that the Government would:

> . . . introduce legislation to implement the final stage of reform of the House of Lords. That will include the removal of the remaining hereditary Peers and put the House of Lords Appointments Commission on a statutory footing. We have given our support to the report and conclusions of the Wakeham Commission and we will seek through consultation to find a means of implementing those conclusions in the most effective way possible.[80]

The Wakeham report included three different options for elected members to represent the nations and regions, comprising 65, 87 or 195 members (representing 12 per cent, 16 per cent or 35 per cent in a second chamber of 550).

---

[75] Constitution Unit Devolution and Westminster survey of MPs, conducted in summer 2000.
[76] *Ibid.*
[77] Interviews with Westminster MPs, February–March 2001.
[78] HL Written Answers, 10 July 2001, Col. WA69.
[79] HL Deb, 20 June 2001, Col. 5.
[80] HL Deb, 21 June 2001, Col. 48.

Such little debate as there has been has focussed on the small proportion of elected members. As important in the devolution context is the nature of their role in representing the nations and regions, and what links if any they would have with the devolved institutions.[81] 'Consultation' has so far been confined to behind the scenes negotiations with the political parties at Westminster. It is to be hoped that the next stage of consultation might take more account of the representative role to be accorded to the elected members, and include the devolved administrations.

The House of Lords Select Committee on the Constitution

To reinforce the second chamber's role as guardian of the constitution and of the devolution settlement, the Wakeham commission recommended that the House of Lords should establish a constitution committee and a devolution committee (with the latter possibly being a sub-committee of the former). The House of Lords implemented this recommendation on 8 February 2001, when the membership of the new Constitution Committee of the House of Lords was announced. Under the Chairmanship of the Conservative peer Lord Norton of Louth the Committee's terms of reference are as follows:

> ... to examine the constitutional implications of all public bills coming before the house; and to keep under review the operation of the constitution.[82]

Figure 9.19. The members of the Constitution Committee at July 2001

Lord Acton	Labour
Viscount Cranborne	Conservative
Lord Fellowes	Crossbench
Lord Holme of Cheltenham	Liberal Democrat
Baroness Howells of St. Davids	Labour
Lord Lang of Monkton	Conservative
The Earl of Mar and Kellie	Liberal Democrat
Lord Morgan	Labour
Lord Norton of Louth	Conservative
Lord Ponsonby of Shulbrede	Labour
Lord Weatherill	Crossbench
Baroness Young	Conservative

The debate over the future role of the Constitution Committee took place in the Lords on 13 February 2001. It was widely agreed that the Committee

---

[81] Russell 2000, chap. 10.
[82] HL Deb, 8 February 2001, Col. 1269.

should play a vital role in scrutinising the workings of the Scottish Parliament and Assemblies in Wales and Northern Ireland[83] and in looking at 'relations between Holyrood and Westminster, the smooth functioning of which is vital to the survival of the United Kingdom.'[84] This is not, however, a point that has been lost on other committees of the House of Lords. The Lords Select Committee on Delegated Powers and Deregulation has observed that unlike the Commons the Lords has no 'obvious first port-of-call for relations with the Parliament and Assemblies'[85] and consequently recommended that the Lords consider the procedural consequences of devolution a 'high priority' issue.[86]

The Constitution Committee's First Report[87] published in July 2001 examined its terms of reference, possible topics for consideration, relationships with the work of other committees and the resources available to the Constitution Committee. In identifying the boundaries of their jurisdiction the Committee defined a constitution as:

> ... the set of laws, rules and practices that create the basic institutions of the state and its component and related parts, and stipulate the powers of those institutions and the relationship between the different institutions and between those institutions and the individual.[88]

Building on this focus on the institutions of the state, the Committee announced that inter-institutional relationships in a devolved UK would form the subject of its second inquiry, to commence after Christmas 2001.

The new House of Lords committee provides the first opportunity for Westminster to address the devolution settlement in the round. Whereas the territorial committees in the Commons remain fragmented and tend to be relatively parochial in their choice of subjects, the new House of Lords committee can think through the issues raised by devolution in a comprehensive and systematic way. Its establishment may come to be one of the most significant steps taken at Westminster towards adapting, and responding to the challenges posed by devolution.

---

[83] See comments of Lord Goodhart, HL Deb, 12 February 2001, Col. 95: '... it is a vital question to study how the devolution is working. Is the balance of devolved and reserved powers satisfactory? Is the partial system of devolution to Wales, which gives power over secondary but not primary legislation, workable?'

[84] HL Deb, 12 February 2001, Col. 97.

[85] Select Committee on Delegated Powers and Deregulation 2000*b*.

[86] *Ibid*.

[87] House of Lords Constitution Committee 2001.

[88] *Ibid*, at para 50.

CONCLUSION

At the end of the second full year of devolution the Westminster response to devolution can still be seen as piecemeal. Significant questions, most notably regarding the English Question and the uncertain future of the territorial committees in the House of Commons, continue to remain unanswered. Inertia on the part of the government has allowed the debate over the English Question to continue without adequate response. Inertia on the part of the Scottish Affairs Committee has led some to question the continuing usefulness of its role. By contrast the Welsh Affairs Committee is trying to forge a new role for itself by deliberately taking an expansive view of its revised remit, while Scots and Welsh MPs are beginning to take a stronger interest in UK-wide matters and are forcing debate over the effects of such matters on the devolved territories.[89] The House of Lords remains part-reformed but despite this has established perhaps the most significant piece of machinery in the UK Parliament post-devolution. The Constitution Committee may yet prove to be the significant factor in bringing Westminster to terms with the developing constitutional settlement.

BIBLIOGRAPHY

Official Documents

House of Lords Constitution Committee (2001). *Reviewing the Constitution: Terms of Reference and Method of Working.* HL 11.
Liaison Committee (2001). *Shifting the Balance: Unfinished Business* (vol II). HC 321-II.
Northern Ireland Affairs Committee (2001). *Annual Report for Session 1999-2000.* HC 148.
Scottish Affairs Committee (1998). *The Operation of Multi-Layer Democracy.* HC 460-I, HC 460-II.
Scottish Affairs Committee (2000). *The Work of the Scotland Office Since Devolution.* HC 390.
Select Committee on Delegated Powers and Deregulation (2000*a*). HL 130.
Select Committee on Delegated Powers and Deregulation (2000*b*). *Thirty-Seventh Report.* HC 180.
Welsh Affairs Committee (2000). *The Work of the Committee since Devolution.* HC81.

Secondary Sources

Cowley, P. and Stuart, M. (2001). 'Parliament: A Few Headaches and a Dose of Modernisation', *Parliamentary Affairs*, 54(2), 238.

---

[89] Interviews with Westminster MPs, January–February 2001.

Hansard Society Commission on Parliamentary Scrutiny (2001). *The Challenge for Parliament: Making Government Accountable*. London: Vacher Dod Publishing.

Hazell, R. (1999). 'Westminster: Squeezed from Above and Below', in R. Hazell (ed), *Constitutional Futures: A History of the Next Ten Years*. Oxford: Oxford University Press.

Hazell, R. (2000). *An Unstable Union: Devolution and the English Question*. London: Constitution Unit.

Kennon, A. (2001). *The Commons: Reform or Modernisation*. London: Constitution Unit.

Osmond, J. (2000). 'The Assembly's Operational Review' in J. Osmond (ed.) *Devolution Looks Ahead: Monitoring the National Assembly for Wales May to August 2000*. Cardiff: Institute of Welsh Affairs.

Osmond, J. (ed.) (2001). *A Period of De-Stabilisation: Monitoring the National Assembly for Wales May to August 2001*. Cardiff: Institute of Welsh Affairs.

Rawlings, R. (2001). 'Quasi-Legislative Devolution, Powers and Principles', 52(1) *Northern Ireland Law Quarterly*, 54.

Russell, M. (1999). *Representing the Nations and Regions in a New Upper House*. London: Constitution Unit.

Russell, M. and Hazell, R. (2000). 'Devolution and Westminster: Tentative Steps Towards a More Federal Parliament', in R. Hazell (ed), *The State and the Nations: The First Year of Devolution in the United Kingdom*. Exeter: Imprint Academic.

10

Hopes Dashed and Fears Assuaged?
What the Public Makes of it So Far

John Curtice

INTRODUCTION

Devolution is a constitutional experiment whose eventual consequences are far from certain. Its advocates hope that it will strengthen the United Kingdom and provide for more effective government. In contrast its critics have argued it will result in more inefficient government and eventually lead to the break-up of the UK. In Northern Ireland at least there is a further source of uncertainty. Advocates of the devolution settlement there claim that it will help to develop more harmonious relationships between the province's two communities. Critics argue that it cannot hope to succeed given the serious ambiguities they believe exist in the Belfast Agreement.

Whether it is the hopes of devolution's advocates or the fears of its critics that are realised will ultimately depend on its impact on public opinion. Devolution will only help strengthen the UK if it helps to convince the public that the Union is worth retaining and if it strengthens an attachment to a British national identity that all four corners of the UK share in common. Equally it will be difficult to argue that devolution has led to more effective government if the public were to come to the view that the new institutions were not helping to bring about a material improvement in their lives. Of course which of these outcomes pertains depends in considerable measure on the actions of the politicians and civil servants who are charged with the task of making devolution work, and these actions are rightly the subject of analysis in much of the rest of this book. But ultimately it is upon the verdict of the public that the fruits of their labours will rest.

However, devolution has not just one audience that it has to convince. This is most obviously the case in Northern Ireland where devolution has to secure the support of both communities there if it is to reduce the tension between them. But even in Great Britain, the success of devolution in Scotland and Wales depends not just on the reaction of those living in Scotland and Wales, but also upon the judgment of those living in England. After all, advocates of devolution hope that the experience of Scotland and Wales will encourage people in England to demand some form of devolution for themselves too. Equally, critics are concerned that as the English public becomes aware of the privileges that the rest of the UK has been granted but they have been denied, some form of backlash will emerge that could weaken the Union further.

In this chapter, therefore, we examine how all of the key publics in the UK appear to be reacting to devolution, two years after Scotland and Wales went to the polls to elect their new institutions. We look not only at the judgment that people in Scotland, Wales and Northern Ireland have formed so far about their own devolved institutions, but also at the reaction of those living in England. While in common with the rest of this book we pay particular attention to the development of public opinion in the second year of devolution, we are often best able to assess the significance of the evidence of the second year by comparing it with earlier findings. After all, we can only examine claims that devolution has changed public opinion by comparing what the public thinks now with what it has said in the past.

The second year of devolution did, however, see one particular event that is of particular interest to any assessment of the impact of devolution upon the public mood. For in June 2001 the first post-devolution Westminster election was held. How the public voted in that election might well provide us with valuable information about their reaction to devolution. Did people in the devolved territories still consider Westminster important enough to turn out for? And would they use the occasion to express their opinion about either the principle or the practice of the devolution settlement? The answers to these questions must comprise an important part of our assessment of devolution's second year.

We begin by looking at the impact of devolution on attitudes towards the Union and the governing structure of the UK. Has support for Scottish or Welsh independence risen or fallen? Are there serious differences in public opinion between the component territories of the UK? We then turn to recent trends in national identity. Is there any evidence that feeling British has become less or more popular? And to what extent do people's identities affect their attitudes towards the future of the UK?

Between them these two sections address the levels of cognitive and affective support for the Union. In contrast, our next section considers how effective the new institutions themselves are thought to have been. Have the new institutions begun to persuade their publics that they are going to improve their lives? What impression have the politicians running the new institutions made? This is then followed by our final section in which we assess what we can learn from the experience of the 2001 election.

We rely upon a variety of sources. We can of course examine the results of the 2001 general election themselves. We also have access to the evidence of commercial opinion polls that have periodically been commissioned by the media. Such polls have the merit of being conducted quickly and published immediately, thereby enabling us to be as up to date as possible. But they often take place at irregular intervals and their content is often guided by what is currently in the news rather than any wish to chart long-term developments in public opinion. Fortunately, however, in England, Scotland and Northern Ireland at least we also have access to the results of more elaborate social surveys conducted during the last two years, including research undertaken in England and Scotland as part of the Constitution Unit's own programme of research on devolution. These surveys are the *British Social Attitudes* survey, *the Scottish Social Attitudes* survey and the *Northern Ireland Life and Times Survey* (NILTS).[1] While the most recently available results for these surveys are less up to date, being based on interviews undertaken up to a year ago, they provide us with a wider range of information than we can obtain from polls.

CONSTITUTIONAL ARRANGEMENTS

Our first task is to examine what has happened to attitudes towards the Union and the way that the UK is governed during the first two years of devolution. Has support for maintenance of the Union been weakened or strengthened? And is there any evidence of disagreement between the different publics of the UK about what the constitutional structure of the UK should be in the wake of devolution?

In Figure 10.1 we have constructed from a variety of sources a time series on attitudes towards their constitutional future in each of Scotland, Wales and Northern Ireland. This reveals that in Scotland and Wales at least, the advent of devolution appears to have had relatively little impact on the level of demand for independence. With just one exception (May 1998) ICM has consistently found since the 1997 referendum that around one in four Scots are in favour of their country leaving the UK and becoming independent.[2] Meanwhile the best time series that we can construct for Wales suggests that support for independence remains constant at around one in ten. To date it appears that devolution in Scotland and Wales has neither helped put the nationalist genie back in the bottle nor has it enabled the independence movement to prosper.

In Northern Ireland, however, attitudes have changed, not least amongst the Catholic community. Here devolution has so far failed to bring about an increase in support for Northern Ireland's continued membership of the UK. Before the conclusion of the Belfast Agreement typically around one in three Catholics said that they felt that Northern Ireland's long-term future lay within the UK. Now that figure has fallen to just one in five, although the

---

[1] Jowell et al 2000; Park et al 2001; Paterson et al 2001; Curtice et al 2001; NILT 2001.

[2] A slightly different question carried as part of the *Scottish Social Attitudes* survey puts support for independence at around 30 per cent, but again fails to show any consistent evidence of a rise or fall in support for devolution. See Curtice and Seyd 2001; Surridge 2001.

Figure 10.1. Constitutional preferences in the devolved territories

Scotland

	Feb. 98	May 98	Jan. 99	Feb. 99	Jan. 00	Feb. 00	Sept 00	Feb. 01	May 01
Independence	28	33	26	24	23	27	24	27	25
Devolution	48	48	53	54	54	46	55	53	56
No Parliament	21	17	18	18	19	22	18	16	17

The detailed question wording was as follows:-

Thinking about the running of Scotland as a whole, which one of the following would you like to see?

• Scotland being independent of England and Wales, but part of the EU

• Scotland remaining part of the UK but with its own devolved Parliament with some taxation and spending powers

• Scotland remaining part of the UK but with no devolved Parliament.

Source: ICM/*Scotsman/Scotland on Sunday*

Wales

Thinking more generally about Welsh politics, which of these statements comes closest to your own views:

	97	99	June 01	July 01
Independence	13	9	8	22
Parliament with tax and law-making powers	18	35	44	38
Assembly without tax and law-making powers	25	35	24	24
No Parliament or Assembly	37	18	18	24

The detailed wording was as follows:

1997, 1999: Which of these statements comes closest to your view?

• Wales should become independent, separate from the UK and the EU

• Wales should become independent, separate from the UK but part of the EU

• Wales should remain part of the UK, with its own elected parliament which has law-making and taxation powers

• Wales should remain part of the UK without an elected Assembly

(The first two categories have been combined in the table.)

June 01: Thinking more generally about Welsh politics, which of the following comes closest to your view?

• Wales should become independent

• Wales should have its own elected parliament like Scotland with law-making and taxation powers

• Wales should continue to have an Assembly with limited law-making powers

• Wales should have no elected Assembly or parliament

July 01: Which of these statements comes closest to your view?

• Wales should become independent

• Wales should remain part of the UK with its own elected parliament, which has law-making and taxation powers

• Wales should remain part of the UK with its own elected Assembly, which has limited law-making powers only

• Wales should remain part of the UK without an elected Assembly

Sources: 1997: Welsh Referendum Study; 1999: Welsh Assembly Election Study; June 01: NOP/BBC Wales July 01 Market Research Wales/Welsh Governance Centre

Northern Ireland					
	1989	1996	1998	1999	2000
% Protestants favouring					
Remain part of UK	93	85	84	87	83
Reunify with Ireland	3	8	3	3	4
% Catholics favouring					
Remain part of UK	32	35	20	16	20
Reunify with Ireland	56	47	48	48	42
% of all respondents favouring					
Remain part of UK	69	62	58	56	60
Reunify with Ireland	24	20	21	21	17

Do you think the long-term policy for Northern Ireland should be for it to remain part of the United Kingdom or to reunify with the rest of Ireland?

Sources: 1989, 1996 *Northern Ireland Social Attitudes Survey*; 1998-2000: *Northern Ireland Life and Times Survey*

most recent reading for 2000 does at least suggest that the fall in support since 1996 may not have progressed any further. So it appears that devolution has undermined support for the Union among the very public where support was already relatively low.

But this is too simple a conclusion. Not only has support for Northern Ireland's membership of the UK fallen amongst Catholics, so also has support for the traditional nationalist goal of reunification with the rest of Ireland. At the beginning of the 1990s over half of Northern Irish Catholics supported reunification.[3] Gradually that figure has dropped, and at the most recent reading has now fallen to a new low of 42 per cent. Evidently the Catholic community in Northern Ireland are increasingly rejecting the idea that Northern Ireland's future simply lies in either membership of the UK or in reunification with the rest of Ireland.

This perhaps should be regarded as a success for devolution and the Belfast Agreement. After all, by creating the North-South Ministerial Council as well as guaranteeing Catholics' involvement in the Northern Ireland Executive the Agreement tried to create a constitutional structure that could accommodate traditional nationalist aspirations while Northern Ireland remained within the framework of the UK. And it appears to have persuaded some Catholics at least that there may be an alternative to the stark choice between the Union and unification.

However, growing uncertainty about Northern Ireland's constitutional future is not confined to Catholics. There is also some evidence that uncertainty is occurring amongst Protestants whose support for maintenance of the Union has fallen by ten points over the last decade. As in the case of Catholics, it appears that the change in mood partly predates the advent of devolution and has been occasioned more generally by the peace process that began earlier in the 1990s and to which the Belfast Agreement was intended to be the conclusion. Together with the change in mood amongst Catholics it does mean that only three in five people in Northern Ireland now clearly support Northern Ireland's continued membership of the UK.

Still, in each of Scotland, Wales and Northern Ireland clear majorities want to remain part of the UK. But what about England? Even if nationalism does not foster demands to leave the UK from the devolved territories themselves, the Union could still be weakened if people in England no longer wish those territories to remain part of the UK. However, so far as attitudes towards Scotland and Wales at least are concerned, Figure 10.2 indicates that at most devolution has only had a marginal impact. Only around one in five people in England think that Scotland and Wales should leave the UK. True, the advent of devolution in 1999 was accompanied by a ten-point increase in the proportion of people in England who thought that Scotland should become independent and a similar seven point increase in respect of Wales.

[3] Curtice and Gallagher 1990.

However, the most recent reading for 2000 has seen that increase reversed somewhat.

Figure 10.2. What England thinks about Scotland and Wales			
	1997	1999	2000
Scotland should . . .	%	%	%
be independent, separate from UK and EU	6	8	8
be independent, separate from UK but part of EU	8	16	12
Remain part of UK with its own elected Parliament which has some taxation powers	38	44	44
Remain part of the UK with its own elected Parliament which has no taxation powers	17	10	8
Remain part of the UK without an elected Parliament	23	13	17
Wales should . . .	%	%	%
be independent, separate from UK and EU	5	6	7
be independent, separate from UK but part of EU	8	14	10
Remain part of the UK, with its own elected Parliament which has law-making and taxation powers	37	34	35
Remain part of the UK, with its own elected Assembly which has limited law-making powers only	18	22	17
Remain part of the UK without an elected Assembly	25	15	20
Source: 1997: *British Election Study*; 1999, 2000: *British Social Attitudes* Survey			

If all the key partners still wish to maintain the Union of England, Scotland and Wales, the same cannot be said in respect of Northern Ireland. For when people across Great Britain were asked by the 2000 *British Social Attitudes* survey whether Northern Ireland's best long-term future lies in remaining part of the UK or reunifying with the rest of Ireland, no less than 57 per cent opted for the latter while only 25 per cent believed it should remain part of the UK. This, however, is nothing new. The *British Social Attitudes* survey has asked this question on a regular basis ever since 1983 and has never found fewer than 52 per cent in favour of reunification. Moreover these figures do not necessarily mean that people in Great Britain believe Northern

Ireland should be ejected from the UK against its will. No less than 65 per cent told NOP just before the June 2001 election that the British Government should guarantee the position of Northern Ireland within the UK for so long as a majority there wished to remain a member. Only 24 per cent back a policy of phased withdrawal. Even so, devolution and the Belfast Agreement have evidently failed so far to persuade people in Great Britain that Northern Ireland is necessarily an integral part of the British state.

Devolution has so far done little to strengthen support for the maintenance of the UK in its current form. Equally it is difficult to argue that it has done much damage. Perhaps though the damage is more subtle than what we have been looking at so far. Perhaps there are growing disagreements about how the constitutional structure of the UK should be organised, and perhaps this could prove to be a growing source of tension that could eventually undermine the Union.

One of the most important features of the current devolution settlement is that it is asymmetrical. Not only do the devolved institutions in Scotland, Wales and Northern Ireland each enjoy different powers, but, with the possible exception of the Greater London Assembly, England does not enjoy any elected form of devolution. So one possible source of tension is that England now wishes to enjoy in some form or other the privileges of self-government that have already been granted to the rest of the UK.

However, it is far from clear that this is the case. In Figure 10.3 we show the results of two recent attempts to gauge English attitudes towards devolution for themselves. In the first case, the *British Social Attitudes* survey invited its respondents to choose between the status quo, an English parliament or regional devolution. It found that over half were happy with the status quo. In contrast a question posed by the Joseph Rowntree Reform Trust's *State of the Nation* survey asked respondents to choose between different ways of delivering some of the aims that lie within the remit of the existing (unelected) Regional Development Agencies in England. This question suggested rather less enthusiasm for rule from Whitehall, but even so, only one in three backed the idea of a regional assembly.

Support for an elected regional assembly does however appear to be somewhat higher in the region of England where there has been the most vociferous campaign, viz. the North East. According to the *British Social Attitudes* survey, a quarter of people in this part of England back an elected regional assembly, seven points higher than across England as a whole. Similarly the *State of the Nation* survey found support running at eleven points higher, while a BBC poll conducted for a series of programmes entitled *Think of England* in September 2000 obtained a similar result.[4] However, even in this region it appears that those who would hope to initiate and win a referendum on the creation of an elected assembly cannot currently be sure of success.

[4] www.bbc.co.uk/england/thinkofengland/survey.html

Figure 10.3. Two perspectives on English devolution		
British Social Attitudes		
	1999	2000
England should be governed as it is now, with laws made by the UK Parliament	62	54
Each region of England to have its own assembly that runs services like health	15	18
England as whole to have its own new parliament with law-making powers	18	19
Source: *British Social Attitudes* survey		
State of the Nation		
Thinking now of your region, which of the following options do you think is the best way of deciding how to generate new jobs, develop major roads and public transport, and other similar issues?		
Government Ministers in Whitehall should decide, taking into account the needs of the country as a whole	12	
An elected assembly for this region should decide	32	
Government officials meeting at regional level should decide	15	
Appointed business and local govt. representatives from this region should decide	29	
Source: ICM/Joseph Rowntree Trust *State of the Nation* Survey, Nov. 2000		

However, even if demand for some form of devolution grows, it is far from clear that it will be a source of tension within the Union. At the moment, support for some form of English devolution is currently higher in Scotland than it is within England itself. When the *Scottish Social Attitudes* survey asked people in Scotland the same question that the *British Social Attitudes* survey administered to people in England, it found that fewer people (45 per cent) favour the status quo than we have already seen do so in England (54 per cent). Perhaps unsurprisingly however, people in Scotland are rather keener on the idea that England should also have its own national parliament (28 per cent) than they are on the proposal that it should have a different system of regional devolution (15 per cent).

Equally, there is little evidence that England is envious of the devolution that has been granted to Scotland and Wales. As Figure 10.2 above shows, just over half of people in England support some form of devolved assembly or parliament for Scotland and Wales, with most preferring the stronger of the two options offered. Only around one in five oppose any form of self government for Scotland or Wales, a figure that if anything has declined since the advent of devolution. Asymmetrical devolution may be untidy, but it appears to reflect what the largest public in the UK actually wants.

One consequence of asymmetrical devolution is, of course, that MPs from Scotland (and indeed Northern Ireland) can vote on laws for England (and Wales) on such matters as health and education that have been devolved to Edinburgh and Belfast while, normally at least, English (and Welsh) MPs do not have any say on the law for such matters in Scotland (and Northern Ireland). This was dubbed as long ago as the 1970s as the 'West Lothian question' by the backbench anti-devolutionist Labour Scots MP, Tam Dalyell. And it has been suggested by Mr Dalyell and others that this would be one of the biggest potential sources of tension between England and Scotland in the wake of devolution.

Figure 10.4. The West Lothian Question

	England	Scotland
Scottish MPs should no longer be allowed to vote on English legislation	%	%
Strongly agree	18	14
Agree	46	39
Neither agree nor disagree	19	17
Disagree	8	19
Disagree strongly	1	4

Source: *British Social Attitudes* 2000; *Scottish Social Attitudes* 2000

At first glance, Figure 10.4 would appear to give some support to Mr Dalyell's claims. For nearly two out of three people in England agree that, 'Now that Scotland has its own parliament, Scottish MPs should no longer be allowed to vote in the UK House of Commons on laws that only affect England', while less than one in ten disagree. However, Figure 10.4 also shows that just over a half of people in Scotland agree that Scots MPs should no longer be voting on English laws.[5] While implementing such a measure

---

[5] Similar results for England were also obtained by NOP for *The Sunday Times* during the 2001 election campaign and for Scotland by System Three in a poll for *The Herald* in January 2001.

may be a source of controversy for Britain's politicians, it is less clear that it is a potential source of division between the English and Scottish publics.[6]

Still, this finding does indicate that while devolution may not have created any significant new tensions between the various publics of the UK, this does not necessarily mean that there is not public support for changing some of the details of the current devolution settlement. People in Scotland and Wales may not have acquired a taste for independence, but they do appear to be acquiring a wish for more self-government.

So far as Wales is concerned, this can be seen in Figure 10.1 above. In 1997 the principality only just voted in favour of the limited devolution that was then on offer. But now it appears that around two in five people in Wales support the idea of the principality having an elected parliament with taxation and law-making powers along the lines of the Scottish Parliament — no less than double the proportion who took that view in 1997. Indeed a NOP/HTV poll conducted just before the June 2001 election found that as many as 49 per cent wanted the National Assembly to have the same taxation and law-making powers as the Scottish Parliament while only 37 per cent believed the Assembly should be confined to its current powers. As John Osmond describes in Chapter 2, the Welsh Assembly has already moved towards methods of working that make it more akin to a parliament, and this change appears to be in line with the changing mood of Welsh public opinion.

But if many people in Wales would now like to emulate Scotland, Scotland itself has also apparently developed a taste for more. The 2000 *Scottish Social Attitudes* survey found that 66 per cent believed that the Scottish Parliament should have more powers, up ten points on when the Parliament was first founded and in line with opinion poll evidence collected at the same time.[7] True, a more recent System Three/*Sunday Herald* poll conducted in February 2001 found that the proportion wanting more powers had fallen by five points since System Three last asked the same question the previous April, but at 57 per cent it remained well over half.

More importantly this latter survey began to give some idea of what powers the Scots public thought their Parliament should have. Just two powers proved to have the support of over half of those polled, that is power over taxation and social security. And further insight into Scots attitudes towards what the Scottish National Party (SNP) dubbed 'fiscal freedom' in its UK general election campaign (see Chapter 3) is provided by two further poll readings obtained by ICM. In a poll conducted in February 2001 for *Scotland on Sunday* fewer than 63 per cent said that they believed the Scottish Executive rather than the UK government should be responsible for setting and collecting taxes in Scotland, with the Executive paying the UK a

[6] However, an ICM/*Scotsman* poll conducted just before the June 2001 election found that over four in five Scots still believed that Scotland should have her own Secretary of State in Cabinet.

[7] Curtice 2000.

grant for the services it provides in and for Scotland.[8] However, a more nuanced question asked by ICM for *The Scotsman* in May 2001 found that while 37 per cent backed the idea of the Scottish Executive setting and collecting all taxes in Scotland, no less than 38 per cent believed that the Scottish Executive and the UK Government should have shared responsibility for the setting and collecting of taxes in Scotland.[9] Still, even the latter would represent a significant departure from the status quo in which the Scottish Parliament has no more than a limited income tax varying power that so far it has not used.

Moreover, despite the more troubled history of devolution in Northern Ireland, there appears to be a willingness to give the new institutions more responsibilities there too. Thus for example, according to NILTS, no less than 57 per cent of people in Northern Ireland believe that the Assembly should have the power to raise or lower income tax while, perhaps even more remarkably, 53 per cent believe that it should be responsible for the highly sensitive area of policing. True, support for granting these powers to the Assembly is higher amongst Catholics than Protestants, but even amongst the latter, 52 per cent favour giving the Assembly income tax powers (and just 27 per cent are opposed) while 48 per cent back giving it powers over policing (36 per cent opposed).

So after two years at least devolution appears neither to have helped save or undermine the Union, though it may have helped change the terms of the debate about Northern Ireland's relationship with the rest of the UK amongst the province's Catholic community. Moreover, there is little evidence that the component parts of the UK disagree significantly about what the constitutional structure of the UK should be. However, this does not mean that there is no support for some change in that structure amongst those living in the devolved territories, though whether England wishes to join the rest of the UK on the devolution journey is still very much open to doubt.

IDENTITY

The ability of a state to maintain the loyalty of its citizens usually relies on more than a cognitive preference to belong to one entity rather than another. It commonly also rests on emotional attachments, a sense of belonging to shared community that acknowledges a common identity. In the UK that common identity has been Britishness, an identity that, it has been argued, has been able to coexist alongside those identities that are associated with the component parts of the UK such as Scottishness or Welshness.[10] In short, people could feel Scottish or Welsh and British and, as a result, the existence

---

[8] See www.icmresearch.co.uk/reviews/2001/scotsman-february-2001-poll.htm

[9] See www.icmresearch.co.uk/reviews/2001/scotsman-may2001-poll.htm

[10] Heath and Kellas 1998.

of the former did not undermine the ability of the latter to provide a common identity for the whole of the UK.

But what has happened to national identity in the wake of devolution? After all by creating separate institutions for Scotland, Wales and Northern Ireland, those in the devolved territories have been given a new symbol of what makes them different from the rest of the UK. The new institutions may even have begun to make people in England more aware that Britain and England are not synonymous with each other. In short, has devolution helped to undermine adherence to a British national identity?

One way in which we can address this question is to examine respondents' answers to the so-called Moreno scale of national identity, a scale that is particularly appropriate where people may have more than one national identity.[11] Rather than being asked to say whether they are either, say, British or Scottish, respondents are asked to place themselves on a scale on which as well as being able to say that they are 'Scottish, not British' or 'British, not Scottish', they can also say that they are 'Equally Scottish and British', or while acknowledging both identities indicate that one is more important than the other. Full details of the scale are shown in Figure 10.5, which also shows the answers that people in England and in Scotland have given in response to this scale since 1997.[12]

These answers suggest rather more people feel wholly or predominantly Scottish and English now than did so before the Labour government embarked on the implementation of its devolution policy in 1997.[13] One in three people in England now describe themselves as either 'English not British' or 'More English than British' compared with one in four in 1997. Meanwhile no less than 68 per cent describe themselves as wholly or predominantly Scottish, compared with 61 per cent in 1997.[14] However, both of these increases have been achieved not at the expense of the proportion feeling wholly or predominantly British, though at just seven per cent in Scotland at least that proportion remains very low. Rather what appears to

[11] Moreno 1988.

[12] Unfortunately, no new information on national identity in Wales has become available over the last year. However, the 1999 Welsh Assembly Election Study confirmed that the level of Welsh identity is lower than in Scotland but remains at a similar level to that which was obtained after the 1997 referendum. See Curtice 2001. Further information will become available when the results of the 2001 *Welsh Life and Times* survey are released next year.

[13] Further evidence that it is the instigation of devolution that has helped foster the increase in Scottishness comes from the fact that more people were already more willing to call themselves Scottish, not British by the time of the 1997 referendum than they were immediately after the 1997 general election (which is when the figures in Figure 10.5 were obtained). No less than 32 per cent said that they were 'Scottish not British' when the Moreno scale was administered on the 1997 *Scottish Referendum Study*.

[14] A Market Research Scotland/*Scotsman* poll undertaken in April 2001 reported that no less than 81 per cent identified themselves as 'More Scottish than British' when offered just a three point version of the Moreno scale. However, this apparent increase in Scottishness over all previous survey readings may reflect the difference in the way that the question was administered.

have declined is the incidence of those who feel equally Scottish/English and British, a development that could perhaps pose a threat to the ability of Britishness to act as a common bond across the UK.[15]

Figure 10.5. National identity, in England and Scotland			
	1997	1999	2000
England	%	%	%
English not British	7	17	19
More English than British	17	15	14
Equally English and British	45	37	34
More British than English	14	11	14
British not English	9	14	12
Other	5	3	6
Scotland	%	%	%
Scottish not British	23	32	37
More Scottish than British	38	35	31
Equally Scottish and British	27	22	21
More British than Scottish	4	3	3
British not Scottish	4	4	4
Other	2	3	4

Sources: 1997: *British/Scottish Election Studies* 1997. 1999, 2000: *British and Scottish Social Attitudes* surveys

But if there has been an increase in the incidence of Scottishness and Englishness in Scotland and England, the same can no longer be said to be true of Irishness in Northern Ireland. As we reported last year and can be seen from Figure 10.6, it appeared that there was a modest increase in the proportion of Northern Irish Catholics who declared themselves to be Irish in the immediate wake of devolution.[16] However, the most recent reading obtained by the NILTS over the course of the last year saw the proportion of Catholics saying that they were Irish fall by nine points to 59 per cent, which is more or

---

[15] We should note, however, that there is no equivalent drop in the incidence of equal identities in readings of the Moreno scale obtained by ICM between April 1997 and January 2000. See Curtice 2000. Moreover, alternative measures of national identity carried by the British and Scottish *Social Attitudes* surveys do not identify any consistent drop in the proportion claiming to be both British and English/Scottish.

[16] Curtice 2000.

less the same level that it was before the Belfast Agreement was concluded. At the same time, however, there is no sign at all that Catholics are becoming more willing to describe themselves as British, or that the stark difference between Catholics and Protestants in their pattern of national identity is narrowing.

	1989	1996	1998 (1)	1998 (2)	1999	2000
Figure 10.6. National identity in Northern Ireland						
% Protestants saying they are:						
British	66	59	77	68	72	72
Irish	4	7	2	3	2	3
% Catholics saying they are:						
British	10	10	10	8	9	9
Irish	60	57	63	64	68	59

Sources: 1989, 1996: *Northern Ireland Social Attitudes Survey.* 1998 (1): Northern Ireland Referendum and Assembly Election Study 1998. 1998 (2), 1999, 2000: *Northern Ireland Life and Times Survey.*

Change in the distribution of national identity is however only one possible way in which devolution could have an impact on the role of national identity on public opinion. Another potentially equally important possibility is that national identity has become a more important influence on people's views about the Union and the constitutional structure of the UK. In other words, national identity could become a more important source of political differences across the UK.

Of this, at least as of yet, there does not appear to be much sign. Some of the evidence for this is to be found in Figure 10.7, which shows the views of those with different national identities in England and Scotland on some of the constitutional issues we discussed in the previous section. We can see immediately that the views of those with a predominantly English national identity towards such issues as English devolution or the West Lothian question differ only slightly from those with a more British orientation. And while those in Scotland who are predominantly Scottish are more likely to be in favour of Scottish independence and English devolution, comparison of the pattern in Figure 10.7 with the results for earlier years shows that the gap has not widened. Thus, for example, in 1997, 36 per cent of those who were predominantly Scottish backed Scottish independence, alongside 15 per cent of those who were equally British and Scottish and 10 per cent of those who were predominantly British, figures that are almost identical to those in Figure 10.7.

Figure 10.7. Constitutional preference by national identity, in England and Scotland			
England	Predominantly English	Equally English/British	Predominantly British
% who favour Scottish independence	23	17	14
% who oppose English devolution	54	52	59
% who believe Scottish MPs should not vote on English laws	69	63	66
Scotland	Predominantly Scottish	Equally Scottish/British	Predominantly British
% who favour Scottish independence	37	14	7
% who oppose English devolution	41	54	55

So far as national identity is concerned then, devolution has not so far apparently achieved much to help strengthen the Union by increasing adherence to a sense of Britishness. If anything the opposite is true. At the same time, however, it has not made national identity any more of a source of political division within the component territories of the UK than it was already. As in the case of constitutional preferences the impact of devolution appears to have been more muted so far than either its advocates hoped or its critics feared.

DEVOLUTION IN PRACTICE

So far we have examined the pattern of support for devolution in principle. But what is it thought to have achieved in practice? Do the various publics that they seek to serve believe that the new institutions are bringing them more efficient and more effective government? Or is there a sense of disappointment in the air? So far as Scotland and Northern Ireland at least are concerned, we are able to bring together a wide range of evidence that addresses these questions, though in the case of Wales the evidence is unfortunately more limited.

Figure 10.8. Perceptions of the impact of devolution

Scotland

% saying Scottish Parliament has achieved:

	Feb. 00	Sept. 00	Feb. 01
A lot	5	11	25
A little	64	56	56
Nothing at all	27	29	14

Source: ICM/*Scotsman/Scotland on Sunday*

Northern Ireland

'Since devolution, many areas of government in Northern Ireland have come under the control of the Assembly. For each of these in turn, can you tell me whether you think it has got better under the Northern Ireland Assembly, has got worse, or is the same as before?'

Under Northern Ireland Assembly % saying has got:

	Better	Worse	Same
Education	16	8	59
Health	9	28	52
Transport	6	16	60
Employment	19	14	52
The economy	22	8	54

Source: *Northern Ireland Life and Times Survey* 2000

Perhaps the most obvious piece of evidence we can bring to bear is whether or not people think that their new institutions have made any difference. In Scotland at least there appears to be a growing perception that the Scottish Parliament has some achievements to its name. As Figure 10.8 shows, in February 2001 one in four Scots said that the Scottish Parliament had achieved 'a lot', well up on the just one in twenty who took that view exactly twelve months earlier. The passage of time thus appears to be giving the Scottish Parliament the chance to prove itself. At the same time, however, we should note that the most common response is still one of the Parliament having just achieved 'a little'. Indeed a Scottish Opinion/*Mail on Sunday* poll in April 2001 found that no less than two in three Scots believed that the Scottish Parliament had not made any impact on their lives at all.

Figure 10.9. Expectations of devolution

Scotland

Percentage saying Scottish Parliament will/is going to:	1997	1999	2000
Give Scotland a stronger voice in the UK	70	70	52
Give ordinary Scottish people more say in how Scotland is governed	79	64	44
Increase standard of education in Scotland	71	56	43
Make Scotland's economy better	64	43	36

Sources: 1997: *Scottish Referendum Study*; 1999, 2000 *Scottish Social Attitudes Survey*

Northern Ireland	1999	2000		
Percentage agree devolution:	All	All	Protestants	Catholics
Will bring prosperity	44	37	29	52
Will secure peace	41	34	26	53
Will bring political stability	n/a	30	20	49

Source: *Northern Ireland Life and Times Survey*

How confident are you that there will be a long and lasting peace in Northern Ireland?

% very/fairly confident will be long and lasting peace in Northern Ireland	1998	2000	2001
Protestants	35	25	19
Catholics	82	59	52
All	55	40	33

Source: UMS/*Belfast Telegraph*

Meanwhile in Northern Ireland we have access to a wide range of evaluations of the impact that the Assembly has had on specific areas of policy. The message is clearly a mixed one. While the economy, employment and education are more likely to be thought to have got better than to have got worse, the opposite is true so far as health and transport are concerned. Moreover, Catholics are more likely to have a favourable view of life under the Assembly than are Protestants, and especially so in respect to health and education, the two policy areas where the responsible Northern Irish cabinet minister is a member of Sinn Féin (SF). But above all, the most common impression across all of the policy areas is that things are much the same under the Assembly as they were before it was created.

The second piece of evidence that we can bring to bear is how far people's expectations of what the devolved institutions might achieve have or have not changed in the light of experience. In Scotland at least, as Figure 10.9 shows, such expectations have fallen considerably from the very high levels they were at when Scots first voted for devolution in 1997.[17] In 1997 clear majorities of Scots expected their new Parliament to achieve all of the apparently laudable objectives set out in the table. But the most recent reading, taken in the summer of 2000, found that now the most common expectation is that the new Parliament will not make any difference either way. It remains to be seen whether the apparently growing perception that the Parliament is in fact beginning to achieve something, as revealed in Figure 10.8 above, is accompanied by any restoration of expectations.

The story appears to be not that dissimilar in Northern Ireland. Among Catholics at least, expectations were also high at the time of the 1998 referendum with over four in five being very or fairly confident that there would now be long and lasting peace in Northern Ireland. Now that figure appears to have fallen to just over half. Expectations were never so high amongst Protestants and this community evidently not only remains less confident than Catholics about the ability of devolution to bring about peace, but is also more doubtful that devolution will bring prosperity. The heady atmosphere that surrounded the 1998 referendum now appears to be a distant memory.

But perhaps the most direct way of ascertaining how much impact devolution is thought to have had in practice is to ask people which institution they believe now has most influence in their part of the UK. Advocates of devolution at least anticipated that the new institutions would become the focus of life in each of the devolved territories. But so far there is little evidence of this. As Figure 10.10 shows, in both Scotland and Northern Ireland two in three people think that it is the UK Government at Westminster that has most influence over their affairs. And in Scotland at least this is in stark contrast to what they thought would be the case when they first went to the polls to elect their new Parliament.[18]

So in Scotland and Northern Ireland, at least, it appears that devolution is not thought to have made a big difference to how well people think they are

---

[17] Surridge and McCrone 1999.

[18] Further evidence of the perceived relative power of the UK government in Scotland comes from an ICM/*Scotsman* poll in May 2001 which found that even when it came to devolved matters such as the NHS and schools in Scotland, 37 per cent believed that the UK government in London had most influence over their quality while 27 per cent said that the Scottish Executive did. (Another 27 per cent said the two bodies had equal influence.)

Figure 10.10. Perceptions of Power: Where do people think power lies?		
Scotland	1999	2000
Scottish Parliament	41	13
UK Government at Westminster	39	66
Local councils in Scotland	8	10
European Union	4	4

The detailed question wording was as follows:-

1999: Who will have most influence over the way Scotland is run once the Scottish Parliament starts work?

2000: Which of the following do you think has most influence over the way Scotland is run?

Source: *Scottish Social Attitudes* Survey

Northern Ireland		
% saying has most power over everyday life in Northern Ireland		
	1999	2000
Northern Ireland Assembly	7	11
British Government	70	66
Local Councils	3	3
European Union	1	1
Irish Government	3	4

Source: *Northern Ireland Life and Times Survey*

governed because they perceive that Westminster still exercises considerable influence over their affairs.[19] But perhaps this is simply the result of disappointment with the individual politicians that are running their affairs in the new institutions. Perhaps we are simply looking at the failure of men rather than institutions.

This, however, is an argument that is difficult to sustain. No less than 43 per cent told ICM in February that they thought that Scotland's new First Minister, Henry McLeish, was doing a good job while only 19 per cent

[19] As we might anticipate, this is not a state of affairs that most people in Scotland or most Northern Irish Catholics find desirable. No less than 72 per cent of people in Scotland say that the Scottish Parliament should have most influence over the way that Scotland is run, while 57 per cent of Catholics say that the Northern Ireland Assembly should have most power over everyday life in Northern Ireland. However, only 35 per cent of Protestants think that the Assembly should be the most powerful body, while as many as 50 per cent nominate the British government.

thought that he was doing a bad job. While this was not as good a rating as was secured by his predecessor, Donald Dewar, at the height of his popularity,[20] it was as least as good as the last reading for Mr Dewar obtained by ICM in September 2000 just weeks before his death, when 46 per cent thought he was doing a good job but 36 per cent a bad one. Mind you, while Mr McLeish might not be unpopular he is evidently not well known, with 37 per cent saying to ICM that they did not know how good a job he was doing.

Equally, although 10 per cent fewer people thought he was doing a good job than did so the previous June, no less than 59 per cent told NOP in October 2000 just after the formation of the Labour–Liberal Democrat coalition that they thought Rhodri Morgan was doing a good job, while just 25 per cent thought he was doing a bad one. Mr Morgan remained more popular than his predecessor, Alun Michael, ever was. Even in Northern Ireland, as many as 53 per cent told Ulster Marketing Services (UMS) in May 2001 that David Trimble was doing a good job as party leader while only 20 per cent rated his performance as 'poor'. Indeed in that same poll the only party leader or cabinet minister of whom more thought they were doing a poor job than a good one was the leader of the anti-Agreement DUP, the Rev. Ian Paisley.

Figure 10.11. Has devolution improved government?			
The way Britain as a whole is governed has been:	*improved*	*no difference*	*made worse*
England	%	%	%
By creating Scottish Parliament	18	54	13
By creating Welsh Assembly	15	57	12
Scotland	%	%	%
By creating Scottish Parliament	35	44	10
By creating Welsh Assembly	18	46	4
Source: *British Social Attitudes* and *Scottish Social Attitudes* Surveys 2000			

Given all of this evidence of the apparently muted impact of devolution in practice, it should then not come as much of a surprise to discover that as of summer 2000, relatively few people in England or Scotland felt that either Scottish or Welsh devolution had improved the way that Britain as a whole is governed. True, as Figure 10.11 shows, just over one in three people in Scotland said that creating the Scottish Parliament had made an improvement, though even they were outnumbered by the 44 per cent who thought it had made no difference. But Welsh devolution had apparently made little impact

[20] Curtice 2000.

John Curtice

on the Scots while neither Scottish nor Welsh devolution had made much impression one way or the other on the English. Here perhaps is one of the reasons why Britain's asymmetric devolution settlement has apparently created so little potential so far for conflict between England and her neighbours. For many people in England there is it seems little of importance to react against.

Figure 10.12. Attitudes towards the Belfast Agreement						
% voted/would vote yes						
	May 98	Autumn 99	May 00	Oct. 00	Autumn 00	May 01
Protestants	54	49	43	47	46	61
Catholics	98	98	96	94	98	94

May 00 figures refer to self-described Unionist/Nationalist rather than Protestant/Catholic. Those who did/would not vote or who did not know how they would vote are excluded.

Sources: May 98: *Northern Ireland Referendum and Election Study*; Autumn 99, Autumn 00: *Northern Ireland Life and Times Survey*; May 00: PricewaterhouseCooopers/BBC; Oct00, May 01: UMS/*Belfast Telegraph*

Equally, it should perhaps also come as little surprise that the perceived day-to-day benefits of devolved government in Northern Ireland have apparently been insufficient to avoid an erosion of support for the Belfast Agreement among Protestants in the wake of continued controversy about certain key features of that Agreement. In Figure 10.12 we chart how attitudes towards the Agreement have developed since the May 1998 referendum. Even at the time of the 1998 referendum only just over half of those Protestants who voted cast a vote in favour of the Agreement. Thereafter there has been slow erosion of support, which while it constitutes far from a dramatic change in the mood of the Protestant community, has been sufficient on most recent readings to put support for the Agreement below the psychologically vital 50% mark. True, the most recent reading by UMS for the *Belfast Telegraph* in May 2001 reported an apparent renewal of support for the Agreement amongst Protestants, but that poll's apparent underestimate of the strength of the anti-Agreement Democratic Unionist Party (DUP) as revealed by the election result a few weeks later casts doubt on whether this can be regarded as a reliable reading of balance of Protestant opinion on the Agreement.[21]

But even this UMS poll gives us a clear indication of what is the principal source of Protestant doubts about the Belfast Agreement, viz the absence of

[21] Only 14 per cent of respondents to this poll indicated that they were supporting the DUP when in the event the Party won 23 per cent of the vote cast across the province as a whole in the general election.

arms decommissioning. No less than nine out of ten Protestants said that paramilitaries — that is both the IRA and the loyalist paramilitaries — should decommission not just some weapons but all weapons (a view shared incidentally by around two in three Catholics). Meanwhile no less than 48 per cent of Protestants agreed with the proposition that, 'The Assembly should be suspended until there has been decommissioning by both republican and loyalist paramilitaries' while only 34 per cent disagreed. Even amongst supporters of David Trimble's Ulster Unionist Party (UUP), no less than 44 per cent agreed (and only 30 per cent disagreed) that those political parties who signed up to the Belfast Agreement should renegotiate the Agreement so that those parties that have links to paramilitary organisations are excluded. Moreover, when in the previous autumn the NILTS asked those respondents who acknowledged that they had switched from being in favour to being opposed to the Belfast Agreement, the most common reason offered by no less than 76 per cent — was the absence of decommissioning.

Perhaps if decommissioning were the only difficulty it would not have proven to be such a thorny issue. But it is not. For example, according to the UMS poll, over a half are opposed to the change of the name of the Royal Ulster Constabulary (RUC) to the Police Service of Northern Ireland. More generally, according to NILTS there is a growing perception that nationalists have gained more out of the Agreement than unionists. As a result decommissioning has probably become the litmus test for many Protestants of whether they are to receive something in return for what many of them regard as the significant 'concessions' that have been made to nationalists elsewhere in the Belfast Agreement and as a result in its absence the current devolution settlement at least remains unacceptable.

So far there appears to have been a muted response to the experience of devolution in practice. It is not thought to have done much harm, but there are doubts about how much benefit it has delivered so far too. Experience appears to have brought about some adjustment of expectations. And in Northern Ireland what the Assembly is thought to have delivered has not been able to insulate the devolution settlement there from other sources of disagreement about the Belfast Agreement. True, in Scotland and Wales, there is no doubt that the new institutions will be granted time and opportunity to prove themselves in the eyes of their public, an opportunity that the Scottish Parliament at least may already be taking. But as of late September 2001 at least, there was no guarantee that the Northern Ireland Assembly would be able to negotiate a safe passage through the rocks of decommissioning.

THE 2001 GENERAL ELECTION

As we noted at the beginning of this chapter, because the 2001 election was the first to be held since the introduction of devolution in Scotland, Wales and Northern Ireland, it gives us some particularly vital clues about the public's reaction to devolution. In Scotland and Wales at least, there appeared to be two crucial questions. First, would people still consider it worthwhile turning out to vote in a Westminster election now that they had their own devolved institutions? And second, would those who did turn out to vote do so on the basis of what was happening at Westminster, or would they instead regard a UK general election as an opportunity to pass comment on how well the Scottish Executive or National Assembly for Wales was performing? In short, was there a danger that Westminster elections would come to be seen as a 'second-order' election in Scotland and Wales?[22]

Figure 10.13. The 2001 general election result in Great Britain				
	Change in % vote since 1997			Change in % since 1999	
	England	Scotland	Wales	Scotland	Wales
Conservative	+ 1.5	– 1.9	+ 1.5	+0.0	+ 5.2
Labour	– 2.2	– 1.6	– 6.1	+5.1	+11.0
Lib. Dem.	+ 1.5	+ 3.4	+ 1.4	+2.2	+ 0.3
Nationalist	–	– 2.0	+ 4.3	–7.7	–14.1
Other	– 0.8	+ 2.1	– 1.1	+1.3	– 2.4
Turnout	–12.1	–13.1	–12.1	–0.1	+15.0

Votes cast for the Speaker in 1997 and 2001 are counted as Labour. Change since 1999 is based on the votes cast in the constituency contests for the Scottish Parliament and Welsh Assembly.

Sources: Butler and Kavanagh 2001; Electoral Commission 2001; Rallings and Thrasher 2000.

We have already noted that people in Scotland at least had come to the view as much as twelve months before the UK general election that the UK government at Westminster had more influence on what happened in Scotland than did the Scottish Parliament. Meanwhile in Wales a NOP/HTV poll undertaken just before the UK general election found that no less than 75 per cent said that a UK general election mattered just as much as it did before the

---

[22] Reif and Schmitt 1980.

National Assembly was created, while amongst the remainder those who thought a UK general election was less important now was more than matched by the proportion who thought it was more important. So in practice we would therefore be surprised if people in Scotland and Wales showed any particular reluctance to vote in a UK general election. And as the last row of Figure 10.13 indicates, that indeed was the case. So while turnout did fall heavily in both Scotland and Wales compared with the 1997 general election, in Wales the fall was identical to that in England while in Scotland it was just one point higher. So the very most that we can claim is that the presence of the Scottish Parliament may have had a marginal impact in lowering the turnout.

Moreover, in Wales there appears to be little doubt that voters are more likely to vote in a UK general election than they are in a National Assembly contest. The 2001 turnout in Wales was no less than 15 points higher than it was in the first National Assembly election in 1999. In Scotland, however, the evidence is more debatable. Here the 2001 turnout was almost identical to that for the Scottish Parliament in 1999. This might suggest that Scottish Parliament elections look set to be capable of securing as high a turnout as Westminster elections. However, when ICM asked voters in Scotland just before polling day how likely it was that they would have voted if it were a Scottish Parliament election that was being held on 7 June, 10 per cent fewer said they were certain to have voted than said they were certain to do so in the Westminster election. If the apparent general aversion to turning out to vote that currently seems to exist amongst voters is still present in 2003, less than half of Scots may vote in their Parliament's second election, as happened in Wales's first contest in 1999.

But what of the behaviour of those who did vote? Did they vote on the basis of how well they thought the UK government was doing? Or were they influenced by considerations closer to home? Polling evidence collected by both ICM and System Three in Scotland during the general election indicated that, as in the rest of the UK, formally devolved issues such as health and education were at the top of voters' priorities north of the border just as they were in the rest of Britain. So there would seem to be good reason why voters should be influenced by the performance of the Scottish Executive, though only of course so long as they considered the Executive to be the body that actually has most influence over the state of schools and hospitals in Scotland.

In Wales at least, people's evaluations of the merits of the parties in the devolved institutions does appear to have had some impact on the way that people voted in the 2001 general election. Labour suffered a calamitous reversal in Wales in 1999; its vote in the Welsh Assembly constituency contests was no less than 17 points lower than it had been in the 1997 general election. And as we can see from Figure 10.13, Labour's vote in 2001 was still no less than six points lower than it was in the 1997 general election, well above the two point drop in support that the party suffered in England. The clear beneficiaries of that drop in support were Plaid Cymru (PC) who with 14.3 per cent of the vote secured their highest ever share of the vote in a Westminster general election. Evidently, some of the unhappiness with Labour at the time of the 1999 Welsh election, most notably over the party's insistence on nominating Alun Michael rather than Rhodri Morgan as the Party's candidate for First Secretary, was still leaving its mark two years later.

In Scotland, in contrast, if the public were using the election to cast a judgment on the performance of either of the parties in the Scottish Executive, it must have been a favourable one. Labour, and more especially the Liberal Democrats, both performed somewhat better than they did in England. However, what is more remarkable both about the result in Scotland and that in Wales is, as the last two columns of Figure 10.13 reveal, the difference between the pattern of voting in 2001 and that in the first devolved elections two years earlier. In both Scotland and in Wales, Labour performed significantly better than it did in 1999, while equally the two nationalist parties found it much harder to win votes.

Of course, one possibility is that the relative popularity of the Labour Party and its two nationalist competitors changed in both Scotland and Wales between 1999 and 2001. However, opinion polls in both Scotland and Wales consistently point to a very different conclusion. This is that voters in both countries are more willing to vote for the Labour Party and less willing to vote for a nationalist party in a UK general election than they were in a devolved election.

For example, in a poll it conducted for *The Scotsman* in the final days of the 2001 election campaign, seven per cent fewer voters told ICM they would have voted Labour in the constituency contest of a Scottish Parliament election. Meanwhile the Scottish National Party's (SNP) support in a Scottish Parliament contest was no less than eleven points higher than it was for Westminster. These differences are in fact greater than the actual change in support experienced by these two parties between 1999 and 2001. In other words, if it had been a Scottish Parliament election that had been held in June 2001 the outcome could well have been very similar to the last result in 1999. Far from indicating that the advent of devolution was changing the way that people would vote in Scotland, the outcome of the 2001 election provided further evidence that voters regard the Scottish Parliament and the Westminster Parliament as two rather separate worlds, each to be evaluated separately on its own merits.

A similar conclusion applies in respect of Wales. Although no opinion poll giving both Westminster and National Assembly voting intention was published during the course of the election campaign, a NOP poll undertaken for HTV in March 2001 found a significant difference in the popularity of the parties for the two kinds of election. Support for PC in a National Assembly election was put at no less than 15 points higher than it was for a Westminster contest, while Labour's support was eight points lower. These differences are more than enough to account for PC's fall in support between 1999 and 2001 and are almost enough to account for the increase in Labour's vote. As in Scotland it appears that if it had been a devolved election that had been held in June 2001 the outcome would have been very similar to that in 1999.

So what is most remarkable about the 2001 election in Scotland and Wales is the lack of impact that devolution apparently had on how people voted. But the same cannot be said of Northern Ireland where within the Protestant community at least, the election became a referendum on the future of the Belfast Agreement. Just how different an election this made the contest in Northern Ireland compared with Great Britain can be gauged from the fact that turnout was slightly higher than in 1997 and almost matched the turnout in the 1998 Northern Ireland Assembly election. Far from depressing turn-out, devolution helped ensure that for Northern Ireland voters at least the election still mattered.

Figure 10.14. The 2001 general election result in Northern Ireland			
		Change in % vote since	
	% vote	1997	1998
Ulster Unionist Party	26.8	−5.9	+5.5
Democratic Unionist Party	22.5	+8.9	+4.4
Alliance Party	3.6	−4.4	−2.9
Social Democratic & Labour Party	21.0	-3.2	−1.0
Sinn Féin	21.7	+5.7	+4.1
Others	4.4	−1.1	−4.6
	100.0		
Turnout	68.0	+0.9	−0.7
Sources: Electoral Commission 2001; Rallings and Thrasher 2000.			

Moreover, the election result was widely regarded as a body blow for pro-Agreement Unionism. The DUP made a net gain of three seats compared with 1997 while the UUP suffered a net loss of four. But if we wish to judge how far the election result was a set-back for pro-Agreement unionism it makes more sense to compare the 2001 results with those of the 1998 Assembly election. The latter took place immediately after the referendum on the Belfast Agreement and thus, in contrast to the 1997 result, gives us a measure of the popularity of the parties at the beginning of the devolution process. Moreover in 1998 UUP and the DUP opposed each other in all eighteen of Northern Ireland's constituencies, a pattern that also obtained in as many as fourteen seats in 2001 but only in seven in 1997.

As we can see from Figure 10.14, this comparison suggests that any swing against pro-Agreement unionism was perhaps more muted than the headlines suggested. In fact the UUP increased its vote compared with 1998 by slightly more than did the DUP. Still, this province-wide comparison is not without its difficulties either. Six prominent UUP candidates were known to be opposed to the Agreement. The DUP fought only 15 seats compared with the UUP's 17. And the UUP were able to profit not only from the decision of other pro-Agreement unionist parties not to stand in most seats, but also from the withdrawal of the pro-Agreement but non-sectarian Alliance Party in a number of key constituencies.

This suggests that the best measure of the changing mood of the Protestant community can be obtained from comparing the total vote for pro- and anti-Agreement unionist candidates in those seats where there were both pro- and an anti-Agreement unionist candidates standing in 2001 together with an Alliance Party candidate.[23] This reveals a clear but small swing against the pro-Agreement cause. On average the vote for pro-Agreement candidates fell by 0.2 per cent while that for those backing the anti-Agreement cause rose by 2.6 per cent. This would appear to be in line with the message of the opinion polls we examined earlier that suggested a modest rather than a dramatic fall in support for the Agreement amongst Protestants. The trouble is that both the level of support for the Agreement and that for the UUP in 1998 were already too fragile to afford even a modest erosion of support.

The outcome of the 2001 UK general election was significant not only for unionism but also for nationalism. For the first time ever SF managed to outpoll the more moderate SDLP both in terms of votes and seats. It appears likely that SF's participation in the Belfast Agreement and the Northern Ireland Assembly has indeed assisted it in its aim of becoming the predominant voice of nationalism. If so, once again devolution in Northern Ireland appears to have had an impact.

Devolution appears then to have had a very varied impact on how voters behaved in the 2001 election. In Northern Ireland the continuing uncertainty about the future of the Assembly and the Belfast Agreement helped ensure both that the election was no less than a referendum on the future of devolution and that the election held an interest for voters that was singularly lacking elsewhere. In Scotland and Wales, in contrast, what was most remarkable

---

[23] These seats are Antrim North, Belfast East, Down South, Foyle and Strangford. We should also note that anti-agreement UUP candidates who were opposed by another unionist secured a 10.4 per cent increase in their vote on average compared with 1998 while the vote for pro-agreement unionists only increased by 4.1 per cent.

was the degree to which voters apparently left devolution and their views about the devolved institutions to one side as they decided whether and how to vote. One consequence of this is that the outcome of the 2001 election in these parts of the UK gave us little guidance about how voters will behave at the next devolved elections in 2003.

CONCLUSION

Devolution may be a major constitutional experiment for the UK. But this does not mean that it was bound to have an immediate or dramatic impact on public opinion, for either good or ill. Certainly two years after the introduction of devolution to Scotland and Wales what is more remarkable is what is unchanged about public opinion rather than what has changed.

Levels of support for the maintenance of the Union across the UK appear to be little changed. There is little evidence that devolution has created new sources of potential conflict between the various publics of the UK or that national identity has become a more important source of division within any of those publics than it was already. Not least of the reasons for this appears to be that the new institutions themselves have, perhaps unsurprisingly, been seen to have made little difference so far to the lives of those they seek to serve.

This of course does not mean that devolution will not still be a source of continuing political debate. That is most obviously so in Northern Ireland where there continue to be significant differences between Protestants and Catholics over identities and the constitutional future of the province, differences that could yet help ensure that the life of the Northern Ireland Assembly proves to be a short one. Even in Scotland and Wales we should not assume that the details of the current devolution settlement represent the 'settled will' of the people even if the principle of devolution apparently is. But as those debates continue, one lesson to draw from the experience of devolution so far is that we should not expect too much of devolution if what we want to do is to bring about a swift and significant change in public opinion.

BIBLIOGRAPHY

Secondary Sources

Butler, D. and Kavanagh, D. (2001). *The British General Election of 2001.* London: Macmillan.

Curtice, J. (2000). 'The People's Verdict', in Hazell, R. (ed.), *The State and the Nations: The First Year of Devolution in the United Kingdom.* Exeter: Imprint Academic.

Curtice, J., 'Is devolution securing nationalism?', *Contemporary Wales,* 14: 80-103.

Curtice, J. and Gallagher, A. (1990). 'The Northern Irish Dimension', in Jowell, R., Witherspoon, S. and Brook, L. (eds.), *British Social Attitudes: the 9ʰ report*. Aldershot: Gower.

Curtice, J., McCrone, D., Park, A., and Paterson, L. (eds.) (2001). *New Scotland, New Society? Are our social and political ties fragmenting?* Edinburgh: Edinburgh University Press.

Curtice, J. and Seyd, B. (2001), 'Is devolution strengthening or weakening the UK?', in Park, A., et al (2001).

Electoral Commission (2001). *Election 2001: The Official Results*. London: Politico's.

Heath, A., and Kellas, J. (1998). 'Nationalisms and constitutional questions', *Scottish Affairs*, Special Issue on Understanding Constitutional Change, 110-27.

Jowell, R., Curtice, J., Park, A., Thomson, K., Jarvis, L., Bromley, C. and Stratford, N. (eds.) (2000). *British Social Attitudes: the 17ʰ report: Focusing on Diversity.* London: Sage.

Moreno, L. (1988). 'Scotland and Catalonia: The path to Home Rule', in McCrone, D. and Brown, A. (eds.), *The Scottish Government Yearbook 1988*. Edinburgh: Unit for the Study of Government in Scotland.

Northern Ireland Life and Times Survey (2001).

Park, A., Curtice, J., Thomson, K., Jarvis, L., and Bromley, C. (eds.) (2001). *British Social Attitudes: the 18ʰ report*. London: Sage.

Paterson, L., Brown, A., Curtice, J., Hinds, K., McCrone, D., Park, A., Sproston, K. and Surridge, P. (2001). *New Scotland, New Politics?* Edinburgh: Edinburgh University Press.

Rallings, C. and Thrasher, M. (1999). *British Electoral Facts: 1832-1999*. Aldershot: Ashgate.

Reif, K. and Schmitt, H. (1980). 'Nine national second-order elections', in Reif, K. (ed.), *Ten European Elections: Campaigns and Results of the 1979/81 First Direct Elections to the European Parliament*. Aldershot: Gower.

Surridge, P. (2001). 'Society and Democracy: the new Scotland' in Curtice, J., McCrone, D., Park, A., and Paterson, L. (eds.), *New Scotland, New Society? Are our social and political ties fragmenting?* Edinburgh: Edinburgh University Press.

Surridge, P. and McCrone, D. (1999). 'The 1997 Scottish referendum vote', in Taylor, B. and Thomson, K. (eds.), *Scotland and Wales: Nations Again?* Cardiff: University of Wales Press.

11

Conclusion

The State of the Nations after Two Years of Devolution

Robert Hazell

This concluding chapter draws together the threads from the preceding chapters and summarises the main characteristics of the devolution settlement as they appear at the end of its second year. Devolution continues to proceed relatively smoothly. Northern Ireland apart, it has not caused the UK government any major headaches. Despite Conservative attempts to raise the issue of 'English votes on English laws', devolution and its consequences did not feature as an issue in the UK general election in 2001.

But below the surface deeper forces are at work, as the dynamics of devolution begin to work their way through. The settlement is still evolving, with Wales wanting primary legislative powers closer to Scotland, and some of the English regions coming together to campaign for elected regional assemblies. The Government has responded by promising a White Paper on regional government in England.

The institutions of central government continue to adapt to devolution, but relatively slowly. In terms of policy, the second year has seen some sharper divergence between the devolved administrations and the UK Government. This chapter opens with the emerging policy differences. It then considers the consequential tensions which are emerging over finance, which are bound to grow with time.

THE BEGINNINGS OF POLICY DIFFERENTIATION

One of the main purposes of devolution was to allow Scotland, Wales and Northern Ireland to get away from 'one size fits all' policies imposed by Westminster and Whitehall, and to develop their own policies better suited to local needs. If devolution does not lead to differentiation of policy then it will prove a serious disappointment to those who voted for it. Reporting on how much policy differentiation takes place is something we will try to do more systematically in these annual volumes in future, and this year we make a start by highlighting the main developments in this final chapter. In one field we have tracked policy developments systematically from the start, and that is in the impact of devolution on health, where we are running a specific research project. During the past year all four governments have announced major changes to the direction and management of the health service. The main points of policy divergence in health are summarised in Figure 11.1. Differentiation in other policy fields is set out below, starting with Scotland which has set the pace.

   Scotland embarked on one policy change early in the first year of devolution, with the new policy on tuition fees in higher education which was insisted upon by the Liberal Democrats as their price of entry into the coalition and a key plank in the coalition's programme for government. In the second year education provided another point of departure for Scotland, when the McCrone Committee on teachers' pay recommended a pay award (of 23 per cent over three years) far higher than the settlement negotiated in England. But the most expensive policy divergence yet in Scotland is likely to be the acceptance by Henry McLeish of the principles of the Sutherland Report on Long Term Care, and his undertaking that in Scotland the elderly will enjoy free personal as well as nursing care. This undertaking was made again partly because of pressure from the Liberal Democrats, and the Scottish Parliament.

   Wales had little to show in terms of distinctive policy in the first year, apart from the Children's Commissioner for Wales. It took the advent of

Figure 11.1 Policy divergence in health[1]

The UK's four health systems have diverged more sharply since devolution. The divergence falls along two axes: the extent to which they rely on planning versus markets, and the extent to which they focus on health care versus health outcomes. They diverge on these axes from a common baseline; the 1991 Conservative reforms which in all four countries introduced an internal market in the health service and pushed attention away from concerns with public health.

England has three characteristics: a strong focus on market-like decision making within increasing centralisation; a focus on health care services and 'delivery' rather than wider determinants of health; and instability. In 1997 the theme was pragmatism and preservation of the good parts of the Conservatives' internal market. Principally, the Government interpreted this to mean that Primary Care Trusts would commission work from NHS hospital and other trusts, acting as buyers on behalf of their patients. Thus England enshrined the market logic most strongly. Then the Government's focus switched to 'modernisation' and 'delivery'. Thus, in mid-2001 came a new reorganisation affecting every level of management, a move designed to give the centre 'a clear line of sight' to the front lines while permitting private firms to do NHS work. Incessant structural reorganisation has been a trait of the NHS for decades and, if anything, has sped up in England since devolution. This raises the question; what is it about the Westminster system that leads to such policy instability?

[1] This analysis is provided by Scott Greer, the researcher on our devolution and health project. Further details about the project from s.greer@ucl.ac.uk

Wales resembles England on paper in that Local Health Groups made up of primary care professionals commission most work (even if commissioning is less important in allocating funds). What is striking about Wales, though, is its attention to the wider determinants of health. The Welsh NHS plan (January 2001) targets outcomes such as lower cardiac disease rates, and uses the health service and schools alike to reduce illness, whether by treating heart patients in hospitals or encouraging children to play sport in schools.

Meanwhile, organisational reforms are trying to flatten further the already-flat Welsh structure in order to permit greater central oversight and local autonomy.

Scotland has moved the furthest toward planning, and is midway between England's health services focus and Wales' health outcomes focus. The Scottish NHS, even before Holyrood began work, was already recreating the older regional planning structure of the pre-Thatcher NHS by putting separate units such as hospitals and family doctors under the same boards. Since devolution, the Scots have continued to amalgamate services so that fifteen regional boards organise and plan all health care. Commissioning and market logics are gone; planning and integration are the new themes of policy. In public health, Scotland has made more progress than England, with programmes such as free fruit handed out in schools. Nevertheless, the public health agenda is not as strong as in Wales, reflecting the competing demands of Scotland's elite tertiary care centres.

Northern Ireland has seen much less policy activity — which means that it has been left behind by the other, faster-changing, UK systems. The 1991 internal market designed by the Conservatives and applied to the entire UK still holds in Northern Ireland, despite the opposition of the Northern Irish parties to fund-holding. The reasons are tied up with the shaky progress of the peace process. Before devolution, the UK Government held off on policymaking so that the devolved administrations' politicians could have a stake in the new administration. After devolution, policy reform fell prey to not only the gridlock of much Northern Irish policy, and the suspensions, but also the controversial politics of its Sinn Féin Health minister, and what the Northern Ireland Assembly's health committee viewed as her inadequately thought-out proposals to replace the market. The only policy moves underway are those in the 'Programme for Government' agreed by the Assembly, and those are biased towards public and environmental health measures. As a result, Northern Irish policy looks set to focus on public health, although there are interesting debates about both health service planning and changing broader health outcomes.

Rhodri Morgan as First Minister, and then the Partnership Agreement which he entered into with the Liberal Democrats in October 2000, for some distinctive policies to emerge. The Partnership Agreement promised free school milk for all children under seven, a freezing of prescription charges, and free bus travel for pensioners from 2002. On 1 April 2001 it delivered free opening of the National Museums and Galleries of Wales and free prescriptions for those under 25 and over 60. In the health service the National Health Plan for Wales in February 2001 announced the abolition of the five Health Authorities by April 2003, and their replacement by 22 Local Health Boards, which will share the same boundaries as the 22 Welsh local authorities. As explained in Figure 11.1 this should enable Wales to tackle the wider determinants of public health in a strategy that will be completely different from the approach adopted in England. And finally in education Wales made a small departure from England by scrapping school league tables in July 2001, following a consultation which concluded they were unpopular with both parents and teachers.

Northern Ireland anticipated this move, with the Education minister Martin McGuinness announcing the scrapping of league tables in January 2001. In February the Executive presented its long-awaited 'Programme for Government', published under the title 'Making a Difference'. This became the ministerial mantra, to emphasise the new policies which ministers insisted would not have been adopted under direct rule. In particular they have highlighted free travel for pensioners (to be introduced from October 2001), a new student finance package to widen access (also from autumn 2001), and the decision to establish a Children's Commissioner. In these last two initiatives Northern Ireland has clearly been influenced by policies adopted by the other devolved administrations. The higher education committee of the Assembly produced a report on student finance in October 2000 which opted for a model closely resembling that in Scotland. And in proposing a Children's Commissioner the Assembly looked to the pioneering model established in Wales.

This is a selective list: in future years we will try to produce a more systematic one (and would welcome help from our readers). But already three points are worth noting. One is the influence of the Liberal Democrats in promoting policy divergence, by putting pressure on their Labour coalition partners. They were the driving force behind the Scottish policy on tuition fees, and on long term care they were part of the coalition of support (with the SNP) for full implementation of the Sutherland report. Similarly in Wales the rate of policy differentiation increased markedly with the entry into government of the Liberal Democrats in October 2000, and their desire to make their mark in the partnership agreement.

The second point worth noting is the beginnings of policy transfer between the devolved administrations. Devolution should encourage greater experimentation in policy, and policy-learning by one government from the pioneering experience of another. It is encouraging that signs of this are beginning to emerge, with the interest shown in Northern Ireland in Scotland's new policy for student finance, free travel schemes for pensioners in Wales and Northern Ireland, and the general interest shown in the new Children's Commissioner for Wales. So far there are fewer signs of the UK government showing much interest in learning from these policy experiments, although there were indications in August 2001 of a possible rethink on tuition fees after their unpopularity had been brought home to ministers during the election. This finally broke the surface in October 2001 when

Estelle Morris, the Education Secretary, announced a dramatic shift in policy on student finance.[2] No reference was made to the Scottish experience, but it is bound to feature in the coming review. When UK governments are willing to acknowledge that they have something to learn from the devolved governments, or Westminster from the innovatory practices of the devolved assemblies, devolution will truly have come of age.

The third point to note about these policy departures is that they mostly involve additional public expenditure; in the case of long term care, and the teachers' pay award in Scotland, very significant additional expenditure. Whether they are sustainable in the long term remains to be seen. That is no doubt one of the main reasons why the UK government has not followed their example; it cannot afford to. And it is the main reason for the tensions which are beginning to emerge over finance, which are discussed in the next section.

THE BARNETT FORMULA COMES UNDER QUESTION

Devolution has exposed the spending differentials between the different parts of the UK; and has put the funding formula under the spotlight . It is now better known amongst the general public that Northern Ireland, Scotland and Wales enjoy significantly higher levels of public spending per capita than in England. It is just beginning to become known, at least amongst the political classes, that those spending differentials are set to decrease. As Chapter 6 demonstrates, the Barnett Formula is becoming the Barnett squeeze. This has led to growing questioning of the Barnett Formula by the devolved administrations.

David Trimble MP, then First Minister for Northern Ireland, put the point with typical sharpness during Questions to the Northern Ireland Secretary in the House of Commons on 9 May 2001:

> In England and Wales, average real terms expenditure is expected to rise over the next three years by 6 per cent in round figures. The equivalent figure in Scotland is 5 per cent; in Wales it is 4 per cent and in Northern Ireland it is 3 per cent. Will he point out [to the Chancellor of the Exchequer] that the formula does not operate very fairly?[3]

And in reply George Howarth MP, Parliamentary Under-Secretary in the Northern Ireland Office (NIO), reiterated the government line on the Barnett Formula, while explaining how it does operate as a squeeze:

> The Government have no plans to change the Barnett formula . . . For Northern Ireland, that delivers a lower percentage increase on the existing baseline because

---

[2] 'Stunning U-turn on student grants' *Guardian*, 'Graduate tax expected to replace student loans' *Financial Times*, 'Students to pay extra tax if grants restored' *Times*, 4 October 2001.
[3] HC Deb, 9 May 2001, Col. 103.

Northern Ireland starts from a higher per capita basis than any other region in the United Kingdom.

In the long term, this position is unsustainable. As David Bell points out in Chapter 6, there is no other country which allocates resources at the sub-national level using a formula based on changes to the baseline, rather than relative need. Lord Barnett himself has accepted that his formula has passed its sell-by date.[4] The question for devolution watchers is when the convergence formula will create a convergence of circumstances which forces a review. That convergence of circumstances will come about when all the devolved governments start to feel the pain. Because of the historically high baseline levels of spending relative to need, particularly in Scotland, there is still some flexibility in their budgets. But the faster the Scottish government ratchets up big spending commitments like the teachers' pay settlement and free long term care for the elderly, the sooner the pain threshold will be reached.

For most of the time the Barnett Formula operates below the political radar. It is never dormant in administrative terms; as Alan Trench explains in Chapter 7, there are frequent negotiations between the devolved administrations and the Treasury over whether in-year adjustments (such as for the tourism effects of Foot-and-Mouth Disease) will attract a Barnett consequential. But in political terms the formula only surfaces occasionally. Two such occasions were in the run up to and during the general election in 2001.

In the run-up to the election John Prescott at the Department of the Environment, Transport and the Regions (DETR) (and batting for England) had been reported to be in favour of a review after the election; but the story was largely speculative, based on publication of the annual Treasury statistics showing the distribution of spending between the nations and regions.[5] (Figures 6.2 and 6.3 in Chapter 6 show how much lower government spending is in the English regions, in particular in the North).

In Scotland the issue was raised in a letter to *The Scotsman* by 12 economists, who called on all parties to address the issue of the Barnett Formula in the election campaign. Greater fiscal autonomy for Scotland has long been espoused by the SNP and the Liberal Democrats, and by *The Scotsman* itself, which continues to contrast Scotland's spending commitments with the greater financial discipline exercised by the UK government.[6] But it is stoutly resisted by the Labour Party in Scotland, for two reasons. The first is purely political; they do not want to concede on this issue to the nationalists.

---

[4] Treasury Select Committee, *The Barnett Formula*, HC 341, 17 December 1997, p1.

[5] *The Guardian*, 'Scots and Welsh face subsidy axe', 24 April 2001.

[6] See for example their Westminster Editor on 3 September 2001, 'Henry McLeish's plans for free personal care for the elderly have been savaged by the UK Department of Health as a wasteful delusion... '. The UK Health department's consultation paper on long term care which provided the pretext for the story contained no reference to the different approach taken in Scotland, and so no justification for this journalistic licence.

And the second is financial; Scotland almost certainly receives more than it would under a needs-based formula (see Chapter 6), and for the moment they do not want to rock the boat.

In Wales the perception is quite different. Wales receives less funding per capita than Scotland, while being significantly poorer in terms of GDP per capita, and almost certainly more deserving in terms of need (see Table 6.4 showing public expenditure relative to need). Ron Davies has been as sharp a critic as David Trimble:

> Whatever the merits of the Barnett Formula over the past years, there is now one inescapable fact: the existing block formula system is disadvantaging Wales. The Barnett block, being historically determined, does not reflect the social and economic difficulties that Wales has experienced over the past 20 years, and is leading to convergence of levels of public spending vis-a-vis England, rather than divergence, as our economic and social needs demand . . . The present system of financing Welsh public expenditure should be scrapped, and replaced with a needs-based system.[7]

Some believe that the Barnett Formula would have to be reviewed if regional government were introduced in England, which could throw again into sharp relief the spending differentials between the English regions, on the one hand, and Scotland, Wales and Northern Ireland on the other. This is not necessarily the case. A separate funding formula could be devised for the English regions, and Scotland, Wales and Northern Ireland could be left (as they are now) to be dealt with as a consequential of spending decisions in England. No one should underestimate the capacity of funding formulae to survive long after the experts have predicted their demise. Because any change creates winners and losers, the political difficulties of negotiating a new settlement are immense. The main loser would be Scotland, which would be likely to receive less under a needs-based formula. But the people of Scotland have a completely different view. When asked about Scotland's share of government spending compared with the rest of the UK, 58 per cent of Scots say that it is less than fair.[8] Nor is the UK government likely to make the first move, so long as the Chancellor and one quarter of the Cabinet come from Scotland.

These are the underlying reasons why the Treasury stoutly maintains that the UK government has no plans to change the Barnett Formula. That will remain the case even though senior politicians in Northern Ireland and in Wales have called for change. Scotland has the swing vote and is the place to watch. Convergence is ticking away there too, and the squeeze will be accelerated by the Scottish Executive's own spending commitments. So far the devolved administrations have not shown much inclination to join together

---

[7] National Assembly *Record*, 13 February 2001.

[8] *Scottish Social Attitudes Survey*, summer 2000, reported in Curtice and Seyd 2001.

in solidarity against the UK government. Only when all three devolved governments line up together, and all three of them call for change, will the British government come under real pressure to concede a review.

DEVOLUTION IS HERE TO STAY . . .

The second part of this chapter shifts back to the constitutional level. It starts with some general observations about the stability of the devolution settlement, and then reviews the pace of constitutional change in each of the devolved nations. The first observation to make is that devolution is here to stay. John Major had passionately opposed it in the 1992 and 1997 elections, urging that it would lead to the break up of Britain. After their 1997 defeat Conservative opposition was more muted during the passage of the devolution legislation in 1998, and in the 1999 elections in Scotland and Wales. Now in the 2001 general election they have made it quite clear that they accept the fact of devolution, and want to work to make it a success.

This policy stance could change under the new leadership of Iain Duncan Smith, noted for being the only member of Hague's shadow cabinet to have urged repeal of the devolution legislation. Opposition to devolution would provoke a split with the Conservatives in Scotland and Wales, who see clearly that if they are to rebuild their party's shattered fortunes they must rebrand themselves as strong supporters of devolution and distance themselves from the national image of the Conservatives as an English-dominated party. Within days of the 2001 election, the second general election at which the Conservatives failed to win a single seat in Wales, Glyn Davies, Conservative AM for Mid and West Wales was arguing:

> Our attitude towards the National Assembly is the key to convincing the Welsh people that we are totally committed to 'sticking up for Wales'. Whether we like it or not, the National Assembly is here to stay and the Conservative Party's commitment to it is the measure by which our commitment to Wales will be judged . . . [9]

In terms of public opinion devolution is also here to stay. That was never in much doubt in Scotland, following the strong endorsement for devolution in the 1997 referendum. Support for independence in Scotland shows no sign of increasing. And support for the Scottish Parliament is equally strong in England. A majority of people both north and south of the border continue to support the idea of a Scottish Parliament. Indeed, in both England and Scotland such opposition as existed to devolution was even lower by summer 2000 (17 per cent in England, 12 per cent in Scotland) than when Labour first came to power in 1997. Support for the Scottish Parliament, which John

---

[9] *The Western Mail*, 11 June 2001.

Smith declared to be the 'settled will' of the people of Scotland, seems to have become the settled will of the people of England too.[10]

But support for devolution could have been in doubt in Wales, where with a 50 per cent turnout in the 1997 referendum only one voter in four had supported the government's proposals. Now the opinion polls suggest that position has been reversed. NOP's June 2001 poll showed just one Welsh voter in five saying that Wales should have no elected assembly or parliament. And nearly half of those polled would like devolution in Wales to go further. Now that Wales has a National Assembly, the people of Wales would like it to have more effective powers.

Only in Northern Ireland is devolution still extremely shaky; but even there public support for devolution has held up while the politicians and institutions have faltered. The end-2000 polling data reported in Chapter 4 show that two-thirds of the people in Northern Ireland would still have voted for the Belfast Agreement. But concealed within this overall majority, Protestant support had slid from 60:40 for the Agreement in the April 1998 referendum to 45:55 against at the end of 2000, which is why David Trimble has come under such pressure from his own supporters.

. . . AND IT IS RESHAPING THE PARTY SYSTEM

Although we have only two sets of elections to go on, the first devolved elections in 1999 and the general election in 2001, we can already see how devolution is reshaping the party system. Whereas Great Britain used to have a single party system, a different party system is emerging in Scotland and Wales, with different election results between the two levels. Most of the political parties now have separate leaders in Scotland and Wales. In future they will be elected by the party members in those countries, which will lead to further differentiation, with all parties learning lessons from Labour's clumsy attempt to foist Alun Michael on the Wales Labour Party. And the parties are presenting themselves differently, with the Scottish and Welsh manifestos in 2001 more clearly different than the repackaged versions of the national manifesto produced at previous general elections. Rhodri Morgan was at pains to make clear that Labour's Welsh manifesto was 'very Welsh, written in Wales to answer Welsh needs, made in Wales and developed in Wales'.[11]

Perhaps most importantly, the devolved assembly elections in 1999 and the UK general election in 2001 produced different results in Scotland and Wales. The devolved elections in 1999 saw a great boost in support for the nationalist parties, with a doubling in the SNP's share of the vote by

[10] Curtice and Seyd 2001.

[11] *The Western Mail*, 10 May 2001. For an analysis of the 2001 election manifestos and their 'devolution literacy', see Trench 2001.

comparison with 1997, and a trebling in the vote share of Plaid Cymru. In the 2001 election the parties' vote share returned to 1997 levels. It is dangerous to make too strong a prediction based on only two results, but this differentiation in voting behaviour between devolved and general elections looks likely to be a permanent feature.[12] The nationalist parties present a real threat to Labour in elections to the Scottish Parliament and National Assembly, and could one day form a government in Scotland or Wales, but at general elections their vote share recedes and Labour dominance is re-asserted.

A different party system does not mean a separate party system. The UK is unlikely ever to see the differentiation which is evident between federal and provincial parties in Canada, or in Belgium (where national parties have ceased to exist). But future general elections will be fought with a strong devolution overlay. Voters in Scotland and Wales who paused to think could have been forgiven for wondering which level of election was being fought in 2001. Labour's five-point pledge card in Scotland contained three pledges which fell within the powers of the Scottish Parliament, not Westminster. The SNP gave great prominence in the election to their new leader, John Swinney MSP, who was not standing as a candidate, while in Wales Labour promoted their leader Rhodri Morgan, also not standing as a Westminster candidate. Although these tactics did nothing to help political education or devolution literacy, they were a rational response to voters' concerns. When voters in Scotland and Wales were asked by pollsters to rank in order of importance the issues which most concerned them in the 2001 general election campaign, in both countries they placed health first and education second, even though both subjects are now devolved.

THE DEVOLUTION DYNAMIC CONTINUES TO UNFOLD

The final part of the chapter reviews how the devolution settlement has continued to evolve in the second year of devolution, and discusses the dynamic forces which will shape it in the future. Given the asymmetric nature of the settlement, there were always going to be strong pressures for leapfrog between the different parts of the UK. These forces were clearly in evidence in 2000-1, with the main developments being in Wales and the English regions; so these are discussed first, followed by Scotland and Northern Ireland.

The Welsh Start to Review the Settlement
In Wales the trajectory is clear. The settlement is not working, and the National Assembly is beginning to put together the case for Wales to be given powers closer to those enjoyed by Scotland. It is going to be a long-drawn-out process, in instalments, over the first five years of the

---

[12] Trystan 2002.

Assembly's life. In his chapter for this volume last year John Osmond suggested that the first year of devolution saw the Assembly gradually turn itself into a constitutional convention. In the second year the convention got down to work. Rhodri Morgan announced an extensive review of the Assembly's internal operation and relationship with Westminster and Whitehall, under the chairmanship of the Presiding Officer. The review is due to report back by December 2001. Reporting on the 43 submissions received by July, and in particular the evidence from the four political parties, John Osmond describes 'a frank acknowledgement on all sides that there are serious flaws in the basic design of the machine they have to operate ... What is also striking is the convergence in many instances of ideas on how to overcome the difficulties'.[13]

Rhodri Morgan also commented on the measure of consensus, including the 'commonplace belief that the Assembly's status as a corporate body is something of a handicap. It is therefore widely accepted that we should use all the scope available to make a distinction between the governmental and parliamentary side of the corporate body'.[14] Since the coalition agreement between Labour and the Liberal Democrats in October 2000, that distinction has become a lot sharper, with a number of changes — some symbolic, some substantive — but all taking the Assembly in a parliamentary direction. A clearer separation of powers has been created between the Assembly and the Executive, with the Presiding Officer being given his own budget of £24 million to run the Assembly. The Assembly Secretaries have decided to call themselves ministers, and Rhodri Morgan is now the First Minister. And within the Assembly there is a clearer separation between the Labour/Liberal Democrat government and the opposition parties represented by Plaid Cymru and the Conservatives.

The 2001 review is confined to improvements in the working of the Assembly within the framework laid down by the Government of Wales Act 1998. More significant in the longer term, the coalition agreement contains a commitment to establish a second review, by 'an independent commission into the powers and electoral arrangements of the National Assembly'.[15] That wider review of the Assembly's powers, which is bound to address the central issue of whether the Assembly should have legislative power, is to be set up by 2003, and to report back in 2004, the first year of the Assembly's second term.[16]

The results of that review can be anticipated now. It will complete the case, being assembled piece by piece, for the Assembly to have legislative power.

---

[13] Chapter 3, *supra*.

[14] Letter to Presiding Officer, 5 July 2001.

[15] *Putting Wales First: The First Partnership Agreement of the National Assembly for Wales*, 6 October 2000.

[16] If the coalition partners can reach agreement on the membership of the commission it may start and finish earlier, starting early in 2002 and reporting in autumn 2003.

A further piece fell into place in June 2001 when the Assembly failed to have most of its bids included in the Queen's Speech. What we don't know is what will be the reaction of the UK government to the commission into the powers of the National Assembly, and to its report. Tony Blair is famously uninterested in devolution, which he regards as a first-term item, and something he has now put behind him. John Prescott will be in charge of the policy, as chairman of the new Cabinet Committee on the Nations and Regions. In his previous incarnation at DETR he was not noted for supporting greater autonomy for the devolved administrations. At official level many Whitehall departments may privately have some sympathy for the Welsh case, because the half-way-house of 'executive devolution' causes them far more problems than the cleaner break of the settlements in Scotland and Northern Ireland. But they will take their lead from their ministers. The attitude of the devolved governments will also be worth watching — will the Scots support the Welsh cause, or will they sit on their hands?

The English Regions Remain in Waiting

In England the long march towards regional government continues; but what form regional government might take, and when English regions might attain it, still remain unclear. But the direction of travel continues to be one way, with several developments in 2000-1 strengthening the regional bodies created in Labour's first term, and laying the ground for further development of the policy in the second term.

The regional bodies created in the first term are the Regional Development Agencies (RDAs) and Regional Chambers which shadow them. The RDAs were given a big increase in resources in Gordon Brown's 2000 spending review, growing from £1.24 billion in 2000-01 to £1.7 billion in 2003-4. They were also given greater financial flexibility (the 'single pot'). In July 2001 Regional Chambers were given financial support for the first time, with each chamber receiving £500,000 per annum for the next three years. The Government Offices for the Regions also saw their roles strengthened, embracing more departments, and in April 2001 a Regional Co-ordination Unit was created in Whitehall to provide them with stronger support. In Chapter 5 John Tomaney describes these changes as 'a significant strengthening of the apparatus of governance in the English regions'.

There has also been a mushrooming of constitutional conventions in the English regions. Figure 5.2 in Chapter 5 summarises the current state of play, and records the launch of two constitutional conventions in 2000 (the North West, and Yorkshire and Humberside) and two in 2001 (the West Midlands and the South West). None has yet come close to producing the kind of detailed blueprint for an elected assembly which came out of the Scottish Constitutional Convention, but it is early days in their campaign. That campaign was launched in 2000 with the creation of the Campaign for the English Regions, to provide a national voice for the individual regional campaigns.

The campaign has a long way to go, in terms of mobilising public opinion. There is little sign yet that the people of England are clamouring to share in the benefits of devolution. Opinion polls show that a majority still believe that England should continue to be governed as it is now, with laws made by the UK Parliament. That majority slid by eight points between 1999 and 2000 (from 62 to 54 per cent), but it is still three times as many as support the idea of regional assemblies (supported by 15 per cent in 1999, 18 per cent in 2000). Even in the North East, the one region of England where less than half wanted England to be governed as it is now, only one in four supported the idea of a regional assembly. Meanwhile, in the southern half of England support for regional assemblies in 2000 stood at only around one in six.[17]

This lack of demand helps to explain the Labour Party's continuing ambivalence towards regional government in England. But the devolution dynamic is ticking away; what is important to watch is the trend, as the English respond to the benefits devolution appears to have brought to Scotland and Wales. Meanwhile the regional campaigns helped to maintain the Labour Party's faltering commitment. Labour's 2001 manifesto repeated the unfulfilled 1997 commitment to introduce elected regional assemblies in England, and promised an early White Paper. However the Queen's Speech in June 2001 made no mention of the English regions, and following the post-election reorganisation of Whitehall the policy lead now lies with three different departments: the Cabinet Office under John Prescott, the Department of Transport, Local Government and the Regions under Stephen Byers, and the Department of Trade and Industry under Patricia Hewitt (which is now responsible for RDAs).

This does not augur well for the White Paper on regional government, first promised by Christmas and then in early 2002. There is no agreed model for the powers and functions of regional assemblies, and the Labour Party and Labour government continue to be deeply divided. In Blair's first term John Prescott was a lone voice on the issue, and there are few signs that he has many more allies in the new government. The Whitehall battles over Scottish and Welsh devolution will pale into insignificance compared to the battles to come over the English regions. Devolving the Scottish Office and Welsh Office left the rest of Whitehall largely unscathed. Devolving powers, functions and, most painful of all, budgets to regional assemblies in England would require sacrifices of all the main Whitehall departments which their ministers are most unlikely to concede. The end result is likely to be an extremely slim-line, strategic model of assembly with powers largely

[17] Curtice and Seyd 2001.

confined to economic development and strategic planning, which voters will find it hard to understand and are correspondingly unlikely to vote for.[18]

Scotland's Policies Threaten the Budget

Scotland saw no major constitutional developments in the second year of the kind emerging in Wales and in England. The Scottish Parliament has come of age and is beginning to record some impressive achievements, especially in the work of its committees. The second year report cards gave the Parliament a much better press than in its first year. Although not as innovative or participatory as some of its creators had hoped, it is a parliament with a purpose and underlying vision which is beginning to be realised.[19] Simply in terms of output, the 24 Acts of the Scottish Parliament in its first two years bear witness to the difference made by devolution; Scotland would have enjoyed one quarter of that output in the pre-devolution days when Scotland was reliant upon legislation passed by Westminster.

But devolution in Scotland is sowing the seeds for a future confrontation over finance. The spending commitments on education, over tuition fees and teachers' pay, and now on health over long term care, raise questions over how long Scotland can afford policies more generous than those in England, especially when the operation of the Barnett Formula means that its budget is converging towards the English norm. If the Scots want more generous public services they will have to find the means of paying for them. The 'tartan tax' will not yield enough to make it worth introducing; the marginal economic gain is not worth the political pain.[20] Chapter 6 brings out how the generous measure of legislative devolution in Scotland is not balanced by an equivalent degree of fiscal responsibility, which may undermine Scotland's ability to develop significantly different policies. A much greater degree of fiscal autonomy is already something espoused by the SNP and the Liberal Democrats, and will be one of the battle lines drawn in the next Scottish elections in 2003.

Those elections will test Labour's static view of the devolution settlement. In Scotland as in the rest of the UK a devolution dynamic is at work. Two in three Scots believe that the Scottish Parliament should have more powers, and this proportion increased by ten points between 1999 and 2000, the first year of devolution. Three quarters of Scots would like the Scottish Parliament to have the most influence over the way Scotland is run, but two thirds believe that the UK government at Westminster currently has the most influence. If those feelings translate into support for political parties which want

---

[18] See Sandford and McQuail 2001, which sets out the slim-line strategic model in more detail.

[19] Winetrobe 2001.

[20] See Hazell 1999, pp 207-8, where four arguments are developed to explain why the Scottish Parliament is unlikely to use its tax raising power.

the Scottish Parliament to have more power, Labour will have to pay heed or face the electoral consequences.

Northern Ireland Falters then Falls: What Next?

The second year of devolution in Northern Ireland saw a continuation of the roller coaster which marked the first year, with a second suspension of the devolved institutions in July 2001, a third in August, and a fourth in September. If the suspension becomes indefinite there is likely to be some kind of review of the operation of the Belfast Agreement, if only as an internal exercise conducted by the Northern Ireland Office. In terms of lessons to be learnt for the future, a number of ideas are beginning to circulate about the design of any new institutions in Northern Ireland.

Some of these were first raised by our Northern Ireland experts, Rick Wilford and Robin Wilson, in an audit of the Northern Ireland Assembly published in May 2001.[21] While their audit covers the whole style and working methods of the Assembly and its committees, they identified certain design features which may not conduce to good government or to political accommodation between the two communities. Central to these is the power-sharing executive which lies at the heart of the consociational model, and which gives a seat in government to all parties which can secure more than 10 per cent of the seats in the Assembly. This makes it difficult effectively to scrutinise or challenge the Executive, and it is impossible to 'turf the rascals out' at an election. Nor is there the usual discipline on coalition partners. Although it might be unworkable in the Northern Ireland context, this has led some to canvass the idea of a voluntary coalition, more akin to European models, rather than the enforced coalition envisaged by the Belfast agreement.

Whitehall and Westminster Carry on Much as Before

At Whitehall and Westminster there has been little change. The devolution dynamic may be working away in the nations and regions, but so far there have been only minor repercussions at the centre. The formation of the new government in June 2001 presented Tony Blair with an opportunity for rationalisation which he didn't take. He instigated major reorganisation of three other Whitehall departments, but the Scotland Office, Wales Office and Northern Ireland Office were left unscathed. Despite predictions of a possible merger, there continue to be three separate Secretaries of State for Scotland, Wales and Northern Ireland, with the same office holders in each case as before the general election.[22]

---

[21] Wilford and Wilson 2001.
[22] Hazell 2001.

The main change in Whitehall following the election is John Prescott's move to the Cabinet Office, where he has acquired overall responsibility for devolution, as chair of the new Cabinet Committee on the Nations and Regions (CNR). This replaces the former Devolution Policy Committee, which was chaired by Lord Irvine. Prescott has also been made responsible for the British–Irish Council, confirming the view we expressed last year that the 'Council of the Isles' belongs to the dignified rather than the efficient part of the intergovernmental machine. On the efficient side, Prescott's first and most important task is to supervise production of the White Paper on regional government in England, a task in which he is supported by the new Nations and Regions Division of the Cabinet Office. This includes the small devolution team from the old Constitution Secretariat, and the much larger numbers in the Government Offices for the Regions and the Regional Co-ordination Unit.

Simply in terms of staff numbers, the 'regions' part of Prescott's portfolio looms much larger than the 'nations'. And in terms of the immediate agenda, he is going to be far more preoccupied with developing the policy on regional government in England than with the wider devolution picture. But when devolution matters intrude, it will be interesting to see how he handles them, and how he develops the 'nations' part of his portfolio. Before the election he seemed to favour a review of the Barnett Formula. Will he carry that through? What is his position vis-a-vis the territorial Secretaries of State? In what respects, if any, is he their devolution overlord? These are some of the things to watch as the new UK government settles in, and devolution issues wash back onto its agenda.

At Westminster there has also been no change, in terms of the committee structures of the House of Commons. Reflecting the three territorial departments, there continue to be separate Select Committees on Scottish, Welsh and Northern Ireland affairs. There continue to be three Grand Committees, although there is precious little for them to do. They are reverting to their old role of being clubs at Westminster for the Scottish, Welsh and Northern Irish MPs. The only new structure was the revived Standing Committee on Regional Affairs, convened on the last day of the last Parliament as a new forum for English MPs to debate regional issues; but it has not been reconvened in the new Parliament, and looks as though it may have been a one-day-wonder. Even if something like it is resurrected, without Government or Conservative support it looks unlikely to command much clout or attention. But with Robin Cook as the new Leader of the House, the pace of change may pick up as part of the wider process of modernisation of the House of Commons. If it does not, the Commons risks being overtaken by the House of Lords, where a faster pace is being set by the new Constitution Committee, also established in the last months of the last Parliament. After a ground-clearing exercise in its first report, issued in July 2001, the committee announced that in spring 2002 it would conduct an inquiry into intergovernmental relations in the light of devolution. That will be the committee's first foray into devolution, and will be an interesting test of the benefits to be gained from looking at devolution in the round, rather than in the segmented way which is prevalent in the Commons.

CONCLUSION

After the excitements of the first year, the second year of devolution was one when the devolved institutions got down to work. The new structures are bedding down and starting to deliver results. New policies are coming on stream which would not have been developed in the pre-devolution era. Slowly but steadily devolution is beginning to make more of a difference. 'Making a Difference' will be the watchword of all the devolved administrations as they embark on the second half of their first term, and face the run-up to the 2003 elections.

How much difference the devolved governments manage to make remains to be seen. How much difference they can make within the current devolution settlement will be increasingly tested. The autonomy of the devolved institutions will be one of the key issues in the 2003 elections, as the nationalist parties seek to show how much more they could do if only they had more power, and more control over their own finances. In Wales and in Scotland the opinion polls suggest they will be working with the grain of public opinion; having been given a taste of devolution, the Welsh and the Scots want more. As Alan Trench says in the opening chapter, the expectation that there would be a genuine and significant transfer of power to the devolved institutions has not yet been fully realised. Devolution is a reform half-completed, and the agenda for the next few years will be to complete the process.

England is the space where devolution is least complete, indeed hardly begun, and everything is still to play for. Although the polls show the English to be firm supporters of devolution in Scotland and Wales, this is not something they yet seem to want for themselves. But the devolution dynamic is working away, with a domino effect beginning to spread from the North through the Midlands down to the South West. Two years ago the North East was the only region with a campaign making plans for a regional assembly. Now five regions have established constitutional conventions, and in the past year they have come together in the Campaign for the English Regions. They need to be prepared for a long haul — in Scotland it took ten years from the launch of the Scottish Constitutional Convention to the installation of the Scottish Parliament. And they need to attract much stronger public demand than is evident at present.

Despite having fought two elections with a promise to introduce regional assemblies in England Labour remains deeply divided on the issue. The most important devolution event — or non-event — in 2002 will be the promised White Paper on regional government. That will show whether Labour still takes a cautious and static view of devolution, being hesitant to run ahead of public opinion, or whether the government is willing to give a lead. John Prescott would like to give a lead, but has little support from his Cabinet colleagues. He will have an uphill battle to persuade them to devolve sufficient powers, functions and budgets to make regional assemblies look credible, or worth voting for. The end result is likely to be a model of regional assembly so slim-line as to be positively anorexic; or one which offers a series of incremental steps towards regional government, starting with building up the indirectly elected Regional Chambers.

For the regional campaigners this will come as a disappointment. But until the people of England find their voice, and begin to demand devolution in the way that the Scots and the Welsh did, it is hard to see the politicians running far ahead. If the people of England have not spoken yet, it is because they are waiting for the politicians to give them a lead.

BIBLIOGRAPHY

Curtice, J. and Seyd, B. (2001). 'Is devolution strengthening or weakening the UK?' in *British Social Attitudes* 2001.

Hazell, R. (1999). *Constitutional Futures*. Oxford: Oxford University Press.

Hazell, R. (2001). *Three Into One Won't Go: The Future of the Territorial Secretaries of State*. London: The Constitution Unit, March 2001.

Sandford, M. and McQuail, P. (2001). *Unexplored Territory: Three Models for Regional Government in England*. London: The Constitution Unit, July 2001.

Trench, A. (2001). *Devolution and the 2001 UK General Election: 'Devolution Literacy' and the Manifestos*. London: The Constitution Unit, June 2001.

Trystan, D. (2002). 'Elections in Wales: Multi Level Voting', *Regional and Federal Studies*. Forthcoming.

Winetrobe, B. (2001). *Realising the Vision. A Parliament with a Purpose: An Audit of the First Year of the Scottish Parliament*. London: The Constitution Unit, October 2001.

Wilford, R. and Wilson, R. (2001). *A Democratic Design: The Political Style of the Northern Ireland Assembly*. London: The Constitution Unit, May 2001.

Index

Acton, Lord 221.

Adams, Gerry 92, 100, 202.

Adamson, Ian 90.

Advocate General for Scotland (see Clark, Lynda).

Ahern, Bertie 80, 81, 82.

Alderdice, John 201.

Alexander, Wendy 51, 53, 54, 57, 72.

Anderson, Reid and Doherty v the Scottish Ministers and the Advocate General for Scotland (see Devolution and the Courts).

Appellate Committee of the House of Lords (see Devolution and the Courts).

Ashton, Joe 219.

Asymmetrical devolution 38, 138, 162, 180, 232, 234, 246, 264.

Atherton, Candy 219.

Baillie, Jackie 54.

Balls, Ed 108.

Barnett formula 8, 21, 65, 66, 67, 68, 97, 124, 136-151, 166, 167, 189, 259-262, 268, 270.

Beddow, Tony 22.

Beckett, Margaret 218.

Beggs, Roy 92, 202.

Belfast Agreement 6, 77, 79, 100, 101, 207, 227, 230, 232, 238, 246, 247, 251, 252, 263, 269.

Bingham of Cornhill, Lord 179.

Birnie, Esmond 93.

Black, Peter 17.

Blair, Tony 58, 66, 79, 80, 81, 82, 111, 154, 155, 177, 189, 193, 265, 267, 269.

Bogdanor, Vernon 217, 218.

Bourne, Nick 25.

Boyack, Sarah 54.

British-Irish Council (see also Intergovernmental Relations) 78, 87, 156-157, 194, 269.

Brown, Gordon 52, 53, 108, 109, 110, 112, 113, 115, 116, 130, 131, 143, 155, 261, 266.

Browne, Des 185.

Buck, Karen 219.

Burnside, David 81.

Burrows, Noreen 6, 15, 195.

Bush, George W. 69.

Butler, Rosemary 20.

Byers, Steven 110, 118, 127, 131, 195, 267.

Cabinet Committee on Nations and Regions (CNR) 126, 194, 266, 269.

Cabinet Office (see also Government at the Centre) 7, 126, 155, 160, 177, 184, 189, 193, 267:
    Central Secretariat 190.
    Constitution Secretariat 160, 189, 190, 270.
    Devolution and Regions Division 160, 194, 270.
    European Secretariat 190.

Campaign for an English Parliament 216.

Campaign for a North East Assembly 123, 124.

Campaign for a West Midlands Assembly 123.

Campaign for the English Regions 122, 266-267.

Campaign for Yorkshire and the Humber 123.

Campbell, Gregory 86, 89, 202.

Chancellor of the Exchequer (see Brown, Gordon).

Chapman, Christine 16.

Chidgley, David 219.

Chisholm, Malcolm 47, 64, 65, 201.

Civil Service 29-31, 161, 176.

Clark, Lynda 182, 183.

Clinton, Bill 79.

Coalition Government:
  in Northern Ireland 84, 269.
  in Scotland 3, 4, 57, 65, 258.
  in Wales 3, 4, 13, 14, 16-20, 36, 41-43, 43.

Comprehensive Spending Review 19, 67, 68, 112-113, 143, 145, 148, 150, 166, 189.

Concordats 156, 157-158, 175, 176, 180, 191, 195.

Connery, Sean 69.

Conservative Party (see Political Parties).

Constitutional Conventions 266:
  North East Constitutional Convention 122, 123.
  North West Constitutional Convention 123, 266.
  Scottish Constitutional Convention 17, 54, 266
  South West Constitutional Convention 266.
  West Midlands Constitutional Convention 266.
  Yorkshire and the Humber Constitutional Convention 266.

Constitution Secretariat (see Cabinet Office).

Consultative Steering Group (see Scottish Parliament).

Cook, Robin 55, 61, 62, 155, 177, 270.

Corus 14, 20, 166.

Cranborne, Viscount 221.

Cubie, Andrew:
  Committee of Inquiry into Student Finance 68.

Cuomo, Mario 53.

Cunningham, Roseanna 201.

Dafis, Cynog 34, 35.

Daintith, Terence 195.

Dallat, John 92.

Dalyell, Tam 234.

Davidson, Jane 17, 24.

Davies, Andrew 17.

Davies, Ron 2, 16, 21, 201, 261.

Davis, Phil 122.

Deacon, Susan 46, 47, 51, 54, 57, 58, 64, 65, 169.

de Brun, Bairbre 88, 89, 93, 156.

Democratic Unionist Party (see Political Parties).

Department for Culture, Media and Sport 119, 120.

Department for Education and Employment (see also Department for Education and Skills) 181.

Department for Education and Skills (see also Department for Education and Employment) 120.

Department of the Environment, Food and Rural Affairs (also see Ministry of Agriculture, Fisheries and Food) 120, 126, 201.

Department of the Environment, Transport and the Regions (see also Department for Transport, Local Government and the Regions) 109, 114, 116, 120, 126, 157, 260, 266.

Department of Health 180, 185.

Department of Trade and Industry 7, 113, 115, 120, 127, 184, 194, 267.

Department of Transport, Local Government and the Regions (also see Department of the Environment, Transport and the Regions) 7, 127, 129, 180, 181, 194, 267.

Deputy Prime Minister (see Prescott, John):

Office of the 126, 177, 193.

Devolution:

and Westminster 7, 153, 197-199, 269, 270.

and Whitehall 175-178, 180-181, 269.

and the Courts 7, 178-180.

effects on machinery of government 7, 126, 176, 180, 186-189, 193-195, 267.

effects on the party system 263-264.

failures of 6-10.

finance (including alternative funding mechanisms) (see also Barnett Formula) 65-68, 136-138, 143-147, 147-150, 268-269.

Guidance Notes 165, 172, 177, 180, 185, 191, 204, 205, 206, 214.

policy divergence 8, 23-24, 38, 46, 63-72, 173, 181, 255-259, 268-269.

sources of tension 232, 234, 235.

successes of 4-6, 230.

support for 232, 235.

Dewar, Donald 46, 49, 51, 52, 53, 55, 56, 63, 154, 156, 183, 184, 245.

d'Hondt mechanism (see also Electoral System: Proportional Representation) 84, 92, 98, 104.

Dimbleby, David 42.

Dodds, Nigel 87, 89, 202.

Doherty, Pat 202.

Douglas-Hamilton, James 201.

Dowds, Lizanne 100, 101.

Duncan Smith, Iain 217, 262.

Durkan, Mark 78, 79, 89, 95, 97.

Elections (see General Election; National Assembly for Wales; Northern Ireland Assembly; Scottish Parliament).

Elfed Jones, John 32-32, 36.

Elis-Thomas, Lord 20, 27, 30, 31, 201.

Ellman, Louise 219.

Empey, Reg 80, 88, 89.

England (see also Constitutional Conventions; Grand Committees; House of Commons; Public Attitudes to Devolution; Regional Development Agencies; Regional Government; Standing Committee on Regional Affairs):

English Question 131, 188, 198, 215-220, 217-218, 223, 234.

English Regions 7, 232, 239, 264, 266-268.

Regional Assemblies 107, 108, 109, 216, 255, 267.

Regional Chambers 107, 108, 109, 115-119, 121, 266.

English Parliament 38, 216, 217, 232, 233.

English Votes on English Laws 216-217, 255.

Essex, Sue 17.

European Convention on Human Rights (ECHR) 179.

European Union 147, 155, 157-158, 168-170, 171:
  Council of Ministers 169.
Evans, Delyth 17.
Evans, Huw 39.
Evans, Nigel 219.
Ewing, Margaret 201.

Falconer, Lord 206.
Farren, Sean 89, 92, 93.
Fawcett, Liz 91.
Fellowes, Lord 221.
Finnie, Ross 53, 54, 71.
Flanders Declaration 55, 154, 170.
Foot-and-Mouth Disease 20, 22, 32, 47, 53, 71, 72, 94, 120, 148, 154, 166, 167, 170-171, 260.
Foreign and Commonwealth Office 168, 170, 180.
Forsythe, Clifford 81.
Foster, Sam 89.
Foulkes, George 183.
Fraser, Christopher 219.
Freedom of Information 99-100.

Galbraith, Sam 48, 53, 201.
General Election 2-4, 24, 38-40, 48, 49, 66, 72-73, 103-104, 112, 126, 130, 154, 186, 199, 226, 248-253, 255, 262, 263.
  turn-out 3, 249.
George, Andrew 219.
German, Michael 13, 14, 15, 16, 17, 18, 40.
Gibbons, Brian 17.
Gildernew, Michelle 104, 202.
Glyn Jones, Dafydd 15, 33-36.
Glyn, Seimon 32, 36, 42.
Gorrie, Donald 201.
Goshen, George 135.

Government at the Centre (see also Whitehall; Cabinet Office; Her Majesty's Treasury) 189-195:
  fragmented nature of 180.
Government Offices for the Regions 111, 112, 119-120, 121, 126, 194, 266, 270.
Government of Wales Act 1998 5, 16, 19, 27, 29, 31, 165, 178, 265.
Grand Committees (see also Standing Committee on Regional Affairs):
  English 219, 270.
  meetings of the 212.
  Northern Irish 211-213, 270.
  Scottish 211-213, 270.
  Welsh 211-213, 215, 270.
Gray, James 187.
Greater London Authority 127, 129, 232.
Greater London Council 127.
Grieve, Dominic 218.
Griffiths, Bruce 33.

Hague, William 177, 188, 199, 216, 217, 262.
Hannan, Patrick 5.
Hansard Society Commission 197, 199.
Harbison, Jeremy 97.
Hart, Edwina 17.
Hayes, Bernadette 100, 101.
Hendron, Joe 93.
Her Majesty's Treasury 71, 135, 137, 143, 144, 148, 150, 166, 167, 189, 260.
Hewitt, Patricia 115, 194, 267.
Holme of Cheltenham, Lord 221.
Home Robertson, John 62, 201.
Home Office 119, 120, 193.
Horowitz, David 78.
House of Commons (see also Grand Committees; Select Committees;

Standing Committee on Regional
Affairs; English Question)
199-220:
   Dual Mandate MPs 73,
    200-202.
   English matters (including
    English Regional
    Government) 124-126.
   over representation of Scotland
    and Wales 198.
   procedure 213-214.
   reform 62, 109, 160, 259.
   role of MPs 7, 214-215.
   state of the parties 199-200.
   territorial committee structure
    7, 198, 207, 270.
House of Lords (see also Royal
  Commission on Reform of the
  House of Lords) 198, 213,
  220-222:
   hereditary peers 220.
   reform 160, 220, 223, 259.
   response to devolution
    270-271.
   representing the Nations and
    Regions 125, 220-221.
Howarth, George 259.
Howells of St Davids, Baroness 221.
Hughes, Beverley 110, 125, 219.
Human Rights Act 1998 179.
Hume, John 202.
Hutt, Jane 17.

Independence:
   for Scotland 2, 51, 52, 227,
    235, 239, 263.
   for Wales 227, 235.
Independent International
  Commission on Decommissioning
  82, 83.
Intergovernmental Relations 50,
  153-173:

   and Westminster legislation
    156.
   and finance 166-167.
   EU and international matters
    168-170.
   informality of 153, 158-163.
   formal machinery of 153,
    154-158.
   Foot-and-Mouth disease
    170-171.
   ministerial co-operation in
    158-160.
   role of officials 160-162.
   role of territorial Offices 158,
    162-163, 181-189.
IRA 78, 80, 81, 82, 84, 85, 86.
Irvine, Lord 194, 216, 217, 219,
  269.

Jamieson, Cathy 47, 53.
Joint Ministerial Committee on
  Devolution (see also
  Intergovernmental Relations) 138,
  154-156, 158, 161, 167, 168, 172,
  173, 175, 176, 194.
Jones, Carwyn 17, 22, 23.
Jones, Derek 20.
Jones, Jeff 18.
Judicial Committee of the Privy
  Council (see Devolution and the
  Courts).

Kellas, James 48.
Kennedy, Jane 185.
Kent, John 118.
Kiley, Bob 128.
Kinnock, Glenys 42.

Labour Party (see Political Parties).
Lang, Ian 70.
Lang of Monkton, Lord 221.
Leigh, Edward 217.

Lewis, Huw 17, 34.
Liberal Democrats (see Political
    Parties).
Liddell, Helen 47, 56, 71, 154, 177,
    183, 184, 187.
Lijphart, Arend 85.
Lipsey, David 64.
Livingstone, Ken 121, 128, 129.
Lloyd, John 27.
London Assembly (see Greater
    London Authority).
Lord Chancellor's Department 193.
Loughran, Gerry 99.
Lynch, Rod 48, 72.

MacKay, Angus 54, 58.
MacWhirter, Iain 48.
Major, John 1, 262.
Mallon, Seamus 80, 87, 88, 89, 202.
Mandelson, Peter 47, 56, 66, 79,
    111, 131, 154, 177, 186.
Mar and Kellie, Earl of 221.
Marek, John 14, 20, 201.
Martin, Michael 199, 213.
Mbeki, President 154.
McAllion, John 201.
McCabe, Tom 47, 54, 57, 58, 62, 68.
McConnell, Jack 46, 51, 52, 54, 55,
    57, 67.
McClelland, Donovan 81.
McCrae, Rev William 81.
McCrone, David 48, 68.
McGimpsey, Michael 89.
McGuinness, Martin 89, 156, 202,
    258.
McIntyre, Robert 60.
McLean, Iain 138.
McLeish, Henry 46, 47, 49, 51, 52,
    53, 54, 55, 56, 57, 64, 65, 68, 69,
    70, 168, 184, 201, 244, 245, 256.
McLetchie, David 62.
McMahon, Peter 53.

Melding, David 25.
Memorandum of Understanding 154,
    156, 158, 160, 190, 191.
Michael, Alun 13, 16, 18, 19, 147,
    167, 200, 245, 250, 263.
Middlehurst, Tom 14, 18.
Ministry of Agriculture, Fisheries and
    Food (also see Department for the
    Environment, Food and Rural
    Affairs) 23, 119, 171.
Ministry of Defence 180, 185.
Mitchell, Austin 125.
Morgan, Alasdair 58, 201, 202. 216.
Morgan, Lord 221.
Morgan, Rhodri 13, 16, 17, 18, 19,
    25, 28, 30, 32, 33, 37, 41, 168,
    201, 213, 245, 250, 256-257, 263,
    264, 265.
Morris, Estelle 258.
Morrow, Maurice 86, 89.
Murphy, Jim 183.
Murphy, Paul 177, 184, 185, 211,
    215.
Murray, Dennis 219.

National Assembly for Wales:
    and education 23-24.
    and the economy 20-21.
    and the Welsh Health Service
        21-22.
    and the Welsh language 15,
        31-36.
    as a legislature 168-169.
    coalition in the (see also
        coalition Government) 245,
        256, 265.
    Commission on the powers of
        16.
    elections to the 4, 5, 16, 41,
        42, 253, 263, 264.
    EU and international matters
        168-169.
    executive devolution 164-165.

involvement in IGR 157, 171.
legislative powers 15, 23, 26,
    31, 36, 41, 205, 235, 255,
    265.
legislative programme 24-26.
legitimacy of 15.
'new politics' 31-32.
Office of the Presiding Officer
    16, 26-27.
Operational Review 14, 15,
    27-29, 264-266.
performance of 248.
programme for government 13,
    256.
relationship with UK
    Government 25, 27, 167,
    265.
National Identity (see also Regional
    Identity) 236-240:
    British 236, 237, 239.
    English 237, 238.
    Irish 238.
    Scottish 236, 238.
    Welsh 236, 238.
Nationalism 2, 69, 77, 101, 104,
    175, 216, 230, 252.
Neil, Alex 46, 60.
Nesbitt, Dermot 89.
North East Constitutional Convention
    (see Constitutional Conventions).
Northern Ireland (see Belfast
    Agreement; Budget; Elections;
    Media Reporting of Devolution;
    Northern Ireland Act 1998;
    Northern Ireland Assembly;
    Northern Ireland Executive; Public
    Attitudes towards Devolution;
    Secretary of State for Northern
    Ireland).
Northern Ireland Act 1998 82, 83,
    87, 178, 211.
Northern Ireland Assembly 89-95,
    210, 242:

budget 94, 97-98.
committees of the 78, 90, 92,
    95, 269.
elections to the 251, 253, 263.
expectations 242, 243.
joined-up scrutiny 94.
legislation 90, 96-100.
media and the 102.
Office of the First Minister and
    Deputy First Minister 78, 86, 87,
    89, 95. Northern Ireland
Executive 84-89, 94, 156, 230:
    administration of government
        83.
    composition of 89.
    'joined up' government 94.
    Programme for Government
        78, 79, 85, 87, 94, 96-97,
        102, 258.
    suspension of devolved
        institutions 77, 81, 82, 83,
        247, 269.
Northern Ireland Office 176, 210,
    269:
    and further devolution 186.
    IGR and 162-163.
    questions to 215.
    role of 185-186.
    staff of the 188.
North-South Ministerial Council (see
    also Intergovernmental Relations)
    78, 79, 80, 81, 87, 88, 156-157,
    230.
North West Constitutional
    Convention (see Constitutional
    Conventions).
Norton of Louth, Lord 221.

Objective One Structural Funds 19,
    147, 167, 189.
O'Brien, Bill 218, 219.
Osborne, Sandra 183.

Page, Alan 195.

Paisley, Ian 90, 202, 245.

Parliament (see House of Commons;
    House of Lords; Scottish
    Parliament; Select Committees;
    Westminster; Westminster Hall).

Patten, Chris 79, 101, 186.

Pearson, Ian 219.

Phillips, Trevor 121.

Plaid Cymru (see Political Parties).

Police Service of Northern Ireland
    (see also Royal Ulster
    Constabulary) 79, 247.

Political Parties:

    Alliance Party 252.

    Conservative 2, 3, 14, 20, 28,
        38, 40, 43, 58, 73, 188, 199,
        200, 207, 215, 216, 217, 219,
        262.

    Democratic Unionist Party 6,
        78, 79, 80, 84, 85, 87, 101,
        103-104, 246, 252.

    Labour 3, 4, 14, 15, 28, 31, 37,
        38, 52, 53, 58, 60, 69, 73,
        107, 199, 200, 216, 250, 251,
        260.

    Liberal Democrats 2, 3, 14, 19,
        20, 24, 27, 30, 37, 38, 40,
        57-58, 64, 73, 149, 200, 250,
        256, 257, 260

    Northern Ireland Unionist Party
        92.

    Plaid Cymru 14, 15, 20, 27,
        31, 36, 39-40, 42, 200,
        202-203, 250-251, 264.

    Progressive Unionist Party 80.

    Scottish National Party 2, 3,
        60-61, 66, 73, 149, 200,
        202-203, 216, 235, 250, 260,
        263.

    Sinn Fein 6, 77, 78, 80, 84, 85,
        87, 103-104, 156, 206.

Social Democratic and Labour
    Party 80, 81, 84, 103-104,
    202.

Ulster Unionist Party 77, 79,
    80, 81, 84, 100, 101, 103,
    104, 202, 247, 252.

United Kingdom Independence
    Party 123.

United Kingdom Unionist Party
    92, 103.

Ponsonby of Shulbrede, Lord 221.

Poots, Edwin 95.

Prescott, John 7, 53, 66, 108, 109,
    110, 112, 115, 116, 126, 127, 130,
    154, 193, 194, 195, 260, 265, 266,
    269.

Price, Adam 203.

Prime Minister (see Blair, Tony).

Proportional representation (PR) 18.

Public attitudes towards devolution:

    in England 122-124, 225-226.

    in the UK 225, 225-253,
        262-263.

    in Northern Ireland 100-101,
        225, 236, 246, 263.

    in Scotland 225, 235, 262-263.

    in Wales 225, 235, 263.

Pugh, Alun 17, 35.

Quin, Joyce 139, 143, 146.

Quinn, Laurie 219.

Raffan, Keith 47, 65.

Randerson, Jenny 16, 17.

Raynsford, Nick 127, 129.

Regional Chambers 107, 111, 112.

Regional Co-ordination Unit 120,
    126, 194, 266, 270.

Regional Development Agencies
    107, 109, 111, 112-115, 116, 121,
    232, 266, 267.

Regional Government:

Labour policies 7, 107, 130-131, 267.
Liberal Democrat policies 123.
White Paper on 8, 107, 108, 125, 126, 127, 131, 194, 255, 267, 270.
Regional Identity 122-124.
Regionalisation 121.
Reid, George 47, 58.
Reid, John 47, 56, 77, 79, 81, 82, 105, 154, 177, 183, 184, 186, 212.
Renton, Lord 216.
Ringwald, Kath 21.
Robinson, Iris 202.
Robinson, Peter 87, 89, 202.
Robson, Euan 47, 58.
Rodgers, Brid 89.
Roy, Frank 177.
Royal Ulster Constabulary (RUC) (see also Police Service of Northern Ireland) 79, 84, 247.
Russell, Muir 161.

Salmond, Alex 46, 49, 60, 61, 200.
Samuel, Bill 118.
Sayeed, Jonathan 218, 219.
Scotland (see Coalition Government; Elections; Independence; Media Reporting of Devolution; Public Attitudes Towards Devolution; Scotland Act 1998; Scotland Office; Scottish Executive; Scottish Office; Scottish Parliament; Secretary of State for Scotland).
Scotland Act 1998 52, 62, 63, 163, 169, 178, 203.
Scotland Office 7, 176, 197, 269:
    developing policy 183.
    IGR and 162-163.
    interface between Whitehall and the Scottish Executive 182.

monitoring legislation 182-183.
    questions to 214.
    role of 182-184.
    staff of 188.
Scott, Tavish 47, 58.
Scottish Constitutional Convention (see Constitutional Conventions).
Scottish Executive 51-57, 156, 248, 261:
    cabinet 51-54.
    European and foreign affairs 55, 69-70.
    institutional innovation 54-55.
    performance of 249.
    policy divergence from Whitehall 8.
    relations with London 50, 54.
    'Scottish Government' 68.
Scottish National Party (see Political Parties).
Scottish Office 30, 50, 70, 71, 72, 181, 187, 267.
Scottish Parliament 57-63, 216, 256:
    as a New Model of Assembly 61-63.
    committees of the 58-60, 62.
    Consultative Steering Group 50, 58.
    elections to the 4, 51, 62, 250, 253, 263, 264, 268.
    Executive-Parliament relations 57-58.
    expectations of the 45-50, 241, 243.
    finance 65-68, 139-143.
    legislation 63, 268.
    'new Scottish politics' 48.

Sewel resolutions 204.
Scottish Qualifications Agency 70, 71.

Secretary of State for Northern Ireland (see Northern Ireland Office; Mandelson, Peter; Reid John).

Secretary of State for Scotland (see Liddell, Helen; Reid, John; Scotland Office; Scottish Office).

Secretary of State for the Union 187.

Secretary of State for Wales (see Murphy, Paul; Wales Office; Welsh Office).

Select Committees (see also House of Commons; House of Lords):
    Catering Committee 203.
    Constitution Committee 199, 221-222, 223, 270-271.
    Delegated Powers and Deregulation 213, 222.
    Environmental Audit Committee 202.
    Liaison Committee 208.
    Northern Ireland Affairs Committee 208, 209, 210.
    Procedure Committee 197.
    Scottish Affairs Committee 202, 208, 209, 210, 212, 223.
    Trade and Industry Committee 202.
    Welsh Affairs Committee 202, 208-210, 223.

Sewel, Lord 203.

Sewel Convention 163, 164, 165, 203, 204.

Shakespeare, David 118.

Sheridan, Tommy 47, 57.

Shortridge, Jon 30, 31, 161.

Sillars, Jim 60.

Silk, Paul 14, 27.

Sinclair, Karen 16.

Sinn Féin (see Political Parties).

Smith, Andrew 143.

Smith, John 262.

Social Democratic and Labour Party (see Political Parties).

South West Constitutional Convention (see Constitutional Conventions).

Spence, Ronnie 99.

Standing Committee on Regional Affairs 124, 199, 218-220.

Steel, David 47, 58, 61, 62, 201.

Steen, Anthony 124, 219.

Stephen, Nicol 69.

Straw, Jack 55, 218.

Sutherland Report 46, 47, 57, 58, 63, 64, 65, 258.

Swinney, John 46, 60, 61, 201, 264.

Taoiseach, the (see Ahern, Bertie).

Taylor, John 92, 201.

Thomas, Simon 203.

Tosh, Murray 62.

Touhig, Don 185.

Travers, Tony 129.

Trimble, David 77, 78, 79, 80, 81, 82, 86, 87, 88, 100, 101, 103, 104, 143, 146, 156, 202, 245, 247, 259, 261.

Tuck, Ron 46.

UKREP 169.

Ulster Defence Association 80.

Ulster Unionist Party (see Political Parties).

Union, The 1, 100, 175, 176, 195, 226, 227, 230, 231, 232, 236, 240.
    unionism 251, 252.

Wakeham, Lord (see also House of Lords: Reform) 220.

Wales (see Coalition Government; Elections; Government of Wales Act 1998; Independence; Media Reporting of Devolution; National Assembly for Wales; Public

Attitudes Towards Devolution; Referendums; Secretary of State for Wales; Wales place in Europe; Wales Office; Welsh Office):
place in Europe 37.
Wales Office 7, 176, 184, 197, 209, 269:
and primary legislation 184-185.
IGR and 162, 165, 171.
Questions to 214.
role of 184-185.
staff of the 188.
Wallace, Jim 54, 65.
Waterhouse Inquiry 185, 205.
Watson, Mike 59, 201.
Weatherill, Lord 221.
Weir, Michael 202.
Welsh, Andrew 201.
Welsh Assembly (see National Assembly for Wales).
Welsh Office 21, 23, 30, 181, 267.
West Lothian Question (see also English Question, the) 175, 217, 234, 239.
West Midlands Constitutional Convention (see Constitutional Conventions).
Westminster (see also House of Commons; House of Lords):
as the parliament of the United Kingdom 217-218.
dominance of 244, 248.
legislation on devolved matters 7, 29, 156, 163-166, 203-207.
response to devolution 197-199, 270.
territorial extent of legislation 203, 219.
Westminster Hall (see also House of Commons) 110, 125, 218.

Whitehall 126-127, 160-162, 172, 180-181, 232, 266, 269.
Wigley, Dafydd 42, 201.
Willett, Alan 129.
Williams, Emyr 20.
Wilson, Andrew 66.
Wilson, Brian 56, 218.
Winning, Cardinal 45.
written constitution 195, 196.
Wyatt, Derek 219.
Wyn Jones, Ieuan 25, 42, 201.

Yorkshire Forward 114.
Young, Baroness 221.
Younger, George 67.